WARDS
of
HANOI

The **Institute of Southeast Asian Studies (ISEAS)** was established as an autonomous organization in 1968. It is a regional centre dedicated to the study of socio-political, security and economic trends and developments in Southeast Asia and its wider geostrategic and economic environment.

The Institute's research programmes are the Regional Economic Studies (RES, including ASEAN and APEC), Regional Strategic and Political Studies (RSPS), and Regional Social and Cultural Studies (RSCS).

ISEAS Publications, an established academic press, has issued more than 1,000 books and journals. It is the largest scholarly publisher of research about Southeast Asia from within the region. ISEAS Publications works with many other academic and trade publishers and distributors to disseminate important research and analyses from and about Southeast Asia to the rest of the world.

WARDS
of
HÀNOI

David W.H. Koh

LᏕᎬᎪᏕ

INSTITUTE OF SOUTHEAST ASIAN STUDIES
SINGAPORE

First published in Singapore in 2006 by
ISEAS Publications
Institute of Southeast Asian Studies
30 Heng Mui Keng Terrace
Pasir Panjang
Singapore 119614

E-mail: publish@iseas.edu.sg
Website: http://bookshop.iseas.edu.sg

The responsibility for facts and opinions in this publication rests exclusively with the author and his interpretations do not necessarily reflect the views or the policy of the publisher or its supporters.

ISEAS Library Cataloguing-in-Publication Data

Koh, David W. H.
    Wards of Hanoi.
    1.   Local government—Vietnam—Hanoi.
    2.   Central-local government relations—Vietnam.
    3.   Vietnam—Social policy.
    I.   Title
    JS7152.3 A3K79   2006

ISBN 981-230-341-3 (soft cover)
ISBN 981-230-343-X (hard cover)

Cover photograph by David W. H. Koh: Hõa Mã Street in Hà Nội, close to the time of Tết, in 2004.

Typeset by International Typesetters Pte Ltd
Printed in Singapore by Oxford Graphic Printers

Contents

List of Tables

List of Figures

Preface

The original questions that underline this book concern first, the extent to which the Socialist Republic of Vietnam, having a communist political system, can sustain its economic growth and development without appropriate political reforms; second, the basis on which the legitimacy of the Vietnamese Communist Party (VCP) lies. Would economic growth be sustained better with a "big bang" of political and economic reforms in tandem, than with an incremental approach that has economic growth and development taking the lead and political reforms trailing behind? In turn, can the legitimacy of one party rule be sustained purely by economic growth and development and minimal political reforms, or is the demise of the communist system inevitable with economic reforms that will spring demands for political reforms? How long can the communist system last in a free-market economy and globalization, with concomitant spread of liberal political values?

These were important questions of the early 1990s when I first decided to become a scholar on Vietnam. They led me initially to study the basis of the legitimacy of the VCP and one-party rule. I wanted to discover how strong the party-state was, and whether economic changes were eroding the iron-handed controls that the party-state had for so many years. I also wanted to find out whether the party itself was changing, by approaching the matter from the angle of how the VCP trained and educated its officials. Neither of these two approaches bore fruit for me in the mid-1990s. I soon discovered that these questions resembled a French traffic circle that had too many avenues leading into and out of it; the project was too big. Furthermore, in the mid-1990s, as a starting graduate student, I did not have the right connections to allow me to do an in-depth study of the VCP schools system that could illuminate internal changes in the VCP. Nevertheless, in search of answers to these two questions, I went to Hà Nội to study the Vietnamese language and to assess the two approaches. I found out that neither approach was feasible, but the stay was fruitful in other ways. Staying among Vietnamese for an extended period of time allowed me to get up close to watch how closely the Vietnamese party-state leaned on society. The results of a period of intense observation for more than a year, combined with archival work, formed the empirical basis of this book. After completing the dissertation, I continued to follow the issues discussed in this book and I have been able to incorporate the latest data.

ANSWERING THE QUESTIONS

Having conducted research into Vietnam for the last nine years, I am no closer to answering the two big questions I had in the early 1990s. But other insights have been gathered that throw some light on the fact that perhaps the questions had inaccurate premises, or that the understanding of the communist system in Vietnam was insufficient, in particular the issue of state–society relations under one party rule of the VCP. For one, a premise was that the Vietnamese political system was communist and therefore the party-state was able to control and direct society effectively. The second premise, following the first, was that state–society relations in Vietnam belonged to the authoritarian type and that was going to change as the country reformed economically and opened itself up to influences of political values from abroad. With the first premise one assumed that people lacked basic freedoms and had to defer to the party-state for every daily activity, every action and reaction. With the second premise, one often looked out for evidence that the controls were going to fall apart.

These premises are true only to a much lesser extent than what they may have implied. The picture of state–society relations in Vietnam is a mixed one and the following pages of this book will demonstrate it. In a few areas, there is truly a denial of freedoms that many other societies have come to regard as basic. On the margins of this big picture, political dissidents toil and suffer by taking on the party-state in the few areas where there are freedoms they deem to be above other sorts of freedoms and are thus *a priori*.

In most other areas, however, the ordinary Vietnamese experience more freedom than other people to do what they want. This book says that the Vietnamese under the one-party state of the Socialist Republic of Vietnam enjoy a fair amount of political, economic, and social space. The immense, penetrating structure of the party-state has been both a control mechanism as well as a mediation mechanism. The control mechanism squeezes tight, but can be loosened by the mediation mechanism. In particular, this book focuses on state–society interaction at the daily level in the City of Hà Nội and shows that at that level the mediation space results from the inefficient party-state as well as from the social dimensions that party-state officials operate when they try to enforce the rule of the one party-state.

The findings of this book contribute to answering the big questions of the early 1990s. If the premise of assuming an omnipotent party-state is not entirely valid, then ironically the party-state can be seen as capable of adapting to changes and demands of society because it has had to accept a reality that works and is different from what its policies prescribe. It has had to adjust and reconceptualize its policies around that reality. That gives people space. Given space, people breathe easier and are less likely to demand for revolutionary political changes. This picture would allow us to cast the Vietnamese political system and state–society relations in the soft-authoritarian camp. In reality, furthermore, the political system of Vietnam has been reforming slowly and that has allowed the venting of frustrations and challenges to the government bureaucracy without challenging in an overt way the power and authority of the VCP. To the dismay of many that wish it ill, the communist political system in Vietnam is surviving through this interplay of control and mediation. The research process of this book can illustrate the simultaneous functioning of control and mediation.

Acknowledgements

I owe a great debt to my teachers. First among them is Professor Benedict Kerkvliet, Professor and Head of the Department of Political and Social Change at the Australian National University. He showed great patience and kindness when I was going through hard times, academically and financially. Way before I enrolled at the Australian National University and after I returned to Singapore to finish writing the dissertation, Professor Kerkvliet had always provided timely advice and nudges in order that I did not take my whole lifetime to complete this piece of work. Now and then, he directly or indirectly reminded himself and me that whatever we have written shall always be just a small piece of the puzzle of knowledge, and life. This is a valuable piece of advice for keeps.

I thank Professor David Marr, from the Department of Pacific and Asian History of the Research School of Pacific and Asian Studies, the Australian National University, for his many criticisms and comments. He always managed to extract from me just a little bit more than what I thought I was capable of. Like Professor Kerkvliet, Professor Marr unselfishly shared many relevant or new materials on Vietnam with me as well as with all Vietnam studies scholars and students of the Australian National University. Professor Harold Crouch of the Department of Political and Social Change gave critical and insightful comments and pointed me to some very basic points that I had missed while this work was at an early draft. Dr Thaveeporn Vasavakul was with the Department of Political and Social Change and I benefited from her detailed comments on my initial ideas and the first draft.

I enjoyed the collegial but critical, nurturing but demanding teacher-student relationships that all these four teachers have provided not just to me but to all their students. I can only repay my debt to them by aspiring to relate to my peers in the same inspirational and unselfish ways.

Among other teachers, friends and colleagues at the Australian National University, I first wish to thank two Vietnamese language teachers, Nguyễn Thị Bích Thuận and Phạm Thu Thủy. My confidence and ability in the Vietnamese language in a big part is due to their dedication and encouragement. In particular, Thủy and her husband Ngô Văn Khoa provided cultural immersion to Vietnamese language students of the University on a frequent, regular and voluntary basis. They laid themselves down as a sturdy, wide bridge across to the world of Vietnam. Choi Byung Wook through frequent discussions and exchanges provided me with much supplementary knowledge not just from his own dissertation topic (on the Nguyễn dynasty in Vietnam) but also about Vietnamese and Chinese history in general. We spent many hours reinforcing, sharing, and challenging what each had learned. Russell Heng Hiang-Khng is very well read and also insightful on politics of Vietnam, thus he has been a good resource person to scholars venturing into the study of contemporary Vietnamese politics. I thank him for his initial comments on my work. Hwang In-Won, Honna Jun, Yoshimatsu Hidetaka, Shannon Smith, Asofou So'o, Morten Pedersen, Drew Smith, Mizuno Kumiko, Elizabeth St. George, Hatmayoshi Kikue, all fellow students of the department, provided a forum for exchange of ideas as well as camaraderie of fellow-travellers. These colleagues also freely provided comparative information about their countries for the subject I study. I also wish to thank Yên Musgrove for letting me lodge at her house in 1999.

Among the support staff of the Department of Political and Social Change, I wish to thank Claire Smith and Beverley Fraser for the generosity and care they showed to students of the Department whenever the latter required help with anything at all. Any day one of them was absent from office, the Department's atmosphere was just not the same.

Many Vietnamese have contributed to this dissertation in no small measure. Among academics, I thank Dr Nguyễn Quang Ngọc for his initial comments on my original topic, as well as for his hospitality and facilitation when I first went to Hà Nội for my first field-trip in 1995. Dr Ngọc was part of the then Centre for Vietnamese and Inter-cultural Studies that sponsored my first two working visas, for the first field-trip and then for a second field-trip in 1996. Then Director of the Centre Professor Phan Huy Lê and his staff Dr Nguyễn Văn Kim did their best to connect me to a few wards as well as arrange interviews with various government departments of the city of Hà Nội. The Institute of Sociology, National Centre for Social Sciences and Humanities, sponsored my third working visa. I thank Professor Trịnh Duy Luân for his assistance and loan of materials he published, and Ms Khuất Thị Hai Oanh for doing the legwork on a survey for Chapter 2. The "sisters" of the library of the Institute of Information and Social Science were very helpful with location of materials and securing a regular seat for me in their crowded library.

Information about the wards gathered from non-written materials, however, came from many ordinary Vietnamese everywhere on the streets of Hà Nội. They allowed me to talk to them in depth about various issues, and they included good friends, neighbours, researchers, hairdressers, shopkeepers, journalists, policemen, housewives, retirees, roaming vendors, officials of the Hà Nội City, Hà Nội's districts and wards, low-level party and state officials, restaurant owners, government bureaucrats, taxi motorcycle drivers, and so on.

The Institute of Southeast Asian Studies, Singapore, provided the main funding for the four years of my studies at the Australian National University, while the Department of Political and Social Change and British Aerospace provided supplementary funding for fieldwork and other expenses. I wish to thank all three institutions.

Words of thanks must also go out to the reviewers who gave very detailed and helpful comments and suggestions. I have tried, in the limited time available amid a very tight schedule at the Institute of Southeast Asian Studies where I work, to accommodate all their suggestions. I agree with their criticisms on the shortcomings of this book. If there is an opportunity to bring out a revised edition, I would explore those suggestions that need more time than I can afford now. I am grateful also to Professor Michael Leaf of the University of British Columbia for his comments and encouragement, and also for allowing me to participate in his Phú Thượng project.

Within my personal circle, I wish to thank my parents and Jancy Yeo for their moral and financial support. Phạm Như Quỳnh, my main Vietnamese language teacher in Vietnam, deserves my life-long gratitude for teaching me so much about Vietnam and giving me so much of her time.

It remains for me to say that in spite of all that help, attention and care, I am still solely responsible for all mistakes and shortcomings of this book.

Abbreviations and Glossary

Acronyms

ĐĐK	*Đại Đoàn Kết*, the thrice-weekly newspaper published by the VFF
ĐTNCSHCM	Hồ Chí Minh Communist Youth Group
ĐLĐVN (Đảng Lao Động Việt Nam)	Vietnam Workers' Party, name of the Vietnamese communist party from 1960 to 1976
ĐCSVN (Đảng Cộng Sản Việt Nam)	Vietnamese name for the Vietnam Communist Party from 1976
DRV	Democratic Republic of Vietnam, name for the state located in northern Vietnam between 1945 and 1976.
HĐND (Hội Đồng Nhân Dân)	People's Council
HNM (*Hà Nội Mới*)	*New Hanoi*, daily newspaper of the Hanoi Party Branch.
KTT (Khu Tập Thể)	collective flats
NXB (Nhà Xuất bản)	short for "publishing house"
SRV	Socialist Republic of Vietnam, name of the Vietnamese state since 1976
TCCS (*Tạp chí Cộng sản*)	Communist Review, the theoretical monthly journal of the VCP
UBND (Ủy Ban Nhân Dân)	People's Committee
VCP (CPV also used in other works)	Vietnamese Communist Party. The name of the Party was changed several times in history, including ĐLĐVN and the Indochina Communist Party.

VFF	Vietnam Fatherland's Front, the united front organization that has the VCP as its dominant member and which includes all social and mass organizations of the country.
WPB (Đảng ủy phường)	Ward Party Branch, the branch of the VCP at the ward level.
WPSC	Ward Party Standing Committee, the standing committee of the WPB

Vietnamese Terms

chi bộ	party cell
Chính phủ	Government
Cụm dân cư	resident cluster
đồng	Vietnam's national currency
Đổi Mới	the process of structural reforms, mainly economic, that have been taking place in Vietnam since 1986. Formally Vietnam is still in the Đổi Mới process.
huyện	the prefecture, the level of state rural administration in between the province and the commune levels.
phường	ward, the lowest level of urban state administration in Vietnam
quận	district, the level of urban state administration between the ward and the city levels. Its rural equivalent is the *huyện*.
thành phố	city
tỉnh	province
tổ dân phố	resident group
tổ phó	deputy head of a resident group
tổ trưởng	head of a resident group

Name Conventions

As far as possible, Vietnamese names are spelt in full. This happens in most situations where Vietnamese names are used, because very few names are mentioned more than a few times in this book. Where repeat mention of a person's name is necessary, or when a person needs to be addressed, his or her given name rather than the family name is used, in keeping with the Vietnamese practice of addressing people by first names. An exception is made with regard to Hồ Chí Minh, who is addressed by his surname by everybody in Vietnam as a sign of respect. Names of frequently cited sources are abbreviated.

As far as possible as well, Vietnamese names and terms are also spelt with their diacritics and tone marks. Exceptions are when such are not used in the original texts that I quote.

Because I want to analyse state effectiveness at the ward level, and because the state and Communist Party are entwined, I use the term "ward party-state machinery", which comprises both party and state offices and officials in the ward. This term is used interchangeably with "ward local administration". Occasionally I use the term "state machinery", which excludes the party component.

1

Mediation Space in Everyday Urban Situations of Hà Nội

PART I: HOW TO LOOK AT STATE–SOCIETY RELATIONS IN VIETNAM

Is the state in Vietnam stronger than society, or is it the other way round? If the answer is for the state, why do party-state objectives in public policy get stonewalled, stalled, and even succumbed to changes and reversals by societal responses? If Vietnamese society has its strengths in this regard, why have the more politically conscious members of society not been able to do more to change the state, the party, and eventually the political system? These questions about the relative strengths of state and society, when they square off and interact, are key questions for understanding the nature of the contemporary political system of Vietnam, especially the question of where the political system is heading towards. They hover in the background of the research and writing for this book. They are interesting questions that can bring forth much debate on Vietnam.

This chapter argues that the present schools of thought on the subject need to move beyond their regular views of the Vietnamese party-state. These viewpoints, while contradictory to each other in some aspects, are complementary to each other; they are competing and complimentary representations of the ways state–society relations in Vietnam really work. Many scholars and writers concerned with Vietnam have a sense of this composite reality, but somehow this view has not been pointed out in a systematic manner. This book marshals facts and viewpoints to demonstrate this reality, and this chapter shows why a synthesis of two seemingly contradictory viewpoints is useful. This chapter argues that the state-disaggregation approach provides a tool to a more comprehensive understanding of state–society relations in Vietnam. This is because it makes us look into specific arenas. It makes us realize that generalizations, such as whether one is weaker or stronger than the other, guide us in the initial steps towards understanding, but they are limited in their usefulness in a situation that is very complex, such as that in Vietnam.

A demonstration of the grounds for the synthesis begins with showing how the schools are each valid in their views. The ground for synthesis is best supported by what can be termed the penumbra of state–society relations in Vietnam. The penumbra is the policy implementation level of the Vietnamese state–society relations. In this penumbra, local officials do not base their dealings with people only on laws and rules of the party-state. A considerable amount of mediation occurs at the everyday basic urban level; as a result, the Vietnamese party-state's policies are often not well implemented on account of this mediation space.

Mediation Space and Schools of Thought on Vietnamese State–Society Relations

I find it useful, following many others who have gone before me, to classify schools of thought on Vietnamese state–society relations into three: the "accommodating state" school, the "structural dominance" school, and the "bureaucratic socialism" school. These three schools have different views about the extent of party-state dominance of society, but all three agree on some general facets of Vietnamese state–society relations. In particular, they agree that the Vietnamese party-state tolerates neither alternative political parties nor social movements outside its structure of political management. Its human rights record has much room for improvement. Elections are not free; candidates have to be approved by the party-state and voters can only choose from among approved candidates. There is little freedom of speech or assembly that is politically against the party-state and one-party rule, because the party-state readily represses them. Any autonomous, organized social activity outside the party-state's control, even in matters such as flood relief, risk being branded as anti-state behaviour and subjected to political attack by the party-state. An apparatus exists to maintain political security for the party-state and to act against dissidents effectively. The administrative structure of the government allows the party-state to intrude into private lives of individuals. Economically, the state sector is dominant although private sector participation and ownership has been growing slowly since the mid-1980s.

The idea of mediation space belongs to a substream of the accommodating state school that focuses on how basic-level policy implementation failures allow mediation and thus qualify party-state dominance of society. While mediation is rooted in the accommodating state school, analysing why people resort to and how people use mediation space requires threads of the other schools of thought, which are the structural dominance and bureaucratic socialism schools.

The Accommodating State

When probing into details of how party-state dominance is maintained in reality, scholars of the accommodating state school of the literature emphasize society having manoeuvering space to do things differently from the party-state's norms, and perhaps even influence the upper levels of party-state authorities in changing those norms to suit practices in society. Therefore, the accommodating state school sees state–society relations as being marked by tolerance, responsiveness, and mutual influence. In its view, the party-state agencies could well have tried to enforce their rules strictly; but partly forced by circumstances, and partly because they want to continue enjoying mass support, they may choose to meet citizens half-way in some situations. Furthermore, the lower levels — or what T. H. Rigby observed to be "action levels" of the party-state (in the ex-Soviet Union) — may have something to do with this appearance or substance of accommodation.[1] They either initiate experiments, or shield people from harsh policies by not following top-level instructions. Sometimes what motivates action levels may be the adaptation of party-state policies so that they work better than their originals; consequently the central level tolerates these practices. For Vietnam, Brantly Womack has characterized the Vietnamese party-state as "mass-regarding" or "quasi-democratic".[2] This view is substantiated by studies that show parts of the Vietnamese party-state "softening" neo-Stalinist economic policies[3] and ignoring under-the-table production contracts among state-owned enterprises;[4] softening of harsh land reforms in North Vietnam in the 1950s after violent protests;[5] allowing some family farming instead of insisting on agricultural collectivization in North Vietnam in the 1960s;[6] allowing experiments with family farming in the late 1970s;[7] tolerance of participation by more social organizations outside the mono-organizational framework (this concept will be referred to in more detail later) in the 1990s;[8] and unplanned urbanization throughout the whole period of communist governance.[9] Many instances of accommodation had taken place before the Đổi Mới national reforms, officially beginning in 1986, thawed the political atmosphere.

Much closer to the heart of this book is the work of some scholars in the accommodating state school who zoom into the basic level as the key action level in shaping the character of state–society relations. These scholars show officials identifying themselves with the local community rather than with the party-state that employs them. Here, two motivations of the officials are found. First, the officials adapt policies or make exceptions for themselves or for people who are able to lobby them based on interests. Second, some of these exceptional decisions may be based on moral/cultural dynamics. For instance, Hy Van Luong found in Bát Tràng village close to Hà Nội that officials employed by the party-state refused to follow orders to increase taxes because that would have busted the village's enterprises and created unemployment, something which they were loathed to do. In fact village officials did the opposite. They reduced taxes, in order to increase business revenues – and to favour some families.[10] Thomas Sikor studied the implementation of reforestation policies in a commune of Son La province and found that local officials and its people colluded to illegitimately obtain more land and money from government reforestation and land allocation programmes.[11] On Hà Nội's streets, Peter Higgs's interviews with street traders revealed that they received their trading licences (for which they were otherwise ineligible) because they were friends, neighbours, or family members of ward officials.[12] In a study of a Hà Nội commune, Shaun Malarney found that notions of leadership, different in some aspects from party-state notions, affected how villagers viewed local politicians living in the commune and who were standing for election to represent the commune. In one instance, a party-state sponsored incumbent candidate was defeated in the commune election because he did not fit into local norms. Malarney found out that party-state officials had to give in to pressures to act more in the interests of members of the local community when implementing policies than sticking to official lines, and they had to be understanding and compassionate when dealing with villagers. Thus officials at the everyday level of the ward and the commune sometimes face a role conflict, because local norms that prescribe decent human — and leadership — behaviour clash with party-state norms.[13]

These studies of local-level mediation in Vietnam strike a chord among studies of village-level state–society relations in China that have emphasized what local authorities and residents do that gives society more space. China's rural situation shows the Vietnamese situation is not unique. This is seen in at least two aspects: state–society relations and the differences in statal leadership norms and societal leadership traditions. For the first aspect, scholars on China have noted that in the rural society of China, villagers have more power than has been credited to them; they have on many occasions refused to follow party-state directions. Sometimes, their refusal is due to anger with corruption and abuses of power at the local level.[14] Furthermore, in relation to the second aspect, both they and local officials act in concert and in accordance with shared interests opposite to that of party-state objectives. For instance, Jean Oi found that village production team leaders and villagers in China, forced by inappropriate party-state policies, co-operated to retain more grain and send less as taxes to the upper level of state authority. For the good of the village, local party-state officials ignored the practice.[15] While villagers were always interested in paying lower taxes, officials were motivated by personal gains or by local community interests that they had the mandate to represent.[16] Richard Madsen has also pointed out that perhaps in China there are diverging conceptions between the state and society on how leaders should behave.[17] This moral dimension is also important in Hà Nội, a point that will be illustrated by Chapters 4 and 5.

What local studies on Vietnam and China show is that officials can stand on the side of residents and make the party-state more accommodating to people at that level without challenging the structural or institutional dominance by the party-state. Accommodation is not an automatic result, but there is a constant process of interaction occurring among the three actors — residents, local officials, and the party-state. This interaction takes many forms, including coercion, resistance, negotiation, and even superficial imposition. In the accommodating state school of thought, therefore, state and society are mutually influencing, and the ultimate outcome of the contest between state and society for space is usually dynamic.

Structural Dominance

The structural dominance school sees little space for society to self-regulate or influence the party-state, except through approved channels in a multilayered hierarchy. Its "mono-organizational socialism" view sees the Vietnamese party-state forcing all social organizations and every individual to become members of the structure that it controls, and in every sector, society is represented by one mass organization, which has a countrywide network.[18] Examples of these organizations are the Women's

Union, the Labour Union, and the Youth Union. These organizations mobilize people to follow the party-state; thus another name for this model is "mobilizational authoritarianism".[19] The extent of political participation by society is limited to feedback on state policies through the corporatist framework, although leading members of these organizations at the central level do aspire to a political career.[20]

Bureaucratic Socialism

Related to the structural dominance view is the bureaucratic socialism view, espoused by Gareth Porter. It sees society playing little if any role in influencing the party-state. Porter argues that bureaucrats make and implement all decisions on behalf of the party-state (which has structural dominance over society) without countervailing forces outside it, with the exception of policy deliberation and debates at the highest level of the VCP. In addition, while Porter identifies the bureaucracy as the key "action level" and notes "creeping pluralism" within it, he sees bureaucrats as essentially unresponsive and authoritarian towards society but yet are equally powerful in relation to each other so that the bureaucratic system is pluralistic and gridlocked.[21] The bureaucracy is thus slow in action. Well-meaning policy proposals from one section usually mired in objections from other sections of the bureaucracy.

Porter's point about "creeping pluralism" within the bureaucracy is well taken if we consider evidence in persistent journalistic, political, and academic writings in Vietnam, which blame the bureaucracy for the lack of state effectiveness in implementing party-state policies. Porter's argument is further strengthened by the fact that political systems similar to Vietnam's also have the same malady of bureaucratism. Scholars' research into different levels and bureaucratic agencies of the USSR and People's Republic of China (PRC) party-states found bureaucrats dominating the party-state, except at the highest political level of decision-making. In those two communist countries, the process of policy-making within the party-state machinery has been marked more by divisions and pluralism among bureaucrats than by an ordered, monolithic view of the communist party.[22] William Taubman, for instance, noted that in the 1970s the USSR party-state's efforts to reform the system of housing provision were undermined by competition among bureaucratic agencies.[23] Cameron Ross also pointed out that there was a consensus-seeking style within the bureaucracy of the USSR because of relative power parity among different agencies.[24] Similarly, in China, rural reforms in the 1980s led to the central state authority, more than before, trying to balance between interests of conflicting state agencies.[25]

Which View Is Appropriate? A Synthesis?

If we want to determine, at the ward level of Hà Nội, who makes the formal decisions and policies, then the structural dominance is a useful approach. The party-state determines the structure of everyday urban state–society relations in Hà Nội's wards, which has as its chief component a party-state machinery in every ward. Most, if not all, leaders of these party-state bodies belong to exclusive groups, and they are vetted for office by the VCP. Under the command of the ward party-state machinery is a network of subward VCP, community and mass organization bodies that act as channels of instruction, mobilization, implementation, and feedback for party-state policies. This network and the ward's party-state machinery bring the party-state into every home, and also facilitate reporting of any dissidence or inappropriate behaviour or activities upwards to the district- and city-level party-state authorities, or ultimately the national government and the headquarters of the VCP, depending on the importance of the matter. Decisions for any ward are entirely made by officials of the party-state machinery. Within that machinery, the chief and senior executives of the wards are officials of the government, but they are always party members as well. They and their administrative and functional subordinates decide and intervene in daily issues of the ward. The ward party-state machinery has power in enforcing administrative procedures that residents are supposed to comply with in order to maintain their relations with the party-state, and in doing so residents are subjected to the ward party-state machinery's direction. Within the wards, therefore, the party-state is structurally dominant, and the party-state machinery is occupied by an exclusive group of party officials and bureaucrats who can make use of power in an authoritarian way.

The structural dominance school and the bureaucratic socialism school, however, do not reflect adequately the reality of mediation at the everyday urban level. Both those schools have three shortcomings. First, they give too little credit to people's use of resistance, in a disorganized way mostly, that can influence bureaucrats at the ward level. Sometimes this influence is channelled up and seen at the highest level of the party-state. Second, they overlook a considerable amount of self-regulation in urban neighbourhoods. Wards in Hà Nội, for example, hand over to groups of residents the power to decide on purely neighbourhood matters among themselves (within the framework of the law and leadership of the ward), such as how much pavement space a shopkeeper should and can have. In such cases, ward officials see no need to closely guide policy implementation, so long as these groups stayed within the boundaries drawn out for them. Third, the structural dominance school is weak in explaining a lack of vertical compliance — that of lower levels towards upper levels. At lower levels of the party-state, insubordination occurs frequently. One of these instances is when ward officials stand on the side of residents rather than on the side of higher up authorities. Although the bureaucratic socialism school recognizes such pluralities among sectors of the party-state, its argument about bureaucrats being unresponsive and authoritarian towards society is only half the picture. When basic-level officials listen to grievances and mediate in favour of local demands and needs, they are far from being "bureaucratic"; instead, they are being responsive without having the intention to influence formal policy-making. In 1996, a survey of thirteen communes (basic-level rural administration) by Trần Nho Thìn in the countryside around Hà Nội revealed, for instance, that 25.1 per cent, a significant number, of respondents thought their commune chairmen listened to people's opinions when performing their duties.[26] The evidence presented by scholars of the accommodating state school shows that bureaucrats do not necessarily stand only on the side of the state, nor only for themselves; when it comes to local, daily administration and solving everyday problems, they may stand up for their locale as well.

I have tried to make clear that the accommodating state school is a major reflection of mediation at the everyday basic urban level of state–society relations within the ward. But the reality as reflected by the other two schools contributes to mediation. Dominance of the party-state at the national level, which those two schools stress, allows it to make policies with little consultation with the masses. These policies are then handed over to wards for implementation. In the implementation process, however, residents of the ward often see problems with the policies. They seek and often receive some mediation space to deal with the problematic aspects of these policies. The existence of that space depends on the co-operation of bureaucrats and party officials who dominate decision-making in the wards. Therefore, the three schools of thought are mutually influencing, reflecting the idea that in reality state–society relations is dialogical.

The State-Disaggregation Approach

What appears also to be useful — a fourth way to look at the matter — is the "state-disaggregation" approach that examines low-level interactions of state–society relations.[27] While examining only "fragments of a nation"[28] has its drawbacks, this disaggregated approach towards state–society relations has its rewards. It allows one to look at different levels of state–society interaction. In the case of Vietnam, this approach reveals fairly different, sometimes even contradictory, patterns from one fragment to another within the whole of state–society relations. With this approach, the right questions to ask are not whether the state is strong, or society weak. Rather, one should ask what the relative strength of each in every particular arena of state–society interaction is. Who has the stronger ability to influence the other in one particular arena and is it only in that particular arena that such an assessment can be meaningful? This attention to arena-specific issues and dynamics is important because agencies of the party-state may not act or think according to what the central level directs; they may not even cooperate well with each other.[29] Therefore, actions of the party-state quite often may not add up to a well-articulated, coherent scheme, designed and directed from the top. If it is, then its ability to influence society is higher, and if not, vice versa.

Furthermore, disaggregating the state and looking closely at certain agencies or levels of government also reveals that the state and society are not necessarily separate and are frequently interactive.[30] In Vietnam and China, at the local level, there is a considerable amount of societal influence on the party-state as well as on the conduct and outcome of politics in which, through mediation and accommodation, new or hybrid ways of doing things arise. These new ways may contradict the directives or values of the party-state and they exist alongside the official way of doing things.[31] Such societal influence on the party-state develops from the lack of clear differentiation between public and private roles. In Vietnam, local officials often have to play dual roles of being party-state agents and of being a part of the local community. When the values of these two roles clash, mediation of state power often occurs. It dilutes local officials' sense of being state officials, but enhances their sense of being part of the local community.

Joel Migdal has suggested a range of four ideal results of state–society interaction.[32] I suggest, from the evidence this book presents, that this range of ideal results can be used to understand everyday state-society relations in Vietnam's urban areas everyday. See Table 1.1. It shows that within each arena to be discussed by this book, evidences show that each contains features of strength and weaknesses of party-state and society. The reader may also note that the party-state is generally stronger where decision-making or policy formulation is concerned, but society usually is able to triumph in policy implementation.

The key element in the varying degree of state dominance of society in Vietnam is the role of the local administrators. What Lucian Pye has said about local administrators in China applies adequately to the state–society relations in Hà Nội: "Playing their part, the local authorities proclaim the superiority of the capital and their obedience to its wishes, then act in terms that make the most sense locally."[33] In Hà Nội, the party-state dominates decision-making, but unpopular decisions are often mediated at the ward level. The mediation takes into consideration individual circumstances, and may have the cumulative effect of either massaging the political tension created by the unpopular policy, or changes to the policy in reality.

Approaching state–society relations in Vietnam from the perspective of everyday urban living interaction contributes to a more nuanced view of Vietnamese state–society relations. Insights gained from the evidence do not negate the structural dominance school of thought regarding state–society relations in Vietnam. Indeed, they confirm that the Vietnamese party-state dominates society in some fundamental ways. At the same time, they show that the party-state machinery, of which the ward is a part, does not necessarily work as prescribed by higher levels. Alongside general compliance of society and lower levels, a significant amount of daily mediation exists. Such mediation not only manifests resistance and evasion of state control, but also shows the capacity of people to use the confusion of roles as well as other weaknesses in the administrative system to influence the party-state. Higher levels of the party-state do not necessarily know about this mediation and their capacity in preventing mediation is limited. Consequently, in addition to being "domineering", the Vietnamese party-state is also "accommodating".

TABLE 1.1
Migdal's Range of Ideal Results

Arena	*(1)* *Total transformation of society by the Party-State*	*(2)* *Party-state incorporates social forces*	*(3)* *Party-state is incorporated by social forces*	*(4)* *Party-state fails to direct or even influence society*
Local administration	Party-state controls the local administration system	Various social forces play a non-decisive, consultative role.	When people lobby the government through the administration system to modify policies.	When officials go against party-state policies or when people simply disobey the administrative system.
Elections	Elections controlled by the party-state	Various social forces have a say in nominations and have their nominees approved by the party-state.	?	Election results show the party-state totally dominant, but there are failures of a few favoured candidates show otherwise. Proxy-voting makes the results hollow.
Traffic order on the pavement	The party-state controls traffic planning. Periodic campaigns obtain good results, but only initially.	Party-state uses social groups to achieve its policy requirements, i.e. volunteer groups, self-regulation.	Shop owners, food operators use various sorts of motivations to urge officials not to apply policy. These forces are disorganized.	At certain times of the day and year, pavement activity suggest defiance against party-state rules.
Housing	Party-state determines land and housing regime	Party-state relies partly on social forces to contribute to housing construction. Gradually allows individuals to build their own homes.	Superficial compliance towards party-state rules. Black economy of bribes for covering up infringements and illegal land/house sale and house constructions flourish.	Land encroachement; building/construction rules ignored. Many rules in land regime changed due to their contradicting popular practice.

PART II: MEDIATION SPACE

Ms Phương

It was the year 1997. Phương smiled and said to me: "Little brother, you have your noodles without prawn paste, more noodles, more shallots, and even more fried onions with a piece of *tofu*, don't you?" It was only my second visit to Phương's pavement noodle stall, but her good memory and hospitality surprised me and made me curious about her work. I soon discovered Phương's cheerfulness hid her many personal difficulties. Close to her forties, she was divorced and lived with her aged mother and an early-teens son on Lý Thường Kiệt Street in Hà Nội. A decade ago, she was retrenched from the textile factory, where she worked for many years and learned her only occupational skill. With neither a job, nor a pension, nor state welfare, she supported her family by selling noodles for breakfast on the pavement of the street where she lived. Her livelihood offended pavement rules of the state and was thus not eligible for a business licence. The more important reason was she was not registered as living in that locality where her mother lived. However, in return for regular "taxes" she paid to the ward, the local urban authority, ward officials informally allowed Phương to trade within certain hours for income to support her mother and son. Phương earned 500 đồng for every bowl of noodles sold. Several times a year since 1995, following orders from higher Hà Nội City authorities, ward (the lowest urban administrative unit of the state) policemen have been enforcing a public order campaign against pavement hawkers. The enforcers always raided in the morning, during the peak hour of business. The raids increased in frequency when important state celebrations or cultural dates approach. Each time, with help from her mother and customers like me, Phương saved first the large pot of hot soup and then the baskets of vegetables and noodles, while ward policemen normally confiscated all of Phương's chairs and utensils and did not go further than that.

Three hours after one such incident in April 1999, tense, tired, and emotional, she told me she had gone to the ward authority to plead, and had gotten back her trade tools after paying a fine of 20,000 đồng (equivalent to profit from 40 bowls of noodles sold, or half-

a-day's profit). The next day, she continued her trade as allowed by the informal understanding with ward officials. But she was always nervous about impending raids, which ward officials could not help except to generally advise her to keep off the pavement at certain hours. In late 1999, she used, without success, her "connection" within a police department to minimize such disturbances by the state to her small subsistence business, which earned on average about a million đồng (around US$65) a month. In a year with many important events held in Hà Nội, her income may be halved. An unfortunate raid may cost her a whole day's earnings, plus costs of replacing equipment and fines. The police connection failed to produce results as the city police department referred the matter back to the ward administration concerned. But in 2001, a turn of fortune saw the plight of this three-generation single-parent family highlighted in a newspaper. This led to an interview with the ward authority, and official recognition of Phương's difficulties. The ward allowed her to continue on the pavement and instructed the policemen to take a lighter touch. In 2002, Phương decided to move out of the city centre and back to another home in suburban Mai Động Ward because selling other things proved more profitable.

Mr Sơn

Much higher up on the social-economic ladder is Sơn, a forty-year-old academic in state employment who lived in a nearby ward from Phương. Sơn also worked part-time arranging for Vietnamese labourers to work abroad. His wife had a profitable toyshop. After saving up for years, in 1998 the family wanted to build a new house in Hà Nội's Thirty-Six Streets, a heritage area that had many restrictions on housing design and construction. They chose that area in order to live close to Sơn's parents-in-law. They faced long bureaucratic delays, one of which was to have the house design approved by the city chief architect. Sơn anticipated these difficulties as he had read and heard much about them. To pre-empt trouble, Sơn asked an architect friend to submit a simple, modest house design for approval, which was secured quickly and which allowed Sơn to obtain a construction licence from the city authority. Sơn then constructed the house according to his own, much more elaborate design that would not have passed government scrutiny. When the house was completed, ward authority officials came to check for design-reality discrepancies. They quickly found out, on arrival, that the house exceeded the height restrictions by 60 centimeters. Although the height exceeded was as short as an arm's length, it would have been a key issue if it were made out to be. Sơn knew he risked hardening the officials' attitude if he argued, and furthermore, many other building code offences in his house were waiting to be discovered by a thorough check. Politically astute, Sơn quickly negotiated a settlement with ward officials: they let his house pass inspection in exchange for a fine of US$700 paid to the ward for the height offence. The certification allowed Sơn to inhabit his house without further troubles from the state. Sơn told me he was lucky. His neighbour paid a few thousand U.S. dollars a few years ago to "pass" the inspection. For Sơn, the fine is affordable. By using the front of house as a retail shop, he can earn that much money in one or two months.

Mediation Space and Vietnamese State–Society Relations

The informal methods that the two ordinary Vietnamese Phương and Sơn used were illegal, but there are benefits in return for the risk. Phương and Sơn evaded regimes of the supposedly dominating Vietnamese party-state.[34]

Every day, thousands of other Vietnamese in Hà Nội use such informal methods, often with the co-operation of ward officials as the "third party" between them and the party-state, in "reworking the state's boundaries".[35] The result is people and ward officials create what I call a mediation space that exists in the penumbra of party-state dominance. Although mediation leaves mostly undisturbed, the overall shape and size of the shadow, which the party-state cast over society, is an important feature of the country's political system.

Mediation space is a daily statement of the equivocality of party-state power. Sometimes the statement is clearly articulated by activities seen on the streets and in the urban neighbourhoods of Hà Nội, such as by Phương's noodles operation. At other times, the statement is hidden by a thin veil of compliance, such as Sơn's deal with construction inspectors. Mediation space, however, has been known and utilized by the majority of people in Hà Nội, as well as people all over Vietnam. Vietnamese authorities lambaste this phenomenon. The printed evidence is a large amount of newspaper reports of actual situations. These reports criticize the lack of state effectiveness in implementing policies and their possible causes. Despite the newspaper coverage, and because much more mediation remains hidden, the true extent of mediation at the ward level may never be known, but it is probably quite large and varies from ward to ward and from activity to activity. The irony is that in their private lives, at their places of their residences, Vietnamese officials and journalists who condemn such infringements also engage in mediation in order that some daily routines and other more important action in their lives can be carried out.

Mediation has to be done by local officials who have discretionary powers to decide whether to apply rules, although residents may well suggest the idea to them. Mediation occurs when ward officials interpose for residents, and treat lightly or ignore their infractions, for which state regimes prescribe punishments. Officials' motivations are varied: from the material, such as bribes or returned favours, to the non-material, such as negligence. There is also, significantly, a set of moral/cultural dynamics that encourage officials to help their family, friends and neighbours and the less fortunate, such as Phương the noodle-seller.

Three Causes of Mediation Space

The Socioeconomic Situation

The socioeconomic situation in Vietnam since the mid-1970s is one major factor that pushed ward officials and residents to do deals in the mediation space. From the late 1970s until the late 1980s and early 1990s, the following economic problems confronted the Vietnamese party-state: the U.S. trade embargo; the end of aid from China (and, later, the USSR); huge military expenditures to counter the China threat in the north and maintain an occupation force for ten years in Cambodia; and severely reduced food production in the late 1970s and early 1980s, caused by a natural disaster in 1979, and disincentives that caused peasants to produce less, such as agricultural collectivization in the Mekong Delta. While the state and collective sectors of the economy sagged due to the conditions above, the private sector in many facets of the economy was banned or greatly restricted until 1987, and did not develop until the early 1990s. All these factors led to a decline and stagnation in real growth. United Nations statistics show Vietnam's per capita real annual income fell from US$101 in 1976 to US$94 in 1981, and returned to the 1976 level only in 1984. While income continued to rise after 1984 by around 30 per cent each year during the remainder of the 1980s, this was offset and left behind by hyperinflation, which reached as high as 800 per cent in one year. In Hà Nội, residents' income had been higher than the national average. But the large majority of people in Hà Nội were employed by the state sector, so they were hit hard by hyperinflation. Their fixed salaries typically paid for only 25 per cent of the average household expenditure.[36] In the early 1980s, Hà Nội residents "became outrightly defiant and complained bitterly about the deteriorating [economic] conditions".[37] In 1999, per capita average annual income in Vietnam was still only about US$300, although in Hà Nội the average per capita monthly income (including salary) was around US$600. In 2005, the Vietnamese per capita income rose to US$800. In the 1990s, the purchasing power of a state salary was weak, being only enough to pay for an employee's breakfasts in Hà Nội.[38] In the north after 1954 social goods such as housing, education, and medical care were supplied by the party-state (because the private sector was banned). But since the late 1970s, in the midst of deep economic difficulties, the party-state could no longer afford to provide the social goods at a level and quality people needed, adding to the economic difficulties in a typical urban household.

Undaunted, however, people in Hà Nội have devised coping strategies. The difficult situation drove many of them to circumvent party-state restrictions and engage in private socioeconomic activities to survive. To supplement household income, many families reared pigs and chickens in crowded dwellings and flats, and sold them on the illegal private markets, thus infringing at least two state rules.[39] Joined by a substantial amount of surplus peasant labour, many urban residents sat on street corners and opened little pavement stalls to offer goods, services, and labour for employment by the underground private economy, infringing economic and traffic regulations.[40] With higher income since the late 1980s, more people demanded better living conditions, such as improved housing, and they were able to find alternative solutions, with the help of officials of the ward and other levels, when the party-state still banned those essentially private sector solutions but could not build enough flats that are of good quality to meet the demand.[41]

These coping strategies, of which I have only mentioned a few, created everyday dilemmas for ward officials who were responsible for enforcing rules and regulations. Not being strict made ward authorities look bad, because of the enormous social disorder that those everyday activities created. Being too sticky about rules, however, made life repressive for their residents, who were merely reacting to economic problems that were not of their own making. Furthermore, requests for mediation became opportunities for ward officials to extract bribes, or answer the call of moral leadership by helping their friends and neighbours. On the part of residents, the price they pay for having mediation has been largely affordable.

Institutional Weaknesses in the Ward System and the Local Administration System in General

The second cause of mediation is institutional weaknesses in the administration system reflected in the wards. The VCP is aware that law enforcement and policy implementation requires an effective state administration. Given the socialist state's desire for control over society, the party-state relies on local administration for policy implementation and law enforcement.[42] In practice, in the post-1954 period the party-state found it difficult to control its bureaucracy.[43] To the extent of sounding contrite, the party-state frequently blamed the bureaucracy as the major fault line preventing proper implementing of policies of the government.[44] The local administration system in general is plagued by an unmeritocratic electoral practice, insubordination, incompetence and corruption, lack of checks and balances, and lack of comprehensive supervision and control by upper level authorities.

Prevailing party-state ideologies of politics and administration contribute to weaknesses in the local administration system. Electing competent people and eradicating insubordination requires changes to the concept and practice of "democracy". Its meaning in Vietnam has overemphasized national unity and communist party leadership (which limits the types of candidates who are allowed to run in elections and become chief executives of each and every level and unit of local administration). Reforms are required to avoid appointing key executive officials based on political (party membership) and other unmeritocratic considerations. Eradication of corruption requires, among other measures, adequate checks on and sufficient remuneration and penalties for bureaucrats and officials; but the party-state has vastly inadequate resources.

In espousing the philosophy of governance in a unitary, democratic state, Vietnamese leaders try to maintain a balance between centralism and the right of lower level administration bodies to make exceptions to central policies in the name of democracy. Often, without adequate checks to prevent abuse, the balance tilts towards the second element of the rights of local authorities to do what they think are better suited to local conditions.[45] The lax supervision and control by the Vietnamese state over the basic level local administration system and its officials' behaviour is probably the most important "leakage of authority" of the Vietnamese administration system.[46] Frequently officials themselves engaged in illegal activities and did not set a good example for people they are supposed to enforce rules on.[47] The economic conditions, after all, affected everyone. One Vietnamese author, writing in the official Communist Journal, noted that

> In the management of the state now we have to overcome one unusual phenomenon quickly, which is many laws after being promulgated are not carried out seriously, or even not carried out. Many cadres, party members offend the law, especially cadres who abuse their position and power in performing illegal activities but who are not dealt with severely. If we do not resolutely eradicate this phenomenon then our state will have laws but without the rule of law, and then we will not be able to manage society according to the law.[48]

In 1988, one source noted, on average about 16 per cent of legal offenders every year were party members, cadres,[49] or civil servants. In Hà Nội in 1996, among 631 offenders who illegally bought and sold 115.6 hectares of state land, 98 offenders (15.5 per cent) were state cadres. Ten per cent of these state cadres were chairmen of communes and wards.[50] In a 1997 newspaper survey 55 per cent of the 4,000 respondents nationwide listed corruption as the second most urgent social problem. Bureaucrats and cadres received 22 per cent of votes as the third top category of people who respondents felt needed to be educated about a civilized way of life that encapsulated virtues such as rule of law, discipline, being responsible and rational, and to do the right thing in fighting social problems.[51]

Other than inadequate checks, the central authority may be providing disincentives to local officials and authorities to obey orders, thus causing them to lose out if they do the right thing. For instance, in 1979, in the attempt to speed up circulation of goods to reduce shortages and inflation, the central authority ordered all highway and road checkpoints set up during the war to be closed because they impeded legitimate goods transport. But the central authority forgot that many local administration units imposed levies on goods transiting these checkpoints in order to gather revenue to make up for the shortfall in state budget allocations. In other words, those checkpoints were a local adaptation strategy circumventing a shortcoming not of their own doing. Closure orders were reissued in 1986 and 1990 apparently because many localities continued to operate the checkpoints.[52] Another example was seen in the early 1980s. Attempting to control the use of video cassette recorders in Hà Nội, the party-state required all owners to register them. Many military, police, local authority and party officials, however, used the machines to screen videos for a fee, which helped them maintain a decent standard of living in the face of hyperinflation. The ban was impossible to enforce without officials first setting the example. Murray Hiebert found more than 20,000 violators in 1989.[53] Presently, no Vietnamese need register their video machines with the government.

Moral/Cultural Context

The third cause of mediation space is that ward officials also operate in a moral or cultural context, not just in the legal or administrative context. Contact with residents on a daily basis is a significant influence on formal as well as informal behaviour of ward officials. One senior Vietnamese government official noted,

> Officials of basic political authorities of the commune, the ward, and the townlets play very important roles as their level reaches the people directly. They relate, live, and contact with the people daily not only on matters relating to the state, but also on matters of relations in families, among neighbours, and customs and habits ...[54]

Ward officials share a common local identity as members of the same neighbourhood and they are expected to help local residents when they face difficulties. These cultural dynamics place local officials in what David

Kelliher calls an "ambiguous political niche" with conflicting roles.[55] First, they are expected to intervene for family and clan members. Referring to this imperative, Vietnamese use the old saying "One of us becomes a mandarin and the whole clan gets favours" (*Một người làm quan, cả họ được nhờ*).

Second, officials often are also inclined, for the sake of feelings and good working and neighbourly relationships, to seek compromise with residents rather than press for full compliance. This cultural trait is encapsulated in a number of Vietnamese folk sayings, one of which is "Nine is accepted as Ten" (*chín bỏ làm mười*).[56] This idea comes quite close to what William Duiker pointed out as governance that emphasizes moral virtues ("the Tao" in Chinese or "The Way") rather than laws.[57] One of these virtues, as Malarney has shown, is local leaders should be forgiving of minor misdeeds of fellow community members.[58]

Third, ward officials sometimes are moved by the difficult circumstances of people and they become compassionate (the Vietnamese words are *thông cảm*) and selective in applying laws and enforcing policies. A vivid example of compassion is the case of a woman living in one ward I was attached to. While I was interviewing a member of the ward people's committee, the woman entered the ward office with her daughter to register her daughter's birth. The child, however, had already reached school-going age. The mother had chosen not to register the child at birth because her "marriage" was unregistered and thus against the law. Schools required parents to produce birth registration certificates of children for enrolment, and only the ward has the authority to issue birth certificates.[59] Instead of imposing a fine on her straightaway for not registering the child, the woman official, the vice-chair of the ward women's association, advised her of a method to evade state penalties: get her marriage and her child's birth "witnessed" retrospectively with the help of her "resident group head" (see explanation of this term in Chapter 2). Once she has done that, this female official would help her register the child's birth retrospectively as well. By a stroke of compassion, state laws on marriage, on rights of women, and its population planning policy were evaded. Yet, none of the other officials in the ward office, all sitting around us and having heard the story, told this mature official of more than fourteen years' work experience that she was doing the "wrong" thing.[60] In 1999, this woman official was asked by her ward party-state machinery to stand for election to the ward's people's council. After she was elected, she was promoted to vice-chair of the same ward people's committee.

The moral/cultural dynamics, when in operation, pose a question for the distinction between state and society. When the terms *state–society relations*, *state*, *party-state*, and *society* are used in this book, they mean the common meanings in political science. State–society relations refers to relations between actors and institutions of governance on the one side, and the subjects of governance on the other, but the distinction between them is not always clear-cut. State and society are separate entities because each of them is an observable independent phenomenon. In many countries, state and society have organizations, interests, and activities independent of each other. State organizations are meant to be impersonal, public organizations. Their officials, while they are members of society, play the role of state agents when executing the will of the state. But as Benedict Kerkvliet has pointed out, making a distinction between state and society should not blind us to instances whereby state and society are intermingled.[61] Jean Oi has argued, and her point is critical to the argument of this book, that officials and people in a locale may stand shoulder to shoulder and act as one "corporate group" in reaction to and in denying the state's objectives which clash with those of the village. Remarking on rural China, Jean Oi said the village "lies at the intersection of state and society; it can be reduced to neither ... Here one can observe how state regulations ... [and] directives are circumvented, twisted, or ignored [by villagers and local officials]."[62] What seems to matter to what we can conclude is, at what level of interaction do we observe state–society relations.

In the wards of Hà Nội, I observed a similar "intersection" where state and society intermingle. This point comes across when ward officials take up the cudgel for the local community they live or work in, and consequently produce policy outcomes at that level which may not resemble what the party-state wants. At most times, and this is important to note, the ward is a part of the party-state, having an organization, an office, and officials who relate with residents as a corporate entity, which is the state. Moreover, it is useful to remember this point to avoid exaggeration, role conflict frequently is resolved in compliance towards the state. Much depends on the actual situation and script of play between the upper levels of the party-state, ward officials, and residents in the ward. But when officials do mediate for residents, their state role becomes hazy, especially when they do so for reasons of informal ties or compassion so that people like Phương the noodle seller can breathe more easily. The line between state and society at the local urban level, I argue, shifts all the time.

Overview of Chapters

The rest of the book will demonstrate the interplay of the three contributing causes of mediation. It takes readers through analyses of the structure, organization, and operations of the ward and implementation by the ward of three sets of party-state policies. In one of these policy areas, the party-state is dominant. In the other two, the power and authority of the party-state are much more equivocal. The choice of the three policy area was dictated by my interests and what I observed to be arenas of state–society relations that would demonstrate contrast and comparison, especially where the roles of local urban administrators were concerned.

Chapter 2 describes and analyses how the typical Hà Nội ward administration unit is organized. It shows the sturdy framework that the party-state has erected in the ward to administer urban society and mobilize it in an authoritative way. Some quarters within the party-state, however, have questioned the usefulness of the ward-level local authority. Some have also argued that the ward is unnecessary. The chapter will examine these discussions about the relevance, purpose, and effectiveness of the ward and outline the development of the ward system from late 1970s to late 1990s. Finally, this chapter will elaborate how institutional weaknesses and the moral/cultural dynamics can expand the mediation space.

Chapter 3 examines elections, an area in which the Vietnamese party-state is firmly in control. Elections are not an everyday matter. But discussing them helps us to understand how the dominance of the party-state is achieved. The chapter outlines how meticulously the party-state ensures victory of its candidates, through control of the election machinery and the screening of election candidates. At each level, the election machinery and screening process are in the hands of that level's top party-state officials. The party-state also tries to beef up the appearance of regime legitimacy by mobilizing a maximum turnout, and to make its notions of what constitute a democratic election — and a democratic political system — prevail. Elections also illuminate how the ward-level authorities carefully toe the line when the party-state scrutinizes implementation closely. Yet even in elections there is a significant degree of informality. Dissent and dissatisfaction among residents with electoral practices are also detectable. Through certain informal practices, as we shall see, ward officials manage to keep these tensions from becoming open and embarrassing to the party-state.

Chapters 4 and 5 look at areas in which the party-state's dominance is much less secure and ward-level mediation is more common. Chapter 4 studies party-state efforts to implement policies regarding traffic, especially pavement usage, in order to reduce traffic accidents. The problems that Phương's noodles business encountered are part of that effort. In the 1980s and 1990s, the party-state repeatedly had to wage new campaigns to impose order on the city's pavements and streets. That several attempts were required meant that the party-state had failed to fundamentally alter the situation until only very recently. Traffic disorder, however, is not simply a traffic problem. In crowded and infrastructure-poor cities such as Hà Nội, numerous daily social and economic issues also affect traffic management. These include lack of employment, public transport, and public space. Wards could not have solved such problems, yet their officials were made responsible for eradicating them. On the formal level, the wards officials often got the blame for pavement disorder, even though macro-level factors constrained their ability to rein in disorderly and illegal behaviour on the pavements. Instead of facing a supposedly straightforward task of getting "illegal" activities off the pavements, wards officials found themselves having to balance between party-state commands and people's need for employment, space, and convenience. They ended up trying to keep things under control during certain times of the day when the party-state is "looking", while at other times leaving people to do what they want.

Chapter 5 examines party-state efforts to maintain its housing regime and prevent unlicensed construction. In the 1950s–1970s, the party-state attempted to provide or manage all housing in Hà Nội. Lack of funding and other reasons forced the state to abandon this. Gradually the party-state established a new housing regime that recognized the role of private housing. The final concession in law to the private sector came around 1990, after a decade of the party-state fighting "illegal construction", during which each new campaign brought worse results. Ward authorities were partly to blame. But their mistakes were also related to the macro socioeconomic issues beyond their control: the phenomenal housing shortage and the unreasonableness of building laws and administrative procedures. Many people were driven to private solutions to the severe shortages. Similar to the traffic order issue, ward officials had to take into consideration people's needs and sentiments. Consequently, ward officials could not enforce rules rigorously. And many officials also participated in illegal construction. Like every one else, they too needed better housing, which the party-state was unable to provide. Top levels of the party-state understood this problem. Like ward officials, decision-makers of the party-state are usually in a dilemma. Ignoring building code offences meant rapid increases in housing stock and political stability. But to have that good result, it also had to tolerate disrespect for the rule of law and for codes that took into consideration safety, land-use, and city-planning issues. Thus, the limits to state capacity in regulating construction is manifested in neglect and deliberate offences against building codes, safety regulations, and zoning regulations. Many Hà Nội residents know that they can circumvent whatever the party-state forbids, as long as they have the financial ability to buy officials' mediation.

Notes

1. T. H. Rigby, "Politics in the Mono-organizational Society", in *Authoritarian Politics in Communist Europe: Uniformity and Diversity in One-Party States,* edited by Andrew C. Janos (Berkeley: Institute of International Studies, University of California, 1976), p. 31.
2. Brantly Womack, "The Party and the People: Revolutionary and Postrevolutionary Politics in China and Vietnam", *World Politics* 39, no. 4 (1987): 479–507.
3. Adam Fforde, "The Political Economy of 'Reform' in Vietnam: Some Reflections", in *The Challenge of Reform in Indochina,* edited by Borje Ljunggren (Massachusetts: Harvard Institute for International Development, Harvard University, 1993), p. 301; Melanie Beresford, *Vietnam: Politics, Economics and Society* (London and New York: Pinter Publishers, 1988), pp. 117–19; Melanie Beresford, "The political economy of dismantling the 'bureaucratic centralism and subsidy system' in Vietnam", in *Southeast Asia in the 1990s: Authoritarianism, Democracy and Capitalism,* edited by Kevin Hewison et al. (St. Leonards, NSW: Allen & Unwin, 1993), p. 218.
4. Stefan de Vylder and Adam Fforde, *Vietnam: An Economy in Transition* (Stockholm: Swedish International Development Authority, 1988), pp. 67–72; Vo Nhan Tri, *Vietnam's Economic Policy since 1975* (Singapore: Institute of Southeast Asian Studies, 1990), p. 17.
5. Tan Teng Lang, *Economic Debates in Vietnam: Issues and Problems in Reconstruction and Development (1975–1984),* Research Notes and Discussions Paper No. 55 (Singapore: Institute of Southeast Asian Studies, 1985), p. 6.
6. Benedict J. Tria Kerkvliet, "Village-State Relations in Vietnam: The Effect of Everyday Politics on Decollectivization", *Journal of Asian Studies* 54, no. 2 (1995): 407; Benedict J. Tria Kerkvliet "Wobbly Foundations: Building

Cooperatives in Rural Vietnam, 1955–1961", *Southeast Asia Research* 6, no. 3 (1998): 193–252.

7. Tetsusaburo Kimura, *The Vietnamese Economy 1975-1986: Reform and International Relations* (Tokyo: Institute of Developing Economies, 1989).

8. Michael Gray, *Creating Civil Society? The Emergence of NGOs in Vietnam* (London: School of Oriental and African Studies, September 1997).

9. Nigel Thrift and Dean Forbes, *The Price of War: Urbanization in Vietnam 1954–85* (London: Allen and Unwin, 1986), pp. 164–65.

10. Hy Van Luong, "The Political Economy of Vietnamese Reforms: A Microscopic Perspective from Two Ceramics Manufacturing Centers", in *Reinventing Vietnamese Socialism: Doi Moi in Comparative Perspectives*, edited by William S. Turley and Mark Selden (Boulder, CO: Westview Press, 1993), p. 139.

11. Thomas Sikor, "Village–State Relations in Vietnam: The Role of the Local State", paper presented at the Annual Meeting of the Association for Asian Studies, Boston, 1999.

12. Peter Higgs, "The Footpath Economy and Beyond: Factors Affecting Social and Economic Change in a District of Hà Nội", paper presented at the Asian Studies Association of Australia Annual Conference, Melbourne, 1996.

13. Shaun Kingsley Malarney, "Culture, Virtue, and Political Transformation in Contemporary Northern Vietnam", *Journal of Asian Studies* 6 (1997): 900. Note that "commune" refers to a cluster of villages and is the smallest rural administrative unit of the state.

14. James Tyson and Ann Tyson, *Chinese Awakenings: Life Stories from the Unofficial China* (Boulder, CO: Westview Press, 1995), pp. 7–36.

15. Jean C. Oi, *State and Peasant in Contemporary China: The Political Economy of Village Government* (Berkeley, CA: University of California Press, 1989), pp. 7–10 and Ch. 6. For similar instances, see Anita Chan, Richard Madsen and John Unger, *Chen Village under Mao and Deng,* Expanded and Updated edition (Berkeley, CA: University of California Press, 1992).

16. Daniel Roy Kelliher, *Peasant Power in China: The Era of Rural Reform, 1979–1989* (New Haven and London: Yale University Press, 1992), pp. 82–88.

17. Richard Madsen, *Morality and Power in a Chinese Village* (Berkeley, CA: University of California Press, 1984).

18. Carlyle A. Thayer, *Political Development in Vietnam, 1975-1985* (electronic copy) (1994); Yeosnik Jeong "The Rise of State Corporatism in Vietnam", in *Contemporary Southeast Asia* 19, no. 2 (1997): 161; Brantly Womack, "Reform in Vietnam: Backwards Towards the Future," *Government and Opposition* 27, no. 2 (1992): 183; William Turley, "Party, State, and People: Political Structure and Economic Prospects", in *Reinventing Vietnamese*

Socialism, edited by Turley and Selden, p. 272; Stein Tonnesson, "What the Vietnamese State Can Do", paper presented to the State and Society network conference in Copenhagen, 27 September 1996, p. 10.

19. Turley, "Party, State, and People", p. 269.

20. de Vylder and Fforde, *Vietnam: An Economy in Transition*, pp. 44–47; Womack, "Reform in Vietnam", pp. 177–89; Carlyle A. Thayer, "Mono-Organizational Socialism and the State", in *Vietnam's Rural Transformation*, edited by Benedict Tria Kerkvliet and D. J. Porter (Boulder, CO: Westview Press; and Singapore: Institute of Southeast Asian Studies, 1995), p. 44. Stein Tonnesson (1996) noted that this corporatist model can be traced back to a system of voluntary associations that mobilized support for the war of resistance against the French. These voluntary associations formed the Viet Minh and metamorphosized into the Vietnam Fatherland Front (VFF) of today. See his "What the Vietnamese State Can Do", paper presented to the State and Society network conference in Copenhagen, 27 September 1996, p. 6.

21. See especially Preface and Chs. 3–6 in Gareth Porter, *Vietnam: The Politics of Bureaucratic Socialism* (Ithaca: Cornell University Press, 1993).

22. See William Taubman, *Governing Soviet Cities: Bureaucratic Politics and Urban Development in the USSR* (New York: Praeger Publishers, 1973); Andrew Coulson "From Democratic Centralism to Local Democracy", in *Local Government in Eastern Europe*, edited by Andrew Coulson (Hants and Brookfield: Edward Elgar, 1995), pp. 1–19; Kenneth Lieberthal and Michel Oksenberg, *Policy Making in China: Leaders, Structures, and Processes* (Princeton, NJ: Princeton University Press, 1988); Xie Weizhi, "The Semihierarchical Totalitarian Nature of Chinese Politics", in *Comparative Politics* 25 (April 1993): 313–30; Zhao Suisheng, "China's Central-Local Relationship: A Historical Perspective", and Luo Xiaopeng, "Rural Reform and the Rise of Localism", both in *Changing Central-Local Relations in China*, edited by Jia Hao and Lin Zhimin (Boulder, CO: Westview Press, 1994) pp. 19–34 and 113–34 respectively. For the role of bureaucracies in determining the effectiveness of states in Third World countries, see Joel S. Migdal, *Strong Societies and Weak States: State–Society Relations and State Capabilities in the Third World* (Princeton, NJ: Princeton University Press, 1988), pp. 209, 252–53.

23. Taubman, *Governing Soviet Cities*, p. 55.

24. Cameron Ross, *Local Government in the Soviet Union* (London: Croom Helm, 1987), pp. 3–4.

25. Luo Xiaopeng, "Rural Reform", pp. 113–34.

26. Trần Nho Thìn, "Đổi mới tổ chức và hoạt động của Ủy ban Nhân dân Xã" [Reform the organization and operation of the Commune People's Committee], Ph.D. dissertation submitted to the Viện Nghiên cứu Nhà nước và Pháp luật,

Trung tâm Khoa học Xã hội và Nhân văn Quốc gia and Bộ Giáo dục và Đào tạo, Hà Nội, 1996, p. 76.

27. Joel S. Migdal, "The state in society: An approach to struggles for domination", in *State Power and Social Forces: Domination and Transformation in the Third World,* edited by Joel S. Migdal, Atul Kohli, and Vivienne Shue (Cambridge: Cambridge University Press, 1994), p. 15.

28. Keith W. Taylor, "Vietnamese Studies in North America", paper presented at the International Conference on Vietnamese Studies, Hanoi, July 1998, p. 8. Keith Taylor was using the term to refer to difficulties of any piece of research on Vietnam being representative of the whole of Vietnam.

29. Atul Kohli and Vivienne Shue, "State power and social forces: On political contention and accommodation in the Third World", in *State Power and Social Forces,* edited by Migdal, Kohli, and Shue, p. 294. For a study of how the socialist bureaucracy may act independently from the party-state, see Kenneth Lieberthal and Michel Oksenberg, *Policy Making in China: Leaders, Structures, and Processes* (Princeton, NJ: Princeton University Press, 1988).

30. Migdal, "The state in society", pp. 9 and 23.

31. Vivienne Shue, *The Reach of the State* (Stanford, CA: Stanford University Press, 1988), p. 25.

32. Migdal, "The state in society", p. 24.

33. Lucian Pye, "The Powers That Be", *Far Eastern Economic Review,* 9 September 1999, p. 42.

34. Migdal, *Strong Societies and Weak States,* p. xiv.

35. Malarney, "Culture, Virtue, and Political Transformation", p. 899.

36. David G. Marr and Christine Pelzer White, "Introduction", in *Postwar Vietnam: Dilemmas in Socialist Development*, edited by Marr and White (Ithaca, NY: Southeast Asia Program, Cornell University, 1988), pp. 4-5; Vo Nhan Tri *Vietnam's Economic Policy since 1975*, pp. 160–68; ĐCSVN, *Chiến lược ổn định và phát triển kinh tế – xã hội đến năm 2000* [Strategy to Stabilize and Develop the Economy and Society until Year 2000] (Hà Nội: NXB Sự Thật, 1991), p. 3.

37. Ng Shui Meng, "Vietnam in 1981", *Southeast Asian Affairs 1982* (Singapore: Institute of Southeast Asian Studies, 1982), pp. 377–78.

38. Vietnam Economic News, "Full Breakfast But Empty Lunch", via Reuters, 22 June 1999.

39. These rules were the ban on private trade, and restrictions on what flats could be used for. Lưu Phương, "Việc làm được ở khu tập thể Nguyễn Công Trứ" [Accomplishments at the Nguyen Cong Tru collective flat area], *Hà Nội Mới* (hereafter *HNM*), 1 October 1975, p. 2; Ánh Sáng, "Nhà máy chế tạo công cụ số 1 xây dựng khu tập thể văn minh" [The Number 1 Tools Manufacturing Factory implements a cultured collective flat area], *HNM*, 18 January 1978,

p. 2; and Trần Hùng "Một số suy nghĩ về 'Hà Nội cải tạo và xây dựng'" [A few thoughts about "Hà Nội being reconstructed and constructed"], *HNM,* 23 January 1983, pp. 1, 3.

40. Li Tana, *Peasants on the Move: Rural-Urban Migration in the Hanoi Region,* Occasional Paper No. 91 (Singapore: Institute of Southeast Asian Studies, 1996). For Vietnamese sources, see Văn Giáp, "Tiểu khu Long Biên vận động những người làm ăn không chính đáng chuyển sang sản xuất" [Small District Long Biên mobilized people to switch from illegitimate work to production work], *HNM,* 7 January 1978 p. 3; *HNM,* "'Bung' sản xuất chứ không 'bung' buôn bán" ["Bursting" of production, not of trade], 16 January 1980, pp. 1, 4; *HNM,* "Chủ tịch phường và những điều lo âu" [The ward Chairman and his worries], 16 November 1988, p. 2; Nguyễn Chí Tình, "Tạm cho sử dụng vỉa hè một số đường phố để quản lý người buôn bán" [Allowing temporary use of pavement along a few roads in order to manage traders], *HNM,* 30 January 1991, pp. 1, 4; and Vĩnh Yên, "Cần giữ cho hè thông, đường thoảng ở mọi nơi, mọi lúc" [Every pavement and every road needs to be clear at all times], *HNM,* 31 July 1995, p. 2.

41. Vương Thức, "Chống làm nhà trái phép ở quận Ba Đình" [Fight against illegal construction of houses in Ba Dinh District], *HNM,* 4 October 1983, p. 3; *HNM,* "Quận Đống Đa xử lý ngay những nhà làm trái phép của cán bộ thuộc quận trực tiếp quản lý" [Dong Da District dealt immediately with cases of illegal housing construction by its own cadres], 30 May 1986, p. 1; P.V., "Quy hoạch xây dựng và quản lý xây dựng ở thủ đô" [Development plans and construction management in the capital], *HNM,* 13 February 1988, p. 3; and Vương Nguyễn, "Để dân an cư" [In order that the people live peacefully], *HNM,* 21 December 1990, p. 3.

42. Nguyễn Ngọc Minh, "Thời kỳ quá độ ở Việt Nam và vấn đề tăng cường hiệu lực của nhà nước xã hội chủ nghĩa" [The period of transition in Vietnam and the problem of strengthening the effectiveness of the socialist state] in *Tăng cường hiệu lực nhà nước xã hội chủ nghĩa của ta* [Strengthen the effectiveness of our socialist state], edited by Viện Luật Học, Ủy ban Khoa học Xã hội Việt Nam (Hanoi: NXB Khoa học Xã hội, 1983), p. 18. See also DLDVN, "Political Report of the Central Committee to the 4th Party Congress", in *4th National Congress: Documents* (Hanoi: Foreign Language Publishing House, 1977), pp. 45–46.

43. The Third, Fourth, and Fifth VCP National Congresses in 1960, 1976 and 1981 respectively called for strengthening of control over the bureaucracy. See Phan Hiển, "Mấy vấn đề về tăng cường pháp chế xã hội chủ nghĩa" [A few issues about strengthening socialist rule by law], *Tạp chí Cộng sản* (hereafter *TCCS*) 10 (1985): 35–36.

44. Nguyễn Ngọc Minh, "Nâng cao ý thức tôn trọng và nghiêm chỉnh chấp hành pháp luật" [Raise the awareness in the respect for and proper carrying out of

the law], *TCCS* 6 (1977): 67; Nguyễn Niên "Tăng cường pháp chế xã hội chủ
nghĩa – biện pháp để nâng cao hiệu lực quản lý của nhà nước" [Strengthen
socialist rule of law: Measures to raise effectiveness of state management],
in *Tăng cường hiệu lực nhà nước xã hội chủ nghĩa của ta* [Strengthen the
effectiveness of our socialist state], edited by Viện Luật Học, Ủy ban Khoa
học Xã hội Việt Nam (Hanoi: NXB Khoa học Xã hội, 1983), pp. 158, 167–68;
Phạm Hưng, "Khắc phục những mặt yếu về pháp chế xã hội chủ nghĩa ở
nước ta" [Overcome the weaknesses in socialist rule of law in our country],
TCCS 10 (1986): 8; Võ Đức Khiển, "Nâng cao hiểu biết về ý thức tôn trọng
pháp luật của cán bộ, đảng viên" [Raise the understanding and consciousness
among cadres and party members in respecting the law], *TCCS* 1 (1988):
44–47; Trần Thế Nhuận, "Bàn về tập trung, phân quyền, tản quyền trong
nền hành chính địa phương" [Discussion on centralism, decentralization of
powers, and separation of powers in our system of local administration],
in *Cải cách hành chính địa phương: Lý luận và thực tiễn* [Reform of local
administration: Theory and practice], edited by Tô Tử Hạ, Nguyễn Hữu Trị,
Nguyễn Hữu Đức (Hanoi: NXB Chính trị Quốc gia, 1998), pp. 51–59.

45. Trinh Duy Luan, "Vietnam", in *The Changing Nature of Local Government
    in Developing Countries*, edited by Patricia McCarney (Toronto: Centre for
    Urban and Community Studies, University of Toronto, and International
    Office, Federation of Canadian Municipalities, 1996), pp. 169–91, and Khoa
    Luật, Trường Đại học Tổng hợp Hà Nội, *Luật Nhà Nước Việt Nam* [Laws on
    the state in Vietnam] (1994), pp. 110–13.

46. The term, first used by Anthony Downs, *Inside Bureaucracy* (Boston: Little
    Brown, 1967), refers to lower level officials preferring to satisfy their own
    goals when implementing upper level policies and having different purposes
    from those of their superiors. See Ross, *Local Government in the Soviet
    Union,* p. 183.

47. Trần Nho Thìn, "Đổi mới tổ chức và hoạt động của Ủy ban Nhân dân Xã"
    [Reform the organization and operation of the Commune People's Committee],
    PTS dissertation submitted to the Viện Nghiên cứu Nhà nước và Pháp luật,
    Trung tâm Khoa học Xã hội và Nhân văn Quốc gia and Bộ Giáo dục và Đào
    tạo, Hà Nội, 1996, p. 31.

48. Trần Lê, "Góp phần thực hiện tốt công tác quản lý kinh tế – xã hội của nhà
    nước ta" [Contribute to implementing well the state's management of society
    and the economy], *TCCS* 9 (1986): 15–16.

49. The term *cadres* (cán bộ) refers to officials who are in permanent employment
    of the party-state and who occupy senior or leading positions in state
    organizations, while ordinary, non-leading state employees are referred to
    as *staff* (viên chức or nhân viên). See Lê Đình Khiên, "Xác định thế nào là
    cán bộ quản lý hành chính nhà nước" [How to define a state administrative
    cadre], *Dân chủ và Pháp luật* 6 (1996): 8–9, and Võ Đức Khiển, "Nâng

cao hiểu biết và ý thức tôn trọng pháp luật của cán bộ, đảng viên" [Raise the understanding and consciousness among cadres and party members in respecting the law], *TCCS* 1 (1988): 44–47.

50. Dương Đức Quang, "Tản mạn về báo chí chống tiêu cực" [Rambling thoughts about newspapers against negativism], *HNM Tết Đinh Sửu,* 7 February 1997, p. 18.

51. Đại Đoàn Kết Cuối Tuần, "Chuẩn mực nếp sống Việt Nam: Đang & sẽ ..." [The good life benchmarks: Present and future], *Xuân Đinh Sửu '97* (1997), p. 12.

52. Tan Teng Lang, *Economic Debates in Vietnam*, pp. 26–7; Beresford, "The political economy of dismantling", p. 230.

53. Cited in Carlyle A. Thayer, *Political Developments in Vietnam: From the Sixth to Seventh National Party Congress* (Canberra: Department of Political and Social Change, Research School of Pacific Studies, Australian National University, 1992), p. 10.

54. Nguyễn Bim, "Một số ý kiến về xây dựng chính quyền địa phương ở Hà Nội" [Some opinions on developing the ward level authorities in Hà Nội], *Tạp chí Quản lý Nhà nước* 7 (1994): 25–26. The author was the Head of the Office of Organization of Local Authorities (Ban Tổ chức Chính quyền địa phương) of the City of Hà Nội.

55. Kelliher, *Peasant Power in China*, p. 81.

56. Last heard spoken by the character of the retired village teacher, Mr Quỳ, in the Vietnamese film *Thương nhớ đồng quê* [Nostalgia for the countryside]. The film is based on two short stories by Nguyễn Huy Thiệp, one with the same title as the film, and the other is "Những bài học nông thôn" [Lessons from the countryside]. Film director is Đặng Nhật Minh. The saying is featured only in the film, and it reminds us of the purpose of nine-pin bowling. In bowling, normally only when ten pins are struck down is the result considered a "strike" and given full points; however, recognizing that most people are less than perfect in skills and luck, and to make these people enjoy the sport even more, nine-pin tap competitions are also organized in which nine pins struck down is considered a "strike", that is, "accepted as ten". For other sources of this deeply-ingrained Vietnamese cultural trait, see the novel by Lê Lựu, *Thời xa vắng,* 4th ed. (Hanoi: NXB Hội Nhà Văn, 1998) and Võ Dũng, Võ Thúy Anh, Võ Quang Hào, *Từ điển thành ngữ và tục ngữ Việt Nam,* 3rd ed. (Hanoi: NXB Văn Hoá, 1997), p. 171.

57. William J. Duiker, *Vietnam: Nation in Revolution* (Boulder, CO: Westview Press, 1983), p. 71.

58. Malarney, "Culture, Virtue, and Political Transformation", pp. 899–920.

59. In Vietnam, doctors certify children born in hospitals, but the state requires parents to register their children's birth within a month at the local authority at the basic level.

60. Fieldnotes 11 June 1997 and 12 June 1997.
61. Benedict Kerkvliet, "Politics of Society in the Mid 1990s", in *Dilemmas of Development: Vietnam Update 1994*, edited by Benedict Kerkvliet, Political and Social Change Monograph 22 (Canberra: RSPAS, Australian National University, 1995), p. 41.
62. Oi, *State and Peasant in Contemporary China,* p. 3.

2

The Ward and Neighbourhood State–Society Relations

Like many other countries, the Socialist Republic of Vietnam has a system of local administration. In socialist countries, where every need of the people is supposed to be taken care of by the state, the local administration system also functions as the channels through which the state dishes out benefits, and both state and society carry out tasks (such as penalties, punishments, compliance, and applications) in public administration.[1] In the interests of efficiency and effectiveness, a large local administration bureaucracy that comprises administrative bodies at different levels is set up. In Vietnam, under the national government there are the province/central city, district, and commune/ward levels of local administration.

This chapter analyses wards (phường), the lowest level of government and administration in Vietnam's cities and smaller urban areas. Ward officials carry out state policies and enforce the law on a daily basis. This chapter examines how the ward local administration is organized to implement policy, and how this machinery of local administration is appraised with reference to its effectiveness in achieving state objectives. In particular, this chapter will contribute to the argument that the ward local administration, set up for effective mobilization of people to follow the leadership of the state and the party, is also a daily tool of mediation that allows society to negotiate state policies and laws. This chapter will demonstrate conditions in the organization and operations of the ward state machinery that makes this possible.

I will first analyse the structure and organization of the ward state machinery as well as the informal but state-directed network of neighbourhood party and residents' organizations beneath the ward state machinery. The second section examines the dilemma surrounding the debate on whether wards should continue to exist, in particular, highlighting how policy-makers, administrators, and academics in Vietnam have been appraising the ward and the obstacles that wards have been facing since their beginning.

PRESENT STRUCTURE AND ORGANIZATION OF THE WARD STATE MACHINERY

In October 1997, Vietnam had 949 wards, compared to 8,823 communes. The country's wards administered around 15 per cent of the national population, even though they covered only about 1 to 2 per cent of the national territory.[2]

Hà Nội is a "central city" (*thành phố trực thuộc trung ương*). This means that it is equivalent to a "province" in scale and status. The jurisdiction of Hà Nội comprises both rural and urban areas. There are thus rural and urban administration at the lower two tiers. At the top of the city's administrative hierarchy are the Hà Nội people's council and people's committee. Both are accountable to central-level state agencies, mainly the National Assembly and the government. At the next lower level after the city level are the districts in urban areas, and prefectures in rural areas each with councils and committees. In 2004, Hà Nội had nine districts. Each district is divided into smaller units, called wards, the third and lowest level of urban government. Hà Nội had 85 wards in 1997, and the number of wards has increased since then.

Each ward has three main administrative and governing components: people's council, people's committee, and ward branch of the VCP. The people's council (resident-elected assembly representing the people and the state) and the people's committee (executive agent of the state and of the people's council) are part of the state apparatus outlined in the nation's Constitution. The ward party branch, technically speaking, is separate from the state structure, but in practice, because the Communist Party has layers of administration that parallel the state all the way down to the ward, and directs the state apparatus, distinguishing the party from the state is very difficult to do.

Therefore, like layers of authority above it, the ward party-state machinery is a three-legged political structure. The most important leg is the ward party branch (WPB). The other two legs are the people's council and people's committee. The people's committee has more political impact than the council, although the council is above the committee in protocol status. The ward state machinery does not have its own court or procurator, unlike levels above it. Below the ward, the state and party project their power through two levels of informal residential organization: at one level the party cells and the residential clusters (*cụm dân cư*), and at the next and last level state agents in the residential groups (*tổ dân phố*). I will now analyse the ward state machinery beginning with the communist party's organization at the ward level, then proceeding to the people's committee and people's council, and finally to the informal residential organizations.

The Communist Party in the Ward

The Communist Party at the ward level comprises two tiers. The upper tier is the WPB, and the lower tier is the party cell (*chi bộ*). The WPB holds a congress every thirty months and elects a fifteen-member executive committee at the congress. The WPB executive committee elects a ward party standing committee (WPSC) and the party inspectorate.[3]

The WPSC normally has six members: (1) party secretary (who is usually chairman of the ward people's council); (2) deputy party secretary (who is usually head of the ward people's committee); (3) head of the party inspectorate (or party inspector); (4) a member from the permanent committee of the WPB (a subcommittee of the WPSC); (5) a member who is usually the chief of ward police; and (6) another member who is usually the leader of the ward branch of a mass organization.[4] The WPSC meets once a week.

The party inspectorate usually has five members: an inspector, a deputy inspector, and three other members. The party inspector must be elected into the WPSC, because this person is supposed to be checking on the top executives of the WPB and should be included in the inner circle in order to know what goes on.[5] If the relationship between the inspectorate and party/government leaders of the locality is too friendly, however, the inspector may have difficulty checking on the WPSC and other party leaders of the ward. Also making oversight of the WPSC difficult is that party and ward-level meetings (except for ordinary meetings of the people's council or ceremonial meetings of each organization) are not open to the public or even to higher levels of party or state authority.

The permanent committee (Ban Thường Trực) is the subcommittee of the WPSC that oversees day-to-day affairs of the WPB. It usually has only one or two members (depending on willingness of the WPSC members to be elected into it), one of whom is the party inspector. If the inspector is the only member of the permanent committee, then the WPSC would in fact have only five instead of six members, because seats (3) and (4) would be held by the same person.[6]

The VCP's budget comes partly from membership fees. Levied at the rate of 1 per cent of each member's nominal income, the average monthly member contribution in 1999 was 5,000 đồng per person per month.[7] The VCP also receives money from either the state or from its business ventures that are organized from the district level onwards. Normally a WPB does not have business ventures and its only source of money is its budget funded by higher party offices.[8]

On a daily basis, the core leadership of the WPB includes the ward party secretary and the permanent committee. Together with the chairman of the ward's people's committee (who is also usually the deputy party secretary, a member of the WPSC) these three or four persons hold the reins of party and state power and authority within the ward. Thus, the party supervises state activities within the ward on a daily basis through the presence of the party secretary and the WPB permanent committee members in the ward office. Other WPSC members hold lesser but still important positions in state and mass organizations. The common pattern of shared leadership at the ward level is seen in Table 2.1.

The pattern of post distribution for the top two posts is not necessarily fixed. It is not uncommon as well to see the WPB secretary become the chairperson of the people's committee, thus giving up the people's council chairperson's seat to someone else, most likely the deputy party secretary or the chairperson of one of the branches of mass organizations such as the Vietnam Fatherland Front (VFF) or the Women's Association.

The Ward People's Committee

The ward people's committee ranks as the second main component of the ward machinery. It attends to the day-to-day governing of the ward, including routine state administration, and also management of community relations.

The ward people's committee is the executive of the ward people's council and is elected from the council. It is the local agent of the state's executive, headed by the central government (*chính phủ*).[9] The people's committee "organizes and directs the implementation of the Constitution, laws, and directives of upper level state organs as well as the resolutions of the people's council of the same level".[10] Table 2.2 tabulates specific functions of the people's committee delineated by different versions of

TABLE 2.1

Common Distribution Pattern of Ward Leadership Posts
Among a Group of Local Party Leaders in the WPB and WPSC

WPB executive committee and WPSC (numbered) members	State post	Mass organizations
(1) secretary	chair, council	
(2) deputy secretary	chair, committee	
(3) party inspector (permanent committee)		
(4) senior member	vice-chair, council	chair of one mass organization
(5) senior member	vice-chair, committee	
(6) senior member	chief of police	
Other WPB executive committee members		chairs and vice-chairs, mass organizations

Source: Gathered from various notes of conversations with wards' party leaders in 1997 and 1998.

TABLE 2.2

General Characteristics of Ward People's Committee
As Seen Over Five Laws and Regulations

Aspect/Year	1978	1981	1983	1989	1994	2003
Frequency of Meeting	Once a month	n.a.	Once a month, at least	Once a month	Once a month, at least	
Length of term	Follows the term of the people's council, but chairperson limited to two terms					
Number of members	1–8	5–7	7–9	7–9	5–7	3–5
Relationship to the Communist Party	Party leads and can determine affairs in every aspect; regular consultations with ward leaders					

TABLE 2.2 (continued)

Aspect/Year	1978	1981	1983	1989	1994	2003
Standing Committee (meets once a week or whenever necessary)	3–4 members comprising chairperson, vice-chairs, secretary of people's committee	n. a.	3 members: Chairperson, Vice-chair, and Secretary			No standing committee
Subcommittees	9 subcommittees: (1) Inspectorate; (2) Labour; (3) Livelihood; (4) Markets; (5) Culture, information, veterans and social affairs; (6) nursery, education of teenagers and youth; (7) Conciliation; (8) Security; (9) Housing (this subcommittee was added only in 1982)[a]					No subcommittees
Manner of decision-making	Majority vote					

Note:

a. DCĐ, "Nội dung phân cấp cho UBND Quận, UBND Phường" [Substance of work delegated to District and Ward's people's committees], *HNM*, 12 May 1982 p. 2. The names of these subcommittees have changed over time but the nature of their work has not changed much.

Source: People's Committee of Hanoi, Quyết định số 5417/QĐ-CQ-UB ngày 21/12/1978 của Ủy ban nhân dân thành phố Hà Nội về Quy định tạm thời về nhiệm vụ, quyền hạn của Ủy ban nhân dân tiểu khu [Decision 5417/QĐ-CQ-UB dated 21/12/1978 of Hanoi People's Council on Temporary regulations on duties and powers of Small Area People's Committees]; SRV, Quyết định số 94/HĐBT, ngày 26/9/1981 của Hội đồng Bộ trưởng Về chức năng, nhiệm vụ và tổ chức bộ máy chính quyền địa phương; SRV, Luật tổ chức Hội đồng nhân dân và Ủy ban nhân dân [Decision 94/HĐBT dated 26/9/1981 of Council of Ministers on role, duties, and organization of local authorities at the ward level]; People's Committee of Hanoi, 3784/QĐUB, 6/8/1986; SRV (1994), Luật tổ chức Hội đồng nhân dân và Ủy ban nhân dân [Law on Organization of People's Councils and People's Committees]; SRV, Luật tổ chức Hội đồng nhân dân và Ủy ban nhân dân (Sửa đổi) [Law on Organization of People's Councils and People's Committees — Amended]; SRV, Nghị Định số 174/CP ngày 29/9/1994 của Chính phủ Về quy định cơ cấu thành viên Ủy ban nhân dân và số Phó Chủ tịch Ủy ban nhân dân các cấp [Decision 174/CP dated 29/9/1994 of the Government stipulating structure and composition of People's Councils and the number of Vice-Chair of People's Committees at all levels].

the Law on Organization of People's Councils and People's Committees and by government regulations between 1978 and 2003.[11]

The size of the people's committee depends on the size of the ward population. According to the 1994 Law, wards with more than 7,000 people have seven members on the people's committee, and wards with less than 7,000 people would only have five.[12] Other than the chairperson, there is one or two vice-chairs (two for the seven-member committee), a secretary, and the rest are ordinary members. Each committee member takes sole charge of one specialized area of ward responsibilities, and usually the chair and the vice-chair also have one special area to take care of, other than being in charge overall.

The ward people's committee has a standing committee consisting of the chair, the vice-chair, and the secretary. The standing committee makes decisions for both the people's council and people's committee (which meet once in three months and once every month respectively) when they are not in session, and in that case decisions made by the standing committee are supposed to conform to the spirit and letter of decisions of the people's committee and people's council. The standing committee of the people's committee is, thus, the core of the state's executive leadership in the ward on a daily basis.

The Ward People's Council

The people's council represents local residents, but it also represents the state at the local level; it is at the same time both a people's organ of representation as well as a state organ of execution.[13] The council does not represent local residents to the state, but instead represent residents to settle local matters among themselves according to laws and policies laid down by the party-state. In its state executive role, it is differentiated from the people's committee by its function in rubber-stamping state policies for implementation by the people's committee.

A list of the characteristics of the ward people's council is presented in Table 2.3. It illustrates changes to the people's council over three versions of the Law on the Organization of People's Councils and People's Committees and subsidiary regulations between 1983 and 2003. The significant changes for the council over two decades were the longer terms of office, less frequent meetings, more power in the standing committee of the people's council, and greater involvement of the VFF in council activities. A new subcommittee instituted in 1989 was for "Rule of Law" to examine widespread disrespect for the law in society.

TABLE 2.3
General Characteristics of Ward People's Council As Developed Over Various Laws and Subsidiary Regulation

Aspect/ Year	1983	1989	1994	2003
Length of term	Two years	Five years		Five years, but chairperson limited to two terms
Number of members	Depending on the population size as stated in election law			
Frequency of meeting	Once per quarter, or twice per year for areas with transport difficulties such as in mountainous regions[a]	Once per quarter, or twice per year for areas with transport difficulties such as in mountainous regions	Twice a year, and when people's committee requests or one-third of council representatives agree.	Twice a year and whenever the chair or vice-chair or one-third of council representatives agree.
Manner of decision-making	Majority vote, through vote by hands or secret ballot. Choice to be exercised by the meeting chairperson. Ordinary meetings are open to residents and invitees, but the council can decide to meet in closed sessions			

TABLE 2.3 (continued)

Aspect/ Year	1983	1989	1994	2003
Subcommittees	• Credentials • Secretariat (introduced by 1983 law) • Other subcommittees related to work of council	• Credentials • Economics, planning, and budget • Culture, society, livelihood • Rule of law • Secretariat[b] • In 1989 law, council does not have a new standing Committee like the other levels but the role of the chairman and vice-chairman of council as *de facto* standing committee of council were emphasized	The roles of the chairman and vice-chairman of council as *de facto* standing committee of council are emphasized No mention of what subcommittees are to be established	Greater emphasis and clarity regarding the right of the council to question the work of the people's committee at meetings No mention of what subcommittees are to be established

Note: For all years, subcommittee members are appointed from council, their numbers to be decided by council; but they cannot be members of people's committee of the same ward as well.

TABLE 2.3 (continued)

Aspect/ Year	1983	1989	1994	2003
Matters that must be discussed and decided in the council	• Agenda of next meeting • Matters of credence • Financial plans and budgets • Economic and social plans • Approve reports on the work of people's committee and on resolution of complaints and suggestions from the people • Elect and dismiss members of the people's committee and subcommittees of the council	• Agenda of next meeting • Matters of credence • Financial plans and budgets • Economic and social plans • Approve reports on the work of its standing committee, the people's committee, and on resolution of complaints and suggestions from the people	The law states ambiguously the areas in which the council would make decisions in: (1) culture, society and livelihood; (2) science, technology, and environment; (3) defence, security, order and public safety; (4) ethnic minorities, religion; (5) enforcement of the Constitution, state laws, and policies; and	No mention; the agenda is set by the standing committee of the people's council but the scope of the agenda contains matters that have been delegated to the local authority to decide. Specific tasks given by upper level authorities to the ward people's committee are not discussed in the people's council.

TABLE 2.3 (continued)

Aspect/Year	1983	1989	1994	2003
	• Consider the resignation or the impeachment of council members • Approve suggestions to redraw boundaries for submission to upper levels • Amend or invalidate any illegal decisions of the people's committee • Dismiss the council of lower level if it is found to have hurt the rights of the people seriously (not applicable to ward)	(• Elect and dismiss members of the people's committee and subcommittees of the council, and chairman of the people's committee^c)	(6) administration and personnel matters of its organs. Chairman and vice-chairman of the ward handle all administrative affairs of the council	

TABLE 2.3 (continued)

Aspect/ Year	1983	1989	1994	2003
Rights of representatives	Cannot be arrested when the council is in session without approval from the chair of the session.			Cannot be arrested when the council is in session without approval from the chair of the session. When arrested at other times, then the chairman of people's committee should be informed. If guilty, loses seat.[d]

Notes:

a. In the 1962 Law on the Organization of Council and People's Committee, the frequency of council meetings was once in six months. The change to one meeting per quarter in 1983 was due to the feeling that the people's councils would be able to operate more effectively if they met more frequently. Despite the 1962 law, in the years before 1983 the people's council of Hanoi and of HCM City were already meeting once every quarter. See Vũ Phụng, "Có những điểm gì mới trong Luật tổ chức Hội đồng nhân dân và Ủy ban nhân dân" [What's new in the Law on Organization of People's Councils and People's Committees], *HNM*, 15 July 1983, p. 2, and 16 July 1983, p. 2.

b. The highlight of the 1989 revisions to the law was the setting up of a standing committee for the people's council of levels above the ward, but not the ward. In the draft version of the law (SRV, Dự án Sửa đổi, bổ sung Luật tổ chức Hội đồng nhân dân va Ủy ban nhân dân [Project to amend Law on Organization of People's Councils and People's Committees], *HNM*, 5 June 1989, pp. 2, 3; article 3) the new body was to be set up at all levels, including the ward. However, in the final version of the law passed by the National Assembly (article 3), the new body only applied to levels above the basic level of local administration.

c. The provision of discussion of the appointment and dismissal of the chairman of the committee as only to be discussed within the council was mentioned in the draft to the 1989 law but omitted in its final version. This change removed a significant power of the people's council over the people's committee, probably for the purpose of more effective administration.

d. Under the 1989 law, if a representative from a ward people's council above the level of the ward is arrested, then the chairman of *that* ward people's council must be informed.

Source: SRV (1983), Luật tổ chức Hội đồng nhân dân và Ủy ban nhân dân [Law on Organization of People's Councils and People's Committees]; SRV (1989), Luật tổ chức Hội đồng nhân dân va Ủy ban nhân dân [Law on Organization of People's Councils and People's Committees]; SRV (1994), Luật tổ chức Hội đồng nhân dân và Ủy ban nhân dân [Sửa đổi) [Law on Organization of People's Councils and People's Committees — Amended].

Under the 1994 Law on Organization of People's Councils and People's Committees, the ward people's council has twenty-five members who must be living in the locality. They are elected for five-year terms and meet once in six months to discuss local affairs, approve reports and plans, review work-in-progress, and examine the work of the VFF. In between council sessions, the people's committee makes decisions on behalf of the council, in consultation with the council chairman.[14] The council can hold extraordinary meetings but only at the request of the people's committee or one-third of council members. The people's council election process emphasizes equitable representation among different social and economic sectors. Members of the council are asked to volunteer or are voted into the subcommittees handling the political, economic, cultural, and secretarial work of the council. A council member cannot concurrently serve on the subcommittees of the council and on the people's committee of the same level.[15] A similar rule applies to the head of any council subcommittee, who cannot be the head of specialized agencies of the people's committee such as the police.[16] These last rules try to prevent conflict of interest, but they do not affect the composition of the top leadership of the ward state machinery.

Other Officials of the Ward Administration

A ward has two groups of expert officials who are employees of government ministries or the ward administration, but who are not members of the people's committee or people's council. Officials of the first group are stationed at the ward by central government ministries and departments to assist the ward in special areas of work. Police officers are a prime example. Others include officials handling taxation, social welfare issues, land, housing, and market inspection. They are directed by the people's committee, but are also accountable to their ministries and departments. The second group of officials comprises the accountant, the clerk, the security guard, and the tea-lady, who are hired directly by the ward.

SUB-WARD PARTY AND STATE ORGANIZATIONS

Indicative of the depth of party and state penetration into daily affairs of the people is that the WPB and the ward administration are not the lowest grassroots organization of the VCP and state representation, respectively. Below the WPB and the ward administration are two organizations that are more informal in nature and operation; below the WPB there is a number of party cells (*chi bộ*) and below the people's committee and people's council there are the resident clusters and resident groups.

The Party Cell and the Resident Cluster

The party cell and resident cluster are discussed together because they are usually mutually associated in the ward party-state machinery. The party cell relates to the resident cluster like the WPB relates to the ward state machinery. Each party cell comprises at least three members, up to a maximum of about thirty-five members. Usually one or more party cells are attached to a resident cluster, depending on the number of party members. The party cell elects its leadership annually. When a national congress of the VCP is to be held once every five years, the party cell starts the process by holding a congress of its own and votes for a number of candidates to attend the WPB congress, which is the next higher echelon. Delegates to the WPB congress then elect delegates to attend the district level congress of the VCP. From the district, the process continues up to the VCP's national congress. When the WPB congress opens, its credentials committee checks that the delegates have been properly elected and have had no political or ethical problems. A party member must attend the WPB congress in order to stand for election to the WPSC.[17]

The party cell elects a standing committee comprising a secretary, a deputy secretary, plus one to three other members. To retain their positions, party cell secretaries must be elected as a delegate of the party cell to the WPB congress. Otherwise, they may as well resign from their party secretary positions.[18] Among the three ordinary members, one is in charge of inspection and answers directly to the ward party inspector. This position is appointed by consensus among cell members at the cell's annual congress. If the party cells are too big, the WPB may create smaller organizations, called party groups (*tổ đảng*), which may or may not have formal leadership.

The VCP has two types of party cells. The first is called basic level party cells (*chi bộ cơ sở*) or street party cell (*chi bộ đường phố*), also known informally as "retiree members' cell" (*chi bộ hưu trí*) because most members are retirees. The other type is the working members' cell (*chi bộ đương chức*). This type comprises party members working in government organizations or state enterprises in the locality. Working people can choose to participate in either or both of these cells, but most choose to participate only at the place of work and to excuse themselves from participation in street party cells, thus contributing to a high average age of members in the latter. The average age of VCP members, however, is also high.[19]

According to one source,

> The party cell usually discusses and passes resolutions on issues such as building a civilized way of life, building a cultured family, securing neighbourhoods, building a new way of life in their area. They resolve contradictions among the people, help in the conduct of activities of the Vietnam Fatherland's Front and other mass organizations; they conduct charity work, look after the aged and the young, and espouse the political line, the policies, and main resolutions of the city, district, and ward authorities.[20]

The resident cluster (*cụm dân cư*) is an informal level of neighbourhood organization situated between the ward and the resident group (*tổ dân phố*) and first established in 1984.[21] It is a collection of several resident groups. The resident cluster sometimes had been misunderstood as a level of administrative authority,[22] but it is not, because it does not have independent state authority that is usually marked by the use of official stamps in documents. Each cluster is the responsibility of one ward people's council deputy and each cluster also has sub-branches of political and social mass organizations (*chi hội các tổ chức chính trị xã hội*). In other words, each cluster is like the constituency of each deputy in the people's council.

The party cell is supposed to lead the resident cluster in producing suggestions to overcome policy implementation difficulties within the ward and to oversee (but not to command or direct) the clusters' implementation of policies decided by the ward. The resident cluster and the party cell have no power to mete out punishments to residents, or to make decisions on their own. They must report to the ward whatever suggestions or unlawful activities they discover and let the ward take action.[23] The WPB holds a monthly meeting with all the party cells of the ward and a regular Saturday meeting with each party cell to delegate tasks.[24] The WPB usually consults the resident cluster on important or sensitive local matters where residents' opinions are sought.

In the implementation of state policies, the party cell has little political authority in the ward state machinery. This is because the heads of resident groups may deal directly with the ward people's committee, in effect bypassing the party cell (and the resident cluster). The party cells have no direct power over the leaders of the resident group within their territory for matters not pertaining to the party, even though protocol-wise, they are placed higher than the resident group.[25] Because it has no say in how the head of the resident group should conduct group affairs or deal with neighbours who resist the state or offend laws, the resident cluster, led by the party cell, can only channel feedback to the WPB. Exceptions occur when relations between a party cell secretary and the resident group head within its area are close. In those situations the party cell can play a leadership role.

THE RESIDENT GROUP (TỔ DÂN PHỐ)

In the urban areas of Vietnam, the term "resident group" is extremely familiar to adults. Resident groups are the smallest formal grouping of contiguous rows of houses and their occupants, with each group comprising 25 to 30 households. Wards determine their numbers, ranging from 50 resident groups (in a newly-formed Hà Nội ward like Phú Thượng (formerly a commune but converted around 1997) to somewhere between 70 and 100 resident groups in matured wards of the inner city.[26] Residents have to deal with the resident group head for matters such as collection of monies on behalf of the ward, and references for matters such as registration of birth, marriage, and residence, mobilization work on behalf of the state, and many other matters. They even have to mediate quarrels among residents.[27]

The resident group of Vietnam, as a state and community organization, has parallels in Indonesian and Japanese cities and in Singapore. In Yogjakarta, for example, the lowest official level of state administration masks numerous networks of semi-formal and informal organization, part-time state agents, and social networks. While the state sets them up, supports them with some resources, and mandates compulsory membership, it also allows them to hold free elections of their leaders, and uses them to promote an ideology of community.[28] In Japan's urban areas, the informality and lack of any active state involvement in urban neighbourhood organizations contrast with the Javanese and Vietnamese types. In Japan, the Resident Association (*chonai-kai*) is territorially based but voluntary in membership. Each association takes care of about twenty-five households and organizes meetings, networks, and social functions. The association has no state funding nor is it under state control; consequently it has no obligation to perform monitoring, integration, or mobilization functions on behalf of the government or any political party, except during election times when the ruling party may request the associations' help in spreading its message. The

Resident Association also runs on voluntary contributions. Its committee has collective responsibility, and residents usually take turns to be members of the committee.[29] The Singaporean model seems to sit in-between forced and voluntary participation. High-rise government flats are the most common type of dwelling in Singapore, and the government organizes one residents' committee for several blocks of flats. Membership is automatic, but participation is voluntary. According to my own experience, one can live in the flats for a long time without ever knowing about residents' committees. According to S. Vasoo, residents' committees in Singapore promote community development through social activities after a period of rapid urbanization broke up traditional communities.[30]

Although Vietnam's Constitution does not mandate the establishment of the resident group or the resident cluster, the government has used these bodies to promote community spirit and ideology as well as to perform administrative duties. Leaders of resident groups are elected from the locality, and their relationship with fellow residents, other than government matters (which dictates a hierarchical type of relationship), include relationships of mutual-help in daily livelihood. As such, resident groups have an informal dimension. On the other hand, resident groups are responsible for the community's self-regulation and mobilization tasks, such as maintaining public health and order, and in realizing the "civilized way of life and the building of new culture families".[31] Resident group leaders' mobilization role is different from that of the party cell in that they do the legwork for the ward and the resident cluster. Accordingly, the ward and the resident cluster rely on them heavily.

Resident groups emphasize informality. They hold an annual election of group heads (tổ trưởng) and assistant group heads (tổ phó) after neighbours have made nominations. Official control of nominations for these two posts are practically zero, thus people can nominate, support, or reject any candidate. Like party members in the ward party cell, most resident group leaders are middle-aged and above. They are usually people who have lived in the locality for some time and have no problems with neighbours. They need not be party members or persons with high socioeconomic standing. Popular candidates are amiable, behave well, and possess good family background; meaning, they are from wholesome family units, and must not have committed offences or crimes against the law or the VCP.[32] My house-mother intimated that group heads and their assistants need to set examples in their daily lives in order to gain the respect and thus the votes of people.[33]

Group heads work directly with the chairman of the ward people's committee rather than the party cell secretary. Group heads are supposed to meet with committee officials once every three months, but work is usually so much that the actual number of meetings is three times a month, indicating the ward's heavy reliance on the resident groups rather than the resident cluster. These meetings are usually held after every monthly meeting of the people's committee, as well as whenever the people's committee has work for them to do.

The job of leading the resident groups is disliked by most people asked to do it. One Vietnamese observer described the status of the group head as having "powers light like straws but responsibilities heavy like stones" (*quyền rơm vạ đá*) meaning that group heads do not have the power to perform their many duties, and are often blamed — by both ward officials and residents — for negative outcomes in their areas.[34] My house-mother, a group head, spoke of the lack of people willing to take over her position even though she, being over sixty years old, would like to retire after being on the job for more than twenty years. This problem seemed to be citywide, and perhaps nationwide as well.[35] Younger people dislike the tediousness of the work and are usually too occupied with their regular jobs. The pay is also very small for such an onerous job.[36] Moreover, group heads often find themselves in the uncomfortable dilemma of having to report on neighbours when the ward requires it. The group head and assistant group head could be blamed for punishments a family receives for minor offences against the law or state policies.[37] He or she may also attract revenge from those who believe they are unjustly treated by the ward.

Nevertheless, the party and the state retain resident groups. Group heads are the only state agents in Vietnam that reach right into homes. They can mobilize people personally, and in this sense, the state is not "faceless" but comes in the form of the eagle-eyed, amiable elderly neighbour, who, even without being the group head, already has some authority over younger neighbours. I do not mean that the old have the ears of the young all the time, but few people are likely to reject reasonable opinions and requests of senior members of the neighbourhood. In Vietnam, the respect for seniors is rather high. A good example is a school-teacher talking about purchasing government bonds (*công trái*). She said she has never taken initiative to buy any. If the group head, however, manages to "catch" her at home (*bắt được ở nhà*) (she worked full-time) when mobilizing people to buy bonds, then she would buy some, so as to be kind to the group head.[38]

For residents, group heads are also important sources of information for the neighbourhood. For instance, when residents apply to register their marriage with the ward, ward officials require them to first ask their group heads to certify their marital status. People also approach group heads for information about many other things. Group heads may also be sources of information about the neighbourhood to higher officials, although they might also protect neighbours from prying officials. My house-mother said that during her twenty years on the job, she was able to avoid telling on her neighbours when asked to do so by ward officials. She advised ward officials instead to have a policeman come to the resident group regularly to patrol and to ask discreet questions of residents.

REMUNERATION OF MAIN WARD OFFICIALS

The ward party-state machinery cannot have more than eight cadres in full-time employment if the ward's population is below 5,000, nine cadres if a ward has between 5,000 to 10,000 residents, and eleven for 10,000 residents and above.[39] People's council members are not state employees but are volunteers, and so they are not paid a salary by the state. They receive a small compensation of 20 per cent of the lowest salary benchmark for state workers.[40] They also receive fringe benefits like health insurance, funeral allowance, and expenses for council work.[41] Leading council members who are also members of the people's committee and of the WPSC receive, in addition, party and executive remuneration for their roles in the party and in the committee.

As of 1993 the ward party secretary and deputy party secretary received 160,000 đồng and 140,000 đồng per month respectively, in addition to remuneration they received from state positions. By 2000, the government raised the minimum salary for bureaucrats to 210,000 đồng per month.[42] A ward party secretary I interviewed in 1997 received in total 450,000 đồng per month, about 1.5 times that of 1993. Such salaries were comparable to what many workers and professionals who worked for the state earned. For instance, one doctor I knew earned a salary of about 150,000 đồng in 1993 and 300,000 đồng in 1997. According to 1993 government regulations,[43] the secretary and deputy secretary also received 40,000 đồng and 30,000 đồng of supplementary payments. In 1993, other posts of the WPB received 120,000 đồng in salary and 30,000 đồng per month in complementary payments.[44] These payments probably doubled by 1997 as well.

As of 1993 the chairman of the ward people's committee received 160,000 đồng per month in salary and 40,000 đồng in supplementary payments.[45] The payment in 1997 was 390,000 đồng, almost doubling the income in 1993. The vice-chairman of the ward people's committee received 140,000 đồng per month, and other posts in the ward received 120,000 đồng per month and supplementary payments of 30,000 đồng.[46] Like the income of the committee chairman, the salary of these other posts in the committee probably doubled by 1997. Cadres involved in special duties or projects of the ward received extra payments for the work done. That money probably came from the budget for the project, which always included payment for work done by project members even though these people were already in employment by the state.[47] When cadres attended ceremonies or events of state organs on behalf of the ward, they also received from the host "envelopes" of lunch and transport money that usually contained amounts ranging from 20,000 to 50,000 đồng.

According to 1993 government regulations the secretary of the party cell received 30,000 đồng a month, while the resident group head received 50,000 đồng. The party cell secretary received a free, daily copy of party newspapers *Nhân Dân* and *Hà Nội Mới*.

Insufficient Pay

The formal income of salaried ward cadres in 1997 thus ranged between 300,000 and 500,000 đồng per month. These amounts were insufficient to support family expenditures in Hà Nội. In 1997, I calculated that a household in Hà Nội where I lived spent around 25,000 đồng per day on food and about 5,000 đồng per day on transport, assuming that all meals were cooked at home, contained the three major food groups, and that the family had a motorcycle. Those monthly expenses equaled 900,000 đồng. Additional expenses included house rental, cooking needs, clothing, repair and maintenance of vehicle, entertainment and leisure, children's school fees of at least 200,000 đồng per month per student in lower primary school, and social exchanges.[48] Official statistics show the average annual expenditure per capita in urban areas of Vietnam in 1993 was close to 2 million đồng. Food expenditure for the same was about 1.11 million đồng. For the whole household, the mean of annual total household expenditure in urban areas was about 9.77 million đồng, which works out to 814,166 đồng per month.[49]

The ward people's committee chairman would have been living in heavy debt in 1997 if his or her family relied only on 390,000 đồng to foot basic family expenditures of at least 900,000 đồng per month. The expenditure–income deficit was about 56 per cent. A ward committee chairman I talked to on many occasions in 1997 stressed that without his wife's tea-stall business his family would not be able to make ends meet. That he chose to make this point to me aroused my curiosity; I made an excuse of visiting his home. I discovered that he was paying for his children to have tuition, had recently bought a new motorcycle, and possessed a number of fairly new electrical appliances including a colour television set and a hi-fi set. Certainly, this ward chairman had other types of income. Tea-stall income alone would not be able to cover the shortfall between his salary and the family's real expenditures.

In part because the pay is low, ward jobs are not well regarded. Every ward faces recruitment difficulties. A conference on the ward in 1997 was told the story of a young man who approached Hàng Gai Ward for a security guard job. Delighted ward officials offered to have the aspiring security guard groomed to become a member of the ward party-state machinery elite; to be the chairman of the communist party vanguard, the Hồ Chí Minh Youth Group, and ultimately a full-time employee of the ward. This job offered security and would have been a good job during the pre-1986 period. But the young man rejected the offer because he was only looking for a temporary position to tide him over until he could find something better.[50]

Overall, there is a movement on the part of the government to improve working conditions for the leading officials who work at the ward level. While these officials' pay are pegged to the nationwide civil service pay scales, the government has also moved to regularize other benefits they enjoyed so that they were on par with those that officials in other parts of the bureaucracy enjoyed.[51]

THE WARD: WHOSE SIDE IS IT ON?

How useful the ward is as a unit of administration and governance for the party-state has long been debated. Examination of the history of this debate helps us to understand not just the history of the ward, but also how the party-state has had both successes and failures in terms of its use of the wards as a governance tool. In summary, supporters of the wards argue that wards provide important services both to residents and to the state's central offices. In between these two poles are those who admit wards are operationally ineffective in many areas, and that the state should review the ward's role and organization.

The 1980 Constitution instituted the ward system of administration. These changes modified the local administration system from a two-level to a three-level system, with the new level being the wards in the urban areas. As discussions on this change to the 1980 Constitution began, there was also debate on whether the new ward level was necessary; Hà Nội City administrators were far from unanimous about the necessity of wards. Anticipating the changes, in 1979 *HNM* published side-by-side two letters about whether the city of Hà Nội should have two levels (city and district) or three levels (city, district, and wards) of local authority. Both letter-writers were cadres of Small Area people's committee (short-lived predecessor or pilot project of the ward). Their timing and placement suggest they might have been encouraged to be sent and published so as to give a semblance of debate contributing to the drafting process of the 1980 Constitution. Orchestration notwithstanding, the chief issue of the debate was the necessity of the ward.

In the first letter, Thanh Đạm, party secretary of the Ngô Thì Nhậm Small Area, noted that his people's committee had held a public discussion on the wards being proposed in drafts for a new Constitution. Among ninety-five persons who spoke, only three supported the proposal, while the rest opposed it. Đạm noted that people were aware of different needs of the inner city (urban) and the rural areas under Hà Nội's jurisdiction. He was referring to the government's desire to have the ward level of administration in the urban area so as to have the urban system resemble the commune level in rural areas. Đạm argued that wards were not real social units; unlike villagers in communes, officials and citizens living in the proposed wards did not feel any sense of belonging to it, a phenomenon already observed in the Small Areas. Therefore, the ward level was unnecessary. Moreover, the Hà Nội City authority was really in charge of policy planning and implementation in every aspect. Therefore, the ward as the enlargement of the Small Area would become an additional bureaucratic level that, like the Small Area, had little to do.[52]

Đào Công Phê, chairman of the Cửa Nam Small Area, presented the opposite argument that was closer to the stand of the central government. Phê justified the ward as a mechanism to take care of citizens on a daily level, a social condition necessary for a big-scale socialist system, the policy line set down by the VCP. The ward was indispensable for tasks such as distributing rationed food. Furthermore, the state relied on the ward to mobilize the people and implement its policies. Phê said his one-year's experience as chairman of the people's committee of Cửa Nam Small Area showed that many administrative tasks were better performed by the people's committee of a level that is lower than the district. Without that lower level, the district's work would be impossible. The Small Area people's committees were relieving the districts of many daily routine matters that needed governmental adjudication, regulation, and supervision. If there were to be only two levels, Phê said, the district would need to be much smaller, and below the district there would need to be an organization resembling the Small Area people's committees to help the district.[53]

Whether the Small Area people's committees were as effective as Đào Công Phê claimed is unclear. The only other evidence I have found is a 1980 report about the Hoàn Kiếm District faulting Small Area people's committees under its charge for not taking initiatives in resolving significant local problems. Instead, they were contented to follow directives and tasks delegated to them. It suggested that Small Area officials were afraid of independent action that could land them in trouble with superiors. On the other hand, contradicting itself, the same District meeting also criticized daring Small Area officials who exceeded their authority by certifying the sale and purchase of houses *ultra vires*, arranging housing for some people without official sanction from the top, and demonstrating a capability, paradoxically, to act independently against rules and directions of upper levels.[54] This report indicated that early on, local officials and people were collaborating to circumvent difficult rules of the party-state. Such actions pre-dated the birth of the ward.

Official Birth of the Ward

Despite criticisms, the government took steps to establish wards. One of the implementing decisions, number 94 of the Council of Ministers, stipulated that

> The ward is the basic administrative unit in the inner parts of cities and towns. Wards are organized according to residential areas and streets, each having 7,000 to 12,000 residents. The main role of the ward is to carry out state administrative duties, manage society, to manage and be responsible in serving everyday needs of the people.[55]

In the administrative jargon of Vietnam the ward is variously referred to as the "basic local authority" (*chính quyền cơ sở*), or "basic administrative unit" (*đơn vị hành chính cơ sở*) of the cities. Decision 94 set out eight broad areas of responsibilities for the ward: (1) politics; (2) security and defence; (3) residence and society; (4) labour; (5) commerce and industry; (6) education and health; (7) housing and land; and (8) planning and budget. But principal "decisions" for these areas are made for wards by central government or Hà Nội authorities. Moreover, most state legislation and government directives leave the job of issuing detailed regulations for implementing laws to the Province level, not to wards. In Hà Nội, that means the Hà Nội City authority, which then leaves only implementation power to the ward. In other words, the people's councils and people's committees of the wards may only alter Hà Nội policies at the margins and decide on purely local matters, usually on unusual matters within their locality or authority (such as helping to organize an election, a donation campaign for natural disasters, or campaigns to solve social problems). Wards also help government departments to carry out regular administrative duties, such as distributing food ration coupons (until 1989) and pensions and registering births, deaths, marriages, and new residents. The specific tasks of the ward are too numerous to discuss. They are listed in Table 2.4 according to categories and sub-categories from one set of legislation to the next from 1981 to 2003. A glance across the table indicates changes in social and economic tasks of the ward over time.

A few years after the wards began, doubts about their usefulness and effectiveness surfaced. After 1981, but before Đổi Mới reforms, state media assessments of the ward were mainly positive, possibly to justify the role of the ward. Typical were reports by Nguyễn Đức Thà, a journalist on the local authority beat. In one of his many articles on the subject, he praised the Cửa Nam Ward as an example of how well the ward model of public administration has worked. According to him, in Cửa Nam Ward the ward authority could do many things its predecessor, the Small Area people's committee, could not. Thà gave some examples, such as the conduct of criticism and self-criticism sessions among the people, and propaganda and mobilization for party lines and government policies.[56] Other press reports gave the ward similar credits.[57] For instance, the Quang Trung Ward created a people's movement to self-police and to reduce crime; wards in Ba Đình District checked to see that businesses in their areas were legal. (The Ba Đình District made its wards responsible because the latter were better able to grasp the local situation then the district.[58]) The wards were also able to receive more people and handle more complaints by the people. In one month, 400 residents (or more than ten per day) went to Cửa Nam Ward to request meetings with local authorities. According to Thà, without

TABLE 2.4

Responsibilities of the Ward As Seen Through Various Laws and Regulations of the State

Responsibilities	*1981*	*1983*	*1986*	*Đổi Mới*	*1989*	*1994*	*1996*
1. Politics							
1.1. Organize, mobilize the people in realizing the ideas and policies of the party and the laws of the state	✔		✔				
1.2. On mobilization, emphasis on mobilizing people to participate in minor repair projects such as repair of lanes; engage them in public health work such as cleaning toilets and collecting garbage; ask the people to manage a section of the road especially painting work, protection of public sources of water[a]	✔						
1.3. Organize elections							✔
Rule of Law[b]							
1.4. Propagate, spread knowledge, and educate the masses on laws			✔				✔
1.5. Ensure that laws are carried out			✔			✔	✔
1.6. Ensure that the Constitution, laws, directives of the state, and the resolutions of the HDND are carried out.						✔	✔

TABLE 2.4 (continued)

Responsibilities	1981	1983	1986	Đổi Mới	1989	1994	1996
1.7. Protect life, property, freedom, reputation, character, and other rights and interess of citizens			✔			✔	✔
1.8. Encourage people to fulfil their responsibilities towards the state			✔				
1.9. Resolve in time the complaints, accusations, and suggestions of the people, and refer them if they are not within the responsibility of the ward	✔		✔				✔
1.10. Carry out work for the people's inspectorate, look out for and report offences against socialist rule of law and to administer the law according to the functions delegated to it	✔						
1.11. Suggest measure to increase compliance and increase management capability of the state.							
1.12. Mobilize the people to obey state laws and rules of the City							

TABLE 2.4 (continued)

Responsibilities	1981	1983	1986	Đổi Mới	1989	1994	1996
2. Security and Defence		c					
2.1. Fight every plot and activity of anti-revolutionaries and criminals, fight their destructive activities	✔		✔				
2.2. Arrest people engaged in anti-revolutionary and criminal activities			✔				
2.3. Manage and educate political detainees and criminals	✔		✔				
2.4. Can recommend to upper-level people to send for re-education	✔		✔				
2.5. Maintain political security	✔					✔	
2.6. Maintain social order	✔		✔			✔	✔
2.7. Eradicate social evils	✔		✔			✔	✔
2.8. Fight all negative phenomena	✔		✔				
2.9. Fight against psychological warfare	✔						
2.10. Preserve traffic order			✔	✔			✔
2.11. Prevent anti-revolutionaries and gangsters from hiding in the ward with guidance from the top	✔						

TABLE 2.4 (continued)

Responsibilities	1981	1983	1986	Đổi Mới	1989	1994	1996
2.12. Create a mass movement to protect the Fatherland			✔				
2.13. Implement measures to protect property of socialism and property of the people	✔		✔				
2.14. Carry out reconciliation of all civil disputes	✔		✔				✔
2.15. Build a people's militia or a self-defence force through enlistment	✔		✔			✔	✔
2.16. Ensure fulfilment of targets in enlistment	✔						✔
2.17. Engage in "hinterland" work for the army	✔					✔	✔
2.18. Mobilize the people to help in "hinterland work"						✔	✔
2.19. Manage families of soldiers							
2.20. Mobilize, educate the youth and the people on their military duties			✔				
2.21. Manage discharged military personnel; educate and manage deserters			✔				

TABLE 2.4 (continued)

Responsibilities	1981	1983	1986	Đổi Mới	1989	1994	1996
2.22. Receive the people regarding their complaints and suggestions					✔		
2.23. Within its capability, resolve complaints and suggestions from the people							
2.24. Spread propaganda about law							✔
2.25. Help the courts collect materials and information							
2.26. Help to carry out court sentences						✔	✔
2.27. Fight natural disasters, protect property of the state, economic units, and society						✔	
2.28. Fight illegal trading, corruption, smuggling, and couterfeit goods.	✔					✔	✔
2.29. Protect state property, protect political, social, and economic organizations.							✔
2.30. Decide on punishments for compoundable offences							✔
3. Residence and Society							
3.1. Register births, deaths, and marriages,	✔		✔				
3.2. Register households' residential status	✔						✔

TABLE 2.4 (continued)

Responsibilities	1981	1983	1986	Đổi Mới	1989	1994	1996
3.3. Serve the people in their daily livelihood, materially as well as culturally, disease prevention and cure	✔						
3.4. The main responsibility is to know about the people, about the number of residents, the types of livelihood, and from there knowing what kind of people need special attention.[d]	✔		✔	✔			
4. Labour							
4.1. Implement the various targets of obligatory labour	✔						
4.2. Introduce employment	✔		✔				
4.3. Achieve targets of student and labour recruitment							
4.4. Ensure employment for every resident							
4.5. Organize various projects in production to employ people							
4.6. Organize public projects to provide employment			✔				
4.7. Mobilize people to go to the New Economic Zones							

TABLE 2.4 (continued)

Responsibilities	1981	1983	1986	Đổi Mới	1989	1994	1996
4.8. Recommend to the District people who should be sent to enforced labour and supervise them in the ward			✔				
4.9. Register labour and monitor the labour migration situation							
4.10. Know the population figures of the locality, handle work on registration			✔				
4.11. Know the number of people who reach the age of labour every year			✔				
5. Economy							
5.1. Register business in industry and commerce	✔ᵉ		✔				
5.2. Check on use of registration of businesses			✔				
5.3. With joint participation from authority directly above, organize and manage co-operatives and private production units to produce light industrial and handicraft goods, transport services, and other sectors decided upon	✔		✔				

TABLE 2.4 (continued)

Responsibilities	1981	1983	1986	Đổi Mới	1989	1994	1996
5.4. Organize and guide the people in pushing for production in the consumer sectors, services according to the plan, and to carry out urban management tasks delegated by upper levels	✔		✔				
5.5. Check on the activities of individual handicraft, other products, and service producers, including co-operatives; and to suggest and to issue licences to them							
5.6. Mobilize individual producers to join co-operatives			✔				
5.7. Check on the sources of supply of primary materials for businesses in the locality			✔				
5.8. Implement the Socialist Reformation policies with regard to the market, fight illegal trading	✔						
5.9. Manage small business according to the law							✔
5.10. Manage markets							✔
5.11. Reform petty traders, encourage them to produce instead of trading	✔		✔				

TABLE 2.4 (continued)

Responsibilities	1981	1983	1986	Đổi Mới	1989	1994	1996
5.12. Manage consumer co-operatives, their services, and self-employed	✔		✔				
5.13. Manage small produce markets	✔		✔				
5.14. Supervise state shops, private shops, stalls, and the distribution and sale of goods to the people	✔		✔				
5.15. Issue food stamps/ coupons			✔				
5.16. Ensure equality and convenience	✔						
5.17. Help in industrial and commercial tax assesment and collection	✔		✔				
5.18. In co-ordination with related agencies ensure that taxes are collected						✔	✔
5.19. Collect directly the abbatoir tax	✔						
5.20. Collect other types of administrative charges	✔					✔	
5.21. Draw up economic plans			✔				✔
5.22. Draw up plans for handicraft and small industry co-operatives, for production groups and for private and family handicraft units			✔				

TABLE 2.4 (continued)

Responsibilities	1981	1983	1986	Đổi Mới	1989	1994	1996
5.23. Develop traditional handicrafts and occupation, and make use of latest technologies							✔
5.24. Draw up plans for trade of consumer, trading co-operatives, service providers			✔				
5.25. Draw up plans for population growth and employment			✔				
5.26. Find/create employment for people			✔				
5.27. Manage the state in the locality with respect to all economic areas						✔	
5.28. Mobilize people to contribute funds to infrastructure building							✔
6. Culture, education, health							
6.1. Implement the civilized way of life, new (this word deleted in 1996) culture family policy	✔		✔				✔
6.2. Create mass movements of culture, arts			✔				

TABLE 2.4 (continued)

Responsibilities	1981	1983	1986	Đổi Mới	1989	1994	1996
6.3. Engage in culture, information, radio broadcast, nursery, kindergarten, public toilets, population planning, sports and physical education, veteran and social affairs, education of teenagers and children	✔		✔				✔
6.4. Protect historical monuments, protect worship houses, Buddhist and Taoist temples in the locality			✔				✔
6.5. Manage cultural and education organizations and recreational facilities	✔						
6.6. Supervise and issue licences to private individuals doing business in this sector	✔		✔				
6.7. Ensure that schools teach according to the rules set up by the state	✔						
6.8. Co-ordinate with the schools and families to look after school children, to manage school children during summer holidays, and mobilize the people to help build, repair, and equip schools.			✔				✔

TABLE 2.4 (continued)

Responsibilities	1981	1983	1986	Đổi Mới	1989	1994	1996
6.9. Manage schools together with upper levels of authority							✔
6.10. Organize and manage nurseries and kindergartens			✔				
6.11. Educate youth deemed "slow to progress"							
6.12. Draw up plans for development of culture			✔				✔
6.13. Fight against superstitution, anti-revolution cultural products, pornography, and social evils							✔
6.14. Organize public health activities, manage the health station, Red Cross, traditional doctors			✔				
6.15. Manage the health station and implement health programmes, publicize health issues							✔
6.16. Draw up or implement plans to help, look after families of injured veterans, families of war and revolutionary heroes, retired cadres, families of serving soldiers, of Young Pioneers			✔				✔

TABLE 2.4 (continued)

Responsibilities	1981	1983	1986	Đổi Mới	1989	1994	1996
6.17. Protect and manage war memorials and cemeteries							✔
6.18. Mobilize the people in helping families in economic difficulties who have many children, the orphans, disabled, unfortunate			✔				
6.19. Manage the locality in all aspects of social affairs						✔	
Religion							
6.20. Implement policies on ethnic minorities and religion							✔
6.21. Ensure freedom of belief and religion according to the law							✔
7. Housing and land							
7.1. Know the housing needs of the locality		✔	✔				
7.2. Supervise building, repair, and use of houses and land	✔	✔	✔				
7.3. Give opinion on the distribution of housing to people and implement such decisions in the ward	✔	✔	✔				
7.4. Ensure that every family meets accommodation needs reasonably		✔					

TABLE 2.4 (continued)

Responsibilities	1981	1983	1986	Đổi Mới	1989	1994	1996
7.5. Supervise the execution of contracts to rent houses		✔	✔				
7.6. Fight against illegal sale, lease of houses		✔					
7.7. Check on building works and implement decisions to demolish illegal construction		✔					
7.8. Draw up plan to manage and maintain public infrastructure in the locality		✔	✔				
7.9. Maintain public works in the ward		✔	✔				✔
7.10. Check on safety of dykes and do repairs							✔
7.11. Check on the usage of water and electricity							✔
7.12. Mobilize the people to manage their own public areas and public works							
7.13. Give opinion, suggest giving permissions for, and check on the use of pavements							
7.14. Manage production on land in the ward still engaged in agricultural production	✔						✔

TABLE 2.4 (continued)

Responsibilities	1981	1983	1986	Đổi Mới	1989	1994	1996
7.15. Manage the locality with respect to land use, natural resources						✔	✔
7.16. Help the locality to make use of the latest technology in agriculture							✔
8. Planning and budget; finance			f				
8.1. Canvass people's opinion in determining the revenue and profit of individual producers							✔
8.2. Educate, mobilize and check on the people especially individual producers to pay the correct amount of taxes and on time							
8.3. Fight tax evasion, and suggest punishments for offenders							
8.4. Help to draw up the budget-expenditure plan and be responsible for implementation of the work and financial plans delegated by upper levels	✔		✔				
8.5. Compile the budget and the final budget, present to the people's council and upper levels for approval							✔

TABLE 2.4 (continued)

Responsibilities	1981	1983	1986	Đổi Mới	1989	1994	1996
8.6. Co-operate with upper levels to implement the budget							✔
9. Miscellanous							
9.1. Collect statistics on the area whenever required by upper levels							
9.2. Be aware of the economic and ideological situation of the area							
9.3. Certify resume and other certificates of the people							
9.4. File reports on illegal activities by anyone							
9.5. Issue orders to stop any illegal activities							
9.6. Issue warnings to repeat offenders and have them criticized in front of the people							
9.7. Prepare for people's council meetings by co-ordinating work of subcommittees of people's council; and prepare people's council resolutions					✔	✔	
9.8. In conjunction with the Chairman of the people's council, prepare for people's council meetings						✔	

TABLE 2.4 (continued)

Responsibilities	1981	1983	1986	Đổi Mới	1989	1994	1996
9.9. Manage organizational and personnel work for the ward machinery						✔	

Notes:
The government may ask the ward to attend to other matters not on this list, such as conducting a particular social campaign.

a. According to Hướng dẫn số 469-TCCP, ngày 2-12-1981 của Ban Tổ chức của Chính phủ Về việc thi hành Quyết Định số 94-HĐBT ban hành ngày 26-9-1981 của Hội Đồng Bộ trưởng quy định chức năng, nhiệm vụ và tổ chức bộ máy chính quyền phương. Cleaning toilets became the job of the Ward UBND in 1986, and it contracted the work out.

b. This area became a new section by itself from 1986.

c. Emphasis on measures to prevent fire, robbery and theft, and smuggling

d. According to Hướng dẫn số 469-TCCP, ngày 2-12-1981 của Ban Tổ chức của Chính phủ Về việc thi hành Quyết Định số 94-HĐBT ban hành ngày 26-9-1981 của Hội Đồng Bộ trưởng quy Định chức năng, nhiệm vụ và tổ chức bộ máy chính quyền phương.

e. Emphasis to be placed on the following: manage a few labour groups and co-operatives, people who are self-employed, and check on and deal with fake goods and phantom shops. Hướng dẫn số 469-TCCP, ngày 2-12-1981 của Ban Tổ chức của Chính phủ Về việc thi hành Quyết Định số 94-HĐBT ban hành ngày 26-9-1981 của Hội Đồng Bộ trưởng quy định chức năng, nhiệm vụ và tổ chức bộ máy chính quyền phương.

f. In 1986, the sources of income for the ward were stated clearly for the first time in an official document on the role of the ward. These comprise three: Income from production and service providing businesses in the ward directly managed by the ward, income from other economic and cultural businesses in the ward managed by upper level by a part of the income given to the ward, and income from subsidy given to budget of the ward. Clearly stated, the ward cannot create new items of taxes or community contribution on its own.

Sources:
1978: Quyết Định số 5417/QĐ-CQ-UB ngày 21/12/1978 của Ủy ban nhân dân thành phố Hà Nội về Quy Định tạm thời về nhiệm vụ, quyền hạn của Ủy ban nhân dân tiểu khu.
1981: Quyết Định số 94/HĐBT, ngày 26/9/1981 của Hội Đồng Bộ trưởng Về chức năng, nhiệm vụ và tổ chức bộ máy chính quyền cấp phương.
1982: DCĐ (1982) "Nội dung phân cấp cho UBND Quận, UBND Phường", *HNM*, 12 May 1982, p. 2
1983: Luật tổ chức Hội Đồng nhân dân và Ủy ban nhân dân
1986: 3784/QĐUB, 6/8/1986 of the People's Committee of Hanoi
1989: Luật tổ chức Hội Đồng nhân dân và Ủy ban nhân dân
1994: Luật tổ chức Hội Đồng nhân dân và Ủy ban nhân dân (Sửa Đổi)
1996: Quy chế hoạt động của Hội đồng Nhân dân các cấp
2003: Luật tổ chức Hội Đồng nhân dân và Ủy ban nhân dân

ward authorities like those of Cửa Nam Ward, the Hoàn Kiếm District, the next higher level of authority that had eighteen wards, would have had the formidable task of receiving more than 200 people per day.[59]

Furthermore, Thả claimed that public opinion about the ward was said to have swung from unfavourable when first proposed to favourable. For instance, when the ward level was experimented upon in Cửa Nam Ward of the Hoàn Kiếm District, two-thirds of all officials of Small Area People's Committees in the same district (only officials voted) were against it. (In Ngô Thì Nhậm Small Area, as noted by Thanh Đạm earlier, the public was also against it.) At the last consultation session for the 1980 Constitution in the Hoàn Kiếm District, only seven officials in the Cửa Nam Ward were still opposed. Nguyễn Đức Thả claimed that the swing was because after two years of operation of the Small District, the people came to realize that the third level of local authority was necessary. According to Thả, officials discovered that people liked the convenience of the proximity of a government office for various purposes: administration, arbitration of quarrels, disputes over house, landownership, and detection of artificial marriages (for the purpose of setting up a false household and getting more rations).[60] Thus, some amount of effort was expended to show that the ward model was successfully achieving objectives the state commanded.

In reality, however, significant problems plagued the ward state machinery, and reporting of these problems soon appeared. From 1983 to 1985, teams of specialists from the party branch of Hà Nội City attached themselves to wards to observe their work and to give recommendations.[61] That the attachment was necessary demonstrated serious concerns about the ward emanating from within the VCP. The party review led to a series of meetings by Hà Nội's urban districts to review their wards' work in 1985.[62] The reviews found, among other problems, that several ward people's committees did not consult with people's councils before taking important action. In part this was because the people's council only met once per quarter. Also the council did not have a subcommittee to oversee daily matters. Consequently, decisions that had to be taken in between council sessions fell into the people's committee's hands.[63] The implication here seemed to be there was insufficient accountability of officials to elected representatives.

Another explanation for this lack of accountability was that although the people's committee was the executive committee of the people's council, it was answerable to government ministries. This was known as the principle of Double Subordination. People's committee members were usually career bureaucrats dispatched by the city to run in people's council elections and then get elected as leaders of people's committee. This situation, in turn, meant that the people's committee could still administer without consulting the people's council. Conceptually the principle of Double Subordination contains contradictions between line and staff organs and power. In practice, executive dominance in daily affairs relegated the councils to a mainly consultative and rubber-stamping role, rather than a supervisory role as intended by the Constitution and laws. In this sense, the role of the Council was seen as "incomplete".

In order to address these problems and institute a "complete" level of state administration, wards established a number of subcommittees within their councils and committees. However, there was either a shortage of manpower or a general unwillingness among residents to serve on the committees.[64] VCP central committee member and vice-chairman cum secretary general of the State Council, Lê Thanh Nghị, noted that a number of local authorities, for some reasons, did not have enough people on their staff and many of the leading members were taking on multiple roles so as to make sure that all the subcommittees' positions were filled up.[65] Furthermore, Nghị noted, most people's committee chairmen did not pay enough attention to the work of the people's council subcommittees, as they should under the 1983 Law on Organization of People's Council and People's Committee.

Criticisms of Cadres' Competence and Morality

Incompetence of officials of both bodies was also criticized by the Communist Party review of 1984/85. An important cause, however, was the party itself. The party claims, then and now, that the Vietnamese state represents the interests of all classes and sectors in Vietnam — workers, peasants, women, youth, intellectuals, military, religion, ethnic minorities, just to name the main ones — and thus it is obliged to ensure that every class and sector is represented in the national assembly as well as in all local people's councils. The result was to subordinate the criterion of competence to political expedience when selecting candidates for election to the people's councils and people's committees. At the aforementioned meeting of leading local authority cadres of Hà Nội in 1985, Lê Thanh Nghị said that numerous council members did not contribute anything throughout their whole term in the people's council, and some could not even say anything when they were meeting in subcommittees and sections.[66] The Hoàn Kiếm District also pointed out that some members of its people's council "were afraid to interact with the voters, because they could listen to the voters but could not tell voters who could solve their problems or whether their problems could be solved …;"[67] it also pointed out that its wards had too many retirees on their people's councils and they could not function effectively. The implication was that the Communist Party, because it controlled nominations, had used the ward as a dumping ground for retired party and state officials.[68]

In the mid-1980s, newspapers reported complaints about ward officials who tended to be authoritarian, rude, and bureaucratic. Another criticism was that some people's committees exceeded their powers while others operated meekly. Too many ward officials lacked initiative and relied on upper levels to give direction. Sometimes, they were not sure what they could do or were afraid to make decisions. Thus very often the districts had to make decisions that wards should have made.[69] These problems were old ones.

Newer problems, however, seemed more critical than bureaucratism. Several other reports highlighted moral degradation of cadres, especially party members, who were linked to the ward administrative machinery. Many cadres had set up illegal businesses, embezzled state property through ruses such as "ghost workers" registered in order to get more rations, helping residents to evade taxes and then splitting the difference. In the Ô Chợ Dừa (Coconut Market Gate) Ward, for instance, more than ten party members were found to have extended the area of their houses illegally.[70] In a major speech on the state management crisis situation in Hà Nội in 1985, Communist Party Political Bureau member Lê Đức Thọ pointed out that an estimated 10 per cent of party members in Hà Nội were "not up to standards" (*không đủ tiêu chuẩn*), and that 75 per cent of people caught watching pornographic films were party members.[71] The ward was unable to either prevent or stop such practices.

Rising Level of Criticisms

Responses to criticisms were lame, and debate about what to do indicated differences in thinking among Communist Party and state leaders. In 1985 writers of the *HNM*, the newspaper belonging to the Hà Nội Branch of the VCP, from the party affirmed the role of the ward in urban management and mobilization work. They questioned whether the district or the Small Areas could have managed the tasks performed by the ward on a daily basis. These included problems such as monitoring markets, maintaining law and order, helping residents with livelihood problems, and especially mobilizing individuals to purchase bonds and participate in other party campaigns.[72] Employment was also a major area that the ward was supposed to have handled well. Several reports also credited wards with helping to create employment for residents.[73] But criticisms against the ward in Hà Nội were too strong to be dismissed, and they intensified as preparations for the 1986 Sixth National Party Congress accelerated.[74]

One such preparation was party rectification. In early 1986, at a time when the party-state was struggling to maintain its governance credibility on many fronts, not just regarding local administration, the VCP launched a "Criticisms and Self-Criticisms" campaign throughout the country. The aim was to improve party and cadre performance and to restore people's confidence in the party's ability to lead. Marea Fatseas argues that the party's leaders sought "in part, to channel public hostility against individual cadres and to divert attention from the failings of the regime as a whole."[75]

The criticism sessions regarding local administration conducted by the Hà Nội party branch on two days in late July 1986 uncovered officially what had been known to people for some time — wards employed numerous ineffective, degenerate, dishonest, and lazy ward cadres and party members. One news report said, "It is quite common to find not a few party members in the inner city breaking rules and regulations, and not following procedures when extending, repairing, building, transferring, purchasing and selling houses; they also take over public land and built houses there illegally."[76] Often, whole groups of party members cum cadres colluded in these illegal activities and succeeded due to their special powers and privileges as public officials in the ward. Party members also, said the account,

> buy valuable goods cheaply. Using what is called "priority internal distribution", they get, for example, motorcycles, sewing machines, electrical fans … They bring their wife and children into permanent employment with the state in those sectors that are regarded as "profitable". A fact which required thinking and review to make its reasons clear is that during the previous two to three years, the living standards of many cadres responsible for economic enterprises and companies have risen to levels impossible to achieve with the income they are supposed to have received.[77]

The criticism sessions also brought out a point made in the early 1980s: party and government lines were blurred. "On the style of leadership of the districts, prefectures, towns, communes, and wards level, the problem is the mixing-up (*lẫn lộn*) of the role of the party with the role of the political authority, of collective leadership and personal responsibility." Because of the lack of differentiation and thus lack of separation of power, local officials holding leadership positions became "dictatorial". For instance, people were especially critical of authorities abusing their power over food distribution. Besides such "common shortcomings" as

> rudeness, being dictatorial, and troublesome, they also reserved the best goods for themselves and their families. The weighing machines were inaccurate, the hours of trade were not guaranteed ... There have been phenomena of cheating on coupons [*quay vòng tem phiếu*], cheating on the rights to rations of customers ... After self-criticism and criticism, it was found that a number of personnel collaborated with customers to transfer, arrange to bring state goods [*tuôn hàng Nhà nước*] out to the black market.[78]

After the Sixth Party National Congress in December 1986, wards in Hà Nội seemed to try to improve their performance in maintaining social order. In Tràng Tiền Ward, for instance, authorities took steps to relieve road congestion by removing about fifty straw huts from the main streets of Hai Bà Trưng and Ngô Quyền as well as the illegal mini-markets that met regularly in front of the Workers' Theatre on Tràng Tiền Street and in front of the General Post Office on Đinh Tiên Hoàng Streets, all in the city centre. The newspaper *HNM* reported, however, that other than these modest achievements, disorder was still the norm: bicycles were still parked haphazardly, and traders removed from Tràng Tiền Street regrouped not far away from there, but were left alone.[79] In other places away from the city centre, such as Kim Liên Ward, there was no improvement in the ward's ability to provide basic services and keep social order. Water and electricity were unreliable. So were food supplies. The food was also more expensive, indicating how poorly authorities managed the ward's trading co-operative, a consumer shop that purchased non-ration goods from the state to resell to people who are members. "Free (private) markets" mushroomed everywhere on the pavement and on the streets, while the state market was not used because of muddy and crowded conditions. Disregard for law and order, even when there were signs and policemen, was common in Hà Nội.[80]

POST-1986 DEVELOPMENTS: REVISING THE LAWS ON LOCAL AUTHORITIES

In view of major criticisms levelled at the operation of local authority in general, the government moved to revise the 1983 Law on Organization of People's Councils and People's Committees as the 1989 local elections approached. The first step towards that goal was to collect feedback from Hà Nội ward cadres. The standing committee of the Hà Nội party branch and the Hà Nội City people's committee held a first-ever conference on the ward in August 1988. At the conference, Lê Ất Hợi, vice-chairman of the city people's committee, made the following points on what had happened to the wards in Hà Nội:

1. The wards had neglected administrative work and management of society.
2. Ability of cadres was still lacking, good cadres were unevenly spread, and thus management results were not good. There was no plan to train cadres. Wards appeared uncaring of the career development of their cadres.
3. Activities of mass organizations were still confused.
4. Co-ordination between different state agencies in the same locality was still not ideal.
5. Upper levels did not supervise wards closely.
6. The wards had too many and heavy responsibilities, beyond the capacity of their resources.[81]

This assessment made the regime realized it was unreasonable to ask the ward to take on so many responsibilities in view of the ward's general lack of capability, in terms of understanding and commitment, financial capacity and supervisory skills. A few city-level officials drew attention to this by emphasizing the state's mistake in asking the wards to open trading co-operatives to procure and sell goods. In doing so, they argued, the state had not only distracted ward cadres from their primary task of administering society on behalf of the state, but also provided opportunities for ward cadres to engage in their own private businesses under the cover of the state. Not surprisingly, ward officials neglected other areas of their work such as administration, infrastructure building and encouraging compliance with the law. Furthermore, control and supervision slackened because the administration of these trading co-operatives gave cadres more power to act independently.

The conference suggested the following changes to allow the ward to focus on administration:

1. Adjust the powers and tasks of the ward to match them with reality. The wards should emphasize administrative responsibilities in their localities.
2. Consolidate the mass organizations.
3. Strengthen leadership of the ward by upper levels.[82]

Column "1989" of Table 2.4 shows that under the 1989 Law on People's Councils and People's Committees, not only were economic responsibilities removed from the ward's hands, but many responsibilities in other areas, especially social control, were curtailed as well, in line with national reforms that took place after the 1986 Sixth Party Congress. Therefore, where legislation was concerned, the state did have a will to improve matters.

Two years after the conference on the ward, in 1990, the government held a National Conference on People's Councils. It expressed through amendments to the 1989 Law on Organization of People's Councils and People's Committees that the fight against "negative phenomena" (*tiêu cực*) — a term usually referring to occurrences against law and order, and social discipline — by local administrators could be more effective. This could come about if people's councils were more effective in their activities and in supervising people's committees. This was the reason the major change in the structure of local administrations under the 1989 Law involved setting up a standing committee of the people's council. At the ward level, however, there was no such standing committee, so the chairman of the people's council had to assume the role of a standing committee. This standing body had the role of ensuring the people's council participation in daily decisions in the ward, and took over from the people's committee chairman the more assertive tasks of preparing for council meetings and liaising between council and committee on ward affairs. At the ward level, however, the above measure merely meant the council chairman, who was usually the party secretary, could now exercise his supervisory role in the name of the state rather than the communist party, apparently in line with the post-1986 political reforms to strengthen the state and the rule of law, but in fact going against efforts to separate the VCP from the state. In reality, however, this standing body of the people's council seldom met and in fact had little or no power to hand out punishments directly, because such work had to be channelled through the people's committee. It also had few resources of its own, relying mainly on the limited government resources that were channelled mainly to the people's committee.[83]

Under a provision of the 1989 Law, the people's council lost power to call a vote of no-confidence in the people's committee, but it was balanced by the power it gained for more supervision of the people's committee. (See Table 2.3.) The purpose seemed to be to increase council's administrative efficiency and to prevent ordinary members of the councils hindering people's committee work and challenging leading committee members.[84]

The abovementioned changes in 1989 in fact strengthened party control in the name of the state and, contrary to the rhetoric of the National Conference, made it even harder for council members to check on the committee. Consequently, at the 1990 conference, there was a call on the party Political Bureau and the VCP Secretariat to clarify the nature of the relationship between party branches in localities, the people's council, the council's standing committee, and the people's committee in official documents and regulations.[85]

Also, in 1990, the Hà Nội City authority held its second conference on the ward, entitled "Building up the Ward". Conference participants noted that opinions regarding the ward reflected the two broad streams of thought that had existed since the early 1980s. On one side were those who thought the ward merely added an additional layer of bureaucracy and should be eliminated by administrative reform. On the other side were those who insisted that the ward was essential in maintaining social order and mobilization, and should be retained.[86] Consequently, reviewing the ward's role and organization according to these two opposing streams of thought led to an impasse. It is, however, difficult to identify who are in the two streams of thought because the names of participants were not provided.

While policy-makers were still struggling to redefine the role and function of the ward level, suggestions to abolish it arose again in 1991, after the Building up the Ward conference.[87] Meanwhile, the political mood swung back slowly in favour of retaining the ward, perhaps reflecting a wave of conservative political opinion at the time of the Seventh Party Congress. In particular, positive assessments of the ward's contribution, seldom heard since the mid-1980s, were reasserted. Contributors of opinion to *HNM* pointed out the ward had been valuable in co-ordinating work to build infrastructure at the ward level. In Ô Chợ

Dừa Ward, for example, the ward administration mobilized the people, the city administration, and the district in contributing money towards paving more than 2,000 metres of lanes with a layer of cement, for the convenience of residents. Other projects included widening of La Thành Road, stabilization in the supply of electricity through installing new transformers, and provision of cleaner water supply and laying pipes to bring water to every home. Many people in Ô Chợ Dừa Ward saw these activities as the efforts of the ward people's council, and supported the existence of the ward machinery.[88]

Moreover, while it has been acknowledged that the ward carried out administrative duties on behalf of the state, a point that was seldom mentioned surfaced, which was that the ward had become a useful tool for averting social problems. This point suggests the usefulness of the group head's local knowledge of residents. For example, at Ô Chợ Dừa Ward someone wanted to mortgage his house to borrow money from a credit society, but the application needed Ô Chợ Dừa Ward's certification of house ownership. Ward officials requested that the views of the applicant's parents and siblings should also be consulted before the loan could be given, because they knew that the house belonged to the whole family. In other words, ward officials through their knowledge of local residents and conditions could help to prevent fraud. In addition to preventing local problems, the ward could resolve disputes as well. Instances of clashes and quarrels among the people in the same ward amounted to several dozens per year. Most of these cases were resolved through conciliation at the ward level.

The comeback of the ward became stronger after the Seventh Party National Congress in 1991, when the ward seemed to have won wider acceptance of its critical role in policy mobilization and implementation. The party-state was held back from abolishing the ward, perhaps because it had no answer to the question: what would replace it? People warned against a hasty removal of wards, despite their weaknesses. As one writer said in the *HNM* paper, officials had to bear in mind the administrative capabilities in the country.

> We paid a high price for the lessons we learnt about being overly eager in wanting to reach big-scale production under Socialism; we integrated provinces, established large agriculture co-operatives for whole Communes, work teams, and large farms, etc. when at that time our management standards were still low, our scientific and technological infrastructure were undeveloped. That lesson taught us absolutely to be

realistic, not to impatiently abolish a regime or a model which was still useful and then not replace it with something better, just because of a few shortcomings.[89]

In fact, there was a suggestion by experts to the 1980 Constitutional Revision Committee to remove the ward level of local authority.[90] It was considered but turned down.

By the mid-1990s, as the ward continued to exist, residents' circumstances also changed significantly as economic reforms transformed Vietnamese society. The explosion of information sources since the late 1980s meant that people have gained access to diversified information beyond the ward. Thus, an experienced ward cadre complained that work at the ward had become more difficult in the early 1990s, because people, being better informed, were more demanding and could assess and challenge the veracity of the ward and its cadres' claims. This new reality eroded the ward's authority as the conveyor of knowledge about governance, hence power. Furthermore, the working of the market economy and the end of the subsidy period gave many people increased opportunities in the private sector rather than depending on the state and the ward to allocate employment. The ward's task of regulating society became more strenuous after reforms because of the "bursting out" (bung ra) of the private economy, especially in petty trade. The new situation caused more disorder in the streets and regulation failures in areas of public policy, for example, control of illegal housing construction, residential registration, and social vices.[91]

In recent years, renewed criticism has come from Vietnamese government academics regarding the system of local administration as a whole. This is a noticeable departure from the past. Before 1996 there was generally a lack of critique by Vietnamese themselves on the Vietnamese local administration system, at whatever level. Most published material about local administration taught cadres the principles and practice of socialist public administration rather than offer critiques.[92]

Latest Developments and Review

Among the various shortcomings recently identified by Vietnamese party and state policy-makers and administrators, two sets of problems emerge as keys to understanding the causes of limits on state dominance of society at the ward level in Hà Nội. The first I call institutional deficiencies, which in the late 1990s are similar to problems that have plagued the ward from the start. The other set contains cultural dynamics, which are seldom elaborated upon by Vietnamese sources.

Institutional Deficiencies

By institutional deficiencies I refer to three main shortcomings in the organization and the operation of the ward state machinery. Senior state officials and academics employed by the state have asserted it is the lack of quality cadres that is the Achilles heel of the local administration system, especially at the basic level in both city and countryside. Recent official statistics indicate that the qualifications of basic level people's committee and people's council members are often barely sufficient to meet the demands of administrative tasks or to understand top-level instructions. A government academic survey found that 60 to 70 per cent of all basic-level cadres expressed an inability to deal with new circumstances in society that have evolved in the thirteen years of reform after 1986. Sixty to 70 per cent of leading basic-level cadres was retirees of the armed forces, and 17 to 19 per cent of them were long-serving cadres recruited from local branches of mass organizations.[93] In other words, if the survey is accurate, close to 90 per cent of these basic-level cadres were not trained as administrators, and indeed 85 per cent of rural commune committee chairmen interviewed felt they needed training to become competent.

Furthermore, at the 1998 national conference on raising the effectiveness of the people's council and people's committee, Vũ Mão, then Director of the Office of the National Assembly, pointed to a survey of the educational standards and work distribution to the people's council chairman in the three levels of local administration across the country (See Table 2.5).

Vũ Mão's statistics show that the lower the level of administration, the less educated people's committee members are, and the less time the people's council chairman has in supervising the people's committee. It is tempting to infer that at the basic level, the ward included, people's committees often have a high level of autonomy because the people's councils do not check them too closely. If that was what Vũ Mão intended to infer, then it is curious, because quite often the people's council chairman's position is occupied by the ward party secretary, senior in the party position to the people's committee chairman (deputy secretary), and therefore the council chairman could exert leadership of the committee leadership via the party hierarchy. Perhaps Vũ Mão wanted to stop the practice of having party secretaries become council chairmen. This would require further

TABLE 2.5
Educational Standard of Leading Ward Cadres

Level of People's Committee	Educational standard of People's Committee cadres			Percentage of People's Council chairman holding a second official job
	tertiary or post-graduate	upper or lower secondary	primary	
City/Province (total 615 cadres)	70-80% (100% in Hanoi)	n. a.	n. a.	68.9% (42, total = 61)
District (total 4,994 cadres)	50–60%	40–50%	0	87.8% (568, total = 603)
Commune/ward (total 62,403 cadres)	0	45.2% and 45.9% respectively	8.9%	90% (9,270, total = 10,300)

Source: Tuổi Trẻ, "Hội nghị về HĐND va UBND: Nâng cao quyền của HĐND và năng lực quản lý của UBND" [Conference on people's councils and people's committees: Raise the power of people's councils and management ability of people's committees] 29 September 1998, pp. 1, 14. See also Nguyễn Văn Thư, "Về đào tạo, bồi dưỡng cán bộ chính quyền địa phương trong giai đoạn hiện nay" [On training and cultivation of cadres of local authorities in the current situation], in Cải cách hành chính địa phương: Lý luận và thực tiễn [Local administration reform: Theory and practice], edited by Tô Tử Hạ, Nguyễn Hữu Trị, Nguyễn Hữu Đức (Hà Nội: NXB Chính trị Quốc gia, 1998), pp. 137–38.

opening of the nominations process in elections to the people's council, or to have the chief state executive of the ward directly elected.

These implications are beyond the limits of the VCP-dominated political system. The Communist Party now allows a limited contest in elections for all people's councils. These council elections are now more open compared to pre-1986. (Chapter 3 examines the issue of elections and the ward.) In spite of this, however, the important leadership posts of the ward are still held by leading party members, state bureaucrats, and mass organization leaders located in the ward. The party and the state are separate entities but intricately joined in personnel and power. No significant persons outside the party-state hierarchy are given meaningful responsibilities to check on the ward machinery (and perhaps act against party wishes). One specific illustration of this is the ward party inspector; while theoretically his task is to check on the top leaders of the ward, he does not have an independent power base, and the party secretary and deputy-secretary guide him, indeed, by the collective leadership of the WPSC. Ward people's council members meet once in six months, while their standing committee is the head of the WPB. Furthermore, if the party officials, heads of mass organizations, and the party cell secretaries in Hà Nội's wards are older and are as poorly paid as reported, then it is unlikely that they will actively check on the ward executive officials, because of their attitudes which will be elaborated towards the end of this chapter. One improvement is in the provision of the 2003 Law on Organization of People's Councils that forbid chairmen of people's committees and people's councils (article 6 clause 3) to hold on to their posts for more than two terms; but this improvement does not address the issue of cadre quality in a basic way. For instance, if a leader has been managing a locality well for two terms, he either retires after that or is transferred to another locality to continue his career. It is at the basic level — in the communes and wards — that many leaders of councils and committees have occupied their posts for more than two terms.[94]

The impact of poor cadre quality — whether morally or professionally — and the lack of checks on the abuse of power limits the effectiveness of the state administration because it allows for a larger amount of space for mediation than otherwise.

In response to this deficiency, the government has in 2004 instituted plans to raise the work capacity of officials of the ward level. The plans followed those already approved for upper level officials. This meant that 70 to 80 per cent of all officials at the ward (as well as the commune) level will undergo training in politics, in public administration, leadership, and specialist training of different degrees of expertise. There would be minimal requirements of post-secondary training for such officials.[95] Furthermore, to make employment with the wards more attractive, the government in 2003 also declared a new scheme of employment for permanent officials of the ward. This new scheme addressed many grievances of these officials regarding the lack of appropriate benefits and security in employment.[96] Limiting the term of the chairpersons of the council and committee to two terms was another show of resolve on the part of the government to improve capacity at local administration level. Concurrent to this was the setting up of a standing committee of the ward people's council.

A second institutional deficiency is the lack of substance to support the rhetoric that the people's council is the supreme local authority organ and acts as a check on its executives. Officially, ward people's councils represent the state in checking on the people's committees and ensuring that they implement state policies and laws faithfully. But several characteristics of their existence prevent them from doing so. From 1981 there have been questions about the people's councils' usefulness, because they meet only a few times a year and are dominated by the executive. One secretary of a ward people's council in a detailed, open report pointed out that not only were the members of his people's council made up mainly of retirees or people who had their main energies directed to other full-time work, the committees of the people's council also seldom met and, therefore, could not contribute much to the work of the people's committee, let alone direct it.[97] It also did not have the time to check if the situation of compliance to law in its jurisdiction was good.

One person I interviewed insisted that the ward people's council plays a bigger role in local affairs and has more power in 1998 than before, even though its powers are still inadequate.[98] I doubt, however, that this person's perception is widespread. My view is symbolically supported by a comparison of the old and new signboards at ward offices of Hà Nội. Old signs tend to emphasize the pre-eminence of the people's committee (in large bold lettering), while only a few new signs emphasize pre-eminence of the people's council (see Table 2.6).

Members of people's councils at the 1998 national conference on raising the effectiveness of people's councils and people's committees pointed out that "the people's councils [at all levels] have the rights but not the power" ("*Hội đồng Nhân dân là cơ quan có quyền mà không có lực*"), and the "people's councils are given blade-less swords" ("*giao gươm mà không có lưỡi*"). In March 1998, I interviewed Mr X, a former people's committee chairman of an urban district in Hà Nội who later became in charge of an internationally funded public administration reform project, undertaken by the Government Committee on Organization and Personnel, investigating reforms to the local administration system. Mr X privately said that the existence of the people's councils is "democracy in form but not in substance", because they can pass resolutions but do not have to consider whether realistically their people's committees can do the job.[99] For improvements in efficiency in state administration, X told me that he may propose the following restructuring and simplification of urban districts and wards' state administrative machinery:

TABLE 2.6
Wording Emphasis on Signs of Selected Ward Offices

Ward	"People's Committee" emphasized	"People's Council" emphasized	Equal emphasis	New or old sign?
Hai Bà Trưng District				
Mai Động	✔			New
Minh Khai	✔			Old
Bạch Mai	✔			Old
Trương Định	✔			Old
Đồng Tâm			✔	Old
Hoàn Kiếm District				
Hàng Bài		✔		New
Hàng Mã	✔			New
Hàng Bông		✔		New
Cửa Nam	✔			Old
Hàng Bạc			✔	Old
Đống Đa District				
Kim Liên	✔			Old
Phương Liên		✔		Old
Trung Tự	✔			Old
Hàng Bột	✔			Old
Văn Chương	✔			Old
Ba Đình District				
Điện Biên	✔			Old
Cống Vị			✔	Old
Quán Thánh	✔			Old
Trúc Bạch	✔			Old
Kim Mã	✔			Old

Source: Thanks to Miss Oanh for her legwork, confirming my preliminary observations, and for her vigorous views. Various e-mail communications, November and December 1998.

1. There will be no people's councils, but only people's committees.
2. Have a minimum of two vice-chairmen instead of one minimum in each committee.
3. The rest of the people's committee would comprise four other members who are in-charge of the following areas: Land, Administration, Rule of law, and Construction.[100]

If Mr X's proposals are accepted, there will be only appointed executives for the wards and the districts. Mr X's proposals would resolve the façade of people's council supremacy over the people's committee, but they do not necessarily increase the accountability or effectiveness of executive officials. Nevertheless, they validate arguments against the ward first articulated in the late 1970s. If we recall earlier pages, arguments against the ward maintained that the city was different from the rural areas and it was not necessary to have the ward people's council or even the ward as well. As late as 2001, the opinion that the people's councils of the ward-level (and the district level) are redundant and that the nature of the ward level administration should be altered from democratic representation (assembly) to one merely being the representatives of a higher level was still being articulated openly, suggesting that the debate was still open. That the 2003 revisions to the Law on Organization of People's Councils and People's Committees did not erase the ward level and the people's council therein shows that there is yet to be found a solution that reassures those who want the ward retained: what would replace it?[101] Thus the debate was temporarily closed, inconclusively.

The argument against a ward-level administration is now made by academics working both inside and outside the government, and articulated in a more open way. They argue that the ward is merely a paper pusher. A joke inserts two Vietnamese words in between the two words forming the compound for "administration" (hành chính) to become the new clause "mainly to torture the people" (hành dân là chính).[102] Echoing the arguments of the late 1970s, these academics now maintain that the administration of a city cannot be easily subdivided, and the government should not divide up the city of Hà Nội into sectors and allow each one of them to have special rules for themselves just as is done for the rural areas. Not only are there fundamental differences in the needs of the city and the needs of rural areas, but the process of subdivision enlarge the bureaucracy unnecessarily as well. However, as a concession to "political correctness", the academics recognize that the wards do have a role in realizing state policies,[103] and they recommend retaining the ward level with modifications. They recommend that a ward should only be a branch of the district executive, organized in a similar way to the Small Areas people's committee model of the 1978–81 period.[104] This compromise seems to be in line with X's proposals as well.

The third institutional deficiency limiting state dominance is that ward authorities adjust state policies to local conditions. Like the two levels of local authorities above them, wards cite local conditions as reasons for administrative practices deviating from national laws and policies. Such discretion is mandated by the Constitution and by the Law on People's Councils.

Catering to local conditions is an essential aspect of local administration in many medium and large countries such as Vietnam. Sometimes, the policies that have been dictated by the higher levels become impractical when attempts are made to implement them at the ward level. This is when the principle of local conditions is useful. For example, the Vietnamese central government has a regulation stating house construction or renovation must be supported by a certificate of land use. This policy attempted to erect a regime of land use based on legally authenticated documents rather than on traditions of use. In Hà Nội, this ruling proved particularly problematic even though it caused few problems in Hồ Chí Minh City.[105] Over recent history the various regimes in Hà Nội did not issue many land-use certificates. The royal government did not issue them and the French issued only a few. Later, during the socialist stage of development most occupants of houses did not have usage or ownership certificates even though they may have been living in the house for several generations. Therefore, these people find it impossible to comply with the state's rule. For residents of houses that are situated outside the dykes of Hà Nội, who need to rebuild or repair annually after damage caused by flooding problems of the Red River, a problem arises because their right to reside outside the dyke has never been recognized by the government. People forced to live on the other side, such as the urban poor, would become homeless if local ward authorities decide to act strictly and evict them, which deepens the city's housing shortage. Therefore, a significant amount of local variation is necessary to make things work.

A number of Vietnamese academics, however, point out that catering to local diversity has meant overriding national laws and standards.[106] Lack of supervision leaves abuse of the discretionary power of ward-level officers unchecked. For instance, while the government's policy may be to clear hawkers from pavements, the policemen responsible for the matter may decide to turn a blind eye to hawkers on streets in his ward. He may provide reasons for his actions in terms of local conditions, but these reasons can become a cover for petty corruption, which most people in Vietnam assume to be the case.[107] (Chapter 4 discusses traffic issues in more details.) In fact Vietnamese academics argue that administrative decentralization to a low level such as the ward is unnecessary and also provides opportunities for corruption.[108] In Vietnamese political discourse parlance, therefore, there is too much democracy leading to a lack of central control.

There is also evidence to suggest that professional state agencies cannot fully control lower level specialist officials. These officials are dispatched to the ward to watch the gates for the ministries. Down at the ward, however, specialist officials are expected to play by the "rules" of the ward; they co-operate with generalist officials in the ward in conceding "special" practices for the locality, with some rewards to them and to the wards.[109] A good example is the enforcement of a building regulation in the Thirty-Six Streets area of Hà Nội. City regulations require retention of old forms of housing and new houses must be not more than three storeys in height, and their roofs must be sloping down to the front, like the other old houses. Most people in Hà Nội, however, would think about exploiting the plot ratio to the maximum, especially if they are building mini-hotels, a big revenue-generating business in the Thirty-Six Streets (a tourism area) on which the wards could levy taxes. The ward has incentives to allow design "mistakes", because the hotel owner's taxes and other contributions to the ward will be higher if the building is a six-storey, flat-roofed hotel complete with a satellite dish (another administration problem[110]), rather than a three-storey private residential building.[111] In allowing those "mistakes" to occur at the stage of design, the ward's generalist and expert officials pursue the law after the building is completed and ask for exorbitant fines and bribes, such as the case of Sơn cited in Chapter 1 showed. As a consequence, upper levels of state machinery have lost control of building height regulation. The same situation applies to the small tour operators in the same Thirty-Six Streets area, according to a source. On the one hand, the city authority wants to close down the small, unlicensed operators to protect tourists; on the other hand, the wards want the tour operators to continue because they create employment for a group of other goods and services providers who work in conjunction with these illegal operators.[112] To this end, ward opposition is legitimate and so the city authority would have to think of another way of solving the problem, and seek a compromise between different goals of administration. In the meantime, however, unlicensed operators continue to tarnish the image of tourism in Vietnam, and the ward is perceived as ineffective in this area too.

The principle of dual subordination in Vietnam has also led to a large degree of overlap of authority in state management. Powers and authority to administer and regulate all aspects of daily life of ward residents are not those of the ward alone; for instance, the ward and the district both supervise housing construction. Therefore, a resident in a ward could go over the head of the ward to ask for permission from the district for a certain construction and in so doing, overrule the ward. These higher officers may respond positively depending on the depth of the patron–client relationship, and whether an exception can be made on the basis of legitimate legal or political reasons arising out of local or special circumstances. Such "guerrilla tactics" by people are possible in many aspects of daily life. Vietnamese academics confirmed this problem in the late 1990s by noting that the principle of dual subordination caused persistent problems of contesting authority and power, especially in creating multiple power channels.[113] As the lower levels, such as the ward (either its people's council or people's committee), try to preserve their legal authority, they often come into conflict with specialized agencies (rather than the people's council or people's committee of the upper levels which had the power to command similar agencies at lower levels) at the upper levels. Even conflicts between the people's council of one level and the people's committee at the next higher level were very common, such as matters pertaining to appointments to the people's committee of the lower level.[114] The contradictions between considerations for local conditions (being "democratic"), and the principle of dual subordination (being "centralized") within the philosophy of the local administration system needs to be resolved if the state wants to increase its effectiveness, as well as balance the right of local administrators to put forward unique and practical solutions for the locality with checks on the abuse of power. It is also possible that these contradictions induce cynicism and alienation among officials and make them more willing to mediate.

The Moral/Cultural Dynamics of Ward Administration

The ward party-state machinery's responsibilities and power are given by the party-state, and ward officials follow a received code of conduct for local administration. Ward officials, however, are also under the influence

of various cultural factors through daily interaction with residents. I call
these cultural influences the moral/cultural dynamics of ward administration,
because they possess moral authority based on cultural arguments.
In identifying reasons for shortcomings in law enforcement or policy
implementation at the ward level in Hà Nội, we need to venture beyond
institutional deficiencies to explain selectivity and unevenness in policy
implementation.

The motif of political life within the ward is the idea of "community"
and its attendant emotional expectations that promote sentimentality and
"fellowship" as a counter to rationality in the administration of law and
party-state policies.

The first trait is the value placed on good neighbourliness, known among
Vietnamese as "sentimentality of neighbours" (Tình cảm làng giềng[115]). It
means that one has to take into consideration the interests and feelings of
neighbours before deciding on a particular course of action. A proximate
expression is "sell distant relatives, buy close neighbours" (bán anh em
xa, mua láng giềng gần[116]), a practical notion of community spirit and
self-interest. (This view is similar to one in Chinese which says that "the
water that is faraway cannot put out the fire close by" or "远水救不了近
火"). No doubt these expressions originated from village life but they are
frequently uttered among urbanites as well.

The second trait is represented by the saying "Nine makes ten" (chín bỏ
làm mười).[117] It exhorts people to accept less than ideal situations, or less
than what they deserve by formal agreements, in their daily transactions
with each other. The idea is not to push one's superiority or advantage too
far, or to obtain the full portion of one's rights over other people, strangers
included. I was given an illustration of this point in one hot afternoon in
Hà Nội in 1999 when returning from Hà Nội's airport to Hà Nội City.

I had fallen asleep in the old Russian Volga, taking me from the Nội
Bài airport. While on the highway, the driver stopped once to check on a
funny smell the engine emitted. We managed to reach the city, nevertheless.
I had already complained to myself that I was paying good money for lousy
wheels. When the car was on the narrow La Thành Street, the driver woke
me up with a pleading voice: "Brother, oh brother!" ("Anh ơi! Anh ơi!")
He wanted to stop by a car mechanic he knew on that street (to check on
the engine problem) rather than send me to my prearranged destination,
a further fifteen minutes' drive through busy traffic. He suggested I took
a motorcycle taxi home. To make his message sound reasonable, he
reduced the fares and asked me to do him a "favour". I was not pleased

but I agreed. Being still half-asleep, I pushed opened the heavy car door quickly to get out, forgetting to look out for pedestrians or bicycle traffic coming on beside the car. "Bang!" A cyclist fell sideways as heavy steel knocked human flesh. The next second, the accident victim, lying on the ground, was looking furiously at me. After experiencing a more serious accident in Hà Nội two years before, I was well prepared to respond. I quickly helped him to his feet, saying "sorry" in every sentence and sincerely asked after his condition. I touched his heart; he got up, brushed dirt and sand off his clothes, and began to look for his cracked spectacles on the ground. He said, "it's alright" and prepared to journey on. I patted him on his shoulder, said "sorry" again, and wished him a safer trip. I had avoided an ugly scene of argument over responsibility and compensation for medical care and injury. The victim saw my apology and concern as reasonable "compensation" for his hurt, even though his bicycle was slightly damaged and he might have had suffered internal injuries. He accepted my nine as ten, just as I had accepted the driver's nine as ten.

Two other aphorisms may also demonstrate this cultural trait. One is literally "everybody in the village breaks even" (*hòa cả làng*[118]). This ideal is often pursued to resolve conflicts quickly and amicably. It usually gives everyone something, and so there would be no absolute winner or loser. The second aphorism is "take harmony as precious" (*dĩ hòa vi quý*), which gives priority to harmony over individual rights, legal or otherwise, as the most desirable outcome.[119]

These two traits compete with rights, logic, and legality as the rationale for resolving social conflicts, and in modifying social relationships, including those between neighbourhoods and their state officials. When dealing with any dispute, persons or officials must demonstrate awareness and consideration for the feelings, sentiments, rights, and interests of other people affected, even though they themselves may be in the right. If possible, a person should also take note of reciprocity. There is correct behaviour perceived in terms of "being both right and sentimental" (*có lý có tình*).

Apart from knowing what is legally right, at the ward level officials also take into account feelings of "compassion"[120] to cultivate good neighbourliness. For instance, sometimes officials of the ward withhold their signatures[121] or avoid making decisions that hurt the residents, because they want to give their fellow residents "face". Also, officials are lenient towards offenders until they are compelled to act. Furthermore, officials or cadres may decide to overlook a certain offence because they would rather not bother with the administration associated with it. Imposing fines on the people who are their neighbours, or who may be people they have to deal with everyday in other situations, undermines the relationship between neighbours. Sometimes, as one official told me, it is unreal to think of imposing fines because quite often the offenders reject the summons by claiming they have no money to pay or would simply be defiant. People expected ward officials to "look the other way" (*bỏ qua*) or be compassionate (*thông cảm*). As good neighbours, officials who recognize that defiance is morally permissible in any circumstances would not pursue minor offences in order to nurture the relationship. We can see, for instance, that one reason residents of Thịnh Liệt Commune voted out its incumbent people's committee chairman was because he was less than magnanimous when dealing with minor law and order offenders in the village.[122] He was probably regarded as someone who was right by the law but wrong by sentiments. As a result, basic-level officials cannot follow the letter of the law strictly when enforcing the law or implementing policies, even more if they risk losing votes and their "authority" within the locality.

Below the ward, informality is even more the order of things. In recent years, there have been discussions in the *HNM* newspaper on the role of the resident clusters, and especially the role of the street party cell in the resident cluster's work. The topic of interest has been how to rejuvenate party cells, because the senior age of the majority of ward party cells' members is hampering leadership of the party at the grassroots and co-ordination of state administration at the resident cluster level (which the party cells are supposed to lead). The reason is, as retirees, street party cell members is happy to contribute to party/community work, but because of their preference for relaxation and distaste for social conflict, they do not like to be too crusading within their party cell and resident clusters, because that may mean moralizing and disciplining fellow members and neighbours on daily matters such as rubbish disposal, or use of public space such as the pavement which the resident cluster is supposed to help regulate. The resident cluster officials may come across, for instance, a certain act by a neighbour or party member which deserves a reprimand from authority, a fine, or even an arrest, but all it can do (and perhaps wants to do) is to report, and not order or ask the police to arrest the offenders. One reporter commented that from the point of view of a party member who is an offender, "To be given a disciplinary record on your party file when you retire towards the end of your life is to live on the high wire."[123]

In this way, the side-effect of having predominantly elderly members in the street party cells is to cushion the neighbourhoods from unwanted impact of party and government policies, or in other words, reduce the ability of the state to maximize its reach and effectiveness in punishing minor offences against social order. At the resident groups as well, cadres are usually senior in age and the job of group heads is not popular because of its tediousness. Group heads see their obligation to their neighbours and to the ward as equally important and may not wish to report on every infringement they see in the group.

The above shortcomings, however, were not enough to convince political and government leaders that the ward is redundant. The Resolution of the Fifth Plenum of the Ninth VCP Central Committee in 2002 decided that the ward should be retained for the very important state function of urban public administration.[124] The VCP decided, and the government followed. In 2003, in anticipation of the local council elections in 2004, the National Assembly passed revisions to the Law on Organization of People's Councils and People's Committees, and the ward was retained as the lowest unit of urban public administration, despite voices in the preceding five years that perhaps the ward was unnecessary.

CONCLUSION

The ward, the lowest unit of government administration in Vietnam's cities, has been controversial. Many discussions since the 1970s have debated its value and whether to retain it. But it has survived despite continued questioning in the mid- and late 1990s of the ward's purpose and how ward officials operate. Among the persistent problems in its operations are such things as the often low quality of ward officials, corruption, and inadequate resources in ward offices to carry out assigned tasks. Another difficulty is tensions due to the ward's position as, on the one hand, that unit of government is the most immediate contact with the people but, on the other, also an agency of the state. Consequently the ward is often the intersection between what the central state prescribes and what local conditions and personal relations prefer. Frequently the two are at odds, even incompatible.

This condition helps to explain an apparent paradox in Vietnam politics, at least in the city of Hà Nội. In the wards of Hà Nội, members of the Communist Party and officials designated by central state departments and ministries hold the most important positions in both the executive (people's committee) and legislative (people's council) bodies. This predominance would suggest that the central offices of the party and state can get ward officials and residents to do what party and state policies require. But in fact this is often not the case. Many rules, regulations, and programmes of the central levels of the party and state are significantly modified, even ignored in ward offices and neighbourhoods. There are many reasons, among them inadequate personnel policies and practices, incompetence, corruption, and socioeconomic constraints. Another is the ward's location at the intersection between central directives and local conditions. According to Vietnamese laws, ward officials are supposed to be attentive to local circumstances and accordingly make some adjustments in how they carry out their administrative and governing tasks. Also, in light of cultural and social conditions where they live and work, ward officials take into account cultural mores involving give and take, being in understanding of individuals' hardships and difficult circumstances. These two factors frequently contribute to ward officials not doing or unable to do what central policies and laws require.

The next three chapters look at particular policy areas to see the other things that the ward level of administration does. In one, regarding elections, the party and the state have been able to stand firm and achieve their objectives using the leverage they have in the wards. In two other areas, regarding traffic and housing, the party and the state are less in control over what happens in the ward and its neighbourhoods.

Notes

1. The politics and economy of Vietnam underwent Đổi Mới reforms in 1986 that saw the state gave up many such functions to the market mechanism.
2. Nguyễn Hữu Đức, "Về cơ cấu bộ máy chính quyền địa phương hiện nay" [On the present structure of local authorities], in *Cải cách hành chính địa phương — Lý luận và thực tiễn* [Local administration reform: theory and practice], edited by Tô Tử Hạ, Nguyễn Hữu Trị and Nguyễn Hữu Đức, (Hà Nội: NXB Chính trị Quốc gia, 1998) pp. 96–97; Hữu Đức, "Về nâng cao hiệu lực của chính quyền phường" [On raising the effectiveness of the political authority of the ward], *Tạp chí Cộng sản* (hereafter *TCCS*) 12 (1985): 70.
3. Interview with a ward VCP official on 2 July 1997 in Hà Nội.
4. This means that the chief of police and leaders of the mass organizations concerned would have to be party members.
5. Interview with a ward VCP official on 2 July 1997 in Hà Nội.

6. Ibid.

7. Interview with a party cell secretary on 10 April 1999 in Cầu Giấy District, Hà Nội.

8. VCP branches from the district and prefecture level and above, however, have business enterprises under their names and control.

9. The Vietnamese term *chính phủ* (government) refers specifically to the central government and not to the entire government or state apparatus across the country.

10. SRV, *Luật tổ chức Hội đồng nhân dân và Ủy ban nhân dân* [Law on Organization of People's Councils and People's Committees], 21 June 1994, Article 41.

11. The law was revised in 2004 but no major changes were made.

12. SRV, *Luật tổ chức Hội đồng nhân dân và Ủy ban nhân dân* [Law on Organization of People's Councils and People's Committees], Article 47.

13. Trường Hành chính Quốc gia, *Về cải cách bộ máy Nhà nước* [On reforming the state machinery] (Hà Nội: NXB Sự Thật, 1991), p. 70.

14. From 1989, the state installed at levels of local authority above the ward a standing committee of the people's council. The people's committee in taking decisions that are within the powers of the council to decide must consult with this standing committee. At the ward level, there is no council standing committee, but the chairman of the people's council is consulted on behalf of the whole council. The purpose of the 1989 ruling was to strengthen control over committee officials by the party secretary, usually the chairman of the council.

15. SRV, *Quy chế hoạt động của Hội đồng nhân dân các cấp* [Regulations on activities of all levels of people's councils] (Hà Nội: NXB Chính trị Quốc gia, 1996), Article 29. *Quy chế* means "regulations", a government document that elaborates on legislation and provides for specific powers mentioned generally or implied in the legislation. In this case, the 1996 Regulations elaborate on the 1994 Law on Organization of People's Councils and People's Committees.

16. Ibid.

17. Interview with a ward VCP official on 2 July 1997 in Hai Bà Trưng District, Hà Nội.

18. Ibid.

19. The average age of communist party members in 1999 was sixty-four. See Voice of Vietnam, "Former party official Pham Van Dong discusses party problems", via Reuters, 16 May 1999. This lack of young members willing to take part in activities of party chapters at the grassroots level has been in sight since the late 1970s at least. See Thái Duy, "Gắn bó hơn nữa Hà Nội", *Đại Đoàn Kết*, 10 December 1977, pp. 10, 11.

20. Văn Chiểu, "Nên tổ chức chi bộ theo tổ dân phố" [Should organize party cells parallel to resident groups], Hà Nội Mới (hereafter *HNM*), 7 May 1997, p. 2.

21. Nguyễn Đức Thà, "Phường Lê Đại Hành: quần chúng tham gia quản lý xã hội" [Le Dai Hanh ward: the masses participate in management of society], *HNM*, 20 February 1985, p. 2.

22. Nguyen Van Canh and Earle Cooper, *Vietnam under Communism, 1975–1982* (Stanford: Hoover Institution Press and Stanford University, 1985), pp. 89–92

23. Presentation by Nguyễn Văn Vách, chairman of the people's committee of Phú Thượng Ward of Hà Nội on 27 May 1997.

24. *HNM*, "Từng bước hoàn thiện cơ chế tổ chức ở cấp phường như thế nào?" [How to perfect the organization and system at the ward level step-by-step?], 29 August 1984, p. 2.

25. Where party matters are concerned, however, party cells are important to party members as party cell officials provide references and reports on members living within the locality or active within the cell, for purposes such as evaluation, admissions, and disciplinary matters at workplaces.

26. Presentation by Nguyễn Văn Vách, 27 May 1997; Fieldnotes 10 July 1997; Nguyễn Bắc, "Mấy vấn đề ở một phường" (A few problems at one ward) *HNM*, 4 June 1987, pp. 2, 4.

27. Nguyễn Trọng Trạc, "Từ suy nghĩ về cơ cấu của Hội đồng nhân dân phường Hàng Bài trong nhiệm kỳ tới", *Đại Đoàn Kết*, 1 March 1987, p. 2.

28. John Sullivan, *Local Government and Community in Java: An Urban Case-study* (New York: Oxford University Press, 1992).

29. Interview with Jun Honna and Kikue Hamayotsu on 16 December 1998, in O'Connor, Canberra.

30. S. Vasoo, *Neighbourhood Leaders' Participation in Community Development* (Singapore: Times Academic Press, 1994), especially Ch. 3.

31. SRV, "Hướng dẫn số 469-TCCP, ngày 2/12/1981 của Ban tổ chức của Chính phủ Về việc thi hành Quyết định số 94-HDBT ban hành ngày 26/9/1981 của Hội đồng Bộ trưởng quy định chức năng, nhiệm vụ và tổ chức bộ máy chính quyền địa phương" [Guideline number 469-TCCP dated 2 Dember 1981 of the Government Commission on Personnel regarding implementation of Decision 94-HDBT promulgated on 26 September1981 by the Council of Ministers on roles, duties, and organization of local political authority at the ward level] II/c.

32. Presentation by Nguyễn Văn Vách, 27 May 1997; see also Đông Phương, "Tổ trưởng dân phố — một trách nhiệm không nhỏ" [The head of the resident group — not an unimportant position], *HNM*, 26 February 1997, p. 2.

33. Referring to an assistant group head in her group, my house-mother said he was unlikely to be re-elected because residents were then recently unhappy

with his family's illegal extension of their home which encroached upon public space. Fieldnotes 17 November 1996.

34. Đông Phương, "Tổ trưởng dân phố" [The head of the resident group].

35. Thái Duy, "Gắn bó hơn nửa Hà Nội", *Đại Đoàn Kết*, 10 Dember 1977, pp. 10, 11.

36. Presentation by Nguyễn Văn Vách, 27 May 1997. In 1997, each group head received 50,000 đồng and the assistant 30,000 đồng per month. Total amount of compensation paid out to all group heads and assistant group heads in a ward I worked with was about 5.7 million đồng per month. In 2005, the compensation was 100,000 đồng and 70,000 đồng respectively but inflation had also gone up in the eight years. Conversation with a former Deputy Resident Group Head, 11 March 2005.

37. Fieldnotes 6 December 1996.

38. I also asked the interviewee how she determined how many bonds to buy. She said she would buy roughly the same amount as her neighbours. If she were the first person asked, she would ask the group head what an appropriate amount would be to fulfil the obligation. Conversation with a school teacher, Fieldnotes 16 April 1999.

39. SRV, *Nghị Định số 46-CP ngày 23-6-1993 của Chính phủ Về chế độ sinh hoạt phí đối với cán bộ Đảng, chính quyền và kinh phí hoạt động của các đoàn thể nhân dân ở xã, phường, thị trấn* [Decision number 46-CP dated 23 June 1993 of the Government on activity allowances for party and political authority cadres, and activity funding for people's organizations at the commune, ward, and townlet level], Article 1.

40. In 1997, the basic starting salary of a state employee was about 300,000 đồng including supplementary payments. The compensation for district and city people's council representatives were 30 and 40 per cent of the starting salary level respectively.

41. *HNM*, "Chủ tịch UBND thành phố ra những quy định cụ thể nhằm bảo đảm thực hiện nhiệm vụ, quyền hạn của HĐND các cấp" [Chairman of city people's committee promulgates specific regulations to ensure people's councils of all levels fulfill their obligations according to their powers], 19 May 1988, pp. 1, 4; SRV, *Quy chế hoạt động của Hội đồng nhân dân các cấp* [Regulations on activities of all levels of people's councils], Article 48.

42. *Lao Động*, "Điều chỉnh mức lương tối thiểu từ 180,000đ/tháng lên 210,000/ tháng" [Minimum salary level up from 180,000/month to 210,000/month] 19 December 2000.

43. That the salary levels of communist party officials are determined by government regulations (probably because a big part of the party budget is funded by state money) reinforces the point that distinguishing between state and party in Vietnam is difficult in practice.

44. SRV, *Nghị Định số 46-CP ngày 23-6-1993* [Decree 46/CP dated 23 June 1993], Articles 2–5.

45. From around 1992 to mid-1997 the U.S. dollar–Vietnamese đồng exchange rate fluctuated little and stayed around 11,000 đồng per dollar. From then on, the đồng readily depreciated against the U.S. dollar, and in mid-2005, it stood close to 16,000 đồng to a dollar, or a depreciation of about 40 per cent over eight years.

46. SRV, *Nghị Định số 46-CP ngày 23-6-1993* [Decree 46/CP dated 23 June 1993], Articles 1–5.

47. One such regular project, for instance, is the monthly disbursement of pension and other government payments to retirees and injured veterans and their family members within the ward. In one ward I was working at, I saw each of the female cadre responsible receiving 50,000 đồng for performing this task, in 1997.

48. One frequent type of exchange is the gifts for wedding invitations, infamously and euphemistically called "Damages Report" (*thư báo hại*). Attendance and a gift of at least 20,000 đồng in cash is usually expected, but many people usually give more. A family may receive two to four invitations during the wedding season. Elaborate wedding feasts and death anniversary commemorations have revived with economic development, and have become a heavy financial burden on low-income households. The trend has come under severe criticisms by the communist party and the mass media. See Ngô Đồng Chiêm, "Cỗ Cưới" [Wedding party], *Lao Động*, 7 January 1997, p. 5; Vũ Quang Du, "Cưới ở Hà Nội qua số liệu thăm dò gần đây [Looking at weddings in Hà Nội through some recent statistics] *Hà Nội Mới Chủ Nhật,* 2 March 1997, p. 3; Nguyễn Văn Truyền, "Nghĩ về mô hình cưới hiện nay" [Thinking about the new model of wedding], *Tuổi Trẻ Thủ Đô,* 24 April 1997, p. 6 (Author was the deputy chairman of the Hà Nội Party Committee on Propaganda and Mobilization [Phó ban Tuyên giáo Thành uỷ Hà Nội]); Lan Thành, "Nghèo vì giỗ, khổ vì đám" [Poverty by death anniversaries, misery by feasts], *Phụ nữ Chủ nhật*, no. 21, 7 June 1998, pp. 5, 9.

49. SRV State Planning Committee and General Statistical Office, *Vietnam Living Standards Survey* 1992–93 (Hà Nội: September 1994), p. 20; Table 6.1.1, p. 179.

50. Tổ PV Ban xây dựng Đảng, "Cấp phường: vai trò Đảng bộ và đội ngũ cán bộ — thực tiễn đang cần lời giải đáp" [The ward: Answers are needed to the question of the role of the ward party branch and cadre], Nhân Dân, 29 April 1997, pp. 1, 3.

51. "Cán bộ xã, phường, thị trấn được hưởng chế độ công chức", VN Express 22 April 03. http://vnexpress.net/Vietnam/Xa-hoi/2003/04/3B9C71A8.

52. *HNM*, "Tổ chức chính quyền mấy cấp trong nội thành?" [How many levels of local authority should we have in the inner city?], 3 October 1979, p. 2.

53. Ibid.

54. *HNM*, "Tổng kết hai năm hoạt động của chính quyền tiểu khu" [Review the activities of the Small District authority in the past 2 years], 17 December 1980, p. 1.

55. SRV, *Quyết định số 94/HĐBT, ngày 26/9/1981 của Hội đồng Bộ trưởng Về chức năng, nhiệm vụ và tổ chức bộ máy chính quyền địa phương* [Decision 94/HDBT dated 26 September 1981 of the Council of Ministers of role, tasks, and organization of ward political authority machinery]. The Constitution of Vietnam sets out the broad and basic principles for the organization of local administration units, while the detailed rules are provided by subsidiary legislation. For the ward, the relevant enabling regulations between 1981 and 1984 were 94 HĐBT 25 September 1983 on the ward, 469-TCCP 2 December 1981, and the laws on the organization of people's councils and people's committees in the communes, wards, and towns. For the last, the earliest version was promulgated in 1945 as Decree 77, 21 December 1945 (although at that time there was still no administrative unit called the "commune"), and then encoded in proper legislation first via the Law on Organization of People's Councils and People's Committees, 27 October 1962. After the 1980 Constitution was promulgated, the Law was revised on 30 June 1983 and on 30 June 1989, on both occasions to meet the needs of local people's council elections held in 1984 and 1989. With promulgation of the 1992 Constitution, the law was again revised in 1994 to serve local elections in that year. The 1999 local council election took place under the 1994 law, even though there were speculations that the 1994 revisions might be amended before the 1999 elections. Similar speculation arosed as the 2004 People's Council election approached, but the result was an anti-climax.

56. Apparently Cửa Nam Ward, like many other places in Vietnam then, also had a few residents who tried to escape overseas. When they were caught and returned, the political authority criticized them in front of their neighbours at these criticism and self-criticism sessions. The facts that they were made to self-criticize, and were criticized, were important enough achievements for the ward, apparently. The journalist did not ask whether these sessions prevented repeat offences, or whether these sessions had any educational impact on other people. Similarly, it was sufficient that the ward was able to produce tiny slogans and pasted them everywhere to remind people of the types of proper behaviour, while the effectiveness of this method in mobilizing the people was not discussed. See Nguyễn Đức Thà, "Phường Cửa Nam từ khi có chính quyền hoàn chỉnh" [After Cửa Nam Ward had a proper political authority], *HNM*, 26 May 1982, p. 2.

57. Phan Tưởng, "Phường Quang Trung làm gì và làm như thế nào để công tác bảo vệ an ninh trở thành phong trào quần chúng" [What and how did the Quang Trung turn work on security into a mass movement?], *HNM*,

2 June 1982, p. 2. For a few other articles with a similar assessment, see S.H., "Phường Hàng Bài càng làm, càng thấy sáng" [Hang Bai does it better every time], *HNM*, 10 September 1982, p. 2; Nguyễn Đức Thà, "Phường Trúc Bạch với công tác thi hành án" [Truc Bach Ward implements court verdicts], *HNM*, 22 October 1982, p. 2; Nguyễn Đức Thà, "Chính quyền phường Đồng Xuân với chức năng quản lý xã hội" [The Đồng Xuân Ward authority in management of society], *HNM*, 3 November 1982, p. 2; Nguyễn Đức Thà, "Hiệu lực của chính quyền phường Ô Chợ Dừa" [Effectiveness of the O Cho Dua ward authority], *HNM*, 26 November 1982, p. 2; Phan Tường, "Phường Phúc Tân bảo vệ tài sản XHCN, giữ gìn kỷ cương xã hội" [Phuc Tân Ward protects socialist property, maintains social discipline], *HNM*, 12 January 1983, p. 2; Nguyễn Đức Thà, "Một năm thắng lợi của phường Cửa Nam" [One year of success for Cửa Nam Ward], *HNM*, 2 February 1983, p. 2; Nguyễn Đức Thà, "Ở một phường mới thành lập" [At a new ward], *HNM*, 4 May 1983, p. 2.

58. Nguyễn Đức Thà, "Quận Ba Đình tiến hành công việc phân cấp cho phường" [Ba Đình District implements decentralization to ward level] *HNM*, 16 June 1982, pp. 2, 4.

59. Nguyễn Đức Thà, "Qua hai năm xây dựng chính quyền phường Cửa Nam" [After two years of operation of political authority in the Cửa Nam Ward], *HNM*, 3 April 1981, p. 2.

60. Ibid. Faking households was a major way to obtain more ration coupons.

61. By authority of Directive 08 on 12 December 1983 of the Standing Committee of the Hà Nội Party Branch. Nguyễn Mạnh Cường, "Mấy nét chủ yếu về hoạt động của các tổ công tác tại các phường" [A few main characteristics of the activities of the special teams at the wards], *HNM*, 22 June 1984, p. 2; Võ Chung, "Người về hưu và công tác ở phường", *Đại Đoàn Kết*, 1 October 1988, p. 7.

62. *HNM*, "Tạo điều kiện cho phường chuyển mạnh vào quản lý kinh tế, có kế hoạch, có ngân sách" [Make conditions possible for the wards to push strongly for planned and budgeted economic management], 26 June 1985, p. 2; Nguyễn Đức Thà, "Vài nét về hoạt động của chính quyền địa phương ở quận Hoàn Kiếm" [A few characteristics of the activities of the wards of Hoàn Kiếm District], *HNM*, 4 April 1984, p. 2.

63. As Trường Chinh said in the Political Report to the Sixth Party National Congress in 1986, "Many people's committees do not really respect the people's councils … Elections were carried out in a forcible manner." Quoted by Carlyle A. Thayer, "Renovation and Vietnamese Society: The Changing Roles of Government and Administration", in *Đổi Mới: Vietnam's Renovation Policy and Performance*, edited by Dean Forbes et al., Political and Social Change Monograph 14 (Canberra: Department of Political and Social Change, RSPAS, ANU, 1991), p. 25.

64. Nguyễn Đức Thả, "Vài nét về hoạt động của chính quyền địa phương ở quận Hoàn Kiếm" [A few characteristics of the activities of the wards of Hoàn Kiếm District].

65. Nghị cited, as typical of the malaise, the two examples of the districts of Thanh Trì and Gia Lâm. In the Thanh Trì rural district, irrigation works were important, but the cadre who was head of the District irrigation subcommittee was also made the head of the District Council Secretariat. In Gia Lâm District, taxation work was important because it was the northern traffic gateway of Hà Nội, with enormous amount of traffic flow and market activity, but the head of the taxation subcommittee was also made the head of the District Council Secretariat. Because this official had many tasks, and because of other reasons such as bureaucratic inertia, many subcommittees were actually not functioning. Lê Thanh Nghị, "Phát huy mạnh hơn nữa hiệu lực của HĐND các cấp ở thủ đô Hà Nội" [Bring into stronger play the effectiveness of people's councils at all levels of Hà Nội the capital], *HNM*, 24 December 1985, pp. 1, 4.

66. Ibid.

67. "HĐND ngại tiếp xúc với cử tri và chỉ biết nghe mà không biết trả lời xem việc đó ai giải quyết, và có giải quyết được hay không, một số phường lập nhiều ban, ngành theo kiểu hình thức, không có tác dụng thiết thực." Nguyễn Đức Thả, "Vài nét về hoạt động của chính quyền địa phương ở quận Hoàn Kiếm" [A few characteristics of the activities of the wards of Hoan Kiếm District].

68. Ibid.

69. Ibid.; Nguyễn Đức Thả, "Phường Ô Chợ Dừa" [Ô Chợ Dừa Ward], *HNM*, 18 June 1986, p. 3. This criticism was repeated at Self-Criticism and Criticism sessions held for the ward after the 1986 Sixth National Party Congress. See Lê Hải, "Sửa chữa khuyết điểm" [Correct the shortcomings], *HNM*, 23 July 1986, p. 2; Nguyễn Mạnh Cường, "Xây dựng cấp phường ở thị xã Sơn Tây" [Building up the ward level in Sơn Tây Town], *HNM*, 7 June 1985, p. 2; Quang Huy, "Phường Cửa Nam chăm lo đời sống nhân dân bằng con đường phát triển kinh tế" [Cửa Nam ward takes care of the people's livelihood via economic development] *HNM*, 2 August 1985, p. 2.

70. Nguyễn Đức Thả, "Phường Ô Chợ Dừa" [At Ô Chợ Dừa Ward].

71. Lê Đức Thọ, *Phấn đấu xây dựng Hà Nội trở thành thủ đô tin yêu của cả nước* [Let us struggle to build Hà Nội into the loved and trusted capital of the country] (Hà Nội: NXB Sự Thật, 1985), pp. 10, 89.

72. P.V., "Phường Quang Trung với hai công tác trọng tâm" [The Quang Trung ward and its two major tasks], *HNM*, 26 February 1985, p. 2; Nguyễn Chí Tỉnh, "Vị trí cấp phường đang được thực tiễn khẳng định" [The position of the ward is being confirmed by reality], *HNM*, 28 June 1985, p. 2; Quang Huy, "Phường Cống Vị: Giải quyết việc làm cho dân" [Cống Vị Ward

finds employment for its people], *HNM*, 28 June 1985, p. 3; Quang Huy, "Phường Cửa Nam chăm lo đời sống nhân dân bằng con đường phát triển kinh tế" [Cửa Nam ward takes care of the people's livelihood via economic development], *HNM*, 2 August 1985, p. 2; Vương Thức, "Tìm việc làm cho dân" [Looking for work for the people], *HNM*, 10 January 1986, p. 2.

73. After the city and the district administrations reviewed the work of the ward in 1984 and 1985, a stronger push was given to economic tasks of the ward level. The wards were asked to initiate economic activities that made use of potential that already existed within its area, meaning home, handicraft, and light consumer, and simple service industries. More importantly, the ward level was thought to be lacking in planning work and in particular should put more attention to planning when constructing its budget. *HNM*, "Tạo điều kiện cho phường chuyển mạnh vào quản lý kinh tế, có kế hoạch, có ngân sách" [Make conditions possible for the wards to push strongly for planned and budgeted economic management], 26 June 1985, p. 2.

74. It is important to note that while the VCP has always talked about separating the party from the government and not allowing the party to substitute for the government, the reality is that the party is intimately linked to the government, and therefore criticism of the party means criticism of the government, and vice versa. This is why in this self-criticism and criticism movement, in the same breath criticism is applied to both government and party institutions.

75. Marea Fatseas, "The Origins and Role of the Self-Criticism and Criticism Campaign in the Lead Up to the Sixth Congress of the Communist Party of Vietnam in 1986", M.A. Thesis, The Australia National University, 1991.

76. *HNM*, "Sơ kết đợt 1 tự phê bình và phê bình" [Preliminary conclusion of Stage One of Self-Criticisms and Criticisms], 25 July 1986, pp. 1, 4.

77. Ibid.

78. Ibid. In the Central Committee's Political Report to the Sixth National Party Congress, party general secretary Trường Chinh only noted in the sections on local governments that party organs usurped the roles and powers of the government machinery not just at the expense of government, but also at the expense of mass organizations — which could not play any role at all — and the roles and powers of the people's committee as well. See Thayer, "Renovation and Vietnamese Society'.

79. Vương Phan, "Phường Tràng Tiền: Những cố gắng và các mặt tồn tại" [Tràng Tiền Ward: efforts made and shortcomings remaining], *HNM*, 24 September 1986, p. 2.

80. Nguyễn Bắc, "Mấy vấn đề ở một phường" [A few problems in a ward] *HNM*, 4 June 1987, pp. 2, 4. For a general lament on the general social order situation in all wards in the mid- to late 1980s, see Vũ Ngọc Anh, "Hiệu lực quản lý của chính quyền" [Management effectiveness of state authority], *HNM*, 19 March 1989, p. 1.

81. *HNM*, "Hội nghị bàn về công tác cấp phường" [Conference discussed work of the ward level], 1 September 1988, pp. 1, 4. See also a report on a District level meeting on the same matter held in the Hoàn Kiếm District, B. V., "Cuộc thảo luận về cấp phường chưa thể kết thúc được" [Discussions on the ward level are still inconclusive], *HNM*, 23 September 1988, p. 2.

82. *HNM*, "Hội nghị bàn về công tác cấp phường" [Conference discussed work of the ward level], 1 September 1988, pp. 1, 4.

83. Trần Hành, "Suy nghĩ về những quy định và việc thực hiện Luật Tổ chức HĐND và UBND đối với cấp phường", *Người Đại Biểu Nhân Dân*, no. 29, 9 October 1993, p. 11.

84. This right to call a vote of no-confidence was restored in 1996. SRV, *Pháp lệnh về nhiệm vụ, quyền hạn cụ thể của HĐND và UBND ở mọi cấp* [Ordinance on tasks, specific powers of people's councils and people's committees at every level] (Hà Nội: NXB Chính trị Quốc gia, 1996), Chapter 4 article 62.

85. *HNM*, "Hội nghị toàn quốc về HĐND kết thúc tốt đẹp" [National Conference on People's Councils successful], 13 April 1990, p. 1. A year later at the third Conference on the People's Council, the government assessed that the changes to the 1989 law had made the people's councils more effective. The criteria for assessment are unknown. See *HNM*, "Hội nghị toàn quốc về HĐND lần thứ III" [Third National Conference on the HĐND], 19 March 1991, p. 1; NĐT, "Hoạt động của HĐND từ khi có cơ quan thường trực" [Activities of the HĐND with a new Standing Committee], *HNM*, 29 March 1991, p. 2.

86. *HNM*, "Hội nghị về công tác xây dựng cấp phường" [Conference on building up the ward], 9 July 1990, p. 1; P. V., "Không bỏ được cấp phường" [The ward cannot be abolished], *HNM*, 30 October 1991, p. 2.

87. P. V., "Không bỏ được cấp phường" [The ward cannot be abolished]; Đinh Phố Giang, "Phường phải là đơn vị hành chính" [The ward has to be an administrative unit], *HNM*, 22 January 1992, pp. 1, 4.

88. P. V., "Không bỏ được cấp phường" [The ward cannot be abolished]. See also Đinh Phố Giang, "Phường phải là đơn vị hành chính" (The ward has to be an administrative unit); Phan Thị Hồng Sinh, "Khi xác định rõ nhiệm vụ của tổ chức Đảng ở đường phố" [When the tasks of the Party on the street level are clear], *Nhân Dân*, 22 February 1997, p. 3.

89. Đinh Phố Giang, "Phường phải là đơn vị hành chính" (The ward has to be an administrative unit).

90. Huỳnh Thanh Luân, "Hội đồng nhân dân các cấp vẫn tồn tại và cần hoạt động tốt", *Người Đại Biểu Nhân Dân*, 1992 (1+2), pp. 11, 12.

91. Vĩnh Yên, "Đầu xuân gặp nữ chủ tịch phường" [Meeting the ward Chairwoman at the start of spring], *HNM*, 8 March 1994, p. 2. See also Kim Dung, "Để nâng cao hiệu quả hoạt động của chính quyền phường, xã" [In

order to raise the effectiveness of the activities of the ward and commune authorities], *HNM*, 20 June 1996, p. 2.

92. See, for example, the volumes Trường Hành Chính Trung Ương, *Những kiến thức cơ bản về quản lý nhà nước: Tập đề cương bài giảng bồi dưỡng cán bộ chính quyền cơ sở* [Basics of State management: Lecture outlines to train basic level political authority cadres] (Hà Nội: NXB Sự Thật, 1989?); Khoa Luật, Trường Đại học Tổng hợp Hà Nội, Luật Nhà Nước Việt Nam [Vietnamese State Law]. (Hà Nội: Khoa Nhà nước và Pháp Luật, 1994); Học Viện Chính trị Quốc gia Hồ Chí Minh, *Nhà nước và Pháp luật Xã hội Chủ nghĩa Tập I, II, III* [State and Socialist Law Volumes I, II, III] (Hà Nội: NXB Chính trị Quốc gia, 1993).

93. Nguyễn Văn Thư, "Về đào tạo, bồi dưỡng cán bộ chính quyền địa phương trong giai đoạn hiện nay" [On training and cultivation of cadres of local authorities at present], in *Cải cách hành chính địa phương: Lý luận và thực tiễn* [Local administration reform: Theory and practice], edited by Tô Tử Hạ, Nguyễn Hữu Trị, and Nguyễn Hữu Đức (Hà Nội: NXB Chính trị Quốc gia, 1998), pp. 140–141.

94. Như Trang, "Chủ tịch UBND không được giữ chức quá 2 nhiệm kỳ", VNExpress, 17 March 2004, http://vnexpress.net/Vietnam/Xa-hoi/2004/03/3B9D0B85/.

95. "Chính phủ phê duyệt quy hoạch đào tạo, bồi dưỡng cán bộ, công chức xã, phường", *Lao Động*, 10 January 2004, http://www.laodong.com.vn/pls/bld/folder$.view_item_detail(90223).

96. This scheme was elaborated in Nghị Định số 114/2003/NĐ-CP. "Ban hành Nghị định về cán bộ, công chức xã, phường, thị trấn", *Thông Tấn Xã Việt Nam*, 14 October 2003.

97. Nguyễn Thái Hùng, "Một số kinh nghiệm tổ chức và hoạt động của Hội đồng nhân dân phường Cửa Đông", *Người Đại Biểu Nhân Dân*, No. 2, March 1989, pp. 27–29.

98. Communication (three e-mails) from Miss Khuất Thị Hải Oanh, 26 November 1998.

99. Fieldnotes 11 March 1998; See also Voice of Vietnam, "Conference on grassroots councils notes poor quality", Reuters, 3 October 1998, for similar views.

100. Interview with Mr X, 11 March 1998.

101. *Lao Động*, "Tổ chức lại bộ máy chính quyền đô thị", 7 April 2001, p. 3.

102. Vũ Huy Từ, "Mấy ý kiến về cải cách thể chế của nền hành chính" [A few opinions on reforming administrative institutions], in *Về nền hành chính nhà nước Việt Nam: Những kinh nghiệm xây dựng và phát triển* [On Vietnam's state administration system: Experiences in building and development], edited by Học Viện Hành chính Quốc gia (Hà Nội: NXB Khoa học và Kỹ thuật, 1996), p. 93.

103. See, for instance, Dương Xuân Ngọc and Nguyễn Chí Dũng, "Ảnh hưởng của kinh tế thị trường đối với hệ thống chính trị ở địa phương" [The impact of market economy on the political system at the level of the ward], *TCCS* 455 (Novêmber 1993): 51–53; Đoàn Trọng Truyền, "Cải cách hành chính địa phương trong cải cách nền hành chính nhà nước" [Reform of local administration in reforms of the state administration system], in *Cải cách hành chính địa phương: Lý luận và thực tiễn* [Local administration reform: Theory and practice], edited by Tô Tử Hạ, Nguyễn Hữu Trị, and Nguyễn Hữu Đức. (Hà Nội: NXB Chính trị Quốc gia, 1998), p. 28.

104. Nguyễn Hữu Trị, "Vấn đề quản lý nhà nước ở đô thị và phương hướng đổi mới mô hình tổ chức chính quyền đô thị" [The problem of state management in urban areas and direction of change in the model for organizing urban political authorities], in *Cải cách hành chính địa phương* [Local administration reform], p. 259.

105. Minh Tuấn and Hương Thủy, "Hà Nội thí điểm cấp giấy chủ quyền nhà và đất" [Hà Nội pilots the policy of granting certificate of usage for land and houses], *Đại Đoàn Kết*, 20 January 1997, pp. 1, 7. The authors estimated that 90 per cent of all construction and renovation of houses in Hà Nội are without licences, thus being illegal, whereas the situation is in the reverse in Hồ Chí Minh City.

106. Trần Thế Nhuận, "Bàn về tập trung, phân quyền, tản quyền trong nền hành chính địa phương" [On centralizing, decentralization, and separation of power in the local administration system], in *Cải cách hành chính địa phương* [Local administration reform], p. 56; Tô Tử Hạ (1998) "Những vấn đề chung: Cải cách hành chính nhà nước trong nền kinh tế chuyển đổi hiện nay" [General issues: Reform of state administration in the context of the present economic transition], in *Cải cách hành chính địa phương* [Local administration reform], p. 13.

107. This is my observation after countless conversations with Hanoians over a one-year period to look for explanations to why certain laws or policies do not apply to certain people within localities. Malarney (1997) also told us that even though there was no proof, Thịnh Liệt Ward committee chairman Đặng Văn Lợi was assumed by people to be on the take when he insisted on completing a road project before Tết (New Year) arrived.

108. Nguyễn Hữu Trị, "Vấn đề quản lý nhà nước ở đô thị và phương hướng đổi mới mô hình tổ chức chính quyền đô thị" [The problem of state management in urban areas and direction of change in the model for organizing urban political authorities], in *Cải cách hành chính địa phương* [Local administration reform], p. 259; Trịnh Duy Luân, "Vietnam", in *The Changing Nature of Local Government in Developing Countries*, edited by Patricia McCarney (Toronto: Centre for Urban and Community Studies, University of Toronto, & International Office, Federation of Canadian Municipalities, 1996), pp. 172, 191.

109. Trần Công Tuynh, "Đổi mới tổ chức chính quyền địa phương đảm bảo thắng lợi công cuộc cải cách hành chính" [Renewing the local authority organization to ensure the success of the public administrative reform] in *Tạp chí Quản lý Nhà nước*, no. 9 (1995), pp. 12. Tuynh, who was the Deputy Head of the Committee of Government Organization and Personnel, was of the view that lower level professional officials usually considered how they could be rewarded before deciding on who to support — their superiors or the local authorities?

110. Mini-hotels lower than two stars in rank have been prohibited since late 1996 from having satellite dishes. Without these dishes, these hotels would face difficulties in retaining foreign customers. In 1998, however, the government reissued the 1996 ban to remind wards and the Ministry of Information and Culture cadres to enforce the rule, since the number of illegal satellite dishes that dotted the skyline of Hà Nội has increased. See Bich Ngoc, "New clampdown on illegal satellite dishes", *Vietnam Investment Review*, 19 October 1998, via Reuters, 19 October 1998. I once asked a close friend who has a satellite dish at home about his experience. He said that when policemen in the ward began to ask questions about his equipment on the rooftop, he built a structure around it to cover up the satellite dish (so that neighbours would not see it) but which still allowed it to work. He worked out a solid deal for the policeman, including the appeal that "Các cháu xin bác, các cháu đang học tiếng Anh cho nên rất cần nghe chương trình nước ngoài một cách thường xuyên." ["We and our children beg you, the children's elder uncle, the favour [of leaving things as they are], the children are learning English and they need to tune in to foreign programmes regularly"]. In 2000, his satellite dish was still operating. I did not know how he did it, but he could have used either or both methods of bribe and/or friendship.

111. Presentation by Trần Hùng from Hà Nội Architecture University on 8 May 1997 at the Institute of Sociology, Hà Nội.

112. Conversation on 4 December 1998 with a Vietnamese participant at the Vietnam Update 1998 conference, Australian National University, Canberra.

113. Nguyễn Đăng Dung, (1997), p. 16, and Nguyễn Hữu Trị, (1998), p. 258.

114. Nguyễn Hữu Trị, "Vấn đề chính quyền địa phương — những xu hướng cải cách" [The question of local political authorities: Directions in reform], p. 37.

115. It is possible that in this well-repeated saying, the tones and order of the last two words have been switched to make the sentence sound better. See Nguyễn Đình Hoà, *Vietnamese-English Dictionary*, (1996) p. 233. The original combination could literally be "tình cảm giếng làng" or "sentimentality around the village well". This means that since villagers drink from the same well, they should be identifying with interests and sentiments of people living around the well.

116. Nguyễn Từ Chi, a Vietnamese ethnologist, translated it as "brothers living at a distance cannot equal close-by neighbours". Nguyễn Từ Chi, "The Traditional Viet Village in Bac Bo: Its Organizational Structure and Problems", in *The Traditional Village in Vietnam*, by Phan Huy Lê et al. (Hà Nội: Thế Giới Publishers, 1993), p. 63.

117. This remark is usually spoken by a third-party mediating in disputes or conflicts. If it is used by one of the two conflicting parties, it may be construed as begging or demeaning. Conversation with Nguyễn Đăng Khoa, 24 May 1999, Canberra.

118. Literally the word "làng" means village, but it is often used colloquially to refer to a group of people with a common purpose, interest, or in the same organization. A small group of gamblers or a small section within an organization can be called a "làng". While the Chinese have a similar concept, *hoà cả làng* is a Vietnamese expression.

119. Douglas Pike, "Informal Politics in Vietnam", in *Informal Politics in East Asia*, edited by Lowell Dittmer, Haruhiro Fukui, and Peter N.S. Lee (Cambridge: Cambridge University Press, 2000), p. 277.

120. This word, translated from the phrase *thông cảm* in Vietnamese, literally means, "to understand difficulties and have sympathies for feelings in the particular situation of other people". *Từ Điển Tiếng Việt* 1994 [Vietnamese Dictionary 1994] (Hà Nội: NXB Khoa học Xã hội và Trung tâm Từ điển học, 1994) p. 919.

121. David G. Marr, "Where is Vietnam coming from?", in *Đổi Mới: Vietnam's Renovation Policy and Performance*, edited by Dean Forbes et al. (Canberra: Department of Political and Social Change, RSPAS, ANU, 1991), p. 18.

122. Shaun K. Malarney, "Culture, Virtue, and Political Transformation in Contemporary Northern Viet Nam", *Journal of Asian Studies* 56, no. 4 (1997): 901–904.

123. Văn Chiểu, "Nên tổ chức chi bộ theo tổ dân phố" [Should organize party cells parallel to resident groups], *HNM*, 7 May 1997, p. 2.

124. "Nghị quyết Hội nghị lần thứ năm Ban Chấp hành Trung ương Đảng (Khoá IX): Về đổi mới và nâng cao chất lượng hệ thống chính trị ở cơ sở xã, phường, thị trấn" [Resolution of the 5th Plenum of the 9th Central Committee: On reforming and improving the grassroots political system of communes, wards, and townlets], *Nhân Dân*, 2 April 2002, pp. 1, 7.

3

Party-State Dominance in Elections and the Ward

INTRODUCTION

Election is one of the many functions that local administrators carry out for the party-state. This chapter investigates the management of elections in Vietnam, in particular the role of the ward state machinery in elections. Elections are an area over which the party-state has strong control. Party-state notions of what elections should be like and how they should proceed are easily achieved, and thus elections in Vietnam are a top-down process. Yet, aspects of elections in Vietnam, while inconsequential for election results, indicate that the ward is more than just an extension of the party-state; it is also an agent in ameliorating tensions in state–society relations that arise out of the regular holding of top-down — and restrained — elections.

In many countries, elections have an aura of formality. Formality is derived from foundational, publicly recognized documents of the political system, such as the country's constitution, electoral laws, and other government regulations. These documents set down how elections are supposed to, or not to, occur. Adhering to the formal procedure — the process — is important for the legitimacy of the electoral outcome. Contestants in an election respect election results not just because they have agreed to the rules, but also because the rules have been acceptably adhered to in electoral conduct. Of course, due to various reasons, informal features of elections also occur. They may include overlooking, bending or breaking the election rules and procedures stated in the formal documents. Reasons for these phenomena vary. Too much informality in procedures can prompt losers to charge electoral fraud and reject the results.

Elections in communist countries such as Vietnam are also formal, but they may not be legitimate elections in the sense that they are not necessarily looked upon with respect and trust with regard to their degree of fairness and justice. The main reason perhaps is that choices in Vietnamese elections are severely restricted by the party-state. On what constitutes a democratic system of elections, the party-state and ordinary people in Vietnam may hold opposite expectations. The former expects people to take elections seriously as a duty of citizenship and as a sign of support for the regime, but it chooses to use power to limit the freedom to stand in elections so that candidates it is agreeable with will emerge as winners. Many people, however, consider freedom to stand in elections as the sacrosanct value of a democratic election. Consequently, many people in Vietnam have responded to the elections with apathy or criticisms. Domestic critics question openly how restrictions could fit the idea of democracy that the party-state uses to legitimize itself, and they even suggested that lack of free choice negates democracy. The party-state, however, denies the validity of these criticisms and emphasizes the merits of its electoral system.

Given that there is little free choice in elections, a way to register protest is not to vote. If too many people do so to produce a low voter turnout, then the standing, and even legitimacy, of the regime takes a beating. Consequently, the party-state attempts to secure a high turnout rate at every election by mobilizing people through the ward state machinery to vote. Yet people may not want to vote because their ballots are rendered meaningless by restrictions or for other reasons, such as needing to or preferring to work or do other things rather than going to the polling stations.

In order to make its elections more respectable, the Vietnamese party-state relies on formality to portray objectivity and fairness of elections. Formality means that electoral decisions, activities, and organizations are based on laws. At the neighbourhood level, the ward administration and election machinery operate according to the law and their officials act according to the formal rules. Nevertheless, ward officials also function informally. Informality underlies many electoral activities that may appear to be formal — from preparations for elections, to voters' meetings to nominate candidates, to the act of voting itself. On occasions, when flexibility in operations is called for, officials may choose to function informally by not adhering to the rules, provided no great harm is done to the objectives of the party-state that have been delegated to them to achieve. Among other consequences, this informality makes it easier for officials to complete their tasks than when only the formal rules are applied. The significance of informality, however, goes beyond the matter of efficiency.

Informal practices at polling stations, usually managed by ward officials, help to conceal contradictions and dissipate electoral tension between state and society over the lack of freedom to contest. Towards the end of this chapter, we shall see how this is so.

First, I will demonstrate the tight grip of the party-state on elections, and then analyse the election machinery. I will then highlight major criticisms that have increased electoral tension and how the party-state has been responding. I will then show how mediation in an election at the ward level may take place, and offer reasons why officials who conduct elections allow mediation.

WHY THE COMMUNIST PARTY-STATE WANTS TO DOMINATE ELECTIONS

The desire of the Vietnamese party-state to control elections is a consequence of Karl Marx's theory of class struggle and desirability of a workers' dictatorship in an industrialized society. The gist of the theory is that workers, as the long-suffering social class exploited mainly by the capitalist class, would triumph after capitalism collapses under its own weight. When that happens, workers have a moral right to form a dictatorial state to not only rule over their capitalist exploiters, but also develop a democratic state for workers. Ultimately, the state as a form of organization of society should also wither away. This theory was adapted in the Soviet Union with significant additions, including the pre-eminent role of the Communist Party in society through elections in which, the Communist Party assumed, the vast majority of voters would naturally vote for the party's candidate.

In reality, of course, the communist party may not win in freely held elections. In order to maintain theoretical integrity and, more importantly, power, the Communist party-state has found it necessary to greatly limit the freedom and openness of elections. This means that the possibility of party-sponsored candidates being defeated is severely circumscribed or even eradicated. This kind of uncompetitive elections in communist countries has become common knowledge, and analysts of such elections have labelled them accurately as "elections without choice".[1]

Vietnam's political philosophy underpinning elections is similar to that found in the former Soviet Union. The SRV party-state views elections held in Western democracies as harmful to the workers' class because they promote the interests of capitalist exploiters and bourgeoisie classes at the expense of workers. An official source says:

This reality is not a strange thing, because elections are contests for representatives' seats or the Presidency to hold state power, to maintain the political line of one's own political party, and to work for the interests of one's clique. In our country, we do not need such an exercise, because standing for election is to voluntarily perform work for the country.[2]

For Vietnam's communist party leaders, therefore, elections should elect representatives of people who will carry out the policies of the party-state, and who would educate the people and lead them to accept state policies, just like in the ex-Soviet Union. Standing for elections is the performing of a national duty delegated by the state.

According to researchers who studied the former ex-Soviet Union, the reasons why the party-state in communist countries wanted to dominate elections went beyond the class struggle explanation. One other reason was that an authoritarian regime "feels the need for popular endorsement, no matter how artificially that endorsement is obtained".[3] Second, Soviet-style elections contributed to socializing of people and integrating them with the regime. By voting, people showed, at least superficially, that they accepted the political system, no matter how authoritarian it is. Otherwise they became targets of repression. Third, the regime used elections to reward loyal followers with seats on people's councils, which brought material benefits. Fourth, the regime used elections to weed out some officials and allow criticism. At nomination meetings, for example, people could vent dissatisfaction with government servants.[4]

Elections in Vietnam have largely the same extended functions and meanings as those in the Soviet Union. VCP officials summarize them under the three principles of legitimacy, socialist legality, and democracy; these mean, respectively, to conduct elections in accordance with the rules, comply with socialist laws and principles, and represent the majority.

VIETNAMESE PARTY-STATE DOMINANCE IN ELECTIONS

Since the end of the war in 1975, elections have been regularly held in Vietnam for the National Assembly and people's councils at lower levels. All citizens eighteen years and older have the right to vote and those twenty-one years or more have the right to stand for election, without regard to religion, race, sex, class, education, occupation, or length of stay in Vietnam. According to the Constitution and election laws, voting is a right rather than a duty. This means voting is legally not compulsory (although in the past skipping the vote could bring unpleasant consequences). Electoral law determines the number of seats for each electoral unit in every election, based on the principle of population size. In 2004, a ward with less than 8,000 people elected twenty-five councillors, and every additional 4,000 people gave the ward an additional councillor, up to a maximum of thirty-five councillors.[5] The government pays for all expenses of elections and actively discourages candidates from using any other resources. In 1997 the total expenses for the national assembly election was US$17,000 or US$25 per candidate.[6] The expenses would include, among other things, payments to election workers — even if the government actually already employs them.

The Vietnamese party-state dominates elections through outlawing and suppressing opposition groups, and through the election machinery it firmly controls, which in turns controls the electoral process. I will examine only the second of these two here.

The shape of the election machinery and how the machinery works in elections for people's councils and National Assembly have changed little since the 1960s.[7] The party-state exercises control of the election machinery at two points. The first point is the party-state's grip on appointment of officials to the Election Council, Election Committee, and Election Section, which are the agencies that run all elections (Table 3.1).[8] For instance, an Election Council for the whole country organizes the National Assembly elections; an Election Council of the city of Hà Nội handles the People's Council election for that city level. Similarly, each district or ward would have one Election Council organizing its own council elections. While the Election Council oversees an election, the Election Committees oversee each electoral unit (or constituency) and Election Sections run the several polling stations in each electoral unit. Members of these three organs are drawn entirely from officials of the party and state machinery (including mass organizations) at every level where elections take place. The quorum for meetings of these election bodies is two-thirds of its members, and all decisions are made on the basis of majority vote. Ward authorities are inevitably involved in every election, local or national, because their officials and semi-officials are the people who oversee the operation of the polling stations of every election.

The Election Council (Hội đồng bầu cử) acts as the supervisory and watchman organ; resolves complaints against subordinate electoral organs; distributes voter cards; receives and reviews reports on the election results submitted by the lower levels; hands over all reports, results, and materials

TABLE 3.1
Election Machinery Members

Election machinery	Appointed by	Composition and eligibility
Election Council	People's committee in the same electoral unit after consultations with standing committee of people's council and the VFF in the same electoral unit	9–21 representatives selected from the VFF, standing committee of the people's council, the people's committee, state organs, and mass organizations in the same electoral unit
Election Committee	ditto	7–13 representatives from state organs, mass organizations and voters in the same electoral unit. At the commune- and ward-level voter representatives are also included
Election Section	ditto	5–9 representatives from mass organizations and voter representatives in the same electoral unit

relating to the election to the people's committee of the same level; and confirms the election results. Its most important political function is to consider whether to accept nominations, and to decide on disputes and complaints against candidates. According to law, its members must be appointed from among representatives of the VFF, the standing committee of the people's council, the people's committee, local-level state organs, and other mass organizations of the electoral unit. Before 1989, an upper level people's committee approved appointments to Election Councils of lower level elections. For instance, the district people's committee approved appointments to the ward's Election Council. From 1994, the people's committee, together with the VFF and the standing committee of the people's council at the same level, appointed the Election Council for elections of the same level. This meant that leaders of the VFF, the people's committee, and the people's council decide who controls the Election Council of their level of elections, and they may indeed appoint themselves. Compared with the pre-1994 situation, the power to appoint the Election Council is now shared more evenly among the party-state elites of each level. But such power has not spread to ordinary citizens in a meaningful way.

For National Assembly elections, party leaders who are leading state officials head and staff the Election Council. The chairperson is usually a senior member of the VCP Political Bureau and head of the highest organ of state. For instance, Trường Chinh (head of the Standing Committee of the National Assembly before 1980, and head of the State Council after 1980) headed the Election Council at many National Assembly elections in the past. In 2002, the chairperson of the National Assembly Election Council was Nguyễn Văn An, Political Bureau member and chairman of the National Assembly. The rest of this Election Council was filled with prominent, Central Committee level, members of the party.

Immediately subordinate to the Election Council is the Election Committee (Ban Bầu cử). This body also has members appointed from within mass organizations and among representatives of voters (usually resident group and resident cluster office holders); at the ward level, those representatives usually are group heads and their assistants. The people's committee, standing committee of the people's council, and the VFF of the same level, make appointments to the Election Committee. The Election Committee oversees the day-to-day election preparations, oversees the finalizing of the voters' register, distributes voter cards and other materials sent to it by the Election Council, supervises the lower Election Sections, supervises the setting up of polling stations, resolves complaints against the Election Sections, reviews the reports of results of vote counts given by the Election Sections, and submits them to the Election Council. The Election Committee resembles most the *agitpunkt* of former Soviet Union elections in the past.[9]

Election Sections are the lowest level of the election machinery. Membership consists of representatives of mass organizations and voters representatives, and they are appointed by the people's committee, chairman of the people's council, and the VFF of the electoral unit. Each Section distributes voter cards to voters, prepares one polling station for voting, manages the station on polling day, ensures security at polling stations, counts votes, resolves complaints regarding vote counting, and submits all reports on electoral matters to the Election Committee. During a ward level election, every 300 to 4,000 voters are allotted a separate ballot box in a separate polling station. The decision on the number of stations is left to the people's committee, which also tries to make it convenient to turn out to vote by having as many polling stations as possible under the rules.

The second point of party-state control over elections is determining who can be candidates. The party-state does this in two ways. First, it sets down the desired characteristics and minimum credentials of candidates, thus greatly restricting who may stand for election. Second, it screens nominees before allowing them to stand as candidates.

Candidate Characteristics and Credentials

At every election, Vietnam's state and party leaders spell out what they think should be the qualities of candidates for the National Assembly and people's councils. Before 1992, these requisites largely resembled those found in the ex-Soviet Union, especially in the priority given to "workers" and "producers" who have contributed significantly to production.[10] The image of the ideal people's representative was a revolutionary and a working-class person. By the mid-1990s, the emphasis in Vietnam shifted from revolutionary, working class to nationalistic qualities, professional qualifications (measured by education standards), and capabilities to be a representative. Qualities of election candidates are highlighted in the following pages.

Qualities of Election Candidates

According to the 1977 electoral law on people's councils, councillors were loyal to the Fatherland and socialism, exemplary workers, able to mobilize the masses for implementation of principles contained in party policies and state laws, had a positive attitude in serving the people, was close to and trusted by, and knew what the people wished, and were with the people in solving all problems and difficulties in production and everyday life.[11] The 1983 electoral law on people's councils changed little of that. A councillor was supposed to be loyal to the Fatherland and socialism. He or she had to have achievements in production, in work, or in armed struggle (*chien dau*) (perhaps reflecting the renewed importance of the military following the 1979 Sino-Vietnamese war as well as the large number of armed forces veterans after the end of the Second Indochina War in 1975). He or she had to enthusiastically serve the people, and carry out the *law and policies of the state* (compared with "party policies and state laws" of the past; thus the special reference to the party disappeared). He or she had to set an example in his or her behaviour, have had a good education, had the ability to discharge his or her duties as a deputy, and had to be trusted by the people.[12] Under the 1989 electoral law for people's councils, production and war achievements were deleted as essential qualities. Councillors were "loyal to the Fatherland and Socialism, enthusiastic in serving the people, straight-forward in fighting for the legal rights and interests of citizens, positively carried out the laws and the policies of the state, well educated and able to fulfil the duties of a councillor, and were trusted by the people".[13] A sentence added to the final legislation of the 1989 law (which was not in the draft) said that the deputy "must know about management of the state, of economics, society". In addition, candidates for elections should be "mature, and must be exemplary in obeying the law; must have ability to fulfil their duties as councillors; and must resolutely fight and protect the interest of the state and the legal rights and interests of citizens".[14] The 1994 Law on Election of People's Councils continued to emphasize loyalty, ability, education, as well as personal example. But these were phrased in terms appropriate for economic renovation, such as a councillor must "be loyal to the Socialist Fatherland, [instead of *Fatherland and Socialism* in the past[15]], were exemplary citizens, struggled to implement the renovation in order to make the people rich and the country strong, morally virtuous, must set a law abiding example, have a good education, have the ability to discharge duties as a people's council representative and local decision-maker, and were trusted by the people". The 2003 Law moved further to place the emphasis on "Vietnam" and to the need for councillors to play their part in solving socioeconomic problems of the locality. In the 2004 People's Council elections, the VFF introduced a set of more detailed criteria to sieve nominees and the following types were considered unsuitable to run for elections:

1. Nominees who have not obtained at least 50 per cent of votes at both Step 2 and 4 of the consultations process (the consultation process is elaborated below);

2. Nominees who have offended laws, especially laws on land use in order to benefit oneself;
3. Nominees implicated in serious crimes under investigation or trial, even if they had not been formally punished or disciplined;
4. Dishonest nominees who did not declare the whole truth in their CVs or who had obtained false certificates of degrees of educational qualifications;
5. Leaders of state agencies and organizations who have allowed many cases of negative behaviour to happen among their subordinates, bringing their agencies into disrepute.[16]

(However, the same directive also says that under (5), the party branch that manages the leaders (who should be party members) must be consulted and have made a decision before the VFF can act on eliminating the nominee.)

Where National Assembly elections were concerned, according to party-state guidelines for the 1987 elections, National Assembly deputies must "have a spirit of renovation, ... must fight every wrong, negative action ..." They were also still supposed to be loyal to the Fatherland and Socialism.[17] The 1997 Law on Election of the National Assembly set out five qualities that deputies must have:

1. Loyal to the Fatherland and the *Constitution*, strives to implement industrialization and modernization to create a rich people, a strong country, and a just and civilized society.
2. Is virtuous, frugal and honest, upholds public interest without private favours, sets an example in obeying the law, resolutely fights bureaucratism, bullying, abuse of power, corruption, and other behaviour against the law.
3. Has the ability to discharge duties of a National Assembly deputy by participating in decision-making on the major issues of the country.
4. Communicates with the people closely, listens to the opinion of the people and is trusted by the people.
5. Is able to participate in all activities of the National Assembly.[18] [My italics]

In 2002, candidates who wished to run in the National Assembly elections "must demonstrate absolute allegiance to the country and its Constitution, and devote their talent and energy to nation-building. Other qualifications include clear political history, ethical conduct, exemplary observance of law and full competence to assigned duties."[19]

One additional criterion is sector representation. Candidates have to fit one of the social sectors and a quota of councillors in the people's council (or deputies in the National Assembly) is set for each sector. People's council (or the National Assembly) in consultation with the VFF decide on the quota. Sectors include those of workers, peasants, bureaucrats, soldiers, army veterans, intellectuals, business people, women, the aged, local representation, and various ethnic minorities. Being members of the councils, they help the state to mobilize people as well as represent the interests of that sector. Having a quota for each sector also helps to avoid alienating groups who otherwise may feel left out. This is what the party-state means by "democracy" in elections, although this preference may be more appropriately called "national unity". The party-state prevents nominees from standing for elections if they do not fit the sector quota, even if they meet all other criteria. The sector quota is party-determined and is enforced by the relevant party branch at every level of local authority election, although the VFF acts as the front for the VCP in "deciding" on this quota for each sector.

There is, however, a way to circumvent the quota if the selectors are keen on a nominee. While each person in society is grouped under one class or sector, rarely does anyone belong to one class alone, because the classification is based not just on the occupation of one's father or on one's origin, but also on one's occupation. For instance, a person who has had tertiary education is considered an intellectual, but if he works as a factory worker, he can be considered a worker. A young woman intellectual can be classified under three valid sectors — being a young person, being a woman, and being an intellectual. Selectors can arbitrate between various sectors and slot a candidate into one sector whose quota has not been used up. Therefore, the quota can be a hard and fast rule (when nominees are not welcomed by the selectors) or a permeable barrier (when selectors are keen on the nominees).

Candidates' qualities stressed in the laws may or may not correspond to what voters look for in their representatives, although evidence on this matter is scarce. Shaun Malarney observed that in rural local elections, moral integrity and leadership abilities were important qualities voters looked for in candidates.[20] The idea of good leadership, Malarney found, rested upon efficiency, honesty, and sensitivity towards the interests and feelings of the majority of villagers and village values. All but one criterion in Malarney's list — the sanctity of village values — are similar to those in official standards.[21]

The Five-Step Consultation Process to Screen Nominees

All candidates must stand either as independents (allowed since 1989 and increasingly common for lower level elections) or as representatives of an organization — a workplace, mass organization, or residential unit (such as a resident group or a ward). To select candidates, the VFF at the level where the election is taking place conducts a five-step process of consultation with relevant bodies, such as organizations of employment, mass organizations, the wards and its resident clusters and resident groups, and the party.[22] Note that people entitled to participate in these consultations are leaders of the VFF, representatives of member organizations of the VFF, in the Election Council, and in the standing committee of the people's council and the people's committee of the same level.

Step 1: The standing committee of the VFF in an electoral unit calls the First Consultation Meeting of its members at that level. This meeting hears reports from the people's council and VFF on the number of seats and the desired sector representation in the electoral unit. The leaders of the people's council and the people's committee attend as "guests", but in fact these leaders control the Election Council that makes the final decision on the number of seats. At the ward level, the ward party secretary is often the chair of the people's council, and the VFF head may be a member of the people's council as well as a member of the ward party standing committee (see Chapter 2).

Step 2: The various mass and work organizations hold their internal, closed staff meetings to nominate people on the basis of the quota of seats at Step 1. (Independent candidates file their papers at this stage.) To continue to Step 3, a nominee must receive a majority vote at the meeting.

Step 3: The VFF and the mass organizations hold a Second Consultation Meeting, and ward party-state machinery officials continue to attend as guests. State and mass organizations present the names of their nominees, and the VFF presents the names of independents. A penultimate nominees' list is drawn up for the next two steps. Up to Step 3, the process is more appropriately called pre-selection because these steps constitute a process to discuss share of seats and for mass organizations to do their nominations, but before the VFF decides on the final list of candidates.

Step 4: Two sessions are held in which every nominee meets voters. One of them is at the nominee's workplace, which is now opened to all colleagues; the other in the ward where the nominee resides. Voters are invited to attend and to express their opinions about the nominees. There, they also vote, by hand or by secret ballot, on who should remain in the final list of nominees. The nominating organization is responsible for any questions regarding its nominee. The ward people's committee handles queries about nominees at meetings held at places of residence. All reports on queries and doubts go to the local arm of the VFF, which compiles a file for each nominee. At this stage as well, the resident group heads in the wards visit the households under their care to publicize the elections and highlight information about the candidates. They then solicit feedback and convey that information to the meet-the-voters session.[23]

The objective of having two nominee-meet-voters sessions is to break down the information barrier between the workplace and the place of residence of the nominee and to obtain information about nominees that would not otherwise be known if there was only one meeting. This information includes, for instance, the nominee's character, sense of neighbourliness, family background, and experience in the revolution.

Step 5: The VFF holds the Third Consultative Meeting with the same participants of the Second Consultative Meeting. The VFF reports on the nominee-meet-voters sessions, comments on dissatisfaction with nominees whom voters have criticized, and filters out unsuitable nominees. This meeting then draws up the preferred list of nominees and presents it to the Election Council. The list is likely to be approved by the Election Council because the Council includes the leaders of the VFF, the people's council and people's committee. Nominees become candidates when the list is announced formally. Table 3.2 summarizes the five steps.

After the five formal steps, however, an occasional monkey-wrench, in the form of public scrutiny or an exposure, may be thrown into the machinery to force a review or a withdrawal of a candidate. This may happen when the unsuitability of a candidate is publicly exposed. An example is the 1981 people's council elections in Hàng Trống Ward. The ward received seventy-three nominations from residents.[24] That list was reduced to fifty-six candidates after Step 5. After this list was presented

TABLE 3.2
Screening Process Summary: Appearance and Substance

	Appearance of objectivity	*Substance of VCP control*
Step 1	VFF, of which the VCP is a member, calls the First Consultative meeting to decide on number of seats and amount of representation from each sector.	The people's council decides on the number of seats and hands the "plan" to the VFF.
Step 2	Organizations hold meetings to decide on their candidates. Independents submit their candidature.	VCP members are in control of organizations and candidates sponsored by organizations have to receive approval of party branches.
Step 3	VFF chairs the Second Consultative Meeting to decide whether to accept or reject nominations.	VFF leaders are also key party officials of the same level.
Step 4	Meet-the-voters sessions. Results of such sessions help to confirm nominations.	VFF invites selected voter representatives, majority are Resident Group Heads who share the same outlook as the regime. Heads of organizations, usually party members, screen out undesirable candidates. "Public opinion" is thus managed.
Step 5	VFF holds the Third Consultative Meeting to confirm nominations after considering feedback from Step 4.	Election Council, comprising members of people's council, people's committee, VFF as the major members decides whether to accept VFF nominations and independents.

to the public, it had to be reviewed because some of the candidates in the list were deemed controversial. Another example is the 1997 National Assembly elections during which one candidate withdrew eighteen days before the election after the public learned he had committed adultery.[25] In the National Assembly elections of 2002, three candidates were withdrawn after the candidates' list (three days before polling day) was finalized because of various issues. One of them had been indicted for criminal trial. A second was found to have abused his office for personal gains, and the third for dishonest behaviour in claiming an honorary award.[26]

In the 2004 people's council elections, for the first time, the polling in some places had to be delayed and not held in tandem with the rest of the polling in the country. These places were three communes of the Bắc Ninh Province. The reason was after Step 4, there were not enough nominees who had received more than 50 per cent of votes at either their workplaces or at their places of residence. The result was insufficient candidates in excess of seats, which failed a requirement of the elections law (minimum of two excess candidates above seats contested).[27]

Such rare mis-steps notwithstanding, the five stages of the candidate selection process are well controlled by the Communist Party through local authorities and mass organizations. The VFF plays the leading role in candidate selection, but the communist party directs the VFF. Election Councils have the final say in deciding whether to force candidates to withdraw in consideration of complaints or denunciations against them.

Steps 2 and 4 of the selection process promote formal voter participation. But the extent of direct participation decreases with higher level elections. For national, city, and district level elections, organization or ward leaders invite one representative from each resident or work group to attend these meetings. Invitees are likely to be resident group heads because they are likely to be senior in age and generally value political stability and peace. Furthermore, the nominee-meet-voters sessions function like criticism sessions, as an experienced informant told me.

> At those sessions, people listen to the biographies, voice their opinions regarding the accuracy of the biographies, and share their personal knowledge about the candidates. They may criticize the candidate for not having done enough for a particular area, such as to eradicate social evils in the locality under his jurisdiction.[28]

At these Steps 2 and 4, if objections towards certain nominees are strong, voters can exert direct pressure and throw serious doubts on a nominee's credentials at the sessions, or raise questions through voters' representatives. If a controversial candidate still manages to stand when voting is conducted, then the only way for people to register displeasure is to cast protest votes.[29] The party-state promotes mass participation in this way in order to receive signals of preferences and acceptability of nominees, rather than receiving these signals at the voting stage and losing face as a result of endorsed candidates' failure to be elected. In order to minimize this, in the 2004 People's Council elections, the party-state decided that nominees who received less than 50 per cent of votes in either Step 2 or Step 4 should not be confirmed as candidates. They must also not have offended the law or acted against government policies.[30]

According to one informant, during National Assembly elections, the districts are the electoral units; wards and the people in general have little or no power to force changes in the list of candidates.

> Once the district has decided on the names, it is impossible for the ward to change the name list at all. The only thing that can be done is to reflect the dissatisfaction through the votes given to the candidates. Those who get the lowest votes would have been deemed unfit for office by the voters. Asked how people assessed and chose candidates, the informant said that people would mainly read each of their biographies. When the district has decided on the nominees, each and every ward would organize meetings for the nominees to meet the people, and in these sessions people would be free to voice their opinions on each and every nominee (if they know the nominee personally or have heard their names) and voice support or rejection. Whatever the outcome, there would be no change to the name list.[31]

On the other hand, anybody on the ultimate list of candidates, after the fifth step in the consultation process, can be removed at the eleventh hour if for some reasons having their names on the list is no longer tolerable for the reputation of the party-state. This was the case in 2002 when three candidates mentioned above were removed from the list.

Nominee-Meet-Voters Sessions

The participatory quality of nominee-meet-voters sessions is uneven and varies with the level of elections. Here are two examples, one for a National Assembly election and the other for a ward election. Election meetings in the ward to consider nominees for National Assembly elections appear to be rather formal, serious, and controlled. Take for example the meeting of voters which took place in the Hàng Bạc Ward on 13 April 1987. People arrived early, attendance was good. Someone suggested that the names of the nominees need not be read out again; people had already heard them many times via the public address system of the ward. Most people agreed, but others urged re-reading to satisfy the formal procedure, and to benefit the discussion.

> After that, the voters expressed their opinion, analysed the names of the six nominees proposed for the National Assembly election. Among them, two were from the TTCN [probably meant *thông tin công nghệ* or information and technology] sector, so voters decided to choose one only. Between the two from the health sector the voters would also only choose one. When a few opinions suggested voting for this or that candidate, immediately the other voters disagreed. The meeting agreed that it only needed to agree on the number of nominees to choose from each sector, and the choice of particular candidates [at the voting stage] would be left to the choice of individual voters.[32]

In the 1992 and 1997 National Assembly elections, evidence emerged that some districts "instructed" voters whom to vote for.[33] The instruction probably came from the communist party or state officials, but it is difficult to tell if there was a central source and whether such instructions were systematically issued to leading officials of the election or administration machinery. Perhaps local officials initiated a push for regime-favoured candidates in their localities.

The selection processes for candidates running for people's councils at the ward level is less formal than elections for higher level offices, with less dictation from the top and more voter participation. At nominee-meet-voters sessions, usually each household can send one representative; the sessions are held at the resident group level. Greater press freedom on such matters in the late 1980s makes possible glimpses of the selection process of ward-level elections, which still takes place behind closed doors. An example is a reporter's story on the front page of *HNM* about such a session at the Khâm Thiên Ward in 1987.

> I [the reporter] arrived at the ward at seven o'clock in the evening as stated in the invitation. ... Even as the tea in the teapot had become diluted over time, in the room, seated all over, there were only a few old men and women; they lived near the house of the group head and so they came over early to accompany each other. I was rather disappointed already. The meeting started just before eight o'clock with about twenty persons, and the representatives of six, seven households were missing. Only a few attendees looked as if they were of a working age. The rest were retirees and old people.

The Group Head told the gathering the purpose of the session, and after that the chairman of the ward read out loudly for everyone to hear the standards required of people to be nominated for election to the people's council. The first resident to speak was an old lady of about 70 years old with a head of silver hair. She looked as if she had thought about the matter before hand, talking for quite a long time on the merits and demerits of the three persons who have been introduced as potential nominees. Finally she cleared her throat and said: "I think all three persons deserve to be people's council representatives. As for me, I still cannot decide whom to choose. I would like to hear the opinion of everyone else."

The three nominees were Ms Tiệm, the chairwoman of the ward Women's Association; Mr Sử, a retiree and a group head; and Mr H, younger than the other two nominees and still working, who was very enthusiastic about community work in the ward. As the meeting got on, a few more voters arrived.

Two persons expressed their wish to nominate Tiệm. When it was sensed that there was an air of unanimity, Tiệm stood up to say that the Women's Association had at a meeting that morning decided to nominate her, and therefore the resident group should really give the place to someone else so that it could exercise its right of nomination. The Chairman of the ward agreed and confirmed what Tiệm had just said. Immediately after that, Mr H asked that he be allowed to withdraw [for various reasons] … After hearing H out, everyday sympathized with him and nobody knew what to say, until one voice spoke out:

"That's it! In that case, we just have to nominate Mr Sử!"

"That's right!" — A few young persons seated far away also said.

It was thus Mr Sử's turn to speak. He also tried to turn down the nomination, but his reasons were not as good as the reasons of the other two. The meeting then became a dialogue between Sử and the people. Occasionally there was laughter, and in the end Sử happily accepted the nomination.

The hands were up in unison to vote for Sử. After that, someone ignited a roll of firecracker to signify that the meeting had concluded successfully.[34]

The nominee here won support by default because two other strong candidates turned down the chance, and because the resident group's right to have a nominee ought to be secured. The criterion used for selection was not so much capability as availability. The mood of the meeting was informal, neighbourly and friendly, and politically unconcerned. The meeting did not debate policy positions of the nominees.

That was in 1987, when the country was beginning to reform. In 1997, an informant who has attended many nominee-meet-voters sessions (not opened to non-voters of the electoral unit, unless invited) told me in a jovial tone that in recent years voters have begun playing a more important role in ward people's council elections. "They really have a go at the people's council elections," ("*Đối với bầu cử Hội đồng nhân dân thì họ làm ghê lắm*") she said. What she meant was people could criticize nominees more openly nowadays than before.[35] What the informant said was evidenced by the 2004 People's Council elections. In that election, voters rejected eleven senior party members of provincial party branches (including the party secretary of Quảng Bình Province) and thirty-two leading officials from state enterprises and organizations who were sponsored by party branches. At the district and commune (including wards) levels, the numbers were 102 and 105, and 2,003 and 943 respectively. These are small percentages no doubt in comparison with the total number of candidates, but this shows a new assertiveness of the electorate and a major weakness in the consultation process that is controlled tightly by local Party chapters and local state leaders.[36] Years ago, this censure by the electorate would have been unthinkable. It was enlightening, however, that the authorities portrayed this setback to be not something unusual and could be expected.[37]

Furthermore, from the 2002 National Assembly elections onwards, candidates were required to "campaign" for votes by speaking directly to voters about their programme of action if they were voted into office. From the 2004 People's Council elections onwards, candidates had to declare their personal assets before the election and to have their declarations compared against another audit when they leave their official posts. These declarations were available to the public for inspection.[38]

VOTERS' MAJOR CRITICISMS

If the electoral process in Vietnam seems to be moving towards more contest and transparency in some aspects, as the above analysis shows, the party-state still controls the important levers to swing electoral outcomes their way. Nevertheless, these improvements are the result of a long process of responding to criticisms of the old ways and finding ways to make the elections much more meaningful to voters without eroding, fatally, party ability to dictate. The following paragraphs trace the criticisms that have been levelled at the electoral process and party-state responses to these criticisms.

Since the Sixth VCP Party Congress in December 1986, the political atmosphere has allowed some election reforms to occur. One impetus for electoral reforms was probably the threat to the "eudemonic legitimacy" (economic performance) of the communist party, to use a term coined by Stephen White. When eudemonic legitimacy is threatened, White said, communist regimes diversify their legitimacy base through several mechanisms, one of which is electoral reform ("electoral linkage"), which mollify pressures for change.[39] Carlyle Thayer has noted that the impetus for electoral change came from within the VCP itself as it responded to the economic crisis.[40]

Yet, electoral reforms in Vietnam pre-dated the Sixth Party Congress, although they had fiddled only with the fringes of the system. Vietnam, like other Communist countries, used to allow only one candidate more than there were seats in each electoral unit. In Hà Nội people's council elections, the candidate-seat ratio was 1.25:1 (176 candidates for 140 seats) in 1977[41] and 1.18:1 (190/160) in 1981.[42] By 1984, in line with the broader trends of increasing electoral choice in Eastern European communist countries, the Vietnamese party-state also decided the number of candidates in elections must be two more than the number of seats in every electoral unit.[43] Consequently, in the 1985 election of the people's council of the city of Hà Nội, the candidate-seat ratio reached a high of 1.66:1 (249/150).[44] The percentage of re-elected councillors in Hà Nội's people's council dropped from 40 per cent in 1977 to 24.7 per cent in 1981, and climbed back up slightly to 28 per cent (42/150) in 1985.[45] For National Assembly elections, the candidate-seat ratio has gone from 1.2:1 (614/496) in 1981 to 1.7:1 (826/496) in 1987 and down to 1.5:1 (601/395) in 1992.[46]

No thorough explanation for these early reforms has yet emerged, but perhaps Carlyle Thayer's concept of regularization of politics is applicable. Thayer means that after the end of the war in 1975, leadership renewal became more regular.[47] Similarly, as part of regularization of politics, the number of candidates in elections increased and the rate of incumbent councillors enjoying a second term declined.

The reform atmosphere in the late 1980s also led to a short burst of printed criticisms of electoral practices. These criticisms were the tip of the iceberg of latent voter dissatisfaction with the electoral system. Broadly, these criticisms crystallized around candidature restrictions and the lack of choice.

Is the Screening of Nominees Democratic?

Many Vietnamese challenge the idea that the screening of nominees is democratic, as claimed by the party-state. One observer said that after 1987, calls came from many quarters to "widen" democracy in two ways: increase the candidate-seat ratio and stop the state from recommending candidates for elections.[48] The challenge from the wider domestic society is represented by two pointed questions asked by a newspaper reporter who interviewed Bùi Mạnh Trung, the Vice-chairman of the VFF Committee of the city of Hà Nội. The first question was "Why is it that consultation meetings [to pre-select nominees and limit the number of candidates], which are not the election, make [our election] democratic?" Trung answered by referring to the official stand that at the voting stage there was still some choice and that pre-selection only screened out unsuitable nominees. The reporter then asked "How are we encouraging people to stand for elections when a person who wants to stand has to be approved and introduced by a majority of people in a collective? Does this make us undemocratic?" This prompted a didactic response:

> Now, we should understand the situation like this. In order to avoid the spread of candidacy which would make voters' choice difficult … all nominations have to arise from the formal list that is produced from consultation meetings. Furthermore, every electoral unit will have more candidates than seats in order that the people can have a choice. As a result, the rights of candidates and the voters are not lost — if the candidate is not trusted by a majority of voters in his backyard [within his own collective] then he would find it difficult to gain the trust of voters within a larger area.[49]

This was the official parry that was also used by Đỗ Mười, a former VCP General Secretary when he responded to a foreign journalist who asked in 1992 why there were so few independent candidates in the National Assembly election that year.[50]

These criticisms, which were found at both the high and low levels of the political system, emerged at the tail-end of more electoral reforms between 1986 and 1989, thus suggesting that the interim changes had not satisfied voters. The reforms included increased opportunities for aspiring representatives, increased candidate-to-seat ratio, restrictions on re-election, and less upper level control of officials who were managing the elections (a point discussed earlier). For instance, in the 1987 National Assembly elections, the candidate-seat ratio rose to 1.8:1, which remains highest ever.[51] After the 1989 revisions to the 1983 Law on Election of People's Councils, candidates could not stand for elections to people's councils of more than two levels at the same time, and two consecutive terms were banned. Consequently, in Hà Nội people's council elections, the re-election rate dropped from 28 per cent in 1985 to 18.5 per cent in 1989.[52] Furthermore, individuals could now nominate themselves or other people in elections for people's councils, even when they were not introduced as candidates of a particular organization at selection meetings. Nevertheless, in the 1989 people's councils elections, the candidate-seat ratio for the commune/ward level was a low 1.15:1 (379,836/330,000).[53]

These reforms did not, however, address the fundamental issue of the legitimacy of the screening process. Readers' letters to the *HNM* newspaper indicated considerable disillusion. People thought the screening process should be abolished and that party-state influence on voters when choosing candidates should be reduced. One voter used the election of January 1946 (National Assembly) as the yardstick to measure the 1989 National Assembly elections. The atmosphere at the local elections in 1989, he said, was not as pleasant as that in 1946 because in 1989 there were unacceptable constraints on democracy, in the form of subtle interventions (in candidate selection) by the Communist Party and the state through the VFF.[54]

Another reader pointed out the high percentage of votes given to the successful candidates (in National Assembly elections) did not mean that people trusted these candidates. He offered two other explanations. First, the state's official biographies of candidates were extensively and favourably written for preferred candidates but sparsely written for the unanointed. Usually people voted for those who had better-written biographies because they did not know the candidates personally and they had no alternative channels of information. Through such subtle manipulations, people knew who the party-state preferred and did their part in adhering to what it wants. In 1997 an elderly informant confirmed this when talking to me.

> I asked K if it was true that somehow the biographies also gave the good side of the stories, and that it is difficult to tell who the better candidate is. K said yes, that is true, but there is nothing that the people can do because people do not have the time to know everything. It is difficult to check on candidates for elections to the National Assembly because

"the people are of thousands of colours and appearances" (*nhân dân muôn màu muôn vẻ*). It is impossible to expect perfection in candidates, so people choose those who are best qualified and to take other points such as sector representation into consideration. K said that "on each hand, there are short as well as long fingers" (*trên một bàn tay, có ngón tay dài, ngón tay ngắn*). So it is not unnatural that there will be some people who are not so well qualified and not so suitable in terms of their behaviour. The people, however, would know who to choose — *especially those who live in the same area or neighbourhood* as the candidate. K added that usually the people introduced by the district are well qualified people and have had some achievements in some areas.[55]

The newspaper reader's second explanation was that pre-selection helped to ensure a high number of votes for government candidates. Another *HNM* reader's letter reinforced this view by pointing out a dilemma that voters faced.

These phenomena [high percentage of votes and pre-selection] often bring to us a state of mind that is negative; the voter feels uncomfortable because apparently he has lost his right to choose his own deputy. If he does not vote in the full number of deputies he would feel that he has lost the right of a citizen; but if he votes this way then he could only vote in those who he thinks have been already decided upon. With such a list of candidates, voters feel that they have lost rights of democracy, and they confide that the election is democratic in form but is obviously artificial in substance.[56]

Two points are noteworthy. First, the passage suggests that a democratic election would not involve compulsion. Second, the passage implies that many candidates sponsored by the party-state were not considered worthy choices.

Party-state responses since 1989 have been instructive. In the two National Assembly elections of 1992 and 1997, the percentage of deputies standing for re-election was modest — 23 per cent (119/496) and 24 per cent (108/450), respectively.[57] A 1994 directive from the VFF said that allocating more candidates than there were seats avoided the situation of insufficient candidates in the event that some would withdraw before polling day. "If the electoral unit has only one excess candidate to replace the withdrawn candidate, then there would be just enough candidates to seats, it is not democratic."[58] Two would be a safe excess number so that if one withdraws, there would still be one in excess. But another senior official said in 1994 that it was important to have only a small number of excess candidates in order to put a limit to "boisterous practices" by independent candidates who were out to capture seats and who served only parochial interests.[59] He apparently favoured a slightly large candidate-seat ratio so long as it was engineered by the party-state. The purpose was to give voters a bit more choice but not to allow competition against the regime.

Nevertheless, the trend is to maintain the present situation. For the 2002 National Assembly elections, the candidate-seat ratio was 1.52:1 (759/498).[60] The People's Council Election Law of 2003 required that every electoral unit should have at least two candidates in excess of seats.[61] Thus, the 2004 People's Council elections had a candidate-seat ratio of 1.59:1, 1.54:1, and 1.55:1 for the provincial, district, and commune/ward levels respectively.[62] The National Assembly expressed a consensus in 2004 that in general the candidate-seat ratio in People's Council elections can improve further to increase competition.

QUALITY OF CANDIDATES

A second major criticism by voters since the late 1980s was that extensive restrictions on who could be candidates, rationalized by the Communist Party's emphasis on equitable sector representation, compromised the quality of candidates. Not until 1987, after reforms became an official policy, did the party-state acknowledge that this was a problem. Later, in 1994, national leaders even said that sector representation resulted in "unavoidable" errors in the quality of candidates.[63]

Despite criticisms, sector representation remains a cornerstone of elections. The party-state still believes it must screen nominees to ensure that elections unite, not divide, the country. What a group head of almost twenty years told me represented the party-state view.

> She elucidated that the elections in Vietnam were unlike those overseas. Representation from different sectors of society were usually guaranteed and preferred, even over other criteria. She also said that the educational standard of the ordinary Vietnamese was still low, such that they could not be aware of the need for overall representation of all sectors and may choose people who simply impress them, either through the candidates' merit or other criteria. There have been instances when capable candidates were rejected in favour of more suitable candidates. [Commenting on sector representation at the ward level election] The composition of the roll of nominees usually included one from the women sector, one from youth sector, one from the VFF, and several others who worked for the people's committee.[64]

Since 1989 independents (not nominated by any organizations or sectors) have been able to nominate themselves. In the 1992 National Assembly elections, there were forty-four independent nominees.[65] Only three got through the screening process, and none won seats. Eleven independent candidates survived the screening process in 1997, and three won seats. In 2002, there were 161 independent candidates out of 759, but only two of them won seats out of 498 seats.[66] In 2004, the independents phenomenon strengthened. Across all levels of the people's council elections, substantial numbers of independents were allowed to compete, as shown by Table 3.3. But in terms of the share of total number of candidates, independents are still a negligible trend. In fact, the government minister in charge of elections complained that there were too few independents, as the party-state expected more.[67]

The percentages for the big cities of Hà Nội and Hồ Chí Minh City, however, looked more promising. For instance, Hà Nội had four independents (4/143 or 2.8 per cent) and Hồ Chí Minh City had six (6/151 or 4 per cent). One of them was elected in Hồ Chí Minh City.[68] Out of sixty-three provinces, twenty-one had independents running in the provincial people's council elections, with the highest found in Lai Châu Province (15).[69]

TABLE 3.3
Independents and Non-Party Candidates in the 2004 People's Council Elections

	Province	District	Communes/wards
Total number of seats	3,809	23,554	284,507
Candidates sponsored by party-state or mass organizations	6,052	36,281	441,856
Independents (% of total no. of candidates)	77 (1.3%)	137 (0.4%)	851 (0.2%)
Non-party candidates	24.3%	25.9%	42%
Candidate-seat ratio	1.59:1	1.54:1	1.55:1

Source: Việt Anh, "Gần 2,000 ứng cử viên bị loại khỏi danh sách bầu cử", VN Express, 21 April 2004, http://vnexpress.net/Vietnam/Xa-hoi/2004/04/3B9D1DF5/.

In time, while treating independents like a "sector" and allowing them a small number of candidates, the party-state have been reducing the influence of the local party branches in recommending candidates. The Political Bureau of the VCP directed in November 2003 that the party branch of any level could recommend only one candidate for election into the people's council in order that person would become one of the leaders of the council or the people's committee. Furthermore, before these nominees could be considered to run for office, they have to be approved by the VFF.[70] The party-state has also increased the number of what was called "non-party candidates". These were people who were not party members and who did not run as independents, but were sponsored by state and mass organizations.

VOTER TURNOUT

Voter turnout has remained high, even though many Hà Nội residents criticized the election process (Table 3.4). The high turnout is despite the fact that sanctions against non-voting are less serious now than years ago. A closer look at how polling is conducted helps to explain this.

I was in Hà Nội during the 1997 National Assembly elections. Although I could not obtain formal permission to conduct interviews at polling stations, I was able to observe how ward officials prepared for the elections and watch what happened on polling day. I was also in Hà Nội to observe the 1999 and 2004 people's council elections.

TABLE 3.4

Voters' Turnout Rate for National Assembly and Hà Nội People's Council Elections

Year	National Assembly	Hà Nội People's Council
2004		98.7%
2002	99.73%	
1999		95%
1997	99.83%	
1994		99.55%
1992	99.23%	
1989		99.10%
1985		99.35%

The party-state is keen to run elections efficiently and according to formal procedures. Doing so, in their view, increases the legitimacy of the elections. Therefore, much attention is paid to getting the process right. Preparations for elections begin as early as three months before polling day when the Election Council and subsidiary bodies are appointed. Once the election machinery is up and running, the government usually issues a special directive that sets out the chronological programme of work for all local authorities and election organizations to follow. Cadres who will count votes, file election reports, identify special ballot papers (such as differentiating between ballot papers in double elections and invalid ballot papers), and so forth, are sent for training.

About a month before the elections, the ward state machinery completes the voters' register for the electoral unit and displays it prominently at the ward office. The ward then reminds voters to check the registers for any errors and refer all mistakes and necessary corrections to ward officials. About two weeks before the election, the officials in the ward I observed, which I call Trung (not its real name), began to prepare voters' cards. I was allowed to help. It was labour-intensive; there were no computers or typewriters. A stack of paper voters' cards had been printed by the Election Committee (at the city level) and distributed to every ward, through the district people's committee. The Trung Ward had about 7,000 cards for around 6,500 voters. I helped Th., the vice-chair person of the ward Women's Association, to process the cards. Every card must have two official stamps — the first was the round seal (used for all official documents issued by the ward); the second had the name of either the ward chairman (Mr N) or the vice-chairwoman (Ms M). The cards also had to be signed by one of those two ward officials. The two stamps had to be in positions specified by regulations, that is, the ward's seal overlaps the signature of the person by about one-third and the name stamp must be directly below the signature. Otherwise, the voter's card may be considered invalid. I had already stamped a few when I was told they did not conform to the regulations strictly, but Th. said: "Never mind, they're small mistakes. We'll use them anyway because there may not be enough cards." As I tried to stamp according to regulations, I noticed that Chairman N had in some cases signed his name too high up, thus overlapping the text above, and therefore the ward's stamp had no choice but to be higher up. I told Th., in jest, that this was the chairman's fault and he should correct his mistakes, because voters would not be able to read the text. Th. responded in a half-shocked and half-amused manner, disbelieving that I had just criticized the chairman. She repeated my words to those present in the ward office and later to the chairman himself. But Chairman N seemed not to mind.

One week before the election, the processed cards were distributed to all resident group heads. Each group head took one card for every eligible voter.

"But the names of the voters have not been filled in?" I said to Th.

"Yes, each group head will ask someone with a beautiful handwriting to write in the names."

"Is there pay for such work?"

"Yes but very little, nevertheless it is important to get beautiful handwriting."

"Why can't the ward get a computer and print it all?"

"Well, we don't have the money. Anyway, it's done once every few years; it's not worth the investment."[71]

A week later, I saw my house-mother sitting on the floor, bending over a list of names taken from the voter's register and a stack of processed voters' cards. She asked her ten-year-old granddaughter to read out the names of voters in her resident group one at a time, and she then labouriously wrote the names on the voters' cards.

Another task that occupied much of the time of the Election Section and the ward was to get the polling station properly decorated for the formal event. I visited a polling station (converted from the ward office) in the evening before polling day. I was able to enter the polling station freely, even though from the eve of the big day it was supposed to be out-of-bounds.

I saw all props were already set up at five-thirty. The room was empty of people, and C, the man whom I later got to know was the chair of the Election Section overseeing the polling station, said that everybody of the people's committee (*uy ban*) had gone off either back home or for dinner, and N, the chair of the people's committee, will be back soon to receive the inspection team from the District to review preparations tonight. Apparently, C and a few policemen of the ward were ready to guard the place throughout the night without sleep. I noticed that two other men whom I had never seen at the ward before were also sitting around waiting for something to do. Later, I found out that they are actually two electricians around to make sure that the lights would not fail in the night. Before anybody could return to the ward from dinner, it began to rain cats and dogs, the heaviest rainstorm I had experienced in Hà Nội. Outside the ward office, floodwater peaked at 0.5 metre high. While waiting for N to return, I copied down the "Rules of the polling station" (Nội quy phòng bỏ phiếu) as well as the "Rules and Regulations of the Election" (Thể lệ bầu cử) handwritten on cardboard pinned on the wall at a few strategic places inside and outside the room. After a while, Chairman N returned in a raincoat on his motorcycle, in slippers because of the rain, and had become all wet from the downpour. He was not surprised that I was there, and he spoke with me with more familiarity and friendliness than before. "The District will come for inspections at seven o'clock," N said. I asked how come the ballot box was already placed in the centre of the voting room. Why wasn't it locked away for security? N said tomorrow morning, there would be an opening ceremony when the ballot box would be inspected to make sure that it was empty. There would be two representatives of voters who would witness the inspection. The box will then be sealed and ready for the polling.[72]

Local authorities are primarily responsible for the percentage of turnout in their areas and do their best to ensure the highest turnout rate. The group heads, in particular, are enlisted to help secure a high turnout. Election Committee and ward officials brief the group heads about how to encourage voters to turnout.

Wards and their superiors also use other tactics to encourage a high turnout. One of them is to provide entertainment and decorations to create a festive atmosphere. Over a period of twenty years, these activities have stayed very much a part of elections, evidenced by descriptions below.

> From yesterday afternoon until this polling day morning, everywhere on the streets, in the villages of the capital bustled with the sound of drums, megaphones, and the teams of lion dancers who were mobilizing for the election. At the districts and wards, convoys of cars and motorcycles have on them slogans, flags, loud hailers that publicized the rules of the election. Every ward in Ba Đình District had a mobilization car. The District used three cars to ferry the artists serving the election.[73] (1981)

> From the afternoon before polling day, teams of cars and motorcycles, which brought with them banners and slogans, and lion dance teams, took to the streets to publicize and mobilize for polling day.[74] (1984)

> Almost overnight the capital, Hà Nội, was ablaze with red flags, while convoys of police motorcycles and trucks adorned with banners drove

through city streets urging people by loud hailer to take part in Sunday's nationwide vote. Early editions of one Sunday newspaper called for people to fulfil their civic duties, and carried photos of Vietnam's spiritual leader, the late president Hồ Chí Minh, and taking part in one of the National Assembly's first elections.[75] (1997)

Other methods to mobilize turnout include using a secondary ballot box, closely monitoring of the turnout, sending cadres out to remind the voters on polling day, and allowing proxy voting.

The Secondary Ballot Box

The Election Law provides a secondary ballot box as a service to bedridden, old, feeble, or disabled voters. I saw it in action coincidentally. I was standing inside the polling station when I saw Little Th., the secretary of the Youth Union who worked on the Election Section, carrying a cardboard box whose colour looked like a ballot box. Little Th. asked C for instructions. I asked C what was happening. C said it was the secondary ballot box, explained its purpose, then looked at a list of voters unable to come to the station and ticked one of the names. Then he said, "Bring your camera and follow me!" Twenty metres away from the ward office, we turned into a lane; C certainly knew where his fellow residents lived. After three turns we went into a house. A young couple brought the four of us to meet an old lady who was assisted to sit up. C went through a short, oral introduction on the election for the lady, and she was then given the ballot paper and asked to vote. But she asked her son who she should vote for, and her son said it was up to her, but he added that perhaps certain candidates may be good. The first candidate the son recommended was the one who ranked highest in official position among the five candidates. After she had voted by placing the ballot in the secondary ballot box, the four of us shook the lady's hand and returned to the ward office. As we walked out, C said: "Although she is old, she makes very wise choices!" The others in the team, walking around me, nodded their heads to agree.

The day 20 July 1997 was polling day. At seven o'clock in the morning the polling station opened. After a simple speech by the head of the Election Section (which managed the polling station), the ballot box was held up high for all present to see that it was empty, and then sealed for use. At every election, VIPs such as members of the VCP Political Bureau might be invited to do the honour of declaring the election open and to cast the first vote. The VIP could and usually, in turn, gave the honour of casting the first ballot to the oldest voter in the area. Already in place at each polling station was a security team that the Election Committee had formed. Each team comprised six middle-aged and older men who guarded the entrance and surroundings of the polling station. Their brief included not allowing people without an official pass or not on official business from entering the station. I observed that the men, familiar faces, were recruited from among neighbourhood communist party and state cadres of the ward state machinery, which explained their high average age.

On arrival at the ward office, I saw the lion dance troupe of the ward ready to move around the ward to stir up the atmosphere in the ward, with Mr Ng. — the culture cadre of the ward — in charge. Riding a small lorry, a group of youths and Ng. moved off amid pulsating rhythms. Their mission was to remind people in the ward to turn out to vote. (When I met Ng. again in 2004, he said he was too old to be going around the ward to mobilize people. But he was nevertheless still participating enthusiastically by overseeing the decoration work at a polling station.)

I stepped into the ward office and saw a "studio" by the side of the entrance. Th. was sitting there with another man. Through the public address system, they took turns to remind voters about turning out to vote. Their message was relayed through speakers mounted on poles, one in every street of the ward's jurisdiction. They read poll regulations, recited poems, played soothing music, and reported on the latest situation on voter turnout. They mentioned by name the resident groups that were doing well and encouraged other groups to catch up. Abreast the entrance stood members of the security team, standing guard to check that nobody not on official business was to enter the polling station. My close friend T, a party secretary in a resident cluster and a member of the security team, was sitting outside the station and waving to me. Strictly speaking I was not allowed by election rules to be inside the polling station.

My eventual trespassing was, however "authorized". When N, chairman of the people's committee, saw me arriving at the polling station, he immediately invited me into his office and asked if I had wanted to look around. His tone of voice was proud of the election being held. (I had told N about two weeks before that I wanted to observe the elections. He

said prior permission had to be applied for, *and* it was too late to do so.)
I nodded my head vigorously at a great opportunity and wondered why
the formal requirement for "permission" had evaporated. N went out for a
moment and came back with C, the chairman of the Election Section for
that polling station whom I met the night before but was not introduced. N
said: "C is the highest authority in this polling state, even I have to defer
to him for permission to be here." On a normal day, C works for N as a
resident group head. Turning to C, N explained my reason for being there,
"to compare Vietnam's electoral system with that of other countries". To
my surprise C readily agreed to my snooping around, and the first thing
he asked me to do was to use my stills camera to capture on film whatever
he thought necessary. He first wanted pictures of the decorations of the
voting room that the Election Section had put maximum effort into. Then
C took a piece of the pink-coloured ballot paper, folded it as if it had been
marked, postured in front of the ballot box, and asked me for a photo of
him mock casting the ballot.

Mid-way through the morning, after I had gone around taking many
pictures of the activities of the election inside the polling station, N
asked me to rest in his office. We had barely drunk our tea when at
about half-past ten a man (introduced to me as being an official from
the district) entered the room, and I began to see the formal reporting
system in action. As a long-standing practice, the city requires the wards
to submit five formal reports on polling day. The first at eight o'clock in
the morning after the opening ceremony; the second and third at eleven
in the morning and six in the evening on the general situation, especially
on the turnout rate; the fourth at eight in the evening, a report on the
closing of the polling station; and the last at midnight to submit the
results for the electoral unit.[76] To submit reports on turnouts, the ward
people's committee chairman collated all the turnout figures from all the
polling stations, which he did hourly by getting onto his motorcycle to
visit the polling stations.

I heard the district official converse with N. The former had a piece
of paper, which had a chart, in front of him. On one axis of the chart
were the names of the wards of the district, and on the other axis were
the hours of report. The ward authorities of the District apparently were
giving *hourly* reports to the district, instead of just five reports for the whole
day; officials everywhere appeared to be anxious about a good outcome
on polling day. N's eleven o'clock morning report about the turnout in
four polling stations is summarized in Table 3.5.

TABLE 3.5
Turnout Report at Eleven O'Clock, 20 July 1997

Polling Station	No. of voters	No. of voters voted	% turnout
1	1,798	1,695	94%
2	1,604	1,420	89%
3	1,696	1,524	90%
4	1,675	1,340	80%
Students[a]	107	82	76.6%
Total	6,880	6,082	88.4%

Note:
a. University students' votes were taken out from every polling station statistics in the ward and collated into a separate category. I do not know the reason for this.

Source: Fieldnotes 20 July 1997.

Most people had already voted between seven and eleven in the morning. The district official told N, in a very disbelieving and amused tone, that some wards had actually reported 37 to 40 per cent turnout at eight o'clock in the morning, which was only one hour just after voting had begun.

At the polling station, voters usually go first to the registration tables to cross out their names on the voters' list by presenting their voters' cards. There were about four tables catering to this procedure, each table manned by one official taking care of about six resident groups. Some of these four officials were heads of resident groups, while others were members of the ward's mass organizations. Voters were then given the ballot paper. Each voter then went to the voting booth, getting behind a curtain to shield him or herself as they ticked on their ballot paper. There were five candidates and only three were to be elected, so voters struck out candidates they did not favour by striking a line through their names.[77] Candidates were listed alphabetically. After dropping the ballot paper into the one and only ballot box, each voter exited the polling room. Before leaving, most voters remembered to present his voter's card to an official for stamping the word "voted". Repercussions for not voting are not stated in the electoral laws and the Constitution, but it may be a black mark against the person and may invite non-co-operation from the ward if in the future the person needs a favour. Every absent voter detracts from the ward's effort to achieve a high turnout. The ward is also able to trace the turnout of every individual via the voters' list.

Allowing Proxy Voting

Proxy voting is illegal. Election regulations say "a voter must vote personally and not ask proxies to vote on their behalf. If the voter is illiterate, he can choose on his own free will another person to write on the ballot paper, but he must cast the ballot paper into the ballot box himself or ask somebody to do so in front of him."[78] (The secondary ballot box was meant to realize this ideal for the sick and aged.) Despite the law, proxy voting has been occurring since before 1989,[79] and I witnessed them in the 1997 elections. In one extreme instance I saw a lone voter carrying eight voters' cards in her hands when she reported for voting. (She was supposed to have held only one, because she only needed to cast one ballot paper in this National Assembly election.) She was given eight ballot papers by one of the officials at the registration table without questions being asked, although the official did check who the voters' cards belonged to and ticked their names in the voters' register. Most of those serving as proxy voters had between two to three voters' cards with them. Proxy voters were also able to obtain the "voted" stamp from the exit official for all voters' cards they held. By my rough count, about one in every five voters were proxies. Subsequent inquiries I made revealed that proxy voting has been a very common practice in the wards throughout Hà Nội. One Vietnamese friend in his early forties, who had seen several elections since the mid-1980s, told me he had never personally cast a single vote, yet had never been reprimanded or punished by his ward. In the 2004 people's council election, many Vietnamese friends when asked said they did not have to be bothered with voting because their family members had gone on their behalf.

If the turnout for ward Trung were already 37 per cent of around 6,500 voters (based on the information from the District official), then it worked out to be 2,405 voters in the first 60 minutes, or about 40 voters in every minute, or about ten voters every minute in each of the four polling stations. This rate requires a polling station to complete voting action by one voter in only six seconds. Either this rate is false, or the ward concerned was unbelievably efficient in moving voters in and out of the polling station and allowing them to cast their ballots at the same time. Proxy voting cannot be ruled out.

Proxy voting probably contributes about 20 per cent to the voter turnout. That reduces real turnout in Vietnam to around 79 per cent, similar to the 75 per cent that had been estimated to be the real rate of turnout in elections of the former Soviet Union.[80]

Looking at from the point of view of the ward, I can see why the Election Sections in Hà Nội facilitated or ignored proxy voting. Although polling day is always on Sunday or a public holiday, many people are actually working anyway and do not want to sacrifice work time to go to the polling station. Allowing proxy voting is a way which the ward is considerate (thông cảm) to those who have other priorities. Besides, it also helps the ward to achieve a high voter turnout. A low turnout not only lowers the standing or the ward and the polling station in the competition on election turnout, but it also casts questions on the mobilizational capability of ward officials in the eyes of higher levels, something not good for bureaucrats' careers. If 100 per cent turnout is achieved early, the polling station can also close early and its officials can enjoy the rest of the day off work. This was indeed what some voters believed to be the right thing to do. From the viewpoint of individuals, families may be occupied at home and see that it is better to send one representative to vote on behalf of every voter in the household. Voters may also believe that personally turning out makes no difference in view of pre-selection and limited choice among candidates. Refusing to vote might be an option some have considered, but they know that would risk a confrontation with party-state officials at the maximum or ill will at the minimum. Proxy voting, therefore, can be a convenient way to fulfil one's duty, avoid possible risks, and avoid having to participate directly in the act of voting — multiple benefits, low risks!

In the former Soviet Union, where proxy voting was also illegal but done, it was a way people used to avoid a distasteful act of meaningless elections. It was also a way to cover over other things or avoid open confrontation. Apartment managers reportedly voted on behalf of those who stubbornly refused so that their own inefficiencies were hidden. Worried family elders voted on behalf of their more idealistic juniors, so that the rest of the family or neighbours would not be targeted for attack by the party-state, and so forth.[81] Reluctant voters less concerned with commodifying their vote used proxy voting as a means of voting avoidance.

Digression aside, after polling is over, each Election Section submitted a summary of vote counts to the ward. Section reports are then collated by the Election Committees, which prepared a report to the district, and from there further reports are made until results reached the Election

Council. The report of the polling station I observed, submitted the day after the election, clustered voters into four groups under the care of the four registration officials on polling day. The number of votes for each candidate by each group was tabulated carefully. Only five out of the close to 2,000 ballots in the polling station was considered illegal, while the turnout was 97 per cent.[82] A district official checked the results while votes were being counted.

Voter turnout for elections in Hà Nội in the mid-1990s, at least in the area where I lived, has been high because the party-state apparatus is geared towards achieving that result. Officials take extensive steps at city, district, and ward levels to prepare for elections, inform voters, mobilize voters, and make it convenient for voters to cast ballots. The latter includes some measures, such as proxy voting, which is supposedly illegal but occur nevertheless as an informal accommodation local officials make with voters in order to get the high turnouts that the party-state leadership wants.

It is also important to note that proxy voting in Vietnam was probably not a new phenomenon that only started recently. Reading reports of polling days of the past, for instance, one could discover the phenomenon had existed for a number of elections already. In the 1992 National Assembly elections, for instance, by twelve o'clock noon on polling day, a number of provinces had already reached high levels of voter turnout: Hà Nội had 75 per cent, Hải Phòng 75 per cent, Thừa Thiên Huế 87 per cent, Khánh Hoà 95 per cent, Yên Bái 85 per cent, Minh Hải 80 per cent, and Nam Hà 89 per cent.[83] Given the large number of votes to be cast and inferring from present practices, this would have been impossible unless people moved like sardines along production lines. Using the statistics provided by the state media, some polling stations were able to move one voter through the polling station every two seconds during the first hour of polling.[84]

In the 2004 people's council elections, a few cases emerged whereby the electoral authorities clamped down on proxy voting. The National Assembly rescinded the results of a total of eight polling stations. The two main reasons were proxy voting, and the number of ballots counted in the ballot box was more than the number of ballot papers given out.[85]

On the other hand, from the 2004 people's council elections there has been the new phenomenon of voters using their votes to voice certain concerns. The way they have done it is to not to turn out, or not to vote for whomever they perceived as the anointed candidates (those who are illustrious as seen in their biography) so that the number of winning votes that the winners get will be marginal. One of the consequences of this has been failure to produce enough winners to fill seats, so that a by-election to elect the remaining has to take place. In 2004, twenty communes and wards in Hà Nội had to organize re-elections, due to this reason.[86] A famous case among them was the Kim Nỗ Commune, where in the mid-1990s a famous peasants' protest took place against a governmental plan to reclaim farmland for a golf course. The voter turnout of the commune on polling day was only 47 per cent.

CONCLUSION: ELECTIONS, INFORMALITY AND LOCAL DYNAMICS

In the example I cited of nominee-meet-voters sessions for ward elections, the atmosphere was informal while members of the resident group strained to do their duty to arrive at a consensus and produce a candidate. When candidates who have obvious shortcomings are selected, it meant that people were willing to give and take, accepting the point that not everybody could be perfect. This tolerance for imperfection strikes a chord in the way ordinary people is willing to sentimentalize their judgements of persons or matters. In the ward office itself, formality and informality were mixed when preparing for and conducting polling. Allowances were made for imperfections on voters' cards, my intrusion into these preparations and into the polling station were overlooked, and proxy voting was approved despite the law saying otherwise. Proxy voting may indicate some discontent among voters, which, if not permitted, could make the discontent become more public in the form of low turnout, which would create problems for officials. At the least, proxy voting is a form of compromise between the party-state, which wants to have high turnouts and many voters who, for one reason or another, does not want to go to the polling stations.

Personal and exchange relationships between voters and local officials are another kind of informality that helps to explain how governments in Vietnam and other communist countries maintain a firm hold on elections and garner high voter turnouts to demonstrate their legitimacy to anyone who believes it. The enthusiasm of local officials involved in running the local election machinery is bolstered by their expectation that doing a good job will help their chances of being promoted or avoiding certain odious duties.[87] Voters in some communist countries squeezed concessions from local authorities — the overdue roof repair or access to special goods — in exchange for voting in a timely fashion.

Some Hà Nội residents who may have hesitated to take part in elections were mindful of the importance of having good relations with local officials whom they might need to call on for special consideration or assistance on some future occasion. Friendship and kinship ties also influenced voters to participate. People in Hà Nội sometimes were motivated to vote out of respect for fellow ward residents who were working hard to mobilize everyone to participate in the elections. They were also mindful of small rewards that might come to them and their families if they showed to local leaders and neighbours that they were co-operative and good citizens. Therefore, in more ways than one, turning out to vote is a task not only about the individual, but also the family, and perhaps the larger community.

Rising above the micro-level at the ward, the Vietnamese party-state is in steady, institutionalized control of the election machinery, and its notions of what, and how, elections should be like prevail in the political system. This situation, coupled with the absence of political opposition, go a long way to enable the party-state to dominate elections. Nobody will be able to stand for election in Vietnam without Communist Party approval, although there are different levels of screening and approval. Another factor helping to assure party-state domination over elections is a degree of informality to accommodate residents' needs.

In other activities, where ignoring or avoiding the will of the party-state would have minor adverse consequences, especially if significant benefits could be gained, party-state dominance may be less pervasive. I shall examine two such areas in Chapters 4 and 5.

Notes

1. Guy Hermet, Richard Rose, and Alain Rouquie, eds., *Elections Without Choice* (London: Macmillan, 1978).
2. "Thực tế này không có gì lạ vì ở đây, bầu cử cũng là tranh cử, là tranh giành nhau ghế đại biểu, ghế tổng thống để nắm quyền lực nhà nước, giữ được đường lối chính trị của đảng mình, mưu lợi ích cho tập đoàn mình. Ở nước ta, không cần thiết một cuộc vận động như vậy. Vì ứng cử là tình nguyện làm việc nước." Phùng Văn Tửu and Ngô Văn Thâu, *Tìm hiểu bầu cử đại biểu Quốc hội* [In search of understanding of National Assembly elections] (Hà Nội: NXB Pháp Lý, 1992), pp. 23–24. See also Gareth Porter *Vietnam: The Politics of Bureaucratic Socialism* (Ithaca and London: Cornell University Press, 1993), p. 153.

3. In my opinion, both left and right of politics do not differ much from each other in their need for popular endorsement. Authoritarian, non-communist regimes of Southeast Asia, for instance, have held elections regularly and have gone to great extents to manipulate votes, including fraud. In some instances as well, these right-wing regimes have admitted and accepted losses in elections. See R. H. Taylor, ed., *The Politics of Elections in Southeast Asia* (Cambridge: Woodfrow Wilson Centre Press, Cambridge University Press, 1996).

4. Howard R. Swearer, "The Functions of Soviet Local Elections", *Midwest Journal of Political Science* 5, no. 2 (1961): 145; Victor Zaslavsky and Robert J. Brym, "The Functions of Elections in the USSR", *Soviet Studies* 30, no. 3 (July 1978): 370–71; Hermet, Rose, and Rouquie, eds., *Elections Without Choice*, p. x; John P. Burns, *Political Participation in Rural China* (Berkeley, CA: University of California Press, 1988), p. 89; James R. Townsend, *Political Participation in Communist China* (Berkeley, CA: University of California Press, 1967), p. 115; (1988) p. 89.

5. Since 1984 but until 2004, the ratio of representatives to voters for all levels of elections has gone down. In the 1984 people's councils elections, each ward people's council had twenty councillors for a population of up to 2,000 people, and one extra councillor for every additional 400 people, up to a maximum of forty-five councillors. In 1984 as well, a commune — the equivalent of the ward in the rural area — that had 2,000 people and below voted for twenty councillors, and one extra councillor for every extra 350 people, but up to a maximum of forty-five councillors. This rate of representation was cut in 1994 — nineteen deputies for 3,000 people, one extra councillor for every additional 1,500 people. The 1994 cuts did not spare Central Cities people's councils, like in Hà Nội and Hồ Chí Minh City. Representation was reduced to a maximum of eighty-five councillors compared to over 150 in the 1980s, although this figure was raised to ninety-five in 2004 probably as a response to higher number of residents in urban areas.

6. Adrian Edwards, "Vietnam reports high turnout in assembly elections", Reuters, 20/7/1997.

7. DRV, "Pháp lệnh quy định thể lệ bầu cử Hội đồng Nhân dân các cấp, ngày 23 tháng 1 năm 1961" [Ordinance on Regulations of People's Councils elections at all levels, 23/1/1961], in *Các văn bản về việc Bầu cử Hội đồng Nhân dân và Ủy ban Hành chính các cấp* [Documents on People's Councils and Adminstrative Committees elections at all levels], by Ủy ban Nhân dân tỉnh Nam Định (Nam Định, 1961), pp. 4–26.

8. This table illustrates the arrangements for people's council elections but the arrangements are similar for National Assembly elections, except that the local of the three main bodies are different from their local in people's council elections.

9. "Agitpunkt" means "agitation point", a temporary electoral office which served as the headquarters for organization and propaganda activities of party personnel and volunteers. It checked voters' list, organized voters' meetings, disseminated literature, and provided lectures on the Soviet system of government. Max E. Mote, *Soviet Local and Republic Elections: A Description of the 1963 elections in Leningrad based on official documents, press accounts, and private interviews* (Stanford University, Hoover Institution Studies 10: The Hoover Institution on War, Revolution, and Peace, 1965), p. 20.

10. Swearer (1961), p. 134 said official Soviet doctrine saw the people's deputy as "a paragon of productive genius, morality, and good citizenship … he is the beneficient and watchful shepherd of his constituents, the pace-setter in virtue and state service, the expounder of official dicta, the organizer of mass activities, the executor of decrees and regulations, and the inspector and courageous critic of hard-hearted bureaucrats." See also Theodore H. Friedgut *Political Participation in the USSR* (Princeton, NJ: Princeton University Press, 1979), pp. 92–93.

11. ĐCSVN, "Làm tốt cuộc bầu cử Hội đồng Nhân dân và Ủy ban Nhân dân các cấp" [Organize well elections of people's councils and people's committees of all levels], *Tạp Chí Cộng Sản* (hereafter *TCCS*) 4 (1977): 36.

12. SRV, "Luật bầu cử đại biểu Hội đồng nhân dân" [Law on Election of People's Councils], *Hà Nội Mới* (hereafter *HNM*), 15 January 1984, pp. 1, 2, Article 3.

13. SRV, 'Luật sửa đổi bổ sung Luật bầu cử đại biểu Hội đồng nhân dân" [Amendments to the Law on Election of People's Councils], *HNM*, 8 May 1989, pp. 2, 3.

14. *HNM*, "Cuộc bầu cử bảo đảm dân chủ hay không, quyết định ở bước hiệp thương do MTTQ đóng vai trò chính" [Interview with Bùi Mạnh Trung, Vice-chairman, VFF Committee of the City of Hà Nội], 8 September 1989, p. 2.

15. Therefore, the change in emphasis from 1977 to 1997 has been from "Fatherland and Socialism" to "Socialist Fatherland" in both local and National Assembly elections, and to "Fatherland" in the 1997 National Assembly elections. The trend has been to emphasize nationalism at the expense of socialism.

16. *Lao Động*, "17.3, hạn cuối loại đối tượng tham nhũng hối lộ … khỏi danh sách ứng cử" [17/3 is deadline to eliminate corrupt officials from the nominees' list], 2 March 2004, No. 62, http://www.laodong.com.vn/pls/bld/folder$. view_item_detail(94244).

17. *HNM*, "Quy định của Hội đồng Nhà nước về cuộc bầu cử đại biểu Quốc hội khóa VIII" [State Council regulations on election of Eighth National Assembly Deputies], 17 February 1987, pp. 1, 4.

18. Bùi Đình Nguyên, "Có gì khác trong Luật bầu cử vừa được Quốc hội thông qua" [What's new in the election law just passed by the National Assembly], *Lao Động Hà Nội*, 9 May 1997, pp. 1, 10.

19. Agence France Presse, "Vietnam warns against abuse of democracy in one-party polls", 1 February 2002.

20. Shaun Kingsley Malarney, "Culture, Virtue, And Political Transformation in Contemporary Northern Vietnam", *Journal of Asian Studies,* no. 6, November 1997, pp. 899–920.

21. One of these village values may be compassion and sentimentality in village leaders, and the fact that it is demanded may be seen from the political misfortune of a village leader. In the village Malarney studied, a reason for the downfall of the people's committee chairman who sought re-election was he dutifully enforced state law in punishing a villager for a light crime, while villages expected less serious crime to be forgiven and overlooked by the local authority.

22. SRV, Quy trình hiệp thương lựa chọn, giới thiệu những người ứng cử đại biểu Hội đồng nhân dân (Ban hành kèm theo Công văn số 193CV/MTTQ ngày 2/8/1994) [Process of selecting and introducing candidates for election to people's council — Appendix to Circular 193CV/MTTW dated 2 August 1994].

23. *HNM*, "Hàng vạn cán bộ làm công tác bầu cử được bồi dưỡng nghiệp vụ" [Thousands of cadres involved in electoral work being trained], 30 September 1981, pp. 1, 4.

24. *HNM*, "Phường Hàng Trống chuẩn bị bầu cử" [Hàng Trống Ward prepares for election], 4 October 1981 p. 1.

25. Reuters, "Adultery charge trips Vietnam Assembly candidate", 2 July 1997.

26. The three individuals and their official posts at that time were: Trần Mai Hạnh, General Director of Voice of Vietnam; Lê Công Minh, Deputy Party Secretary (Standing) of Quảng Bình Province; and Trần Trung Am, Deputy Party Secretary and Chairman of People's Committee, Nam Định Province. Vietnam News Agency, "National Assembly Office explains elimination of three candidates", 17 May 2002.

27. P. Linh, "Giải quyết vướng mắc trong bầu cử đại biểu HĐND 3 cấp", *Lao Động*, 5 April 2004, No. 94, http://www.laodong.com.vn/pls/bld/folder$. view_item_detail(97397).

28. Fieldnotes 16 May 1997.

29. Protest votes, for whatever reasons, are classified as "white ballots" and "illegal ballots". The former refers to ballot papers that do not have any candidate's name or have all the names of candidates on it cancelled out. Illegal ballots are those that do not conform to the design of the official ballot paper, or that are not stamped, or have more candidates than there are seats in the ward. In fact, the election mobilization propaganda emphasizes education of the

voters to vote properly so as to minimize white and illegal ballots. Every Election Council, Committee, and Section in their reports to the upper levels have to report on the numbers of white and illegal ballots. I could not obtain statistics on them, unfortunately.

30. Đỗ Lê Tạo, "Ba tiêu chỉ trong hiệp thương" [Three criteria in consultations], *Lao Động Điện Tử*, 16 February 2004, No. 47, http://www.laodong.com. vn/pls/bld/folder$.view_item_detail(92794).

31. Fieldnotes 16 May 1997.

32. *HNM*, "Họp cử tri ở một phường" [A ward voters' meeting], 14 April 1987, p. 1.

33. Carlyle Thayer, "Recent Political Developments: Constitutional Change and the 1992 Elections", in *Vietnam and the Rule of Law*, edited by Carlyle Thayer and David G. Marr, (1993), pp. 50–80; Reuters, "Cheating reported ahead of Vietnam election", 16 July 1997.

34. Hữu Mạo, "Chọn người ra ứng cử ở một tổ dân phố" [Selection of election candidates in a resident group], *HNM*, 22 March 1987, pp. 1, 4.

35. Fieldnotes 16 May 1997.

36. Như Trang, "Một số cán bộ chủ chốt không trúng cử HĐND" [A number of key cadres not elected into People's Councils], *VN Express*, 28 June 2004, http://vnexpress.net/Vietnam/Xa-hoi/2004/06/3B9D3FF7/.

37. "Bí thư tỉnh ủy không trúng cử đại biểu HĐND" [Provincial Party Secretary not elected into People's Council], *Tuổi Trẻ*, 30 April 2004, http://www.tuoitre. com.vn/Tianyon/PrintView.aspx?ArticleID=30842&ChannelID=3.

38. D.L.T., "Người ứng cử đại biểu HĐND các cấp phải kê khai 5 loại tài sản" [People's Council election candidates of all levels have to declare five kinds of assets], *Lao Động*, 19 March 2004, No. 79, http://www.laodong.com. vn/pls/bld/folder$.view_item_detail(95819).

39. Stephen White, "Economic Performance and Communist Legitimacy", *World Politics* 38, no. 3 (1986): 471–74.

40. Thayer, "Recent Political Developments", p. 74.

41. *HNM*, "Danh sách những người ứng cử đại biểu Hội đồng Nhân dân Thành phố" [Nominees for election to the People's Council of the City of Hà Nội], 24 April 1977, pp. 1, 3.

42. *HNM*, "Hội đồng bầu cử HĐND Thành phố công bố danh sách 190 người ứng cử HĐND Thành phố khoá VIII" [Hà Nội Election Council of Hà Nội People's Committee announced list of 190 candidates for 8th City People's Council elections], 7 April 1981, p. 1; *HNM*, "Danh sách những người ứng cử đại biểu HĐND thành phố khoá VIII" [Name list of candidates for election of the Eighth City People's Council], 8 April 1981, pp. 1, 4 and 9 April 1981, pp. 1, 4; and *HNM*, "Danh sách các vị trúng cử đại biểu HĐND thành phố khoá VIII" [Names of candidates elected into the 8th City People's Council], 30 April 1981, pp. 1, 4.

43. *HNM*, "Nhìn lại cuộc bầu cử đại biểu HĐND hai cấp" [Review of people's council elections of two levels], 25 July 1984, p. 2.

44. *HNM*, "Kết quả cuộc bầu cử đại biểu Hội đồng nhân dân thành phố Khoá IX" [Results of Ninth City People's Council elections], 27 April 1985, pp. 1, 4.

45. *HNM*, "Hội đồng Bầu cử Hội đồng Nhân dân thành phố công bố kết quả cuộc bầu cử ngày 15-5" [Election Council of the Hà Nội People's Council announced 15-5 election results], 19 May 1977, p. 1; *HNM*, "Hội đồng bầu cử HĐND Thành phố công bố danh sách 190 người ứng cử HĐND Thành phố khoá VIII" [Election Council of Hà Nội People's Council announced list of 190 candidates for 8th City People's Council elections], 7 April 1981 p. 1; *HNM*, "Kết quả cuộc bầu cử đại biểu Hội đồng nhân dân thành phố khoá IX" [Results of Ninth City People's Council elections], 27 April 1985, pp. 1, 4.

46. Cat@coombs.anu.edu.au, "VN: Implications of Electoral Change?", Message sent to vnforum@saigon.com, 3 December 1994.

47. Carlyle A. Thayer, "The Regularization of Politics: Continuity and Change in the Party's Central Committee, 1951–1986", in *Postwar Vietnam: Dilemmas in Socialist Development*, edited by David G. Marr and Christine White (Ithaca: Cornell Southeast Asia Program, 1988).

48. Such criticisms were articulated openly by Nguyễn Hữu Thọ, a lawyer who nominally led the southern resistance during the American war. He later became acting President of the National Assembly of unified Vietnam. He asked for the uncapping of total number of candidates. William Turley, "Party, State, and People: Political Structure and Economic Prospects", in *Reinventing Vietnamese Socialism: Đổi Mới in Comparative Perspective*, edited by William S. Turley and Mark Selden (Boulder, Colorado: Westview Press, 1993), p. 264.

49. *HNM*, "Cuộc bầu cử có bảo đảm dân chủ hay không, quyết định ở bước hiệp thương do MTTQ đóng vai trò chính" [Whether the elections are democratic is decided at the consultations stage led by the VFF] (interview with Bùi Mạnh Trung, Vice-chairman, MTTQ Committee of the City of Hà Nội), 8 September1989, p. 2.

50. Đạm Minh Thụy, "Dân chủ là thực hiện việc trao toàn bộ quyền lực tối cao vào tay những đại biểu xứng đáng của nhân dân" [Democracy means handing all the highest powers to deserving representatives of the people], *Lao Động*, 23 July 1992, pp. 1, 2.

51. Gareth Porter, *Vietnam: The Politics of Bureaucratic Socialism* (Ithaca: Cornell University Press, 1993), p. 154.

52. *HNM*, "Công bố kết quả bầu cử và danh sách trúng cử đại biểu HĐND thành phố khoá X" [Official results of elections and list of elected representatives of the Tenth City People's Council], 24 November 1989, pp. 1, 4.

53. Phan Trung Lý, "Suy nghĩ về kết quả bầu cử đại biểu hội đồng nhân dân ba cấp" [Thoughts about results of the 3-level People's Council elections], *Người Đại Biểu Nhân Dân*, No. 9, May–June 1990, p. 45.

54. Minh Ngọc, "Điều mong muốn chính đáng" [A legitimate wish], *HNM*, 3 November 1989, p. 2.

55. Fieldnotes 16 May 1997. Italics are mine.

56. Đào Quang Cát, "Về danh sách ứng cử viên" [About the list of candidates], *HNM*, 3 November 1989, p. 2.

57. Adrian Edwards, "Former S. Vietnam Soldier elected to Assembly", Reuters, 28 July 1997.

58. SRV, Quy trình hiệp thương lựa chọn, giới thiệu những người ứng cử đại biểu Hội đồng nhân dân (Ban hành kèm theo Công văn số 193CV/MTTW ngày 2/8/1994) [Process of selecting and introducing candidates for election to people's council — Appendix to Circular 193CV/MTTW dated 2 August 1994].

59. Interview with Phùng Văn Tửu published in the *Đại Đoàn Kết* newspaper, in Reuters, "Assembly Vice-Chairman views People's Council elections", 21 September 1994.

60. David Thurber, "Vietnam votes for National Assembly", Associated Press, 19 May 2002.

61. *Vietnam Express*, "Nội dung chính và những điều còn tranh cãi trong Luật Bầu cử đại biểu HĐND" [Main contents and remaining controversies in the Law on Election of People's Councils], 5 July 2003, http://vnexpress.net/Phap-luat/2003/07/3B9C96B7/. Nghĩa Nhân, "Thu hút đông đảo nhân dân tham gia, giám sát bầu cử" [Attract the people to participate in and supervise elections], *Vietnam Express*, 8 January 2004, http://vnexpress.net/Vietnam/Phap-luat/2004/01/3B9CEC98/.

62. Việt Anh, "Gần 2,000 ứng cử viên bị loại khỏi danh sách bầu cử" [Close to 2,000 nominees removed from electoral roll], *VN Express*, 21 April 2004, http://vnexpress.net/Vietnam/Xa-hoi/2004/04/3B9D1DF5/.

63. See Note 59.

64. Fieldnotes, 17 November 1996.

65. Murray Hiebert, "Letting off steam", *Far Eastern Economic Review*, 30 July 1992, p. 10.

66. Voice of Vietnam, "Vietnam officially announces election results", 27 May 2002.

67. L.H., "DBSCL: Dự kiến 50% chủ tịch HĐND, UBND các cấp tái cử" [Mekong Delta: 50% of People's Council and Committee Chairmen of all levels could be re-elected], *Lao Động*, 24 February 2004, No. 55, http://www.laodong.com.vn/pls/bld/folder$.view_item_detail(93584).

68. Huy Giang, "Chỉ có 6 đại biểu trẻ dưới 35 tuổi, 20 đại biểu nữ" [Only 6 youth representatives below 35 in age, and only 20 female representatives], *Tuoi Tre*, 28 April 2004, pp. 1, 3.

69. Như Trang, "Giảm 34 ứng cử viên đại biểu HĐND cấp tỉnh" [34 candidates less for provincial People's Council elections], *VN Express*, 29 March 2004, http://vnexpress.net/Vietnam/Xa-hoi/2004/03/3B9011A2/.

70. Nghĩa Nhân, "Thu hút đông đảo nhân dân tham gia, giám sát bầu cử" [Attract the people to participate in and supervise elections], *Vietnam Express*, 8 January 2004, http://vnexpress.net/Vietnam/Phap-luật/2004/01/3B9CEC98/.

71. Fieldnotes, 10 July 1997.

72. Fieldnotes, 19 July 1997.

73. *HNM*, "Cử tri thủ đô hăng hái đi bỏ phiếu bầu cử đại biểu HĐND quận, huyện, thị xã, thị trấn và phường xã" [Voters of the capital enthusiastically votes in representatives for people's councils of urban and rural districts, commune towns and towns, and wards and communes], 5 October 1981, pp. 1, 4.

74. *HNM*, "Cử tri toàn thành phố hăng hái đi bỏ phiếu bầu cử HĐND hai cấp" [Voters of the whole city enthusiastically votes in elections for two levels of people's councils], 7 May 1984, pp. 1, 4.

75. Adrian Edwards, "Hà Nội ablazed with red on eve of elections", Reuters, 21 July 1997.

76. *HNM*, "Trên 1 triệu cử tri của thủ đô đi bỏ phiếu bầu đại biểu HĐND các cấp" [More than 1.5 million voters of the capital vote for people's council representatives of all levels], 4 October 1981, p. 1.

77. In the 1950s, voting in favour of the only candidate listed on the ballot papers in communist countries meant that voters only needed to insert the ballot papers into the boxes after receiving them without making any marks. Thus, entry into the voting booth to cancel names indicated openly the desire to vote against the candidate. However, in Vietnam in 1997 all voters in the ward I observed entered the voting booth, which is the standard practice now that there are more candidates than seats, making cancellation of names necessary.

78. *"Cử tri không biết chữ hay vì tàn tật không thể tự ghi phiếu được có thể tùy ý nhờ người ghi hộ nhưng phải tự bỏ phiếu, nếu không thể bỏ phiếu được, cử tri có thể nhờ người bỏ giúp trước mặt mình."*

79. *HNM*, "Cuộc bầu cử có bảo đảm dân chủ hay không, quyết định ở bước hiệp thương do MTTQ đóng vai trò chính" [Whether the elections are democratic is decided at the consultations stage led by the VFF] (interview with Bùi Mạnh Trung, Vice-chairman, VFF Committee of the City of Hà Nội), 8 September 1989, p. 2.

80. Victor Zaslavsky and Robert Brym, "The Functions of Elections in the USSR", *Soviet Studies* 30, no. 3 (1978); 366; Zaslavsky and Brym, "The Structure of Poser and the Functions of Soviet Local Elections", in *Soviet Local Politics and Government*, edited by Everett M. Jacobs (London: George Allen & Unwin, 1983) p. 70.

81. Theodore H. Friedgut, *Political Participation in the USSR* (Princeton, NJ: Princeton University Press, 1979), p. 115.

82. "Báo cáo" (Report) by Mr C, chairman of the polling station, 21 July 1997.

83. *Lao Động*, "Hà Nội, TP Hồ Chí Minh, Khánh Hoà và nhiều tỉnh, thành phố đạt tỷ lệ bầu cử cao" [Hà Nội, Hồ Chí Minh City, Khánh Hoà and many provinces, cities achieved high election turnout], 23 July 1992, p. 1.

84. *Lao Động*, "Cử tri Hà Nội" [Hanoian voters], 23 July 1992, pp. 1, 2.

85. N. Linh, Đức Quang, "Huỷ bỏ cuộc bầu cử tại một số đơn vị, khu vực" [Election results in a few electoral units rescinded], *Tuổi Trẻ*, 5 May 2004, http://www.tuoitre.com.vn/Tianyon/PrintView.aspx?ArticleID=31498&ChannelID=3.

86. Việt Anh, Thiên Nguyên, Lê Cương, "Bầu cử lại tại một số địa phương" [Elections at a few localities to be reorganized], *VN Express*, 9 May 2004, http://vnexpress.net/Vietnam/Xa-hoi/2004/05/3B9D2611/.

87. Zslavsky and Brym, "The Functions of Elections in USSR", pp. 367–68.

4

Wards' Implementation of the Pavement Order Regime in Hà Nội

Since the early 1980s, many people in Hà Nội have taken to the pavement to sell goods and services. They include many former state employees, and they do so for basic livelihood and to supplement income. These needs came hard and fast in the mid and late 1980s, the years of hyperinflation and economic restructuring. The biggest blow to the economy then was the drastic reduction of the state sector, which had provided most, if not all, the employment in Vietnam. Here went a four-liner that slightly exaggerated and teased:

On one end of the street, a senior colonel pumps tires
On the other end, a lieutenant colonel sells black beans dessert
Thought he was a stranger but turned out a friend as we went near —
Our brigadier presses a horn to sell ice-cream.[1]

People in Hà Nội were joined by roaming vendors (*hàng rong*), who came into the city from the villages to peddle farm produce, especially after 1988.[2] In addition, though mainly in the older parts of the city where housing space for each family was tight, many Hà Nội residents reluctantly did their personal, family, and business chores on the pavement, including activities such as washing, cooking, recreation, and storing and displaying goods. A journalist of the *Hà Nội Mới* (*HNM*) newspaper criticized a typical scene he saw, whereby the pavement, a public space, became a yard for many families:

Around the [submerged] water tanks on the pavement many thoughtless and shocking acts take place that hardly show the refinement of Tràng An [an old alias of Hà Nội] people! Foreign guests walk by and are very surprised because they have never seen, in the capital of any country in this world, a stranger method to keep water. People even turn the pavement around the water tanks into their own private yard and do anything they want without a thought for others. They brush their teeth; wash their faces in the morning. They wash rice and vegetables at noon and in the evening. In time, they also do their laundry and bathe right there -- first the children, then the adults ...

I have gone past these "yards under the sky". The men would be in shorts, top-naked, and the women and girls in untidy clothes. There was even one woman who rolled her pants up above her knees and helped her son to wash up. The sound of splashing water echoed around. All types of clothes, mats, and blankets were brought out for the wash. The sound of women scolding their children inter-mixed with shouts at husbands. Dirty water flowed all over the pavement. Pedestrians felt discomfort as they found no places to land their feet and therefore had to walk on the street, which made them easy victims of vehicles.[3]

These spontaneous vending and household activities make scenes on the pavements of Hà Nội more colourful, but they have had consequences for traffic safety. Many pedestrians prefer to walk on the road because those pavement activities interrupt their walks on many busy streets (see Figure 4.1 and 4.2). Pavement vending also causes interruptions and obstructions that are hazardous to traffic when many motorists stop to make purchases. Therefore, streets and pavements crowded with vending and household activities are more likely to cause traffic jams and accidents. Increased pavement vending, combined with huge increases in the number of vehicles on the road, poor driving habits, and poor road infrastructure, were partly responsible for a big increase in the number of traffic accidents, especially serious and fatal ones.

Given these imperatives, the Vietnamese party-state has been enforcing order on the pavement in Hà Nội, with mixed results. We know of this effort through a large number of newspaper reports about party-state and public dissatisfaction with traffic and pavement disorder in Hà Nội. Two major campaigns, in 1986 and 1991, achieved much less than ideal results. The government was disoriented and merely coping until the third major campaign in 1995 managed to restore some sort of order. Since then, the good situation in the inner parts of the city of Hà Nội has been maintained, especially in areas where the population densities are the highest, and the traffic conditions most congested. The results have also been uneven when comparisons are made across wards. Some wards do better through the day and even into the night, whereas some others witnessed enormous amounts of disorder throughout the day. On the other hand, in a very few

FIGURE 4.1
Fruit vendors occupying pavement.

FIGURE 4.2
A vendor carrying out business on pavement.

areas where important people of the country live and work, such pavement and traffic disorders are unheard of.

The question at the heart of this chapter is: why has a supposedly pervasive and penetrating Vietnamese party-state been unable to enforce the pavement regime consistently and thoroughly? Three explanations are explored.

The first explanation is that perhaps the Vietnamese party-state did not want to be thorough. In the early 1980s the party-state was aware of the difficulties people faced in the difficult times. In early traffic and pavement order campaigns of the 1980s, it was willing to allow some degree of vending on the pavement, although it also insisted that the pavement regime must be respected. In the two campaigns of the 1990s, this awareness became embedded in pavement and traffic order regulations, which instructed local authorities to make exceptions where necessary and to reserve some pavement and road space for vending. In the process, however, for various reasons some local authorities were too liberal in their interpretation of the exceptions to be allowed.

A second explanation could be that in the traffic and pavement order campaigns, the party-state had relied too much on mobilization and education, and too little on actual enforcement to condition good habits of pavement usage. This tendency had some limitations in economically difficult times, when the objective of behavioural change competed poorly for attention with urgent measures required to secure livelihood and market conveniences. For instance, vendors had no choice but to vend on the pavement because there were no markets for them to congregate in; vending on the pavement incurred less fixed costs, and consumers wanted their services as well. Apparently, the benefits of vending illegally outweigh the costs of the occasional fine.

A third explanation is the one I wish to focus on in this chapter. It is weak implementation by the ward level party-state machinery. Ward officials have been asked to restore and maintain order on the pavement. They have to prevent roaming vendors from trading on busy streets, and restrict non-pedestrian use of pavement space by residents. Campaigns to restore order to the pavement usually started well, indicating the willingness of ward officials to carry out orders when supervision of upper levels was strong. The campaigns, however, usually fizzled out after a few months, returning the pavement and streets to the pre-campaign chaotic state. Implementation lacked consistency and persistence.

The reason behind wards' lack of consistency and persistence is the conflicting demands placed on their role as implementers. Ward officials have obligations to the party-state and residents who want a more orderly street. In principle, they can be strict with people who offend the pavement regime, because decision-making about implementation of the pavement regime in their jurisdiction is completely in their hands. But bureaucratic dominance is not the only determinant of decision-making in the ward; when implementing pavement order campaigns, ward officials have also been influenced by personal gains, by their personal ties with residents, and by their feelings for those who need pavement activities to survive. They are aware of the links between political stability and street order; thus, there is some political utility for the party-state in allowing ward officials to mediate for vendors, both roaming and fixed types. Ward officials may allot more mediation space to residents who are in genuine difficulties, who need exemption from the pavement regime in order to survive. This measure helps to maintain jobs for the needy and contribute to political stability. This balance between conflicting demands is seen in answers to the question why the ward officials of Phương the noodle seller (see her story in Chapter 1), enforced the law against her only occasionally and ignored her activities on most days. Ward officials then accounted for them as their right to make those exceptions in policy implementation for the very good reason of moral economy that even the highest levels of government would support.

This chapter emphasizes the role of the ward authorities in trying to achieve a balance. It starts with an outline of how the traffic and pavement situation evolved after 1975, which sets the socioeconomic, and also political, context that ward officials operate in. Campaign by campaign, I will then outline how wards implemented the traffic and pavement order campaigns and explore the reasons why the campaigns could not be consistent and persistent. I will attempt to draw out the salient reasons for repeated pavement disorder. I end the chapter by highlighting the conceptual implications of mediation by ward officials in the pavement order regime.

THE SERIOUS TRAFFIC SITUATION
AFTER 1975 AND ITS CAUSES

There are many causes for the serious traffic situation after 1975. Some of the causes are direct, while others are indirect but provide the context in which the direct causes, one of which is pavement activities, are played out.

One reason that has directed the Vietnamese government to install traffic and pavement campaigns has been the high losses of lives and serious injuries caused by the increasing number of traffic accidents. As shown in to Table 4.1, the number of traffic accidents, the number of deaths and injury to persons in traffic accidents that occurred in Hà Nội rose rapidly from 1991 and made a big leap in 1995. A similar trend is observed nationwide (Table 4.2). Compared with figures on all accidents in the whole country in the years when a direct comparison is possible (such as the years 1991, 1995, 1996) the number of accidents, deaths, and people injured in Hà Nội comprised from 10 to 20 per cent of corresponding phenomena at the national level.

Authorities often cite bad driving habits and disregard for traffic rules and regulations as the direct causes of accidents. In between 1981 and 1997, the following causes of traffic accidents dominated: speeding (34 per cent), failure to observe rules (12 per cent), and drunk driving (12 per cent).[4]

The indirect causes of accidents in Hà Nội have been the lack of road space and pavement space. In 1981 roads took up only a 6 per cent share of the total built-up area of the city. A Vietnamese source claimed this share was low when compared with 15 to 20 per cent in many other foreign cities.[5] By 1994, the share increased in Hà Nội, but only to 8 per cent.[6] In Hà Nội, very seldom do new urban areas constructed after 1954 have pavement spaces as wide as those seen in the "Western" urban areas ("Western" meaning that they were planned and constructed during the colonial period) of downtown Hà Nội. High-rise flats built from the 1960s planned for wide space in between flats but later residents took much of the space over for private purposes.

Compounding the problem of constricted road space since the mid-1980s, there has been a very strong preference among Vietnamese for private over public transport, and for motorized over pedal vehicles. The trend has been related to increases in income as well as, in the last five years, affordability of motorcycles imported from China. Table 4.3 correlates income levels to changes in use of state-owned transport services and private transport means, up to the year of 1995. In 1997 the share of passenger traffic among the different medium of transport within Hà Nội was: motorcycles 60.3 per cent, bicycles 30 per cent, taxis 2 per cent, three-wheeled motorcycle taxis 1.8 per cent, buses 1.5 per cent, and the

TABLE 4.1
Traffic Accidents Resulting in Deaths and Injury in Hà Nội

Year	No. of accidents	No. of deaths	No. of injured
1983–87		935 (average 186/year)	
1988 (Jan – June)	283	100	176
1991 (Jan – June)	307	129	234
1993	657	243	608
1994	653	297	424
1995	3,100	1,249	2,326
1996	3,321	314	3,434
1997	2,985	304	3,136
1998	2,614	281	2,970
2003	1,418	549	1,138
2004 (Jan–Jun)	787	262	755

Sources: Phan Tương, "Trật tự và an toàn giao thông của thành phố hiện nay" [Traffic order and safety in the city at present], HNM, 8 September 1982, p. 2; Nguyễn Thành Lập, "Độ phức tạp tại các nút giao thông trong thành phố" [The complexity of the traffic junctions in the City], HNM, 2 November 1988, p. 2; HNM, "Tai nạn giao thông chưa giảm" [Traffic accidents have not decreased], 9 August 1988, p. 1; Văn Thành, "Tai nạn giao thông vẫn là nỗi lo của mọi nười" [Traffic accidents are still everybody's worry], HNM, 30 August 1991, p. 3; Kim Liên,"Tuyên truyền nhiều nhưng trật tự an toàn giao thông vẫn kém" [Much mass education but traffic order and safety still far from ideal], HNM, 11 May 1994, p. 2; Bùi Văn Sưởng, "Hà Nội có những chuyển biến tốt" [Hanoi sees positive changes], HNM, 5 June 1996, p. 3; Vũ Đình Hoành, "Làm gì để thực hiện Nghị Định 36/CP của Chính phủ có hiệu quả cao?" [What is to be done to ensure implementation of 36/CP of the government is highly effective?], HNM, 1 August 1995, pp. 1, 4; Nguyễn Mẫn, "Tai nạn giao thông vẫn cần nhắc lại" [Need to remind people about traffic safety], Lao Động Hà Nội, 18 April 1997, p. 8; information for the years 1997 to 1998 provided by an informant working in An Ninh Thủ Đô newspaper, e-mail 27 February 1999; Quang Hiếu "Chính thức đề nghị tạm ngừng đăng ký xe máy tại 5 quận còn lại" [Formal request to stop registration of motorcycles in 5 remaining Districts], Lao Động, no. 51, 20 February 2004, http://www.laodong.com.vn/pls/bld/folder$.view_item_detail(93296); Quang Hiếu, "6 tháng gần 300 người chết vì TNGT" [300 dead in traffic accidents in 6 months], Lao Động Điện Tử, 12 June 2004, No. 194, http://www.laodong.com.vn/pls/bld/folder$.view_item_detail(106559).

TABLE 4.2
Traffic Accidents Resulting in Deaths and Injury in Vietnam

Year	No. of accidents	No. of deaths	No. of injured
1978–1980	3,664 (average 1,221/year)	397 (average 132/year	3,001 (average 1,000/year)
1987	5,517	2,549	6,033
1988	4,497	2,776	5,871
1989 (Jan – Mar)	791	591	1,123
1991 (Jan – June)	3,149	1,223	2,974
1992	>8,000		
1995	15,376	5,430	16,920
1996	19,638	5,962	21,718
1997	>20,000	6,152	>22,000
1998	19,975	6,067	22,700
1999	21,420	>7,000	<24,000
2000	23,184	7,882	25,678
2001	26,874	10,548	30,175
2002	29,933	13,186	25,953
2003	20,738	11,800	>19,000

Sources: Trọng Nghĩa, "Có thể bảo đảm an toàn giao thông được không?" [Can traffic safety be assured?], *HNM*, 24 July 1981, p. 3; Nguyễn Quang Hoà, "Có thể giảm tai nạn giao thông?" [Can traffic accidents be reduced?], *HNM*, 20 January 1989, p. 3; P.V.,"Tai nạn giao thông vẫn còn nghiêm trọng" [Traffic accidents still at serious level], *HNM*, 14 July 1989, p. 3; Văn Thành, "Tai nạn giao thông vẫn là nỗi lo của mọi người" [Traffic accidents are still everybody's worry], *HNM*, 30 August 1991, p. 3; Nguyễn Xuân Yêm, "Vi phạm hành chính và công tác giáo dục ý thức, lối sống theo pháp luật cho công dân" [Administrative offences and work on education for citizens to cultivate consciousness and way of life that respect the law], in *Xây dựng ý thức và lối sống theo pháp luật* [Build consciousness and way of life that respect the law], edited by Đào Trí Úc [Hà Nội: Đề tài KHCN cấp Nhà nước KX-07-17, 1995], p. 216; Hồng Vy, "Tai nạn giao thông đường bộ chưa giảm" [Road traffic accidents have not decreased], *HNM*, 19 February 1997, p. 2; Minh Tuấn, "Mục tiêu chủ yếu của Nghị Định 36/CP vẫn chưa thực hiện được" [The main objective of 36/CP has not been achieved], *Lao Động,* 4 March 1997, p. 3; Xinhua News Agency, "Traffic accidents claim 15 lives a day in Vietnam", 6 July 1998, carried by Reuters, 6 July 1998; Vietnam Economic News, "Road Accidents Now Claim 6,000 Lives Per Year", carried by Reuters, 7 July 1999; Vietnam Economic News, "21,420 traffic accidents reported in 1999", 7 January 2000; Xuân Quyết, "Thêm một cách nhìn về tai nạn giao thông" [One more way to look at traffic accidents], *Nhân Dân*, 8 February 2001, pp. 1, 5; Xinhua News Agency, "Traffic accidents in Vietnam rise in 2001", 31 December 2001, Chu Thượng, "Tăng cường xử lý nghiêm minh" [Strengthen enforcement], *Lao Động,* 11 November 2002, http://www.laodong.com.vn/pls/bld/display$.htnoidung(46,50352); Deutsche Presse-Agentur, "Traffic fatalities in Vietnam down 10 per cent in 2003", 23 December 2003; AFP, "More than 11,800 killed in Vietnam road accidents in 2003", 3 January 2004; Quang Hiếu, "Vi phạm tăng, tai nạn cũng tăng" [Offences and accidents increased], *Lao Động Điện Tử,* No. 110, 19 April 2004, http://www.laodong.com.vn/pls/bld/folder$.view_item_detail(98743).

TABLE 4.3
National Income/National Product Growth Rates Correlated
with Changes in Rate of Use of State-Owned and
Private Vehicles Nationally

Year	National income/ product growth rate[a] %	No. of passenger trips using private vehicles (million)	No. of passenger trips using state-owned vehicles (million)	No. of passengers on 1+ trips using state-owned vehicles (million)	No. of passengers on 1+ trips using private vehicles (million)
1985	5.7	104.0	275.0	11,215	2,272
1986	0.3	120.2	268.4	12,700	2,683
1987	3.6	135.5	284.8	13,716	3,001
1988	6.0	150.9	268.1	11,825	3,352
1989	4.7	171.7	177.6	8,002	3,718
1990	5.1	193.4	133.4	6,191	5,639
1991	6.0	325.8	110.7	6,875	6,040
1992	8.6	396.0	97.0	8,191	6,409
1993	8.1	457.5	58.9	8,373	6,899
1994	8.8	491.5	64.0	8,968	7,789
1995	8.8 (est)	535.6 (est)	66.8 (est)	9,965 (est)	8,485 (est)

Note:

a. Before 1986, the concept used by the source was "national income", and after 1986 it
   was "national product".

Source: Tổng Cục Thống Kê, *Động thái và thực trạng kinh tế - xã hội Việt Nam qua 10
năm Đổi Mới (1986–1995)* [Socio-economic dynamics and realities in Vietnam after 10
years of Đổi Mới, 1986–1995] (Hà Nội: NXB Thống Kê, 1996), pp. 5, 9, 12, 396, 399.

rest (4.4 per cent) was taken up by other types of vehicles.[7] In Hà Nội
and Hồ Chí Minh City, the share of public transport in transport needs
ranged from only 3 to 7 per cent, in 2001.[8] Corresponding to these figures
were huge increases in the population of motorcycles, much more than
increases in other means of transport since early 1980s. Table 4.4 shows
that compared with the situation in 1954, the motorized vehicular population
in Hà Nội in 1981 and 1994 had increased by around 50 times and 333
times respectively. The increase in 1994 over 1981 was 28 times, and

TABLE 4.4
Vehicle Population in Hà Nội

Year	Private car	Car Taxis	Motorcycle	Bicycles	Trishaws and pulled bicycles
1954		1,500		50,000+	"A few hundred"
1981	18,000		56,648	600,000	2,000
1990	8,319		212,302		
1993	16,232		380,917		
1994	50,000		406,000		more than 10,000
1996	52,051		492,190		
1997	60,200 (including 200 buses)	1,200	600,000+	1,000,000	8,000 (trishaws only)
2000	92,000		700,000	1,000,000	6,000
2002 (9)	109,932		1,076,581	1,000,000	6,000

Sources: Trọng Nghĩa, "Có thể bảo đảm an toàn giao thông được không?" [Can traffic safety be assured?], *HNM*, 24 July 1981, p. 3; Vũ Minh, "Hãy cố gắng khắc phục nguyên nhân chủ quan" [Let's try to overcome the subjective causes], *HNM*, 19 April 1981, p. 3; Trần Sơn, "Đỗ xe ở Hà Nội – bài toán nan giải" [Parking in Hanoi – a complex problem], *Pháp luật và đời sống*, 28 October 1996; Bùi Văn Sướng, "Hà Nội có những chuyển biến tốt" [Hanoi sees positive changes], *HNM*, 5 June 1996, p. 3; Thịnh Giang, "Chẳng lẽ người Hà Nội cứ cam chịu mãi cảnh giao thông như thế này?" [Do Hanoians really want to continue to tolerate the present traffic situation?], *Nhân Dân*, 15 January 1997 pp. 1, 7; Minh Quang and Phạm Hiếu, "Chuyện trang: xíchlô Hà Nội" [Special Report: the xíchlô in Hà Nội], *Lao Động*, 15 April 1997, p. 6; Quang Hiếu and Đức Trung, "3 năm nữa ra đường chỉ còn đi ... bộ," [Three more years and there will only be space for ... walking], *Lao Động*, 7 December 2000; *Lao Động*, "Dự thảo cấm xe máy, ôtô – liệu có khả thi?" [Plan to ban motorcycles and motorcars – is it feasible?], 1 November 2002. http://www.laodong.com.vn/pls/bld/folder$.view_item_detail(49325).

motorcycles accounted for most of the increases. In 1997, the Hà Nội City authority allowed registration for an additional 6,000 motorcycles every month, which were about 72,000 motorcycles every year.[9] In comparison, the number of bicycles had increased by only twenty times between 1954 and 1997. In August 2003, Hà Nội City authorities decided to cease motorcycle registration in inner city districts as one measure to curb the rise of traffic accidents caused by traffic congestion.

Vending activities on streets and pavements in Hà Nội have also contributed to constriction of road space. Trading on the pavement is not something new. For instance, the selling of food on the pavement has been seen in Hà Nội for a long time, at least since the beginning of the twentieth century.[10] In the late 1950s, pavement food operators numbered more than 10,000 across the city.[11] With socialist economic reforms, which banned all purely private enterprises in the commerce sector, by 1960 the pavement food-stalls had largely disappeared.[12]

From the late 1970s, two other factors have been present to make pavement trading an important cause of traffic accidents. The first factor was the rapidly increased and higher speed vehicle population. That made the overflow of pavement activities and pedestrians onto the road much more likely to lead to serious or fatal accidents than before. The second factor was rapid expansion of private, pavement trading activities in the 1980s, especially the sale of second-hand goods. These activities began mushrooming in small lanes of Khâm Thiên Street. On page 48 of William S. Turley (1980) "Hanoi's Domestic Dilemmas" there is a vivid photograph of a scene of a thriving pavement market in Hà Nội in early 1978. In 1981, there were reports of new markets that were spontaneously formed on the pavement and on the side of several roads in Hà Nội.[13] In the middle of 1982, observers noted illegal pavement markets along main streets such as Ngô Thì Nhậm (where the Hôm market that sold fresh produce was located), Nguyễn Công Trứ,[14] and Trần Nhật Duật (beside the old railway station at Long Biên Bridge). Later on, the range of goods went beyond second-hand goods to the full range of fresh produce as well as cooked food, snacks, beverages, and even controlled items such as beer. Sellers took over the whole pavement, and on some streets where traffic was still not too heavy, they even traded on the streets.[15] In the Ngô Thì Nhậm Ward, vendors gathered on streets and made some of them barely passable to traffic. In the case of the Chợ Trời Market, only motorcycles could crawl between stalls. The activities there had spilled over to several other streets and roads in the vicinity.[16] A bursting out of spontaneous trading activities on the streets and pavements was witnessed in many places of the old city area, traditionally an area where petty traders congregated.[17]

Official figures on the number of private traders on the pavement are not available, but figures on the private sector's share of trade and the number of private traders as a whole may provide some clues. The share of the private sector in the total volume of trade in Hà Nội jumped from 25.8 per cent in 1975 to 50.6 per cent in 1983, showing a temporary slowdown in increases only in 1981.[18] The party-state looked upon the growth in private sector trade disapprovingly but could not stop it.[19]

After 1975, the Hà Nội City authority repeatedly promulgated pavement and traffic regulations, beginning with 971 QĐ/UBHC of April 1981. In particular, in 1984, for the first time the city authority stated that pavements were for walking on; other uses must have approval from the Hà Nội Department of Transportation and Urban Public Works (Sở Giao thông Công Chính, henceforth GTCC) and would be charged a fee. That indicated the beginning of state efforts to deal with the pavement problem. Before 1995, there had been at least three significant national campaigns to mobilize the people to help keep the streets clear and traffic orderly.

THE FIRST TWO TRAFFIC AND PAVEMENT ORDER CAMPAIGNS: 1983 – DECEMBER 1991

The first known large-scale campaign which had a traffic and pavement order component in the post-1975 era in Hà Nội was one called "Tidy houses, Clean streets, Beautiful capital" (*Gọn nhà — sạch phố — đẹp thủ đô*) in 1983. It was a part of the national "Cultured way of life, New culture families" (*Nếp sống văn minh, gia đình văn hoá mới*) campaign to imbue persons and families with socialist culture. Clearing the pavements for pedestrians was one of many objectives of the Hà Nội campaign.[20] Ward authorities in Hà Nội had responsibility for implementation and enforcement, with the help of their self-defence militia and mass organizations. Pavement appropriators and squatters were given reprieves and a deadline to clear out. Not much else is known about this campaign unfortunately, but at that time the traffic situation was not as serious it was in later years.

In 1986 the national government started a new pavement and traffic order campaign called "404". No reason was given officially for the campaign but it was probably a response to the worsening traffic order situation. The 404 campaign, named after the serial number of the government directive, mandated every ward in Hà Nội to set up a "Team 404". Each team consisted of ward officials, including the police, public works, and market management sections; neighbourhood leaders such as party cell and resident group leaders and mass organization representatives within the ward. The policemen received their orders directly from the district; they then co-ordinated their work with the 404 teams.[21]

The tone of implementation, however, was to educate rather than punish; ward authorities sought to establish practices in each resident cluster that promoted education, awareness, as well as peer pressure. Resident group heads and mass organization representatives briefed households under their charge of the traffic rules and penalties, and what to do or not do within their locality. Another method used was mobilization by mass organizations and neighbourhood leaders. For instance, the Hồ Chí Minh Youth Group roped in its members to patrol the streets (around thirty members per ward) during the peak hours of traffic.[22] Mobilization was only reinforced with regular patrols by a team of regular ward inspectors, directed by the police.

PROBLEMS OF THE 1983 — DECEMBER 1991 CAMPAIGNS

In 1988, the city legislated heftier fines for offences against its "Regulations on fines for traffic order and safety in the City of Hà Nội", indicating that a stronger deterrent was required and the pavement and traffic situation probably got worse.[23] Also reflecting the situation were vigorous complaints from journalists about the huge growth in number of pavement vendors who operated without licences from the city authority. The GTCC, the city-level agency responsible for overseeing implementation of 404, was criticized for the worsening situation.[24] A GTCC official explained to the *HNM* that his office was short of hands, and sometimes pavement situations were out of control and had to be ignored. However, the media and the public were of the view that the disorder on the pavement was due to the GTCC and the ward administrators, especially the ward police "selling" pavement space. GTCC and ward officials, according to critics, were turning a blind eye in exchange for bribes for the individual law enforcers or kickbacks for their organizations.[25]

Corruption, however, was only part of the picture. At least four other reasons explain why the situation worsened. First, the GTCC officials were unable to cope with the growth in the number of pavement vendors. Private sector trade was legitimized after the Sixth VCP National Congress in 1986. The growth in pavement vending was also due to many people turning to trading on the pavement to fight hyperinflation and job retrenchment using the quickest, if not the most effective way. A report in *Đại Đoàn Kết* pointed out that the reality was not only that streets traditionally providing trade and services had their pavements taken over; the phenomenon was spilling over to almost all streets and roads in Hà Nội, including those that were at the periphery of the city and quiet at that time.[26] In 1991, an estimate put the pavement economy as employing 23,000 people, more than double the number of pavement breakfast operators in the late 1950s.[27] Whether to crack down strictly on unlicensed operators posed a big dilemma for authorities. Vendors on the pavement were being gainfully employed in the difficult economic environment. The vendors were of course causing much disruption in social order on the streets, but the trade-off for a more orderly pavement was fewer jobs, which would have undermined political stability.

Second, the GTCC bureaucracy was hindering applications for licences to use the pavement for trading. The bureaucratic delays they caused persuaded many pavement vendors that they should not bother with the wait to apply for official licences, and success of application was not guaranteed anyway. Instead of waiting, vendors bribed ward officials to mediate and ignore their activities. Potential licence applicants saw many unlicensed vendors not being fined or not being dealt with, or they were dealt with by the ward only periodically and sparingly; so these vendors decided that formal licences were inferior to the mediation method.[28] Some illegal vendors received special treatment based on family ties and friendship, whereas other illegal vendors paid the ward or ward officials in order to stay open for business.[29] Many vendors with neither licences nor connections were willing to be "fined" periodically, indicating that their profits were quite attractive and far outweighed the benefit of applying for a formal licence, or the cost of fines or bribes. One report said that many ward officials under-reported the number of licences issued to pavement traders; the number of actual traders on the pavement was many times more. Apparently it was also the case that many vendors, while putting in their applications to trade on the pavement, simply put the matter out of their minds and continued to trade, with or without approval.[30]

Third, law enforcers were also facing stiff resistance from pavement vendors, many of whom persisted on the pavement because there were not enough proper markets that could house them.[31] Many vendors, especially roaming vendors, did not want to obtain a regular seat in the regular markets because high overheads jacked up their prices. There were also not enough places, and allocation of places usually gave priority to Hà Nội residents.[32] A policeman of the Trương Định Ward referred to the roaming vendors from the villages that faced a similar situation:

Soon, when we enforce the new regulations on fines [in 1988 for traffic and pavement order] it would be easy to deal with motorists or with people with pushcarts, but as for the women who are selling vegetables and fruits [on the pavement] in the early mornings beside the Mơ market, it would be very difficult to enforce rules. They strive to sell as much as possible so as to get back to their farm work. They could not find places in the market. When we chase after them and they move on to sit at the junctions, they then become the victims of petty thievery. Every ward is facing the same problem and trying to look for a solution.[33]

Ward policemen were also afraid of pushing the pavement people too hard. For instance, a government official said a good way of maintaining police authority on the pavement was to make sure they did not have to face challenges from both consumers and vendors at the same time, especially during the peak hour of traffic and market activity. Ward policemen thus usually operated two daily shifts to patrol the pavement. The first shift started well before six o'clock in the morning and focused on preventive action: they let roaming vendors and residents use the pavement, but asked the users to tidy up before the peak hour period — the time of the second shift — from eight to nine o'clock in the morning.[34] Furthermore, there was evidence that ward officials were collaborating with pavement traders by informing them of impending raids.

Fourth, ward officials were lax because they were responding to local needs. To them and their residents, pavement vendors brought the convenience of a large array of goods and services to their doorsteps. This convenience was important for housewives and shopkeepers who did not want to go too far to the market for their daily marketing. People who were on their way to or from work usually preferred to do their daily marketing on their motorcycles or bicycles for convenience, and they preferred to stop where there were pavement vendors rather than to park and walk into markets. They shared these interests with pavement vendors.[35] The case of Tràng Tiền Ward was an example. In that ward, a regular but illegal and disorderly fresh produce market met on Nguyễn Khắc Cần Street. Roaming vendors there often took over the whole street as well as its pavement. On average, there were two to three traffic accidents a day whose causes were traced to the market crowd. However, instead of clearing the vendors from street market, the ward made its own internal decision against city regulations to allow the market to continue operation, with the condition that it conducted business in an orderly fashion. The ward's reason was that residents in the area needed the street market, as there was no proper market in that area.[36] In another ward, officials in charge of pavement order were reported to have hidden themselves at home in order not to have to face the pavement people and be caught in the difficult position of having to enforce the law in the face of people living and working in the same neighbourhood.[37]

Poor results of implementation of the 404 campaign, therefore, was related to the overwhelming socioeconomic situation and the effectiveness of enforcement officials at the ward.

Pavement regime rules, such as requiring formal licences for vending activities, were not making life easier for various groups of people in society who needed income badly. Consequently, voices for changing the pavement regime emerged from the middle of 1990. The *HNM* reflected public opinion that the 1984 central government regulation of allowing only pedestrian activity on the pavement was unrealistic.[38] Following that, the GTCC experimented with allowing licensed vending on certain streets and lanes in Hà Nội, but not on Hà Nội's major roads. In the middle of 1991, the Hà Nội City people's council debated on GTCC's experiment and agreed the GTCC could issue licences for limited business use of the pavement. The criteria to be used by the GTCC for deciding which roads to exclude or include were the condition and width of the pavement.[39] This change in policy generated an immense response from society. Trading business licence applicants increased from only 28,000 in 1989 to 53,000 in 1991, and a large number of them applied to operate on the pavement.[40] From mid-1990 when the GTCC began its experiment until December 1991, the GTCC issued 9,000 pavement vending licences, or sixteen per day, which was about 37 per cent of the total number of pavement vendors.[41]

These city-level adaptations that softened the pavement regime were, however, reversed several months later in December 1991 by a new nationwide traffic and pavement order campaign (Decree 135/CT). To implement the national government decree, the Hà Nội City people's council issued an order called the 57/UB.

THE 57/UB (DECEMBER 1991)

The objectives of 57/UB were to prevent further growth of pavement vending and to restore order on the pavement. The city directive stopped the issuing of new pavement vending licences, except for applicants whose families were in genuine financial difficulties. Furthermore, the 57/UB required business entities to have a shopfront if they wanted to provide services,[42] but it was clear the government could not apply the rule to thousands of petty service providers such as bicycle repairers, and motorcycle taxi drivers, just to name two of them. The policy reversals were probably caused by the fear that licensed traders would overwhelm the pavement, making the problem worse, not better. By then, licensed business users of the pavement could prove difficult to remove from the pavement, if it was ever necessary to do so.

To implement 57/UB, however, the city administration emphasized mobilization and education rather than strict enforcement. In thirty-five localities across Hà Nội where the traffic situation was particularly pressing, the city police patrolled with thirty-five "self-management teams". Each team member received 30,000 đồng per month (about US$3 at that time) for helping the police patrol streets, dealing with traffic offences and accidents, and resolving social conflicts among residents (caused by competition in the use of the pavement).[43] The teams worked only during peak hours in the morning and in the late afternoon to early evening.[44] They did not have legal powers to enforce the law; the maximum extent of their capability was to remind people of the rules and to threaten reporting the offenders who did not follow the rules.[45] The city authority also asked the wards to use a few other mobilizational methods. One method, which has stayed a feature of mobilization in the implementation of many party-state policies, was asking all residents and people in work places to sign a pledge (giấy cam kết). Its signatories acknowledged in it that a ward official of the 57/UB rules had briefed them. They promised compliance, and if they were found wanting, they had to accept punishment without complaints (because they were aware of the rules). Other than individual residents, people in workplaces, including private businesses, were also asked to sign the pledge.[46] Another method of mobilization was to use the public address system to announce daily messages, reminders, and important notices of the ward to residents. The timing of addresses was usually at half-past seven in the morning, and half-past four in the afternoon. Each address lasted about half an hour.

Effectiveness of the 57/UB

Most newspaper reports on implementation of the 57/UB by Hà Nội's wards saw immediate changes in the pavement situation for the better. The city administration claimed initial successes for the 57/UB campaign.[47] The combination of mainly mobilizational methods, peak hour direction by the police at busy junctions and roads, and daily attention from the wards and the districts extracted results. Immediately after 57/UB took effect, appropriation of the pavement almost ceased, indicating the effectiveness of the ward party-state machinery if it was focused on the job. In the Hoàn Kiếm District the transformation was particularly stark, because pavement offences and traffic disorder were most serious in this centre of trade.[48] Some wards such as Cát Linh reported a more orderly traffic situation after the self-management teams went into action.[49]

Most of the same reports, however, were pessimistic about the 57/UB campaign remaining effective for long. True enough, around three months after implementation started, complaints about the return to disorder began to pour in.[50] Wards officials were reportedly "tired" and not paying attention to the daily routines of supervision and checking on management of pavements; diligence separated wards who had implemented the 57/UB effectively from those who had not. Because of the shortage of hands, follow-up action by ward officials to maintain order was very weak.[51] A few interviews I conducted among Hà Nội's residents who witnessed the pavement situation in the early 1990s suggested at that time the pavements of streets such as Lò Đúc and Nguyễn Công Trứ were full of stalls, so much so that one could never stroll smoothly without coming across obstacles or being forced to walk on the street.[52] These two streets were, moreover, not the hottest spots of disorder in Hà Nội.

Weaknesses of the 57/UB

There were two main weaknesses of the 57/UB. The first was the unevenness of implementation. The observant noted that policy implementation had been "administratized" (*hành chính hoá*), meaning that the policy had an impact only during office hours, when ward policemen and inspectors were still present on the streets.[53] After office hours, pavement vendors came back onto the pavement in full force. Furthermore, when offenders were caught, some were dealt with strictly, while others were let off. In some wards, officials even completely ignored the pavement situation. The unevenness happened sometimes on the same street, such as when two or several wards shared one long street. For instance, on the eastern side of Lê Duẩn Road was the Cửa Nam Ward of the Hoàn Kiếm District. The ward was strict in preventing spontaneous street markets from forming around the legitimate Cửa Nam market. On the western side of the same stretch of the road 200 metres away, however, the Văn Miếu Ward of

Đống Đa District ignored disorganized markets at the entrance to the Trần Qui Cáp railway station, less than 100 meters away from the Cửa Nam Market. "This made the people have different opinions about law enforcers – that this one was good, the other was bad..."[54] Unevenness devalued the impact of mobilization, because people saw no need to obey government policies if officials played favourites. There were also indicators that the unevenness was because ward authorities "sold" pavement space, such as in Nguyễn Du Ward where the owners of a cafe took over the recreation space previously reserved for school students but they were never dealt with by the ward authority. Ward officials may have used their position to grant licences to pavement traders who were familiar people or who were relatives.[55]

While the unevenness was thought by journalists to be caused by ward officials "selling" pavement space, it was not necessarily so all the time.[56] Instead, unevenness might have reflected the contradictory pulls in different directions by public opinion, city-level decision-makers, and ward implementers. Essentially the tension was about a choice between enforcing rules strictly or in a flexible manner. Some people favoured a total ban of pavement vendors, but their opposition thought a total ban meant that housewives had to walk further to satisfy daily marketing needs, and had to subject themselves to higher prices in the proper markets if there was no competition from the pavement. Furthermore, where would the pavement vendors go, and what would they do to earn a living? Housewives and vendors were happy with lax wards such as Nguyễn Du, but residents who did not earn their living on the pavement complained of congestion and disorder and wished that the Nguyễn Du Ward authority were stricter.[57]

Evidently, the wards have had a role in fine-tuning the party-state policy. According to journalists and officials, ward officials could assess the needs of each and every neighbourhood and decide whether some roaming vendors should be allowed total freedom on smaller streets at marketing hours if they were not likely to affect traffic conditions.[58] They could report on the situation to the upper levels and made suggestions to fine tune policy.

The result of such feedback led to a suggestion by the city police department to the city authority to allow some twenty street markets, which had been formed by pavement vendors, to be recognized as permanent markets. Fifty-two other such markets were classified as temporary (meaning they were illegal but tolerated) and thus also allowed to continue operations.[59] In two years of implementation, in the Hai Bà Trưng District,

62,790 pavement businesses were relocated successfully into legal markets from the pavement.[60]

Part of the "credit" for the continued freedom of pavement vendors went to the vendors themselves. Because of their experience with previous campaigns, most vendors were able to gain the upper hand over policemen and inspectors. They adopted a wait-and-see attitude when the 57/UB began;

> several days after the [57/UB] campaign started, at the stalls that had appropriated [the pavement], at the sheds that had been taken apart, their owners used nylon [sheets] to cover or close up temporarily. Who can be sure that the sheds would not become active again, or return to these places, when the private businesses [insist to] carry on displaying their wares for sale at the same places as well?[61]

After the initial "hot" days of the campaign were over, pavement vendors reverted to their old ways, slowly and cautiously.[62] Using a method similar to the way people built illegal sheds and houses on public land,

> They appropriated upon the pavement using the "impose and extend" method, a little bit every day, and slowly becoming bolder, making the situation "comfortable to the eye" not just to the business owners but also to enforcement personnel as well. When the latter bothered to stop and look closely, the pavement was already full of goods. Everybody wanted to expand their spaces, people fought with each other for places to sit that caused disorder, traffic jams, and traffic accidents. Ward police numbers were just too few and spread too thin, and they were often ineffective.[63]

A survey done in two Hà Nội wards (not mentioned by name in the source) by the Hà Nội Police Department in 1992 revealed that 100 per cent of vendors gathered in illegal markets, on pavements and streets in those two wards showed "lack of concern" (*không quan tâm*) for the 57/UB, and 35 per cent of respondents knowingly offended rules that prohibited pavement vending.[64]

The situation in 1994 was worrisome to the government. In 1993 as well as 1994 the accident figures showed that, on average, every five days in Hà Nội traffic accidents killed four persons and injured six.[65] In the first half of 1995, the number of traffic accidents in Hà Nội ballooned to 3,100 while the number of dead and injured persons was 1,429, and 2,326 respectively. These figures, if correct, meant an average of thirteen traffic accident deaths per day in those six months. The government linked the worsening situation to pavement vending, with a new government campaign, the 36/CP, continuing to target pavement vendors as a cause of traffic accidents.[66]

THE 36/CP (MAY 1995)

The preparatory work for the 36/CP was extensive. The government promulgated the decree in late May 1995 but, in contrast to the style of implementation in past campaigns, delayed the effective date till 1 August 1995. It was to give people and state agencies more time to prepare and get used to the new campaign. During the month of transition, the mass media did its part by holding special programmes and quizzes to promote awareness. Everyday, television stations fed audiences with traffic rules and news on the major traffic events. The government also used long-established propaganda methods, such as putting up huge posters, hanging red banners with slogans across streets, and erecting painted panels on all major roads.[67] A 36/CP Steering Committee was established at every level of state administration and every government agency.[68] The 36/CP was implemented at all levels well before the effective date; in the approximately two months leading up to the effective date of 1 August 1995, all offences were forgiven. All efforts were taken to make sure that on the effective day, a fundamental change in traffic order was already in place.

In terms of market management, the 36/CP granted city authorities the right to make some exceptions on designated streets to allow display and sale of goods, although in principle all pavement and roads could only be used for the purposes of commuting and traffic. The Hà Nội administration managed to disperse twenty-one illegal street markets causing traffic jams.[69] Plans were to disperse another sixteen that had caused less urgent traffic problems, although this matter had to wait for local authorities to draw up plans on relocation of vendors, indicating possible resistance from the districts and wards who were more concerned with the livelihood and convenience issues.

At the neighbourhood level, the government continued to ask wards to use mobilization methods. Many meetings to publicize the 36/CP were carried out at that level.[70] Wards distributed materials published by the city to publicize the 36/CP, and utilized the street-level loudspeaker system to remind residents of the "dos and don'ts" at particular points of congestion in the wards. On a daily basis as well, groups of volunteers of the ward, especially the "storm troopers" (*đội xung kích*) patrolled streets and reminded people about pavement and traffic rules.[71] All households, especially those who had a shopfront facing the street, were asked to sign the pledge, requiring them to ensure that there was always a corridor wide enough for pedestrians to walk on.[72] During the grace period, offenders who were forgiven were asked to sign the pledge and to promise no repeat offence.[73]

But under the 36/CP, Hà Nội's wards went beyond mobilization to emphasize self-regulation at the neighbourhood levels, through further development of the "self-management" model. Making households responsible for the portion of the pavement in front of their houses is a method already mentioned. Several other variants of the "self-management" teams, first used under the 57/UB, also appeared. One variant was called the "self-managed family groups" (*nhóm liên gia tự quản*). Each of these mutual-help and self-policing groups consisted of between seven to ten neighbouring households. Its members adopted rules of the 36/CP as well as, where necessary, provided separate rules based on agreements among themselves to tackle special pavement order problems specific to the group's area. With the backing of the ward's authority, these groups were able to enforce 36/CP rules on fellow residents. In this way, the police were kept out, and minor offences were dealt with within the group. The authorities hoped that such self-policing would cultivate considerate pavement habits for the future,[74] and no doubt they also hoped to be relieved of some work. The same self-management method was extended to private businesses, and state agencies and enterprises.[75] Another variant of "self-management" was an "alliance" between schools and the ward authority to deal with traffic and pavement problems caused by schools. Most schools of Hà Nội are located on narrow streets and the crowd of students and parents in front of the school gate waiting for pickup or for friends pose traffic hazards and jams. Learning and tuition centres also produce the same problems in the early and mid-evenings. In August 1995 the Hàng Trống Ward pioneered the "alliance" model by arranging to have the schools publicize the 36/CP and using citizen education periods to promote compliance. The schools informed the ward of the timing of end of school days and even arranged for parents to pick up their children at a place that was further away from the school, but possessed wider space for parking and waiting. The schools helped the wards by spacing out the dismissal times at fifteen minute intervals.[76]

Effectiveness of the 36/CP

One member of the public commented that the 36/CP was the best public policy ever implemented in terms of effectiveness because it had the personal attention of the Prime Minister of the day.[77] Indeed, in its first month the 36/CP proved much more effective than all its predecessors and much credit went to its intensive and extensive preparations. The Minister for Traffic and Transport noted that the 36/CP had created a mood of voluntary compliance, something that the government had failed to accomplish in the past. The good result was unexpected (*bất ngờ*).[78] Most of the newspaper reports on implementation of the 36/CP in Hà Nội noted its success. Many foreigners on return visits to Hà Nội after the 36/CP started have told me that traffic order and cleanliness had improved tremendously. The success of the 36/CP could be measured quantitatively by the fact that in Hà Nội, one month after implementation began, there were only twenty-seven accidents, causing fourteen dead and twenty-four injured, a substantial reduction compared with monthly averages before the 36/CP was implemented.[79]

Limitations of the 36/CP

However, the media and members of the public also did not believe that the good, orderly situation in the early days of the 36/CP would last, even though generally people supported the policy. They called the expected phenomenon "elephant head, rat tail" (*đầu voi đuôi chuột*), a term that described something that started with a bang but never followed up or done thoroughly.[80] That worry was later proven valid. Two months into the campaign, many readers of the *HNM* wrote in to complain that streets and pavements of Hà Nội had become disorderly again. In many places, vendors and residents again openly flouted rules right under street signs of prohibition.[81] After adopting a "wait-and-see" attitude for two months, during which they stayed low, unlicensed vendors cautiously re-emerged. Their new setups became more modest and mobile so as to be ready for any police swoop that they no doubt kept a keen look-out for.[82] Upon seeing the police within 50 metres away, they packed up quickly and dashed for the small lanes, or got up and pretended to be walking and carrying their products somewhere, which was not an offence. In the evenings when dusk fell, however, fresh produce sellers usually could stand on street corners without fear of being harassed by police. Policemen and "self-management" team members did not work overtime, so cooked food stalls usually emerged in the evening to take advantage of "administratization".[83] Basically at certain times of day and in the night, the pavement was unaffected by the 36/CP. I frequently observed implementation of 36/CP around the Ngô Thì Nhậm, Đồng Nhân, Nguyễn Công Trứ wards, the Hàng Da and Hôm markets, and within the city centre. I found that the police and "self-management" teams were very active between eight o'clock and eleven o'clock in the morning and between four o'clock and six o'clock in the evening. They were usually not seen at all in these areas at other hours.

The city police department did informal surveys across the whole city five months after the 36/CP began, and found that all pavements on 180 streets surveyed usually saw the pavement economy came back to life in the early mornings and late evenings.[84] Evidently, the local authorities have no choice but to allow the situation to return to spontaneity after office hours because of the lack of manpower.

Here, I would like to divide up the analysis of reasons for the limitations of the campaign into those that pertain specifically to the 36/CP and those that underlain every major traffic order policy in the city of Hà Nội.

FACTORS SPECIFIC TO THE 36/CP

One of the problems with the 36/CP was that while the high level of fines was meant to deter offenders, this had no effect on the intention of vendors to trade on the pavement. Because the minimum fine was 50,000 đồng, roaming vendors who sold cheap fresh produce usually did not bother to retrieve their goods after the goods were confiscated. The cost of their products was less than 50,000 đồng, a more bearable loss than the fines when we consider that their daily profit was only 10,000 to 20,000 đồng.[85] Furthermore, because inspection work was uneven and irregular, vendors knew that if they kept off the well-inspected streets during office hours and were sharp enough, they stood a good chance of not ever being caught. Even when the policemen were on hand, they were able to wrangle with the police in order to free themselves.

While people applauded efforts to clear the pavements and make roads safer, many people were also unhappy with the many inconveniences the 36/CP caused. People had to take care of how they parked their vehicles to keep the walkways clear, when before there was no such need and nobody

FIGURE 4.3
Properly parked motorcycles. The white dotted line provides
demarcation for parking on the pavement.

had any authority to tell them how to park their vehicles (see Figure 4.3). People could no longer carry out activities on the pavement that they would rather not do within their homes — such as washing of vehicles or clothes. Even though they could still do so at night, after office hours, the day restriction was inconvenient. Businesses could no longer use the pavement as their daytime warehouses or workshops. Having to move things into the house during the day limited the scale of their business and pushed them against size constraints within the house.[86] At the household level, the 36/CP also reduced convenience for some housewives because not every street and ward allowed vendors.

The view from the ward was that it was given a huge task impossible to enforce properly and faithfully without adequate manpower. "Administratization" and unevenness in implementation were related to inadequate compensation for ward policemen and ward patrol team members. For example, a member of the "self-management team" — not considered a state employee — in 1995 was paid 200,000 đồng per month.

TABLE 4.5

Approximate Salary Levels of a Sample of Ward Officials and Some Other Low-Salary Earners in Non-Ward Employment

Job	Approximate official salary per month (*đồng, 1997*)
Trishaw drivers	300,000 to 500,000
Roaming vendors	300,000 and above (10,000 to 20,000 per day)
Road sweepers	700,000 to 1,000,000
State cadres	200,000 starting salary (Head of a section got around 450,000)
Ward policemen	300,000 onwards (A policeman in service for about 10 years already receive close to 1 million per month)
Chairman of people's committee	390,000 (after twenty years of service)
Ward doctor	300,000 (about five to ten years of service)
Resident group head	50,000
Assistant resident group head	30,000
Ward party secretary	450,000 (more than twenty years of service)
Party cell secretary	30,000
Retirees	200,000 (retired senior ranks from the armed services, such as a Senior Colonel (*Đại tá*) got about 1,000,000 đồng)

Note: Jobs in italics are directly in party-state employment. Road sweepers are employed by state companies and I consider them to be indirectly under state employment.
Source: For trishaw drivers, see Minh Quang and Phạm Hiếu, "Chuyện trang: Xích lô Hà Nội" (Special Report: The Xíchlô in Hà Nội), *Lao Động,* 15 April 1997, p. 6. For road sweepers, see Thu Thủy, "Xíchlô thành phố Hồ Chí Minh sau một năm cấm đường" (The Trishaw in Hồ Chí Minh City after one year of road ban), *Lao Động,* 21 December 1996, p. 6. The figures for the others were gathered through interviews and conversations with ward officials and many friends who were state cadres.

Compare that with the "official" monthly remuneration of ward officials and some other wage earners in 1996/97, in Table 4.5.

Chapter 2 already discussed the income-expenditure gap of bureaucrats. The amount of formal income that ward officials, ward policemen, and members of the "self-management teams" earned was not enough to maintain decent living standards for a household of four persons. The open secret in Vietnam is that most party-state employees at any level of government would have some kind of side income that they spent time on after or even during office hours. For this fact, Vietnamese has an idiom that says "The outer leg is longer than the inner leg" (*Chân ngoài dài hơn chân trong*). The "outer leg" refers to the informal economy, and the "inner leg" referring to formal employment. Most officials of the ward would be no different. Furthermore, because of the lack of funds, "self-management" team members were not required to do a whole day's work, let alone overtime. Some wards even reported shortage of funds to pay overtime to policemen, or to buy printed copies of the 36/CP (each ward had to buy its own from the official publisher, the NXB Chính trị Quốc gia) to distribute to every policeman.[87]

Such a situation encouraged many pavement vendors to switch to vending at night or during certain daylight hours when ward officials paid no attention. For instance, one only needed to walk, during breakfast time as well as lunchtime, around government offices in the middle of Hà Nội to see temporary food stalls appearing on the pavement at lunchtime. Food stalls or shops also appropriated the pavement with extra tables and chairs. In fact the operator of my favourite noodles stall, Phuong, operated the whole morning and early afternoon, but between half past eight and eleven o'clock in the morning, which were the hours of police inspections, she moved into a small lane. From six o'clock to half past eight in the morning, and from eleven o'clock to two in the afternoon, she mostly operated without harassment. Her working hours were the result of an informal understanding between her and the ward on how best to balance her economic needs and the need to maintain order on the pavement. She had to meet with the leadership of the ward once a month "to work" (*làm việc*), a term for the monthly meeting with the ward to assess her situation. At the meeting, she also paid formal and informal taxes. On a 300 metres section of the Giảng Võ Street (the dyke section between the Láng Hạ junction and the Heritage Hotel), cooked food stalls took over the whole pavement when night fell till the early morning hours. The district police carried out only occasional inspections in the night. One vendor-friend along that stretch of road told me that ward policemen always acted as informants for the district's raids. In return, the ward policemen received some compensation from the pavement vendors.[88]

UNDERLYING FACTORS

The chief difficulty experienced by the Hà Nội City in ensuring order on the streets and pavements is still the road infrastructure of the city.[89] Major traffic arteries attract people to set up businesses as well as attract vendors. Therefore, expanding the present carrying capacity of roads and streets within the city heavily used by traffic is the major task. Official measurements of present road usage rate may underestimate the real situation. In 1995, a Hà Nội City official cited a government survey of 137 Hà Nội traffic junctions. This survey found that 46.3 per cent of traffic junctions had a flow rate of 300 vehicles per hour (five per minute), 34.55 per cent had 300–500 per hour (5–8.3 per minute), and 13.5 per cent had the highest range of 500–800 per hour (8.3–13.3 per minute).[90] People who have lived in Hà Nội along busy streets and know its major roads at busy hours may consider these figures low. Take my own estimation, for instance. In December 1995, at about four o'clock in the afternoon, close to evening peak hours, I stood on Lò Đúc Street, across from the walls of the then Ministry of Forestry and Development of Agriculture, to count the traffic flow rate. The road width was about six metres with traffic going in two directions. I counted an average of 60 vehicles (all types included) per minute passing in either direction. That amounted to 3,600 vehicles per hour, about four times the highest official estimate. Lò Đúc was a fairly busy street with schools, markets, lots of shops, and was a major artery linking the city centre to the southeast corner of the city.

The second major, underlying difficulty is that a vast number of people depend on pavement vending in varying degrees for their livelihood. Economic difficulties in the late 1980s forced many people to "burst out" (*bung ra*) onto the pavement to make a living or to make enough to cover what was lost through inflation. As a result, whether it was a deliberate directive from the top or merely the awareness of officials at lower levels, ward officials believed that people must be given some breathing space in these extraordinary, difficult times. One ward chairman noted that "The people can row the boat; they can overturn the boat as well … The political authority must be flexible, the people cannot take it if it is too tough."[91] At the same time, however, the policemen were also afraid to produce adverse reactions from large groups of people who depended on the pavement for livelihood, although it also depended on the ability of the vendors to stay their ground. When I asked an informant why she thought traffic order in Hà Nội was not ideal, she said that

In Vietnam, it is difficult to order people around. The law is only for people who are obedient. Those who are not obedient often have a powerful way to escape compliance. The simplest example to illustrate this difference is to contrast the women selling vegetables, with two baskets hanging from a pole, with the man selling fruits on pushbikes. When the ladies are ordered by the policemen to clear the pavement or the streets, they would usually move on. But the men, being men and stronger, could refuse. If the policemen try to use force, force would be used in return, and so the policemen have no choice but to leave those men alone. Such daily occurrences are a reminder to people that if one has power, one may stay above the law.[92]

The awareness that people cannot be pushed too hard is now evident in the decisions that the party-state makes. The 36/CP contained a provision whereby city authorities should make sure that adequate amount of pavement space is allocated to vendors to cater to marketing conveniences and livelihood for roaming vendors. On 20 October 1995, via Decision 3814/QĐ-UB, the city authority officially allowed some vendor trading on fifty-seven streets and small lanes of Hà Nội, on the condition that the conduct of vending followed five guiding principles.[93] These principles were not published but I gathered from observation they were the following: vendors should be from poor families, they should not contribute to traffic disorder (and thus would be allowed only at certain times of the day), they should not be allowed where the pavement is too narrow, they should clean up any rubbish at the end of the day, and they should pay taxes to the ward. The city also allowed retirees (whose pensions were not sufficient to sustain basic livelihood) to sell lottery tickets on the pavement stall. Motorists stopped at their stalls freely without being harassed by policemen. But the retirees' plight was only addressed after the media urged the city authority to consider giving them special concessions.[94]

The awareness of being careful with people's livelihood penetrates the ward level of administration. For instance, at a ward meeting convened for my formal visit, the chairwoman of the ward's Women's Association said the reason why the roaming vendors were driven off from the pavement while vendors who were residents could stay was because the ward had to help residents in economic difficulties. Women's Association officials also acted as guarantors for poor families when the latter asked for permission from the ward to have a vending stall on the pavement, and their requests were given special consideration by the ward.[95]

One other way to gain further insight into how ward officials see the need for them to be flexible towards vendors is to see the conditions of work of two groups of people — the roaming vendors and the ward policemen.

Roaming Vendors

Mixed feelings exist among the public and the government regarding whether to allow vendors to ply the streets.[96] One view says that modernity is not compatible with the business nature of roaming vendors. They pollute and congest the city, and in the process the urban landscape loses its beauty. The opposite view, such as that represented by the newspaper articles that called for breathing spaces for hard-pressed people, want the roaming vendors to remain but under control and management. What have roaming vendors done to evoke such views?

Most roaming vendors in Hà Nội are from the excess rural work force in their villages. Some also come to Hà Nội in between planting seasons to look for a temporary job, such as selling cooked food and durables to supplement the family income. A substantial number who live nearby come to Hà Nội and stay a few days at a time to sell farm produce directly to customers for greater profit than if they were sold through middlemen.[97] When their own goods are sold out, these roaming vendors return to their villages to procure more, or they buy more from the wholesale markets in Hà Nội to resell. Their petty trade usually does not attract the taxmen and their overheads are low, so they are serious competitors to traders sitting in the markets.[98] Pavement vendors usually know that their trading activities on the pavement are against the law. "They do not protest, they do not wish to apply for a shop house to trade in, they just want the state to allow them to live off the pavement."[99] But to survive, they have to be conversant with "guerrilla" tactics in avoiding law enforcers. Fresh produce roaming vendors thus have to use the tactic of perpetual walking and sticking close to shops' end of the pavement if they have to stop. Consequently, their lot is hard; each day, they may walk within the city while shouldering the weight of goods for multiple kilometers.[100]

The first reason for the mixed feelings people and the government have about roaming vendors is that while on a daily basis they bring conveniences to a large number of people, they also cause traffic to slow down considerably and become more hazardous. The roaming vendors tend to stand on the pavement of busy streets at peak hours of traffic to attract as many commuters as possible. Pedestrian traffic would then overflow onto the streets. This behaviour holds up traffic flow, and is greatly disliked by the majority of commuters.

On the other hand, the risks to the vendors for doing so are great. Streets with busy traffic are usually well patrolled by traffic order policemen during peak hours (see Figure 4.4 and 4.5). Therefore, when police patrols arrive to corner the vendors,

> Many scenes bring tears to eyes. One policeman is sighted, and the sellers shout: "Police! Police!" The roaming vendors scamper in all directions. Shoulder poles hook into each other, spilling fruits and vegetables onto the road. Everyone tugged and pulled to disentangle from another. Noisy arguments drew people to assemble and watch. Sounds of rushing and nagging intermixed with sounds of abuse and crying.[101]

The unlucky ones, whose poles and shoulders the policemen could reach, argue, resist, beg, and at the same time pull away from the policeman. If they were lucky the policemen might let them go. As long as the vendors' over-the-horizon reconnaissance is good, their trading arrangements mobile, and they are not hemmed in by the patrol teams, they can usually move on without being detained by the policemen. Those with slower reflexes are

FIGURE 4.4
Law enforcers on a lookout for roaming vendors.

FIGURE 4.5
A roaming vendor looking helplessly at her goods
being confiscated.

less lucky, such as the woman vendor I came across on one late afternoon in early January 1997.

I was strolling southwards along Ngô Quyền Road on the way home from the library. Leading from the Metropole Sofitel Hotel in the centre of Hà Nội City, the wide road ended at the Hàm Long junction and led into the narrower Ngô Thì Nhậm Street. The local ward with the same name was famous for its strict enforcement of the 36/CP, a point I read in the newspapers. As I passed by house number 70 at four-thirty in the afternoon, I witnessed a typical scene repeated everyday at peak trading hours across the city of Hà Nội.

> I saw a woman hawker's goods being confiscated by the ward police. The enforcers came in one three-wheeled motorcycle, which surprised the woman who was sitting down on the pavement, her baskets beside her. There were two ward policemen and one self-management team member. I heard the woman shouting at the law enforcers: "I was not selling anything here! I was merely squatting to rest!" It was rush hour and it would be difficult to believe her. The police loaded everything

she had except a basket of some cooked food. They even took away the weighing scale (quite expensive to buy so every roaming vendor always fought to grab back the weighing scale first from the police) as well as the bamboo stick that all hawkers use to balance two baskets on their shoulders. The woman kept pleading for mercy and even used force to try to take back some of the things to be carried away. One of the local policemen found her too resistant, twisted her arms to her back and cleared the way for his colleagues. But he did not use additional force. His manner and words were stern. As the police was about to drive away (at this time the woman's arms were already released) the woman stood beside the motorcycle and kept trying to retrieve the bamboo stick from the vehicle, and at last managed to do so. The police left, by now the woman's courage was gone, and she sat down sobbing. "What an evil!" (*Sao màa ác thế!*) she judged. She showed the few people who had already crowded around her injured fingers (through struggling over the goods). A street cleaner was on hand to clear up some rubbish. She saw some of the hawker's goods that fell from the police motorcycle onto the street, gathered them, put them in a red plastic bag, and gave it back to the hawker. Not a word was exchanged between them, and nobody felt any urge to say anything. There were not many people around who were watching because I believe people have become used to such scenes. One old man (clearly a resident on the street because of the pajamas pants he was wearing) who watched the whole episode had said loudly to the police while they were clearing out the hawker that they were doing right because these hawkers occupied the whole pavement every morning, making it very difficult for people to walk. He said the hawkers deserved it because "they never listened to advice" (*nói mà không nghe*).[102]

Everybody understood and respected the legality of the action, and yet there was, in the overall, lingering sympathy for the young woman. Even after their products were confiscated, however, the roaming vendors usually poured in fresh capital to continue trading on the streets. They did this simply because the profits were irresistible when compared with the fruits of labour in their villages.[103]

A second reason why roaming vendors evoke mixed feelings among city folks is they tend to leave rubbish behind wherever they stop to trade. Road sweepers of the City Environment Company exert great effort and patience in cleaning after roaming vendors. I came to know the magnitude of the work only after waking very early one morning. I had decided to ride my motorcycle to Trần Xuân Soạn Street to check out a daily "market" of roaming vendors from outside the city that I had heard about. It always started outside the Hôm Market building from around three o'clock pre-dawn until half past seven in the morning. By the time I reached there at seven o'clock, the street was filthy and everywhere littered with unwanted food wastes that vendors had left behind. I rode into the street, winding through scattered piles of rubbish, and went for breakfast. When I returned to the street at eight o'clock, the street was clean again because of efficient work by road sweepers. Every day, in the later afternoon and early evening, a similar situation occurred on Hàng Khoai Street outside the Đồng Xuân market, and in the pre-dawn hours outside the Mơ market of Bạch Mai Street.

The Views of the Ward Policemen

Ward policemen were the main law enforcers, and they did not like enforcing the 36/CP. They faced pressure from four sides: superior officials, the media, the residents, and the roaming vendors. The pressures generally are of two types: pressures of performance and accusations of corruption, and pressures of "moral economy" arising from sympathy for roaming vendors.[104] The first type of pressures make the policemen work hard on a daily, endless task. The second type of pressure makes them shy about performing their duties. Whether they did well or neglected the situation, they were abused by any one of the four sides. The more the policemen carried out their duty, the more they felt helpless in the face of problems that recurred everyday, involving the same people at the same spots. It was troublesome dealing with the roaming vendors when they were arrested because the traders usually cried and begged, caused attention to the situation, and even abused policemen if they felt they had been treated unfairly.[105] The policemen were aware of the guerrilla tactics of the roaming vendors but there was nothing more they could do except to make their presence felt, and to hope that the city government resolved the problems of infrastructure and livelihood as soon as possible.

THE WARDS' ROLE IN THE TRAFFIC AND PAVEMENT ORDER CAMPAIGNS: SOME IMPLICATIONS FOR STATE–SOCIETY RELATIONS

In this chapter we have seen that the party-state has mixed ability in enforcing a pavement order regime in Hà Nội. All its campaigns were effective at the start; they altered the traffic and pavement situation for the better initially, but their impact usually did not last long.

Lack of persistent and consistent results in the party-state's traffic and pavement campaigns is partly explained by the lack of changes in direct and some indirect factors contributing to traffic accidents. These factors are road space, bad driving behaviour, employment opportunities to attract people away from pavement vending, enough markets to cater to convenience of buyers and sellers, and the policy choice to emphasize mobilization and education, tactics that were limited in their impact during times of economic difficulty.

The second explanation was the lack of will of the party-state and its implementing officials. On one hand, the party-state insisted that its pavement regime ought to be conformed to; but on the other hand, it conceded, as a varying principle, that local authorities ought to allow some form of pavement vending for residents' and vendors' convenience. The two campaigns of the 1990s demonstrated the situation.

A third explanation for the mixed results was the role of ward officials. They operated under difficult conditions; they lacked funds to sufficiently patrol and enforce pavement rules persistently throughout the day. Ward officials were also accused of corruption. Probably a significant number of accusations are true, because officials were paid miserly rates, many rungs below a decent living standard, and because ward officials had exclusive powers to mediate for people under "escape clauses" that the traffic and pavement regulations provided. In many instances as well, ward officials adopted a "live and let live" attitude towards offenders, and, for reasons of compassion, were willing to mediate for fellow residents who needed to earn a living on the pavement. These local-level policemen stationed at the ward were obviously told by much higher levels that they should not come down too hard on people and should rely on mobilization and education. This quote from way back in 1977 set the tone:

> There was a time when public opinion in the whole city said that the police had been too far right in its approach [towards traffic and pavement disorders], why not punish and fine. A police comrade explained:

> The precious part about our system is democracy. While enjoying this democracy, many people misinterpreted things and did not obey authority. We were told by upper levels that we should not rely on punishments and fines; after all the people had fed us, hid us in their underground cells, suffered strikes of the enemy just to defend us [during wartime],

now they come to the city, offends this rule and that rule, and we target them for fines and put them behind bars – really? And the youth who had gone overboard: a few months later, a few years later, they will become soldiers, cadres ... should we the police just heedlessly punish these brothers? We should be persistent only in educating them.

The matter of evacuating the Đinh Ngang Market [in Hà Nội] demonstrated the importance of persistence, as shown by the cadres of Cửa Nam (Small Area). The disorder and lack of public hygiene at that market was more than clear. But we had to consider the livelihood of the people there, the ordinary people who needed to buy their daily fishes and vegetables, and they would only need to take a few steps to reach Đinh Ngang Market.[106]

Characteristics of state-society relations found in the implementation of traffic and pavement order campaigns in Hà Nội reflect the different schools of thinking about state-society relations in Vietnam. The structural and bureaucratic dominance schools reflect the party-state having the right to determine pavement rules and regulations independent of influences from society. The state also possesses the capability to order local authorities to implement the campaigns. Furthermore, decisions of implementation have been made purely by bureaucrats working at different levels of local authorities.

At the same time, however, the Vietnamese party-state is also less capable and less dominating than what the structural and bureaucratic dominance schools suggest. In fact state authorities are often ambivalent and accommodating to society when they enforce rules. The state is also open to feedback from people seeking policy changes. On at least two occasions in the 1990s, the party-state was proactively accommodating when erecting rules for society. In the latest 36/CP campaign of 1995, the party-state also allowed more self-regulation at the neighbourhood level, indicating a willingness to allow people to play a larger role in their own affairs, albeit still on a miniscule scale. Another cause of the accommodating state, however, is weaknesses in the workings of the administration system. These weaknesses persisted through the whole period under study; they showed up clearly when the role of wards in Hà Nội in implementing the pavement order campaigns as examined.

Chapter 5 will discuss the problem of illegal housing construction in Hà Nội. It will further elaborate on the weaknesses of implementation and strengthen the observations I have already made about state-society relations characteristics at the everyday level.

Notes

1. *"Đầu đường đại tá bơm xe*
   Cuối đường thiếu tá bán chè đỗ đen
   Nhìn xa tướng lạ hoá quen
   Đến gần thiếu tướng bán kem bóp còi"

2. In 1988 the state liberalized the agriculture procurement system. New rules allowed peasants to sell their surpluses directly to the market after fulfiling state contracts.

3. Vương Thức, "Hè đường kêu cứu" [The pavement is calling for help!], *Hà Nội Mới* (hereafter *HNM*), 14 March 1987, pp. 1, 4.

4. Trọng Nghĩa, "Có thể bảo đảm an toàn giao thông được không?" [Can traffic safety be assured?], *HNM*, 24 July 1981, p. 3; Bùi Văn Sương, "Hà Nội có những chuyển biến tốt" [Hà Nội sees positive changes], *HNM*, 5 June 1996 p. 3; Hồng Vy, "Tai nạn giao thông đường bộ chưa giảm" [Road traffic accidents have not decreased], *HNM*, 19 February 1997, p. 2; Trần Đào, "Làm thế nào kiềm chế sự gia tăng tai nạn giao thông?" [How to stop the increase in traffic accidents?], *Nhân Dân*, 24 June 1997, p. 3. The majority of traffic offenders were also the young — 75 per cent in Hà Nội (compared with 76 per cent in Hồ Chí Minh City). See Nguyễn Xuân Yêm, "Vi phạm hành chính và công tác giáo dục ý thức, lối sống theo pháp luật cho công dân" [Administrative offences and work on education for citizens to cultivate consciousness and way of live that respect the law], in *Xây dựng ý thức và lối sống theo pháp luật* [Build consciousness and way of life that respect the law], edited by Đào Trí Úc (Hà Nội: Đề tài KHCN cấp Nhà nước KX-07-17, 1995), p. 215.

5. Ngô Huy Giao, "Giao thông đô thị" [Traffic in urban areas], *HNM*, 19 April 1981, p. 3.

6. Kim Liên, "Tuyên truyền nhiều nhưng trật tự an toàn giao thông vẫn kém" [Much mass education but traffic order and safety still far from ideal], *HNM*, 11 May 1994, p. 2. By the end of 1993, in the four inner city districts of Hà Nội there were 496 roads and streets, of which 410 had pavements of varying widths. See Vũ Đình Hoành, "Sau gần 20 tháng thực hiện chỉ thị 57" [After close to 20 months of implementation of Directive 57], *HNM*, 9 July 1993, p. 2. See also Tổng Cục Thống Kê, *Động thái và thực trạng kinh tế - xã hội Việt Nam qua 10 năm Đổi Mới (1986–1995)* [Socioeconomic dynamics and realities in Vietnam after 10 years of Đổi Mới, 1986–1995] (Hà Nội: NXB Thống Kê, 1996).

7. Thịnh Giang, "Chẳng lẽ người Hà Nội cứ cam chịu mãi cảnh giao thông như thế này?" [Do Hanoians really want to continue to tolerate the present traffic situation?], *Nhân Dân*, 15 January 1997, pp. 1, 7.

8. Xuân Quyết, "Thêm một cách nhìn về tai nạn giao thông" [One more way to look at traffic accidents], *Nhân Dân*, 8 February 2001, pp. 1, 5.

9. Lý Sinh Sự, "Đâu lại đóng đấy" [Back to square one], *Lao Động*, 23 February 1997, p. 1.

10. Thạch Lam, *Hà Nội băm sáu phố phường* [Thirty-Six Streets of Hà Nội] (Saigòn?: Đời Nay, 1943). Most parts of the, if not the whole, book described the various types of breakfast food sold on and off pavements of Hà Nội, where to eat the most delicious, food origins, and the methods of cooking those foods.

11. Trần Huy Liệu et al., eds., *Lịch sử thủ đô Hà Nội* [History of Hà Nội the capital] (Hà Nội: NXB Sử Học, 1960), p. 290.

12. Lý Kiến Quốc, "Ba mươi năm cải tạo và xây dựng kinh tế, phát triển văn hoá của nước Việt-Nam Dân chủ Cộng hoà (1945–1975)" [30 years of reform and building of the economy, developing the culture of the Democratic Republic of Viet-Nam [1945–1975]], *Học Tập* 8 (1975): 23.

13. Trần Thông, "Sớm có biện pháp" [We should act early], *Đại Đoàn Kết*, 27 May 1981, p. 2.

14. The streets of this apartments area have developed into the famous and sprawling Open Market (Chợ Trời), specializing in second-hand, stolen, and smuggled goods, as well as electrical tools and appliances. In the day, the many streets within this market vanish and consolidate into a huge market area, making the whole area impassable to traffic. The market still operates.

15. Nguyễn Xuân, "Phố...chợ!" [Street...Market!], *HNM,* 11 June 1982 p. 1.

16. Linh Lanh, "Chuyện 'vỉa hè' Hà Nội" [The Pavement in Hà Nội], *Đại Đoàn Kết,* 4 December 1985.

17. Trần Hoàng Trâm, "Một trong 5 phường khá nhất thành phố" [One of 5 best wards of the City], *An Ninh Thủ Đô*, 15 June 1986, p. 3.

18. "Tổng mục và cơ cấu bán lẻ thương nghiệp xã hội" [General index and structure for social retail trade], in *Thủ Đô Hà Nội: 30 năm xây dựng và bảo vệ chế độ Xã hội Chủ nghĩa* [Hà Nội the capital: 30 years of building and protecting the Socialist system], edited by Cục Thống Kê và Sở Văn hoá Thông tin Thành phố Hà Nội (Hà Nội, 1984), p. 91.

19. Tô Hữu, "Mấy quan điểm cơ bản về mấy vấn đề lớn trong công tác phân phối lưu thông" [A few basic points and a few big problems in distribution and circulation of goods], *TCCS* 8 (1980): 10–20, and Trần Hỗ, "Một số vấn đề về phân phối lưu thông" [A few problems on distribution and circulation], *TCCS* 3 (1984): 27–33.

20. Trần Dũng and Vũ Long, "Từ phường Hàng Bông ... đến phường Phan Chu Trinh" [From Hàng Bông Ward ... to Phan Chu Trinh Ward], *HNM,* 19 April 1983, pp. 2, 4.

21. P.V., "Phường Hàng Bài xây dựng nếp tự quản đường phố, làm chủ số nhà" [Hàng Bồ Ward builds self-managed streets and houses], *HNM,* 12 March 1986, p. 2.

22. P.V. and Quang Nghĩa, "Hơn 5.000 lượt thanh niên, thiếu niên và các lực lượng an ninh tham gia tuyên truyền giáo dục nếp sống mới, lao động xây dựng thủ đô và kiểm tra trật tự trị an ở nơi công cộng" [More than 5,000 youths, children and security forces participate in mass education on the new way of life, labour to build the capital, and checks on order and security in public places], *HNM,* 20 April 1983, p. 1; Đỗ Sơn, "Phường điểm về trật tự vệ sinh công cộng" [Model Ward in public order and hygiene], *An Ninh Thủ Đô,* 28 December 1986, p. 6; and Nguyễn Triệu, "Trên một trục đường trọng điểm" [Along the axis of a few busy streets], *HNM,* 9 November 1988, pp. 2, 4.

23. People's Committee of Hà Nội, "Quy định về việc phạt vi cảnh đối với những vi phạm trật tự an toàn giao thông trong thành phố Hà Nội" [Regulations on penalties for common nuisance offences against traffic order and safety in Hà Nội], *HNM,* 8 October 1988, p. 3

24. Nguyễn Chí Tình, "Tạm cho sử dụng vỉa hè một số đường phố để quản lý người buôn bán" [Allowing temporary use of pavement along a few roads in order to manage traders], *HNM,* 30 January 1991, pp. 1, 4.

25. These allegations were neither denied nor confirmed by the same GTCC official, who evaded answering directly. See also allegations against Hà Nội's wards, in Thanh Chi, "Trật tự đô thị, một việc cấp bách" [Urban order – an urgent matter], *HNM,* 18 March 1991, p. 2; Nguyễn Quang Hoà, "Vỉa hè, đường..." [Pavement, Roads...], *HNM,* 16 August 1991, p. 3. According to official figures quoted in the last source, the entire GTCC annual budget was not enough to cover the expenses for repair and improvement of the pavement and its pavement.

26. Nguyễn Thị Nương, "Vì sao những lộn xộn trên vỉa hè Hà Nội kéo dài?" [Why does disorder on Hà Nội's pavements still exist?], *Đại Đoàn Kết,* 12 November 1988, p. 7.

27. Nguyễn Quang Hoà, "Vỉa hè, đường..." (Pavement, Roads...) .

28. Ibid.

29. Nguyễn Chí Tình, "Tạm cho sử dụng vỉa hè một số đường phố để quản lý người buôn bán" [Allowing temporary use of pavement along a few roads in order to manage traders], *HNM,* 30 January 1991, pp. 1, 4.

30. Thu Phương, "Lại chuyện vỉa hè Hà Nội" [It's the Hà Nội pavement story again], *Đại Đoàn Kết,* 7 November 1989, p. 5.

31. Đinh Hương Sơn, "Lý và tình trong việc chấp hành pháp luật, bảo vệ trật tự và kỷ cương xã hội" [Reason and sentiments in carrying out the law, in protecting social order and discipline], *HNM,* 12 February 1990, p. 2; Nguyễn Chí Tình, "Tạm cho sử dụng vỉa hè một số đường phố để quản lý người buôn bán" [Allowing temporary use of pavement along a few roads in order to manage traders].

32. Presentation by Trần Hùng from Hà Nội Architecture University on 8 May 1997 at the Institute of Sociology, Hà Nội.

33. Kim Dung, "Qua một số chốt trật tự giao thông thuộc quận Hai Bà Trưng" [At a few traffic order hotspots in Hai Bà Trưng District], *HNM,* 30 October 1988, p. 1.

34. Nguyễn Chí Tỉnh, "Tạm cho sử dụng vỉa hè một số đường phố để quản lý người buôn bán" [Allowing temporary use of pavement along a few roads in order to manage traders], *HNM,* 30 January 1991, pp. 1, 4.

35. Presentation by Trần Hùng from Hà Nội Architecture University.

36. Tôn Xuân Thích, "Phường Tràng Tiền giữ gìn trật tự công cộng" [Tràng Tiền Ward keeps public order], *HNM,* 28 October 1988, p. 2. I rode my motorcycle through Nguyễn Khắc Cần Street many times from 1995 to 2000. It was only about four metres in width. There was hardly any pavement, so vendors had to stand on the street to trade. At peak hours, such as in the early mornings and in the evenings, it was difficult to get through the street. Other than serving the residents there, the main customers of the market were civil servants who worked in several state organs such as the Office of the National Assembly, the Ministry of Trade, Maternity Clinic "A", the General Company of Petroleum, and a big number of other state agencies and foreign institutions. Till this day, the city administration has yet to build a proper wet market for the area.

37. Thu Phương, "Lại chuyện vỉa hè Hà Nội" [It's the Hà Nội pavement story again].

38. *HNM,* "Về quản lý đường, hè phố" [On management of roads, pavements], 2 July 1990, p. 3.

39. Nguyễn Chí Tỉnh, "Tạm cho sử dụng vỉa hè một số đường phố để quản lý người buôn bán" [Allowing temporary use of pavement along a few roads in order to manage traders].

40. Tiến Phú and Phan Tưởng, "Qua 2 năm lập lại trật tự hè, đường phố" [After 2 years of restoring order on pavements and roads], *HNM,* 29 October 1993, p. 2.

41. Nguyễn Quang Hoà, "Vỉa hè, đường..." [Pavement, Roads...].

42. HNM, "Tăng cường quản lý hè, đường phố ở thủ đô" [Strengthen management of pavements and streets of the capital], 23 December 1991, pp. 1, 3.

43. Most if not all the team members were people who were middle-aged, army veterans, unemployed youths, or members of families who were poor. Thus, the exercise also looked like one that sought to create employment. Instead of establishing "self-management" teams, some wards chose to utilize the existing "people's defence force" (dân phòng), which comprised mainly war veterans, to assist the police.

44. Bùi Bá Mạnh, "Đội tự quản giao thông Nhân Dân" [The Traffic Self-management teams of the people], *HNM,* 17 April 1991, p. 2.

45. Lê Phương Hiên, "Đội tự quản giao thông — trật tự phường Cát Linh" [The Traffic and Order self-management team of the Cát Linh Ward], *HNM,* 8 January 1992, p. 2.

46. Trần Quế Thương, "Nhìn lại hai tháng thực hiện chỉ thị 57 ở Quận Hoàn Kiếm" [Review of two months of implementation of Directive 57 in Hoàn Kiếm District], *HNM,* 28 February 1992, p. 2; Trần Quế Thương, "Phường Hàng Đào thực hiện có hiệu quả chỉ thị 57 của UBND Thành phố" [Hàng Đào Ward implements effectively Directive 57 of the City People's Committee], *HNM,* 17 January 1992, p. 2.

47. See Phan Thị Bội Hoàn, "Phường Kim Liên với chỉ thị 57" [Kim Liên Ward and Directive 57], *HNM,* 13 January 1992, p. 2; Trần Quế Thương, "Phường Hàng Đào thực hiện có hiệu quả chỉ thị 57 của UBND Thành phố" [Hàng Đào Ward implements effectively Directive 57 of the City People's Committee], *HNM,* 17 January 1992, p. 2; Kim Dung, "'57' làm được, phải giữ được" [Achievements of 57 must be maintained!] *HNM,* 9 March 1992, p. 2; Phan Tương, "Sau hai năm lập lại trật tự hè, đường phố ở quận Hai Bà Trưng" [After two years of restoring order on the pavement and roads in Hai Ba Trung District], *HNM,* 13 October 1993, p. 2.

48. Vũ Đình Hoành, "Sau gần 20 tháng thực hiện chỉ thị 57" [After close to 20 months of implementation of Directive 57] *HNM,* 9 July 1993, p. 2.

49. Lê Phương Hiên, "Đội tự quản giao thông - trật tự phường Cát Linh" [The Traffic and Order self-management team of the Cát Linh Ward], *HNM,* 8 January 1992, p. 2.

50. Nguyễn Văn Xây, "Rất cần 'ba kiểm tra' trong thực hiện chỉ thị 57" [Real need for "three checks" in implementing Directive 57], *HNM,* 5 March 1992, p. 1.

51. Kim Dung, "'57' làm được, phải giữ được" [Achievements of 57 must be maintained!], *HNM,* 9 March 1992, p. 2; Tường Anh, "Tổng kiểm tra, duy trì kết quả thực hiện chỉ thị 57/UB về giữ gìn trật tự hè, đường" [General inspection to maintain results of Directive 57/UB on maintaining order on pavements, roads], *HNM,* 16 September 1992, pp. 1, 4; Thanh Hùng, "Trật tự, kỷ cương đô thị lại bị buông lỏng" [Urban order and discipline are loose again], *HNM,* 4 September 1992, p. 2.

52. Fieldnotes 26 November 1996; 28 November 1996; and 18 December 1996.

53. Phan Thị Bội Hoàn, "Phường Kim Liên với chỉ thị 57" [Kim Liên Ward and Directive 57], *HNM,* 13 January 1992, p. 2; Thanh Hùng, "Trật tự, kỷ cương đô thị lại bị buông lỏng" [Urban order and discipline are loose again] *HNM,* 4 September 1992, p. 2; Thúy Hằng, "Trật tự đô thị ở phường Tràng Tiền" [Urban order at the Tràng Tiền Ward], *HNM,* 26 February 1993, p. 2.

54. Kim Dung, "'57' làm được, phải giữ được" [Achievements of 57 must be maintained!], *HNM,* 9 March 1992, p. 2.

55. Thanh Thủy, "Thử xem tham nhũng cấp phường đến đâu!" [Let's see how deep corruption is at the ward level!], *HNM,* 1 July 1994, p. 2. Peter Higgs, "The Footpath Economy and Beyond: Factors affecting Social and

Economic Change in a District of Hà Nội" paper delivered at the Asian Studies Association of Australia Annual Conference held in Melbourne, 1996.

56. Thanh Mai, "Xung quanh việc thực hiện chỉ thị 57" [About implementation of Directive 57], *HNM,* 6 January 1992, p. 2.

57. Trần Quế Thương, "Nhìn lại hai tháng thực hiện chỉ thị 57 ở Quận Hoàn Kiếm" [Review of two months of implementation of Directive 57 in Hoàn Kiếm District], *HNM,* 28 February 1992, p. 2, and Vũ Đình Hoành, "Sau gần 20 tháng thực hiện chỉ thị 57" [After close to 20 months of implementation of Directive 57], *HNM,* 9 July 1993, p. 2. Thương was a policeman working in the Hoàn Kiếm District while Hoành was the Deputy Chief of Police of Hà Nội City.

58. The best example of such a peak-hour only market after 1996 would be Lê Ngọc Hân Street, which was not a major traffic artery but parallel to one. During marketing hours, the whole street was turned into a market and vehicles were not allowed in. This market was used to channel all roaming vendors from the very busy Lò Đúc Street just next to it.

59. Vũ Đình Hoành, "Sau gần 20 tháng thực hiện chỉ thị 57" [After close to 20 months of implementation of Directive 57], *HNM,* 9 July 1993, p. 2.

60. Phan Tường, "Sau hai năm lập lại trật tự hè, đường phố ở quận Hai Bà Trưng" [After two years of restoring order on the pavement and roads in Hai Bà Trưng District], *HNM,* 13 October 1993, p. 2.

61. Thanh Mai, "Thực hiện chỉ thị 57 ở một con đường" [Implementing Directive 57 on one road], *HNM,* 8 January 1992, p. 3.

62. Tường Anh, "Tổng kiểm tra, duy trì kết quả thực hiện chỉ thị 57/UB về giữ gìn trật tự hè, đường" [General inspection to maintain results of Directive 57/UB on maintaining order on pavements, roads], *HNM,* 16 September 1992, pp. 1, 4.

63. Lê Phương Hiên, "Đội tự quản giao thông - trật tự phường Cát Linh" [The Traffic and Order self-management team of the Cát Linh Ward], *HNM,* 8 January 1992, p. 2.

64. Nguyễn Xuân Yêm, "Vi phạm hành chính và công tác giáo dục ý thức, lối sống theo pháp luật cho công dân" [Administrative offences and work on education for citizens to cultivate consciousness and way of live that respect the law] (1995), p. 218.

65. Kim Liên, "Tuyên truyền nhiều nhưng trật tự an toàn giao thông vẫn kém" [Much mass education but traffic order and safety still far from ideal], *HNM,* 11 May 1994, p. 2.

66. SRV, *Chỉ thị của Thủ tướng Chính phủ Về tăng cường công tác quản lý trật tự an toàn giao thông đường bộ và trật tự an toàn giao thông đô thị* (Directive of the Prime Minister on strengthening management of traffic order and safety on roads and urban traffic order) numbered 317/TTg, promulgated 26 May 1995.

67. K.D., "Tích cực chuẩn bị cho ngày đầu tiên thực hiện Nghị Định 36/CP của Chính phủ" (Enthusiastic preparations for the first day of implementation of 36/CP), *HNM,* 29 July 1995, pp. 1, 4.

68. *HNM,* "Thủ tướng Chính phủ họp với các ngành, đoàn thể bàn biện pháp triển khai Nghị Định 36/CP và Chỉ Thị 317/TTg về bảo đảm trật tự an toàn giao thông đường bộ và trật tự an toàn giao thông đô thị" [PM discussed with branches and organizations on measures to implement 36/CP and Directive 317/TTg on traffic order and safety on the roads and in the cities], 16 June 1995, pp. 1, 4; and Bùi Danh Lưu, "Kết quả bước đầu thực hiện Nghị Định 36/CP và Chỉ Thị 317/TTg trong cả nước" [Initial achievements of the nationwide implementation of the 36/CP ordinance and the 317-TTg Instruction], *Quản lý Nhà nước* (10/1995) 13:9-12, 20; p. 10.

69. K.D., "Tích cực chuẩn bị cho ngày đầu tiên thực hiện Nghị Định 36/CP của Chính phủ" [Enthusiastic preparations for the first day of implementation of 36/CP], *HNM,* 29 July 1995, pp. 1, 4.

70. K.D., "Tích cực chuẩn bị cho ngày đầu tiên thực hiện Nghị Định 36/CP của Chính phủ" [Enthusiastic preparations for the first day of implementation of 36/CP], *HNM,* 29 July 1995, pp. 1, 4; *HNM,* "Thủ tướng Chính phủ họp với các ngành, đoàn thể bàn biện pháp triển khai Nghị Định 36/CP và Chỉ Thị 317/TTg về bảo đảm trật tự an toàn giao thông đường bộ và trật tự an toàn giao thông đô thị" [PM discussed with branches and organizations on measures to implement 36/CP and Directive 317/TTg on traffic order and safety on the roads and in the cities], 16 June 1995, pp. 1, 4.

71. Vĩnh Yên, "Cần giữ cho hè thông, đường thoáng ở mọi nơi, mọi lúc" [Every pavement and road needs to be clear at all times], *HNM,* 31 July 1995, p. 2.

72. Nhóm Phóng Viên Hà Nội Mới, "Ngày khởi đầu" [The first day], *HNM,* 2 August 1995, pp. 1, 3; P.V., "CA phường Ô Chợ Dừa làm tốt vai trò nòng cốt thực hiện NĐ 36/CP" [Ô Chợ Dừa Ward police performs its pillar role well when implementing 36/CP], *HNM,* 2 October 1996, p. 2.

73. Thu Hương, "Các cấp, ngành, đoàn thể tích cực triển khai thực hiện Nghị Định 36/CP" [All levels, branches, and organizations enthusiastically prepares to implement 36/CP], *HNM,* 31 July 1995, pp. 1, 4, and Mạnh Hùng, "Liên kết thực hiện Nghị Định 36/CP" [Joint implementation of 36/CP], *HNM,* 28 July 1995, p. 1.

74. Kim Dung, "'Nhóm liên gia tự quản ở cụm dân cư số 2 phường Ngô Thì Nhậm" ["Self-managed family groups" in Resident Cluster no. 2 of Ngô Thì Nhậm Ward], *HNM,* 22 September 1995, p. 2.

75. P.Q., "Hoàn Kiếm nhân điển hình cơ quan xí nghiệp tự quản thực hiện NĐ 36/CP" [Hoàn Kiếm District uses self-management model for state agencies and enterprises in implementing 36/CP], *HNM,* 10 August 1996, p. 1.

76. P.Q., "Liên kết trường - phường một mô hình cần được nhân rộng" [School — Ward alliance — a model that needs to be spread widely], *HNM,*

15 November 1996, p. 2. Other wards with schools on busy streets also practised this method, such as Phạm Đình Hổ Ward with a school on the Lò Đức Street, Nguyễn Du ward with a school on Trần Xuân Soạn Street, and Hàng Bài ward with a school on Lý Thường Kiệt Street.

77. Even though previous national traffic order campaigns were also ordered by the Prime Minister, the 36/CP was one in which the Prime Minister paid the most personal attention. See Vĩnh Yên, "Cần giữ cho hè thông, đường thoáng ở mọi nơi, mọi lúc" [Every pavement and road needs to be clear at all times], *HNM*, 31 July 1995, p. 2.

78. Bùi Danh Lưu, "Kết quả bước đầu thực hiện Nghị Định 36/CP và Chỉ Thị 317/ TTg trong cả nước" [Initial achievements of the nation-wide implementation of the 36/CP ordinance and the 317-TTg Instruction]; Nguyễn Quang Hoà, "Lục cục '36'" [Internal conflicts of "36"], *HNM*, 18 October 1995, pp. 1, 3.

79. P.V., "Sơ kết một tháng thực hiện Nghị Định 36/CP của Chính phủ" [Preliminary review of the first month of implementation of the Government's 36/CP], *HNM*, 14 September 1995, p. 1; Bùi Danh Lưu "Kết quả bước đầu thực hiện Nghị Định 36/CP và Chỉ Thị 317/TTg trong cả nước" [Initial achievements of the nation-wide implementation of the 36/CP ordinance and the 317-TTg Instruction]; Nguyễn Quang Hoà, "Lục cục '36'" [Internal conflicts of "36"].

80. Minh Đức, "Trật tự an toàn giao thông" [Traffic order and safety], *Nhân Dân*, 13 January 1997, p. 2. The feedback received through fieldwork interviews revealed the same doubts about persistency of the good results.

81. Thanh Chi, "Trật tự giao thông đô thị ở Hà Nội trước và sau NĐ 36/CP" [Urban traffic order in Hà Nội before and after 36/CP], *HNM*, 16 October 1995, p. 2.

82. Nguyễn Trường Giang, "Quán Thánh, 2 tháng thực hiện NĐ36/CP" [Two months of 36/CP at Quán Thánh Ward], *HNM*, 9 October 1995, p. 2.

83. Nguyễn Quang Hoà, "Lục cục '36'" [Internal conflicts of "36"]. The Hàng Da Market area is the best example. Shops there normally displayed their wares within shops in the day and put goods out on the pavements in the evenings. Cafes all around the city put out their stools and coffee tables onto the pavement when night arrived.

84. Tiến Chính, "Không nên hỏi: 'Tồn tại hay không tồn tại?'" [We should not ask "Should it or should it not exist?"], *An Ninh Thu Đô*, 9 Decmeber 1996, pp. 1, 3.

85. Nguyễn Quang Hoà, "Lục cục '36'" [Internal conflicts of "36"]; Bích Hậu and Bích Hương, "Long đong … hàng rong" [Hard times fall on street vending], *Lao Động Hà Nội*, 17 January 1997, pp. 1, 10.

86. Conversation with a family operating a business in the Hà Nội neighbourhood I lived in. Fieldnotes 28 November 1996.

87. Nguyễn Quang Hoà, "Lục cục '36'" [Internal conflicts of "36"].
88. Conversation with Ms T, grilled chicken seller on Giảng Võ Street. Fieldnotes 23 April 1997. Cooked food and fresh produce sellers operated from the early evening on the following streets: Nguyễn Công Trứ Street (supper); Hàng Điếu Street (supper, drinks) Lò Đúc (supper, fresh fruits), Bạch Mai Street (supper, fresh produce), Lý Văn Phúc Street (grilled chicken), Đội Cấn Street (supper, fruits), Láng Trung Street (fruits), Nguyễn Trãi Street (supper, fruits), and many other streets. Also a particular feature of street vending culture in Hà Nội was the mini-petrol stations, marked by plastic bottles empty or filled with petrol and placed near the kerb. Only when the motorist stopped by the bottle would the "station" operator emerge from the house or the shadows to sell the petrol, and the profit margin was about 500 to 1,000 đồng per liter. If two liters were sold each night, it could fetch 30,000 đồng in additional monthly income for the family (late 1990s prices).
89. The city was obstructed in developing roads and social infrastructure within the urban area partly because land requisition was usually burdened with long delays and problems of people's distrust of local authority officials. Road-widening projects such as the one in Đại Cồ Việt Road, Thái Hà Road, Cầu Giấy Road had given rise to charges of ward officials' corruption, incompetence, and high-handedness. People refused to move and demanded market rates (in a real estate market bubble) as compensation, thus delaying urgent improvements to the city's roads. See Quang Nguyễn, "Mở rộng đường Hùng Vương – Cầu Giấy có dễ hay không?" [Widening the Hùng Vương – Cầu Giấy Road - easy or not easy?], HNM, 24 February 1993, p. 2; Tổ PV Điều Tra, "Dân đòi hỏi quá đáng, hay thực hiện chưa công bằng" [Do the people demand too much, or is the implementation unfair?], Đại Đoàn Kết, 21 April 1997, pp. 1, 7. Similar cases also emerged in other provinces regarding compensation deemed insufficient by the people in lieu of losses of land and livelihood. See Lao Động, "Vì sao không đền bù thỏa đáng cho dân?" [Why are people not compensated appropriately?], 9 January 1997, p. 6 for a case in Vĩnh Long province; Lý Quốc Khánh, "Chính quyền xã Tân Phú cưỡng quyền với dân, vì sao?" [Why did the local authority of Tân Phú Commune compel people?], Đại Đoàn Kết, 13 January 1997, p. 6 for a case in Cà Mau province; Cát Bình, "Vì sao việc giải phóng mặt bằng đường 18A chậm?" [Why is land requisition for road 18A slow?], Đại Đoàn Kết, 1 June 1998, p. 6 for a case in Quảng Ninh province.
90. Vũ Đình Hoành, "Làm gì để thực hiện Nghị Định 36/CP của Chính phủ có hiệu quả cao?" [What is to be done to ensure implementation of 36/CP of the government is highly effective?], HNM, 1 August 1995, pp. 1, 4.
91. "Dân là người chèo thuyền, cũng là người lật thuyền … Chính quyền phải biết co giãn, quá cứng thì người dân không chịu nổi." Official meeting at

one ward with ward officials to discuss 36/CP implementation in that ward. Fieldnotes, 17 May 1997.

92. Fieldnotes, 10 March 1997.

93. *HNM*, "Thành phố cho dùng hè ở 57 tuyến phố để sắp xếp các hộ kinh doanh" [City allows traders to use pavement on 57 roads], 26 October 1995, pp. 1, 4.

94. Tuấn Anh, "Nỗi niềm những người làm kinh tế vỉa hè" [The feelings of those working in the pavement economy], *Lao Động Hà Nội*, 10 January 1997, pp. 1, 7. See also Hương Thủy, "Các đại lý xổ số sẽ bán vé ở đâu?" [Where would the agents of lottery sell their tickets?], *HNM*, 10 July 1995, p. 3.

95. Briefing held at a ward. Fieldnotes 17 May 1997.

96. See, for example, Chí Thành, "Tự do, dân chủ và pháp luật, kỷ cương" [Freedom, democracy, and law, discipline], *HNM*, 25 October 1988; Đinh Hương Sơn, "Lý và tình trong việc chấp hành pháp luật, bảo vệ trật tự và kỷ cương xã hội" [Reason and sentiments in carrying out the law, in protecting social order and discipline], *HNM,* 12 February 1990, p. 2; Nguyễn Chí Tỉnh, "Tạm cho sử dụng vỉa hè một số đường phố để quản lý người buôn bán" [Allowing temporary use of pavement along a few roads in order to manage traders], *HNM,* 30 January 1991, pp. 1, 4; Thanh Chi, "Trật tự đô thị, một việc cấp bách" [Urban order – an urgent matter], *HNM*, 18 March 1991, p. 2; and Nguyễn Trường Giang, "Quán Thánh, 2 tháng thực hiện NĐ36/CP" [Two months of 36/CP at Quán Thánh Ward], *HNM*, 9 October 1995, p. 2.

97. Đỗ Ngọc Dương, "Cần có những biện pháp cụ thể và phù hợp thực tế để bảo đảm thực hiện nghị định 36/CP" [Need for specific measures closer to reality to ensure that 36/CP is implemented], *HNM,* 30 October 1995, p. 2.

98. Nguyễn Chí Tỉnh, "Tạm cho sử dụng vỉa hè một số đường phố để quản lý người buôn bán" [Allowing temporary use of pavement along a few roads in order to manage traders], *HNM*, 30 January 1991, pp. 1, 4; Nguyễn Quang Hoà, "Vỉa hè, đường..." [Pavement, Roads...], Tran Thanh Tuong, "Street vendors and taxes killing off markets" *Vietnam Investment Review* 8 June 1998, carried by Reuters, 8 June 1998.

99. D.T. Phương, *Lecture on Development of Hà Nội* (Hà Nội: Institute of Sociology), 5 May 1997.

100. Tuấn Anh, "Nỗi niềm những người làm kinh tế vỉa hè" [The feelings of those working in the pavement economy], *Lao Động Hà Nội,* 10 January 1997, pp. 1, 7.

101. Mai Hoa, "Hàng rong: chuyện nhỏ mà không nhỏ" [Hawkers: apparently small but actually big matter], *An Ninh Thủ Đô,* 13 December 1996, p. 3. See also Xuân Hà, "Giải quyết nạn hàng rong quả thật không dễ!" [Really

not easy to solve the *hàng rong* problem!], *Lao Động Hà Nội*, 10 January 1997, p. 2; Hải Yến, "Ngõ hay chợ?" [A lane of a market?], *An Ninh Thủ Đô*, 8 April 1997, p. 5.

102. Fieldnotes, 7 January 1997.

103. Xuân Hà,"Giải quyết nạn hàng rong quả thật không dễ!" [Really not easy to solve the *hàng rong* problem!].

104. Ibid

105. Mai Hoa, "Hàng rong: chuyện nhỏ mà không nhỏ" [Hawkers: apparently small but actually big matter]. The roaming vendors felt that way because they could not accept why local residents were allowed to trade on the pavements while they were disallowed to do the same, especially when local residents who were roaming vendors were also offending the 36/CP but were never dealt with. They were even of the opinion that the injustice arose out of their inability to bribe off officials. See Xuân Hà, "Giải quyết nạn hàng rong quả thật không dễ!" [Really not easy to solve the *hàng rong* problem!].

106. *"Có hồi đã có dư luận ồn cả thành phố là công an ta hữu khuynh quá, tại sao không phạt. Có đồng chí công an phân tích:*

    — Cái quý của chúng ta là dân chủ. Được hưởng quyền dân chủ ấy, nhiều người nhận thức không rõ, hoá nhờn, quá trớn. Chúng tôi được trên nhắc nhở, không được lấy phạt làm chính, không nhẽ bà con nông thôn vừa nuôi mình, cất giấu mình dưới hầm, chịu đòn địch để bảo vệ mình, nay bà con ra thành phố, vi phạm này nọ, mình lại nhắm bà con mà phạt tiền, phạt giam ư? Với ngay anh em thanh niên quá trớn nữa. Chỉ vài tháng sau, vài năm sau, anh em thành bộ đội, cán bộ... không nhẽ công an chúng tôi cứ nhằm nhằm phạt anh em. Phải kiên trì vận động thôi.

    Vụ dẹp chợ Đình Ngang cũng nói lên tinh thần kiên trì, <<tư công phu>> của cán bộ cơ sở Cửa Nam. Mất trật tự, mất vệ sinh từ cái chợ Đình Ngang này thì rõ quá rồi. Nhưng phải tính đến đời sống của bà con buôn bán ở đây, phải tính đến đời sống của nhân dân cần mua con cá mớ rau, chỉ vài bước ghé vào chợ Đình Ngang.

    "Vài nét về Khu phố Cửa Nam – Hà Nội" [A few characteristics of the Cửa Nam area], *Đại Đoàn Kết*, 10 December 1977, pp. 6, 7.

5

The Housing Regimes and
Hà Nội Wards' Role

INTRODUCTION

This chapter discusses the role of Hà Nội's wards in enforcing the housing regimes of Vietnam from 1954 to 1998, and how that role affects Vietnamese party-state–society relations. It argues that Hà Nội's wards play a critical role in mediating between the party-state and ward residents. It examines illegal housing construction in Hà Nội from 1975 to 1995, and what the wards did to deal with it. While the time-frame is so limited, the problems of illegal construction is still a current problem of law and order in urban areas and it represents the disregarding and/or negotiation of party-state boundaries. Along with raised living standards and new areas of urbanization, illegal construction has spread beyond Hà Nội.

By "housing regime" I mean official "answers to questions such as who may use [housing units], do what with [them], and with what rights and obligations."[1] Therefore, a housing regime has official rules aimed at regulating various housing issues and activities, such as ownership, purchase, use, construction, and renovation. There are two distinct Vietnamese housing regimes from 1954 to the present in the Democratic Republic of Vietnam (DRV, 1945–75) and the Socialist Republic of Vietnam (SRV, from 1975). The first, which I call the socialist housing regime, lasted from 1954 to 1990. Its main feature was heavy state regulation in all housing matters. Housing demand was mainly to be satisfied by the state. The second, which I call the liberalized housing regime, began in 1991 and continues until now. Its main feature has been allowing the private sector to participate in the housing sector.

The socialist housing regime drastically and negatively affected housing conditions, especially after 1975. It discouraged private construction by requiring numerous licences and permits. Moreover, the state bureaucracy took many months, even years, to issue those licences and permits. At the same time, the state attempted to provide housing but did so poorly. People who needed housing urgently were caught in a bind: it was nearly impossible to construct a dwelling privately, yet the state could not provide the accommodation people needed urgently. To overcome these obstacles many people in Hà Nội boldly built or renovated their flats and houses without licences. A large number went out of the inner city to take over vacant land to build their dwellings. Others took over a large amount of open space that existed between houses and buildings, and also spaces that belonged to places of worship and historical legacy that were neglected by the state. The Hà Nội History Association said that there were 1,774 points of historical legacy in Hà Nội; out of this number, 267 have vanished due to such a reason, while 1,163 have suffered severe encroachments.[2]

The problems at Hà Nội's historical sites were the tips of a giant iceberg. Illegal housing construction in Hà Nội is several times in magnitude to that. From 1975 until late 1990s, recorded illegal construction cases in Hà Nội amounted to tens of thousands of cases. The party-state took action and succeeded in making its rules stick in many cases. But in a substantial number of other cases, it did not succeed. Moreover, numerous violations of housing regime regulations could have gone undetected.

Scholars who studied other socialist countries have explored various features of housing regimes of those countries, such as urban planning, urbanization, inequalities in distribution, and finance. But they say little about illegal construction.[3] Yet illegal construction did occur in those socialist systems. John Sillince says, without much description, that one of the effects of housing shortage in socialist countries of Eastern Europe was illegal and poorly built homes and shanty towns.[4] Frank Carter notes that in Bulgaria some illegal construction of second homes in coastal areas or in urban areas took place contrary to state rules on urban planning and the housing regime in general.[5] But these studies of other socialist countries have not examined the political significance of illegal construction for state–society relations.

Illegal housing on a large scale has political significance, especially when it occurs in a political system like Vietnam's in which the state has tried to keep firm control. It raises questions about the ability of the state to enforce its own laws. There are also issues of socialist property rights (all land belonging to the state) and whether the state can defend this land property regime. Another set of issues concerns relations between central and local officials who are supposed to see that people obey the housing regime's rules and regulations. Then there are questions to explore about what, if any, political reasons motivate those people who violate the housing laws.

An informant called C said that people in Hà Nội who had very low standards of housing openly defied ward officials who tried to enforce construction rules.

> People illegally extended small flats against building safety regulations because they needed the extra space. For example, it was hopeless to tell a family of three generations with six to eight people living in a 30 m. sq. flat that they ought not to extend their living area. When the officials approached and talked to the offending family, they were told that they did not understand what it was like to live in such a crowded place and therefore they had no authority to tell the family what to do.[6]

Delving into all these political issues is more than my research can handle. What I will concentrate on is how local officials handle the infringements, relations between those infringing on the housing regime and those who are supposed to uphold that regime, and the ways in which infringements occur. One question I address in this chapter is why, when, and where are informal rules applied? Another question is to what extent does the "fence- breaking" and the informal rules at the ward level in Hà Nội undermine the housing regime?

This chapter has two parts. Part I analyses chronologically how the housing regime evolved. It highlights the severe housing shortages in Hà Nội and their causes and effects. This logically leads to Part II, which analyses the various stages of the illegal construction movement in Hà Nội, showing how people had gone fence-breaking and sought mediation from the ward or other levels of authority, and support from neighbours.

PART I: BACKGROUND TO ILLEGAL CONSTRUCTION IN HÀ NỘI

What is Illegal Construction?

The word "construction" is used here to mean activity that either builds a house or other dwelling from scratch, or any extension or renovation to either the interior or exterior of a house or a flat. In Vietnam all such activities that are without official licences or permits are called "illegal construction" (*xây dựng trái phép*). Some studies estimate that, using a strict interpretation of the relevant laws, 90 per cent of all construction in Hà Nội could be considered illegal.[7] (The authority in Hồ Chí Minh City estimated that on average 65 per cent of about one million houses already built did not have construction licences. In some districts of the city, the illegal construction rate was 95 per cent.[8]) By 2004, the rate of illegal construction in Hà Nội reportedly improved but only to 60 per cent, mainly because of the reduction in bureaucratic procedures.[9]

Like urban housing regimes in other countries, Vietnam's urban housing regime has rules for construction and renovation of buildings in line with current regulations on land-use and ownership rights, safety and aesthetic standards, and safety of public works installations. Under the socialist housing regime, residents also needed certification from the ward office that additional housing space was warranted, as necessary documentary and political support for requests for a larger living area. During the war and in times of economic shortages, the Vietnamese state also regulated supplies of building materials; getting those materials required appropriate resource control and release documents. In the 1970s and 1980s, separate construction licences were also needed for work on different parts of houses, inside and outside, and for minor maintenance work such as painting a door. In the 1990s, many of these permit requirements were dropped. Yet, some official papers are still supposed to be obtained. The district remains responsible for issuing licences for building or renovating dwellings that face the main streets. The ward (lower level to the district) issues licences for housing along the lanes and small streets. For flats in collective apartment buildings both local authorities and the state enterprises that own these buildings are supposed to authorize alterations. The Hà Nội Chief Architect issues licences for construction in the Thirty-Six Streets area as well as in areas near the dykes that meander through Hà Nội.

In 2000, a Hà Nội resident related the usual troublesome experience in trying to obtain a licence for construction:

> Why should I apply for a licence? I have to make so much effort to get all sorts of documents to support the application. I have to get up to the offices of the ward, the district, and the city Land Office, and while there I also have to pay for expenses, presents (such as cigarettes, drinks). But the biggest deterrent is to be made running around these offices so many times, to wait, and to attend upon the officials. And we have not even mentioned the formalities of being polite in spite of all that! Well, forget it! The informal way is the lightest way, because I do not have to be obsequious.[10]

Here, the "informal way" meant that the lady interviewed decided to allow herself to be fined by various authorities three times, for a few hundred U.S. dollars, at the end of which her illegally built house was allowed to stand. That was the less troublesome experience than the legal licence route.

Even if one had all the necessary documentation to build or renovate a dwelling, the construction project could still be illegal if the work done does not conform to the specifications stated in the construction licence, or if zoning regulations are violated. Thus, official inspections of the construction work are supposed to be conducted after the work is completed.

Anyone building or revamping a house or flat is also expected to approach every household in the vicinity who might be affected to exchange technical notes and discuss compensation due to collateral damage, or to alter construction plans and take neighbours' interests into consideration. Neighbours have the right to reject construction plans or ask for alterations. If not properly consulted in advance, or compensated for a valid inconvenience, neighbours are more likely later to insist on bigger compensation or that the construction is undone. It is wise, therefore, to consult neighbours.[11] Neighbours' approval is necessary because in crowded housing situations in many parts of Hà Nội, especially in the 1980s, living space is a highly-valued asset. Many people share houses and flats, and most houses found in older parts of Hà Nội have shared walls. Consequently, a renovation by one household affects the safety, living space, and rights of other households, temporarily or permanently. Interests of neighbours include damage to shared walls; intrusion of privacy (for instance windows and doors of two units of dwellings should not face each other); use-rights of shared toilets, kitchens, and courtyards; and many other details.[12] Agreement and co-operation of neighbours ensure that collateral damage or loss of rights caused by construction work or unacceptable design is compensated.

Furthermore, neighbours' support is crucial if construction is illegal. If it does not offend neighbours but simply violates the law, neighbours may help the family in persuading the ward that no harm is done to anyone and no further action should be taken. Authorities can refuse to issue a construction licence if neighbours oppose the construction plans; but when neighbours approve and support an application, then wards may turn a blind eye.

But as we shall see later in this chapter, neighbourly goodwill is exhaustible, especially when issues of public or private interests may lead either neighbours or local authorities to insist that construction rules be respected strictly.

The Ward's Role

The ward's official role on construction matters is to be the eyes, ears, and hands of the state. Ward officials issue construction licences (for houses not facing a main street), monitor illegal construction, investigate cases to report to the district (which has the authority to decide on demolition and appeals) and carry out district orders.[13] The ward people's committee usually delegates these tasks to its construction section, with the ward people's committee chairman directly in charge. The wards are crucial especially when illegal construction interferes with public work installations (for instance high voltage electricity cables), and they usually have to depend on resident group heads and residents to help report those offences. Electricity cables in Hà Nội run on poles above ground and they are an inconvenience in house construction work. For instance, in the ward I lived in, a co-operative tried to extend its members' living area on the second storey outwards to align the second storey window with the road kerb. In doing so, it had to make the electrical wires of the neighbourhood, hang above the pavement and along the road, run into and then out of the extended part of the second storey. This was illegal and also dangerous to house occupants and neighbours. Once residents reported the problem, ward officials took immediate action to stop construction.[14]

Besides its official role, ward offices often have informal functions regarding housing. Dealing informally with ward officials rather than the district (which also issues construction licences) allows residents involved in illegal construction to enjoy some advantages. Residents frequently turn to ward officials for sanctioning of such activities, even if their project requires district approval. Indeed, often they ask ward officials to mediate with the district authorities or ask ward officials to help them entirely avoid dealing with the district.[15] Informants say there are three grounds on which ward officials could decide to help residents on this matter: a construction activity is accepted by neighbours, it does not offend major public works (which would catch the attention of most residents and higher level supervisors), and there is a pay-off for the officials or for the ward. Paying officials a bribe keeps offences under wraps, or has the ward cite residents for lesser offences than what actually happened, as in Sơn's case (see Chapter 1). For other types of construction that do not need district approval, ward officials have considerable discretion, although neighbours' approval is still necessary.

When assisting their residents, ward officials may use a number of methods. On construction licences issued by the district, ward officials and not district ones carry out the required post-construction inspection. Ward officials may visit a home when construction is done and issue a certificate of inspection for licensed construction work and certify that the conditions of the dwelling conform to regulations and the construction licence, regardless of its real condition.[16] Informant C said that when the ward officials come to conduct the inspection and find infringements of construction regulations, the house owner often can

> give the local police or official concerned an envelope (containing a bribe) so that the authority above the ward does not hear about it. If the authority above the ward comes to check, the local authority then help their client by stating that they have checked the house and that it is alright.

Ward officials, be them the policemen, or the ward leaders, or construction affairs officials stationed at the ward, are often on the take. The number of cases is numerous and it is also often assumed by residents that this is the reason why many offences go unpunished.

A second way ward officials may help a resident is to levy a fine on the illegal construction, keep the money as ward income, but never require the household to remedy the construction anomaly. This way of dealing with illegal construction is called "fine for existence" (*phạt cho tồn tại*).[17] A third way is to pretend ignorance of an illegal construction while its work is in progress, and then appear at the site when work is almost complete. In that way, the illegal builder would plead for compassion from officials because the construction work is almost done, and ask the officials to treat the offence as a "fine for existence" type. Pay-offs is also given to the officials as part of the deal.

The Socialist Housing Regime in Hà Nội, 1954–75

One of the main reasons for the large amount of illegal housing in Hà Nội is the housing shortage. Reasons for that shortage, in turn, are often traceable back to the socialist housing regime. This requires some explanation, which I will do in two sections. The first looks at the socialist housing regime in North Vietnam between 1954 and 1975. The second will look at the situation in Vietnam between 1975 and 1990.

Beginning in 1954, the Communist Party government in North Vietnam nationalized all dwellings whose ownership could not be proven with appropriate papers. Private ownership was allowed if it had been registered before 1954 (in the north) and before 1975 (in the south), and if it could be proven with ownership papers. Because only a small minority of houses in Hà Nội, perhaps only 10 per cent, ever had ownership papers, this meant most housing in the city belonged to the state.[18] The socialist housing regime also nationalized all houses of families who had more than one room. Original occupants of those houses then had to rent their rooms from the state. The "excess" housing was then "redistributed" or rented out to those without homes. Consequently many big villas and houses in the ancient and western quarters of Hà Nội were each divided into several living quarters shared by many families. Rents paid for these rooms were at modest rates. Employees of the state typically had such housing for free as part of their remuneration packages.

In this socialist housing regime, the state severely restricted private construction. The state had its own housing construction agency that built flats as ordered by the party-state's five-year socioeconomic plans. No significant housing market survived in this housing regime, and any transfer of housing among people was supposed to be approved by and registered with the state.

This North Vietnam socialist housing regime resembled what existed in Eastern European countries and China between 1945 and the 1980s. Except in Yugoslavia and Hungary, private housing in these socialist countries was virtually gone.[19] In China, the state tolerated private ownership and construction until 1958, after which state housing became predominant. Over time, nationalization and new state construction projects gradually crowded out private construction, although some degree of private ownership remained.[20] In the USSR, private housing construction was formally possible after the 1950s, yet in practice it faced many difficulties such as regime confiscation of dwellings deemed ostentatious, scarcity of building materials, and reels of red tape.[21]

Given strong pressures against private construction in Hà Nội between 1954 and 1975, state-built collective flats (Khu Tập Thể) were in great demand. To be allotted a unit in the collective flats in the 1960s to 1970s was considered good fortune. In Hà Nội, the collective flats were in four and five-storey blocks located in planned self-contained satellite areas, such as Nguyễn Công Trứ and Kim Liên built in the 1960s, and Trung Tự, Khương Thượng, Giảng Võ, Thành Công, Thanh Xuân Bắc and Vĩnh Hồ built in the 1970s. All units within these collective flats were distributed to people working in the same economic sector or enterprise, or the same state agency.[22] The 1960s flats had common toilets and kitchens, each shared by four to five households. Flats built in the 1970s had individual facilities for each household. Each flat was usually designed for use by one household of four persons; housing space per person was supposed to be at least 4 square metres. Actual space per person was quite often only about 2 square meters because many flats were shared by two families.[23] In some collective flats, as many as ten to twenty households shared a common toilet. This was even before mentioning the difficulties of water pipes and waste drains that were often choked because of the severe lack of maintenance over long periods of time.

The socialist housing regime in the DRV had had both good and bad times. We can see this through changes in the rate of housing space per person in Hà Nội between 1954 and 1975, presented in Table 5.1.[24]

In 1955 in Hà Nội, housing space per person reached 6.5 square metres, the highest achieved for Hà Nội ever since. This high rate was probably boosted by mass emigration out of the city following the change in the political regime in 1954. Between 1954 and the first five-year plan that began in 1960, the state constructed very little new housing. By 1960, the rate of housing space per person in Hà Nội dropped by more than 30 per cent, accompanied by a 1 per cent increase in the housing stock but a 4 to 20 per cent increase in population. Under the country's first five-year plan between 1960 and 1965, however, housing stock increases were more than sufficient to meet an 80 per cent increase in population, thus lifting the housing space per person back to 6.2 square metres in 1965. By 1975, due especially to destruction by bombing during the war and lack of resources for civilian construction during the war, Hà Nội's housing space per person dropped drastically to 2.15 square metres.[25] While peace was returning to the country, a serious housing shortage crisis was brewing in Hà Nội in the mid-1970s.

The Socialist Housing Regime in Reunified Vietnam and Housing Conditions in Hà Nội, 1975–90

After reunification of Vietnam in 1975, the socialist housing regime was extended to the whole of Vietnam, and housing redistribution was carried out a second time in Hà Nội.[26] But the new situation of general peace began to exert a greater impact on the housing situation.

As returned soldiers and reunited families looked to peace and to improved living standards, housing demand increased, and thus the housing shortage crisis persisted and grew worse. Between 1976 and 1980 and

TABLE 5.1
Housing Space in Hà Nội, 1954–75

Year	Population	Total housing stock (million sq. m.)	Housing space per person (sq. m.)	Compared with China's national average (sq. m.)[a]
1954	445,529	1.79	4.84	
1955			6.5	3.5 (1957)
1960	462,000	1.8	3.89	
1965	840,000	2.07	6.2	3.7
1969	1,164,198			
1975		2.51	2.15[b]	

Notes:

a. Peter Nan-shong Lee, "Housing privatization with Chinese characteritics", in *Social Change and Social Policy in Contemporary China*, edited by Linda Wong and Stewart MacPherson (Aldershot: Avebury, 1995), pp. 113–39.

b. I arrived at this figure by dividing the housing stock in 1975 with the population in 1969. It is likely to be much lower in reality.

Source: K.O., "Xây dựng nhà ở theo phương châm 'Nhà nước và nhân dân cùng làm'" [Building houses according to the line of "State and people work together"], *HNM*, 8 March 1985, p. 3; Cục Thống Kê và Sở Văn hoá Thông tin Thành phố Hà Nội, *Thủ Đô Hà Nội: 30 năm xây dựng và bảo vệ chế độ Xã hội Chủ nghĩa* [Hà Nội the capital: 30 years of building and protecting the Socialist system] (Hà Nội, 1984), p. 51; Xây Dựng, "Chương trình phát triển nhà ở của Hà Nội đến năm 2000 và 2010" [Programme to develop housing in Hà Nội from now until 2000 and 2010], November 1997, p. 9; Nguyễn Văn Uẩn, *Hà Nội nửa đầu thế kỷ XX. Tập 3* [Hà Nội in the first half of the twentieth century: Volume 3] (Hà Nội: NXB Hà Nội, 1995), pp. 704–707.

between 1981 and 1985, the differences between housing demand (as indicated by state targets) and supply in these two periods were 53–56 per cent and 71 per cent respectively (see Table 5.2). Because the state was the only legal producer of new housing, non-state suppliers did not plug the shortfalls. According to a survey, in the 1970s and 1980s, each applicant for housing waited, on average, twenty-seven months before being allotted a flat.[27]

TABLE 5.2
State Housing Production in Hà Nội, 1976–85

Year/s or Period	Target (sq. m.)	Output (sq. m.)	Shortfalls (%)
1976	340,000	66,000	80
1977		121,543	
1978		108,095	
1979		40,159	
1980		33,033	
1976–80	**800,000 to 850,000**	**368,830**	**53–56**
1981		36,689	
1982	70,000	42,410	40
1983		45,497	
1981–85	**800,000**	possibly **229,596** (Assuming 1984/85 outputs were 10% over 1983 level)	**71.3**
		(1985–1990 statistics n.a.)	

Sources: Hàm Châu, "Hà Nội mùa thu xây dựng" [Hà Nội in autumn and construction season], *Đại Đoàn Kết,* 2 September 1978, pp. 16, 17, 33; Nguyễn Văn Cừ, "Phát huy mọi tiềm năng xây dựng nhà ở" [Realize every potential in building accommodation], *HNM,* 29 October 1982, p. 3; *HNM,* "Về vấn đề phân phối nhà ở hiện nay" [On distribution of accommodation at present] (Interview with Vũ Quốc Huy, Director of Public Works, Hà Nội), 27 November 1977, pp. 3, 4; Tuổi Trẻ Thủ Đô, "Hà Nội: Bước ngoặt giải quyết nhà ở" [Hà Nội: turning point in solving housing problems], 20 November 1996, pp. 1–2; Cục Thống Kê và Sở Văn hoá Thông tin Thành phố Hà Nội, *Thủ Đô Hà Nội: 30 năm xây dựng và bảo vệ chế độ Xã hội Chủ nghĩa* [Hà Nội the capital: 30 years of building and protecting the Socialist system] (Hà Nội, 1984), p. 50.

One major cause for the output shortfall was a state funding shortage (see Table 5.3A). Between 1976 and 1980, funding for housing construction was on average only 3.24 per cent of all state investments. Vietnamese officials considered this level of investments low compared with the norm of 8 per cent on average in socialist countries.[28] In Vietnam between 1985 and 1990 (Table 5.3B), the share of state investment in housing among total state investments is difficult to determine because official statistics lumped state investments in housing with those in public welfare and tourism, but they were likely to be lower than the levels of the late 1970s.

TABLE 5.3A
State Investment in Housing Construction, at Constant Prices, 1976–80

Year	State investments in housing (million đồng, constant prices)	State investment in housing as a percentage of all state investments (%)
1976	88.6	3.0
1977	143.6	4.0
1978	165.0	4.3
1979	103.7	2.8
1980	76.0	2.1
1981–1984	N.A.	N.A.

Source: Nigel Thrift and Dean Forbes, *The Price of War: Urbanization in Vietnam 1954–85* (London: Allen and Unwin, 1986), p. 127.

TABLE 5.3B
State Investments in Housing, Public Welfare, and Tourism, Current Prices, 1985–90

Year	State investments in housing, public welfare and tourism (billion đồng, current prices)	State investment in housing, public welfare, and tourism as a percentage of all state investments (%)
1985	3.10	0.32
1986	2.63	8.53
1987	9.70	8.21
1988	37.99	5.68
1989	120.96	6.30
1990	232.11	0.58

Source: Tổng Cục Thống Kê, *Động thái và thực trạng kinh tế — xã hội Việt Nam qua 10 năm Đổi Mới (1986–1995)* [Socio-economic dynamics and realities in Vietnam after 10 years of Đổi Mới, 1986-1995] (Hà Nội: NXB Thống Kê, 1996), Table 148.

A second cause of the low output of housing was the state continued to strongly discourage private housing, made worse by the state strongly disapproving differences in income and wealth expressed through the quality of housing people enjoyed. During the early 1980s in Hà Nội, the state repressed private builders who used income obtained from corruption or from illegal economic sectors such as private trading to build opulent houses.[29] Consequently, households were unlikely to improve their housing irrespective of their sources or amount of income, wealth, or savings. People who built better homes for themselves risked being investigated by the state, and if guilty of inappropriate economic activities, have their houses confiscated.[30]

Given the low investment and output in the housing sector in the 1980s, Hà Nội residents, on average, had smaller and smaller living space (Table 5.4).

According to one source, in Hà Nội between 1981 and 1985 three households frequently shared the same flat. This was worse than the situation that existed in the period before 1975. Nevertheless, housing space per person (3 square metres) in Hà Nội was larger than what it was in two smaller northern Vietnamese cities, Hai Phòng (2.7 square metres) and Quảng Ninh (2.5 square metres).[31] Compared with several other socialist and a few selected (based on the availability of statistics) developing countries, Hà Nội's housing space per person in 1981 was average among socialist countries, above what existed in India, Pakistan and Sri Lanka, and slightly above United Nations' norms (Table 5.5). But compared with China's national average rate, Hà Nội's rate of housing space per person began to lag behind from about 1982 (Table 5.4).

More importantly, after the war and reunification, Hà Nội residents began to expect higher quality housing conditions than the state could satisfy. Family sizes grew, yet the size of their allotted flats did not.[32] Many families in collective flats built in the 1960s now wanted separate kitchens and toilets, not shared ones. The demand for more space and privacy was a major reason why families encroached on available public space (hallways, walkways), and divided already small rooms and flats into even smaller ones.[33]

Meanwhile, upkeep by the state of its housing stock deteriorated.[34] The state's housing agencies could neither maintain the flats nor upgrade them to meet changing needs. For instance, in 1979, the Hà Nội city housing authority could complete only 20 per cent of the work necessary to maintain the city's housing stock properly. Only 9 per cent of the money

TABLE 5.4

Housing Conditions in Hà Nội, 1980–90

Year	Population (inner city only)	Total housing stock (million sq. m.)	Average space per person (sq. m.)	Compared with China's national average (sq. m.)[a]
1980	876,000	2.25	5.8	3.9
1981			4.2	3.7
1982			2.3	4.4
1984	905,400	2.75	3.04	4.9
1985		3.26	2.65?[b]	
1989			3.6	
1990			4.6	6.7
2004	3,500,000	14	4	

Notes:

a. Peter Nan-shong Lee, "Housing privatization with Chinese characteristics", in *Social Change and Social Policy in Contemporary China,* edited by Linda Wong and Stewart MacPherson (Aldershot: Avebury, 1995), p. 122.

b. Because it is not clear what the population of Hà Nội in 1985 was, I added 322,509 (the average per annum growth in population between 1980 and 1984) to the population figure of 1984 to arrive at a possible population of 1,227,909 in 1985. The total housing stock was then divided by this population figure of 1985 to arrive at the average space per person figure.

Source: Cục Thống Kê và Sở Văn hoá Thông tin Thành phố Hà Nội, *Thủ Đô Hà Nội: 30 năm xây dựng và bảo vệ chế độ Xã hội Chủ nghĩa* [Hà Nội the capital: 30 years of building and protecting the Socialist system], (Hà Nội, 1984), p. 51; Thanh Lan, "Lực cản tại cơ chế" [The obstruction is from the mechanism], *Đại Đoàn Kết,* 19 February 1998, pp. 1, 7; Nigel Thrift and Dean Forbes, *The Price of War: Urbanization in Vietnam 1954–85* (London: Allen and Unwin, 1986) pp. 148–151; Xây Dựng, "Chương trình phát triển nhà ở của Hà Nội đến năm 2000 và 2010" [Programme to develop housing in Hà Nội from now until 2000 and 2010], November 1997, p. 9; Thu Huyền, "Nhiều dự án, thiếu nhà ở", *Lao Động Điện Tử,* 16 February, 2004, No. 47, http://www.laodong.com.vn/pls/bld/folder$.view_item_detail(92798).

TABLE 5.5
Urban Housing Space Per Person in Selected Countries *circa* 1981
(unless stated otherwise)

Country/City	Persons/Room	Sq. m. per person
Soviet Union (1978)		12.8
N. Korea (Pyongyang) (1978)		12
Romania		10
S. Korea (Seoul, 1970)		5.9
Việt Nam (Hà Nội)		4.2
Cuba	1.0	4
China/Shanghai		3.7/4.52
Bulgaria (Sofia, 1985)	1.3	3.08
Poland	1.57	2.55
Sri Lanka	2.3	1.74
India	2.6	1.54
Pakistan	3.0	1.3

Notes:
The UN Standard of 4 sq. m. per room is indicated by the double line.

Sources: For Bulgaria, Cuba, India, Pakistan, and Sri Lanka, see Statistics Division of the UN Secretariat and United Nations Centre for Human Settlements (Habitat) (1995) Compendium of Human Settlement Statistics 1983, and Compendium of Human Settlement Statistics 1985 (http://www.un.org/Depts/unsd/social/housing.htm, 1998.) The figures given in the UN source were based on persons/room, and I derived the probable sq. m. per person figures by dividing the standard measure of 4 sq. m. per room by the number of persons per room. For Poland, see, Kazimierz Jose Zaniewski, "Housing Inequalities under Socialism: The Case of Poland", Ph.D. dissertation, University of Wisconsin, 1987. For the Soviet Union, Pyongyang, Romania, and China figures, see Sun Jin-lou and Liu Lin, *Zhu zhai she hui xue* [The Sociology of Housing] (Chi-nan: Shan-tung ren min chu pan she, 1985), pp. 7, 138–52. For Seoul, see Simon Chu-Hsung Wen, "A cross-national study on housing development in Asian transitional countries — Hong Kong, Korea (South), Singapore, and Taiwan (The Republic of)", Ph.D. dissertation, University of Michigan, 1988, p. 67.

it used came directly from state coffers, while the rest was paid for mainly by state enterprises.[35] The quality of state collective flats was also poor; many of them had technical problems not long after they were completed, with some of them even sinking by a metre or two. Some blocks of flats even had to be abandoned.[36] On the other hand, individuals who preferred privately repairing and upgrading their dwellings were hindered by multiple permit requirements and very long waits for licences.[37]

Rising demand, severe shortages, higher expectations, and illegal construction together stimulated the underground housing sector. A 1986 government survey of house ownership found that 91 per cent of all families in Hà Nội had bought or sold housing without registering with the state.[38] This was possible with a practice that circumvented the legal housing regime. To trade housing space and avoid the long bureaucratic screening process and the political danger of questions from the state about one's source of wealth, people erected a separate, informal documentation system which used scrappy handwritten notes to document transfers.[39] Everyone accepted these papers. Many people even used unauthorized copies of official forms for the purpose and affixed fake seals.

As the underground housing sector in Vietnam grew bigger, it met some of the demand. Simultaneously, the state's will to repress private construction weakened. By the early 1980s pressure was growing to reform the socialist housing regime, the major cause of the housing shortage crisis.

In many socialist countries in the 1970s and 1980s, severe housing shortages forced government leaders to revamp their housing regimes in order to boost housing production. The most important change common to these countries was the recognition of private housing to a modest degree. In 1979, the government of China decreed that improperly confiscated private homes would be returned to their owners, as the first step towards recognizing the sanctity of private property. Four years later, in 1983, it officially recognized private ownership of new houses.[40] The USSR lifted the ban on new private housing in 1985. In the USSR and Bulgaria, the state also made available more funds for loans to individuals to construct houses, whereas previously state banks were unwilling to give credit for such a purpose. The USSR also decentralized state housing construction, and emphasized quality instead of quantity of houses built. In Poland, housing rents were allowed to fluctuate with the market in the hope that income surpluses could finance private construction activities.[41] By the mid-1980s a sort of mixed state and private housing regime had arrived in the communist bloc.

In the case of Vietnam, Nigel Thrift and Dean Forbes argued that the Sixth Plenum of the VCP Central Committee held in 1979 was the political launching pad for a private sector role in the economy, housing included.[42] An axiomatic change in thinking took place because Vietnam's leaders realized that state resources for housing were insufficient for satisfying housing demand and ought to be complemented by private resources, which were plenty but hidden away due to fear of seizure by the state. The change in thinking and policy was in fact popular, as confirmed by the Bãi Bằng paper mill incident. The state took pains from 1980 to plan a foreign-funded, state-designed housing estate for workers of the paper mill, but the project took too long to begin, due to bureaucratic difficulties and long delays in negotiations with the Swedish sponsor. In 1983 workers of the mill clamoured for the district administration to give them land reserved for the housing estate to build their own houses and in return waived their entitlement to company housing. The district authority gave in and granted 100 plots of the reserved land to the workers.[43]

In the spirit of tapping private resources as an urgent solution to the housing shortage crisis, in the early 1980s the Hà Nội City administration initiated models of state–private co-operation. One model was "state and people working together" (*nhà nước và nhân dân cùng làm*) projects, in which people contributed capital and labour, and the state contributed land and building materials.[44] There were several variants of the model, distinguished by different degrees and nature of contribution from both parties.[45] Although the houses built were reported to be better in quality, and were registered as privately owned, all construction had to follow the state's macro plans for housing.[46]

The second model was house repair co-operatives; members pooled funds for tasks such as repainting and building toilets and other amenities in older flats.[47] The city sold these difficult-to-obtain building materials to the people-initiated co-operatives, and contributed some money. Co-operative members contributed their own labour as well as money.[48]

The Transitional Period Leading to a New Housing Regime

After Đổi Mới was officially announced in 1986 many more liberalizing changes to the socialist housing regime in Vietnam began. In 1987, Hà Nội housing authorities directly sold, rather than rented out as had been the prevalent case in the past, newly-built state flats in pilot areas such as

Nghĩa Đô (northwest outskirts of the city) to families. The buyers had to agree to various conditions, among them promising not to resell within a stipulated period of time.[49] The owners were then able to renovate their flats without having to overcome bureaucratic procedures regarding ownership. The pilot project was the beginning of state-sanctioned private ownership of new housing. In 1988, the state began distributing land to state enterprises to let them build houses, giving them full rights to manage and to approve renovations without needing local authorities' approval. Most enterprises, however, redistributed the land to employees for them to build their own houses.[50] In 1989, the state began to recognize the purchase and sale of private houses in Hà Nội, but tied such transactions to anti-speculation conditions.[51] In June 1990, the state formally allowed private builders to employ labour for constructing houses, but the size of such new houses were limited to a certain scale in order to obtain approval under employment controls.[52] Common to these transitional period changes, it seemed, was not just the purpose of eliminating red tape to boost incentives for housing production, but also the concern on the part of the party-state that unfettered privatization might create an out-of-control housing market that could inflate prices beyond the reach of many people, or create too big a gap between the haves and have-nots of housing.

THE LIBERALIZED HOUSING REGIME
FROM 1991

In March 1991, the state issued the Ordinance on Residential Housing that formally recognized the right of private ownership and participation in the housing sector.[53] A key provision stated:

> The State encourages and makes conditions favourable for every organization and individual to maintain and develop the residential housing stock. Any organization or individual can conduct businesses in residential housing through building, renovating houses for sale or for rent, and other housing business activities as stipulated by law.[54]

Consequently, according to scholars, between the years 1991 and 1994 "new houses sprouted like mushrooms". About two-thirds of all new housing was privately built and owned (see Table 5.6).[55] Government policy was to privatize the housing stock by selling dwellings under state control to occupants. The state also brought into the salary structure housing allowances instead of providing free accommodation to its employees.[56]

TABLE 5.6
New Housing Output in Hà Nội, State and Private, 1991–95, and Share of Housing, Public Welfare, and Tourism Sectors in State Investments for the Whole Country, 1991–94

Year	New Housing (sq. m.)	Private sector share (%)[a]	State investments in housing, public welfare, tourism sectors for the whole country	
			Billion đồng (current prices)	Share of total state investments (%)
1991	140,000	68%	224.5	4.98
1992	170,000	64%	330.3	4.37
1993	220,000	68%	425.8	2.54
1994	225,000	n.a.	512.1	2.42
1995	252,000	n.a.		
1996[b]	n.a.	40%		

Notes:
a. See these figures in Trịnh Duy Luân and Nguyễn Quang Vinh, *Tác động kinh tế xã hội của Đổi mới trong lĩnh vực nhà ở đô thị* [Socio-economic impact of Đổi Mới on urban housing] (Hà Nội: NXB Khoa học Xã hội, 1998), pp. 148, 177.
b. Trịnh Thi, "Building blocks: Where is the Vietnamese identity in the new architecture?", *Heritage* (January/February 1996), p. 27.

Sources: Housing figures come from Tuổi Trẻ Thủ Đô, "Hà Nội: Bước ngoặt giải quyết nhà ở" [Hà Nội: turning point in solving housing problems], 20 November 1996, pp. 1–2; investment figures are from Tổng Cục Thống Kê, *Động thái và thực trạng kinh tế — xã hội Việt Nam qua 10 năm Đổi Mới (1986–1995)*, [Socio-economic dynamics and realities in Vietnam after 10 years of Đổi Mới, 1986–1995] (Hà Nội: NXB Thống Kê, 1996), Table 148.

Meanwhile, from 1991 to 1994, state investments in housing, public welfare and tourism increased in absolute amounts but decreased as a proportion of total state investments (Table 5.6). With private sector participation no longer illegal, the housing situation in Hà Nội recovered from the 1980s' doldrums and the amount of housing space per person increased (Table 5.7).

Another aspect of the liberalized housing regime was that the state changed how it handled the housing it owned. In 1992 the state stopped providing housing directly to its employees; instead it gave state employees monthly monetary supplements to help them pay for dwellings rented from either the state or from the private housing market.[57] Second, in 1994, the state began to sell existing government houses (a policy called 61/CP) and to lease out (rather than allow use for free as before) residential land to users (60/CP). These policies were piloted in several areas of Hà Nội to assess their feasibility. Divestment was deliberately slow, in order to assess how the new policy might affect the wealth gap.[58] The state began with lower quality, or outer-city types of state accommodation and state land.[59] In 1999, however, preparations were being made to sell collective flats in the city centre, such as those belonging to armed forces' employees in the Trần Phú Road area, indicating privatization of state housing stock was gaining ground.[60] By 2002, the state agency responsible for privatizing the state's housing stock appeared to be impatient in wanting to complete its

TABLE 5.7

Housing Space Per Person in Hà Nội, 1991–98

Year	Population	Average space per person (sq. m.)
1991		3.2
1992		4.5
1994		5.3
1995	2,315,000	5.2
1996	2,364,000	4.5
1998		4.7
Forecast		
2000	2,570,000	5.5
2010	3,500,000	8.10–10.0

Sources: Quân Đội Nhân Dân, "Hà Nội's living space expands", quoted in Avsl-IVNA, 19 December 1997; Thanh Lan, "Lực cản tại cơ chế" [The obstruction is in the mechanism], *Đại Đoàn Kết,* 19 February 1998, pp. 1, 7; Tuổi Trẻ Thủ Đô, "Hà Nội: Bước ngoặt giải quyết nhà ở" [Hà Nội: turning point in solving housing problems], 20 November 1996, pp. 1–2; Xây Dựng, "Chương trình phát triển nhà ở của Hà Nội đến năm 2000 va 2010" [Programme to develop housing in Hà Nội from now until 2000 and 2010], November 1997, p. 9; Trung Thành, "Tìm giải pháp đồng bộ cho nhà ở đô thị đến năm 2000" [Looking for co-ordinated solutions for urban housing between now and the year 2000], *Đại Đoàn Kết,* 14 May 1998, pp. 1, 7.

task, but reported that bureaucratic difficulties slowed down the process. By June 2002, the total number of applications approved was only 30 per cent (of 800,000 applications).[61] By the end of that year, only 35 per cent of applications in the urban areas were approved.

By the mid-1990s, therefore, the new housing regime had not only permitted private housing, but also reduced the state's role in providing housing directly to employees. By legitimizing the private sector, the party-state in Vietnam resolved, at least temporarily, the housing shortage crisis. The liberalized regime, however, came at a cost for the party-state. Its ability to regulate buildings and construction has been greatly reduced, a matter I shall examine in the next section.

PART II: ILLEGAL CONSTRUCTION

1975 to Mid-1980s

Illegal construction of dwellings has long challenged the authority of the state's housing regimes. In this section, I will examine that for the post-1975 period with an eye primarily to analyse informal, "fence-breaking" methods by ward officials and residents.[62]

Much of the illegal construction in this period reportedly happened in the collective flat areas. On open areas between blocks of flats in Nguyễn Công Trứ, for example, people erected straw and bamboo structures, testing state resolve to enforce construction rules. Building on the vacant space between housing blocks was called "squeezed-in construction" (*xây chen*). If the ward and higher levels of state authority demonstrated inattention and indecisiveness, which was often, then offenders replaced the straw and bamboo with bricks and other stronger materials, and encroached on more land as well. Illegal structures, such as sheds, were used to keep children's toys, raise chickens, cook meals, park vehicles, and set up warehouses and production lines.[63]

In response, the Hà Nội City administration emphasized the political, mobilizational approach rather than the legal approach. It launched the "Civilized Way of Life and Family of New Culture" campaign (*nếp sống văn minh, gia đình văn hoá mới*), which the wards implemented in 1978. Expanded from the previous "Five-Good Family" (*Gia đình Năm tốt*) social education campaign, this new campaign exhorted people to voluntarily comply with rules and regulations governing daily living, including public health, sanitation, public awareness and consideration, traffic and courtesy. The state claimed the campaign was successful. The results in terms of stopping illegal construction, however, were mixed. Many of the illegal structures were still in many collective flat areas in the 1990s.[64] (see Figure 5.1). There was evidence that some wards tried to enforce state rules on construction but these were not successful in general as people ignored ward authorities or co-opted them.[65]

Squatting and illegal construction in Hà Nội also occurred on vacant land elsewhere in the city. A typical offender was Đặng Duy Hải who initially built a single-storey house on state land in Ngọc Hà Street. After the state demolished the house, Hải rebuilt it quickly, added a second storey, and even began to sell noodles downstairs, in the hope of strengthening his claim to stay there because he was making a living. In Hàng Chiếu Street, Lê Thị Bình's family built their house illegally on vacant public land in 1978. Instead of complying with the local authority's demolition order, Bình improved on the condition of the house and built a second storey. Other such cases occurred in the same District. It took ward officials two to four years to successfully enforce demolition orders in these cases.[66]

FIGURE 5.1
Illegal structures in collective flats.

Despite some success in stopping or destroying squatting and illegal construction, offences grew in number and spread to many parts of Hà Nội. Three locations had more illegal construction than others: Giảng Võ-Thành Công, Cao Sà Lá, and Trung Tự-Kim Liên areas.

Along Giảng Võ Street beside the Giảng Võ Exhibition Centre area, squatters began in 1982 to build houses and sheds. They usually completed construction in one night or one day, presenting an accomplished fact to the authorities by the time ward inspectors had heard of it. On a piece of vacant land at the nearby Thành Công area, twenty sheds appeared in 1982, days after the government said it was being reserved for a future market. An illegal private land and housing market quickly developed. "Rights" to land (marked by physical markers and guarded by their owners) and to houses were bought and sold. Squatters were motivated by future compensation for resettlement, either in the form of money, or in the form of a retail stall in the proposed market. Amazingly, some people were able to demand successfully that the state compensated them for resettlement, even though the squatting and housing construction were illegal in the first place.[67]

The second area was also vacant public land, along a 500-metre stretch of Nguyễn Trãi Road and beside the Cao Sà Lá factories.[68] An observer claimed "one only needed to rent a vehicle to transport materials to the area and one would be able to build a house immediately". The claim was probably valid, as local authorities had to demolish as many as fifty sheds in 1982. Yet people rebuilt many of them after the authorities had gone away.[69] The motive of squatters, other than creating much-needed living space, was to take part in the local economy surrounding the factories. From those sheds, people supplied factories and workers with products and services, and traded in goods smuggled out of the factories. The sheds then became legitimized houses as time went by and all of them remained standing.

Meanwhile, ward officials encountered numerous difficulties when trying to enforce rules in these two areas. First, ward officials had to refer all cases to the district for decision. This prevented ward officials from taking immediate demolition action, although they could order that construction be suspended. Because the district office took a long time to decide, offenders usually took very lightly ward orders to stop construction. While the wards waited for instructions the illegal construction problem widened as more squatters joined in. Many offenders were also able to complete and inhabit their building, and by that stage, the issue had become emotional. People saw the state as uncaring for the welfare of the needy, because it demolished inhabited houses when there was a shortage of accommodation everywhere in the city.[70]

Second, ward officials were vulnerable to vetoes from authorities higher than the district, which made them hesitant about carrying out district orders too quickly or acting too strictly towards offenders who could appeal to the district and levels above. According to a 1982 source,

> Recently, the District of Đống Đa decided on demolition [of the numerous sheds around the Sao Vàng rubber factory], and a few wards had already prepared for it. However, there was suddenly a directive from the City that suspended demolition, thus causing confusion among the people and the local authorities.[71]

Sometimes, higher levels over-ruled the district and the ward when dealing with people who absolutely needed more space. But there were many such cases in the early 1980s, and giving special treatment to one family with genuine circumstances, while politically expedient, made it difficult for the ward and district officials to insist on demolishing other illegally built houses. This was because other offenders reminded officials of the principle of equality and cited their circumstances of hardship, even though the second reason was not always genuine for the other cases.

The third and most important problem for wards was the complicated and long approval process for construction licence application. In the collective flat areas, for instance, approval of multiple government agencies with equal powers to decide on matters within the area often landed renovation and maintenance issues in gridlock. Responding to complaints, in 1982 the city administration streamlined the construction licence application process. Among other measures, it specified the number of days within which relevant agencies had to reply to applicants.[72] City officials also emphasized criminal and civil penalties for offenders. These were: stoppage of work with compensation for state losses, withdrawal of construction licence (if found to have violated terms of licence), confiscation of land being used, compensation for damages done through illegal action, and prosecution under the law.[73]

These regulations proved quite insufficient to deter illegal construction, and in fact illegal construction began to spread, with higher intensity than before, across Hà Nội City. One month after the new regulations were issued, the city administration ordered an enforcement exercise and found 1,432 cases across the city of Hà Nội. Outlying wards such as Cống Vị,

Yên Thái, Ngọc Hà, and Thanh Xuân — because they had large tracts of vacant state land closest to the city — were the hot spots.[74]

Crisis at the Trung Tự and Kim Liên Collective Flat Areas

The illegal construction that occurred in the third area Trung Tự-Kim Liên during the early 1980s marked a shift in the kind of illegal activities.[75] In the late 1970s, problems of illegal construction in the collective flat areas were mostly structures external to the buildings. From the early 1980s, extensions and renovations to individual flat units were beginning to be detected. A survey of all of Hà Nội's collective flat areas in 1983 showed that 75–83 per cent of people living on the ground floor and 50 per cent of those living on the upper floors of collective flat areas had knocked down walls of their flats without asking for permission from relevant authorities. A large number of people living on upper levels built suspended balconies (called "tiger cages" or *chuồng hổ* by Vietnamese), without concrete support below (see Figure 5.2). These renovations or extensions threatened building safety because they added weight to the buildings without reinforcement of building foundations.[76] Compared with the late 1970s, in the 1980s many offenders in the collective flat areas did not bother to test the responses of the authorities by first building modestly. Instead, they used strong, lasting materials straightaway, indicating the belief that their renovations would outlast the will of the state.[77]

Evidently, the state's political mobilization and education approach of the late 1970s was not working. Hence, it changed emphasis. In 1983, the Hà Nội City promulgated a set of regulations (Decree 11/XDCB) governing construction and renovation in collective flat areas.[78] Despite the regulations being publicized in the newspapers, many people in Trung Tự-Kim Liên took no heed. Before 1982, the government had recorded only 51 cases of illegal construction in the Trung Tự-Kim Liên areas, yet after Decree 11/XDCB, there were 16 cases in 1983, 41 in 1984, and 33 in January–June, 1985 (total of 127 cases from 1976 to June 1985), and probably an additional 473 cases between July 1985 and 1989. The total figure of 600 cases was equivalent to about 26 per cent of all households who lived in Trung Tự-Kim Liên. The majority of offenders had created space, from 3 square metres to 23 square metres, for another bedroom, a new kitchen, or a bathroom.[79] In 1985, the Council of Ministers (the national government cabinet) demanded that local authorities in Trung

FIGURE 5.2
Flats with suspended balconies.

Tự-Kim Liên enforce construction rules without exceptions. Yet, ten more illegal cases were recorded, and a further twenty families were preparing to start construction illegally.[80]

There were at least four reasons for such illegal construction. First, many residents had the co-operation of ward officials, by virtue of their own positions in the state bureaucracy. Except for one, all families living in Trung Tự-Kim Liên were state employees of senior and middle rank. In 1985, 51 families among the offenders in the year belonged to the "B" to "C" ration coupon classes.[81] Their official positions allowed them to easily obtain co-operation from Trung Tự-Kim Liên ward officials. Wards officials had a vested interest not to be too tough on offenders so that they, their neighbours, colleagues, and fellow party members who needed extra space could build and extend without being encumbered by permits and licences.[82] This is shown by the fact that prior to 1989, party officials in the Kim Liên ward party branch kept silent on the situation of illegal construction, despite its seriousness and the large degree of publicity. From

1984 (when ten cases involving party members appeared) until 1988, party cells in Kim Liên ward did not discuss the matter seriously, and imposed no disciplinary action on any party member, even though they knew that forty out of 600 illegal construction cases in the area before 1989 involved fellow party members.

Co-operation between officials and residents was not the only explanation for the break down of the housing regime authority in Trung Tự-Kim Liên. Ward officials were also negligent and incompetent; they did not deal with illegal construction proactively. "Responsible agencies like the ward, its committee on housing, the inspection team … usually stopped at the stage of filing situation reports … the most they did was to impose fines, they never sent people to demolish houses. That's why people could do what they liked."[83]

Another part of the explanation is that the "penetration" of society that ward officials should have in theory was absent. Ward officials had difficulties penetrating the "walls" that residents erected to block investigations. Residents refused to entertain ward officials' visits to inspect houses or to meet heads of families responsible. Some families forged alliances to keep the ward out of the matter completely. They co-constructed (if they shared the same wall or floor/ceiling, for instance) and therefore persuaded the ward to ignore their case, because nobody suffered any damages or would complain to higher authorities.[84] Ward officials managed to enforce order in a few cases, but generally they could not be persistent in enforcing regulations without engaging in heated, emotional arguments with people or meeting with intense lobbying from other officials to forsake investigations. One 1985 account gives a flavour of the defiance ward officials encountered:

> … the [demolition] orders were not carried out, or when the ward managed to send its men down to enforce the demolition order, they met with decisive and strong responses [from the people]. There were cases where a few days after demolition, the demolished houses [on the ground floor] were rebuilt in an even more open manner.[85]

A fourth reason is residents could ask higher level officials directly for favours and, therefore, they could adopt a defiant attitude towards ward officials. When the district or higher authorities would ask ward officials for favours for some residents, wards could not say "no", despite knowing that it was not the right thing to do. Consequently wards did not want to be too tough on residents, in case residents asked district officials to intervene. That would mean ward officials having to back down from a tough position. That would be a loss of face, and thus authority. In a number of cases in Kim Liên for instance, the ward could not enforce regulations because high officials who were relatives or friends of offenders asked ward officials to ignore the cases as a favour.[86] Informant C told me that

> Connections are useful when the local policemen or official is insistent on stopping the construction or in carrying out the law to stop the illegal work. Somebody higher up the local authority would be contacted so that he can speak to the local official to give the family concerned some leeway, either for reason of compassion or for the authority of the person requesting the favour, even if that person is not a specialist in construction matters. I was also an illegal constructor, and in my case, a high official in my department called up the local authority official and asked for the favour.

Such exceptions provided justifications for other illegal constructions. The unprivileged retorted to the ward's demand for demolition that "only after the government demolishes the house of Mr X [the protected offender], will we demolish our houses as well." ("*Bao giờ phá được nhà ông X., thì nhà chúng tôi mới phá.*")[87]

The Illegal Construction Situation from 1987 to 1995

In a renewed attempt to restore order on construction matters in many places of the city, the city people's committee issued new construction regulations (Decision 4637/QĐ-UB, dated 31 October 1987).[88] Two provisions are notable. First, Decision 4637 forgave illegal houses built by squatters on vacant public land, provided they paid land taxes, and vacated the land when the state required it. This was a major concession from the party-state. In effect the decision legitimized the existence of whole neighbourhoods built against urban planning and housing regime and construction rules. In hindsight, this measure may have encouraged more squatters because it showed that the state would give in eventually if squatters held out long enough. Second, the regulations gave more powers to the ward level. The district and the city levels of authority, the regulation stated, should be the levels of appeal. The ward was to be the first authority to deal with illegal construction. The objective was to reduce frequent instances whereby offenders went straight to levels above the ward and used political connections to obtain authoritative decisions in their favour. To protect against abuses by ward officials, the new regulations specified significant punishments of ward officials if they distorted the truth about people's housing situation.[89]

Despite Decision 4637, the illegal construction situation in Hà Nội worsened. In 1988 the four inner city districts recorded 1,768 offences, 300 more than in 1983. The 1,768 offences were more than twice the number of construction licences (769) issued in the same year. Many other offences had gone unrecorded.[90]

There were probably four reasons for the worsening situation. First, economic liberalization in the late 1980s provided another push for illegal construction. When petty private businesses became legal in the late 1980s, many households wanted to open shops for which they needed space. Many households living on the ground floor of collective flats walled up vacant public space in front of their flats and turned them into family shops to earn a living.[91] In areas of the city where there were no collective flats, many households had to renovate their living space into shop space as well.

A second reason was the general bureaucratic situation and the wards' ineffectiveness. Decision 4637 did not significantly change licence requirements, nor did it create conditions to give officials incentives to enforce rules strictly. Being at the bottom of the bureaucratic hierarchy, with no increased protection for taking tough action, ward officials continued to look up. They had to guard themselves against what higher officials might do to them if they adhered to the rules. For instance, one ward chairwoman said that her fellow officials suffered low morale because of the district's ambiguous attitude towards illegal construction cases. Districts did not act swiftly or decisively to reinforce ward decisions when residents appealed. By taking a long time to act, district offices gave people reason to think that either the officials were incompetent or some lobbying was taking place behind the scenes. Whichever the case, the delay or silence allowed illegal construction to stand. Without district support, ward cadres became confused about right and wrong when similar cases occurred. They generally, therefore, delayed acting or, if they did take steps to enforce the law, they did so in such a weak manner that the political will was unconvincing to the offenders.[92]

Wards officials also responded to informal pressures and inducements from residents and others. Some ward officials discriminated among illegal constructors, thereby arousing suspicions about their honesty and integrity. For instance, at the Tô Hiến Thành and Mai Hắc Đế Streets junction, the Hà Nội City Tourist Company built a shed with a zinc roof and used it as a commercial bicycle parking lot. It was an eyesore but the ward did not order its demolition, whereas bamboo sheds that had been on the same street for decades were demolished for the reason that they were offensive aesthetically.[93]

A third reason was that ward officials often sheltered offenders. As long as the illegal construction did not bother neighbours or adversely affect public installations, officials and residents were often willing to keep the whole matter under wraps. These cases are illustrative. A Mr Hoàng Văn M had a ground floor flat at 11 Vọng Đức Street. His sons who were living with him had all grown up and his 12 square metre flat was getting too small. Thus in 1991, without a construction licence, he had his flat extended beyond the perimeters of the building. In this way he added 15 square metres of living space and brought the total area of the dwelling to less than 4 square metres per person, around the average standard of Hà Nội in the early 1990s. All of M's neighbours and the local authorities feigned ignorance (làm ngơ), even though the protrusion was obvious to everyone, because they understood M's dire needs.[94]

I have more knowledge of the second and third cases. The second case took place in my neighbourhood in 1997. A lady called Hoà living five doors away complained to my house-mother that her immediate neighbour had built a high wall in front of her balcony door and window, and this denied her rights to ventilation and a view. Before building the wall, the neighbour had neither consulted her nor asked her permission. Hoà said she was determined to see that the ward order the wall dismantled, but she also said if her opinion and permission had been sought before the construction had began, she would have been willing to concede out of goodwill.[95] Eventually, nothing happened to the offender.

The third case took place in Cống Vị ward. M and O, a young couple who are my friends, got married in the early 1990s. They planned to live on the earnings of O's hairdressing skills. Because their parents' houses were too small to accommodate them, they constructed a small house at the end of the collective flat block where her parents lived, on Kim Mã Thượng Road. The small, 10 square metre dwelling was their only shelter and served as both shop and home. They were in fact squatting on public land. But ward officials only charged them a fine and did not demolish the place. They managed this arrangement largely through O's father. He was of middle-rank in the state agency that managed the collective flats; he pleaded with his superiors and the ward officials to let the couple stay.[96]

Such informal methods do not always work. When Hoàng Văn M later became overambitious and started work to build a second storey on top of the protruding ground area (which would have doubled his housing area), his neighbours opposed him. They said he was being greedy and was threatening building safety. Furthermore, he was usurping the space rights of his upstairs neighbours. M's neighbours complained to the ward, and ward officials stopped the construction.[97] Similarly, in the spring of 1997, M and O told me that in one or two years' time they would like to extend their house outwards to align the front walls of the house with the road kerb ten metres away. This would double their living space. But it would also turn much of the open, public space in front of the house, now enjoyed by residents, into their own private space. If that were to happen, the lane beside the house would be very narrow, creating a hazard for traffic there. When I last visited M and O in spring 2004, they had not carried out their plan. Instead they had added a second storey to their 10 square metre shed, and the construction was "fined" by the ward. They had not proceeded with their original plan because in 1998 neighbours had voiced opposition, including appealing to ward officials to stop it.[98] In fact M and O's immediate neighbour had the same ambition to extend his house out to the road kerb. This neighbour disregarded residents' and officials' objection by beginning construction. Incensed neighbours got tough and had the ward send down officials to stop construction work and ensure that this new structure was dismantled. In 2002, I found that their neighbour had already extended his house and turned much of the sidewalk space into the family yard. In 2002, however, the neighbours succeeded in pushing the perimeters of the house gate out to very close to the kerb, apparently succeeding in part.[99]

The last reason why Decision 4637 failed to curb illegal construction was that it did not reduce possibilities of bureaucratic manipulations of construction licence applications. The number of permits required for construction was not reduced; and opportunities for corruption were as many as the number of permits required. From the mid-1980s, hyperinflation was already rife, and people on fixed incomes faced tremendous pressures to obtain extra income from any avenue. Many bureaucrats of all levels extracted bribes from licence applicants. As a result, some people took the risk of offending the law. One source described it sarcastically:

> At present, in many places, the maximum time required for approving applications for construction and renovation licenses was not fixed [despite the 1982 regulations]. The speed was dependent on the level and unit of government involved, as well as the attitude of the applicant, and dependent on whether the applicant knew how to play the game

"beautifully" or not. The price for such play varied. If the price were wonderful then it would be fast, but if the price was only sufficient to satisfy one player among the many, then the applicant's file was left to rot! As a result, from the time the application was lodged to the time approval was received, the time passed could have been a few months, half-a-year, or even one year. People were afraid of delays and they took the risk to construct even before approval was given; they were willing to accept the fines or whatever punishment given so long as they could move into the new place as soon as possible.[100]

In June 1990, the city authority responded to the worsening situation by issuing Decisions 2704 QĐ/UB and 2771 QĐ/UB, which reduced the number of permits required. Under Decision 2704, people no longer had to obtain wards' certification of their housing need, thus getting rid of a channel for grease. Furthermore, small-scale repairs, such as replacing parts of doors, painting, and changing of roof tiles, were liberated from permit requirements, provided there was no extension of living space.[101] Decision 2771 also, once again, granted different degrees of amnesty to all illegal construction, provided local authorities agreed.[102] The last provision, therefore, opened a new channel for grease while another was closed.

Thus it was no surprise that evidence showed that Decisions 2704 and 2771 could not reduce illegal construction between 1990 and 1992, because two years later, in August 1992, the Hà Nội City people's committee issued Decision 1431 which urged more vigilance among officials in catching illegal construction.

But there was another twist to Decision 1431. In an attempt to overcome bureaucratic manipulations and the strength of informal methods people employed at the neighbourhood level, it transferred to the ward police the powers of inspecting construction sites and imposing administrative fines. These powers had belonged to the District Land, Construction and Housing Inspectorate. According to one source, the reason for the transfer was that the District Inspectorate had become too powerful and corrupt. The city authorities thought that ward policemen, with their close supervision of neighbourhoods, could better the Inspectorate in enforcing construction rules.[103] This assessment proved erroneous. After the transfer of power, ward officials in general were still accused of being in coterie with offenders.[104] On the other hand, some ward policemen also reported that they found it difficult to deal with people in the ward whom they met on a daily basis and had good relationships with.[105] In fact, ward policemen referred more cases to the districts after Decision 1431 than before, because it was a good way to avoid lobbying from residents. In effect, Decision 1431 created an extra layer of bureaucracy, the ward police, in the fight against illegal construction.

Realizing these problems, four years later in 1994, the city people's committee transferred the powers of inspection and enforcement from the ward police back to the District Land, Construction and Housing Inspectorate.[106] However, the reversal could have been driven by another rise in the number of illegal construction cases to a new, higher plateau in the early 1990s, which suggested that ward policemen were ineffective. Compared to 1987 when there was an average of 142 cases of illegal construction per month in *all* the four inner city districts, in the eight months after Decision 1431 in 1992, there was an average of 109 cases per month *in just one district* (Hai Bà Trưng) alone.[107] In 1993, the district of Ba Đình (which usually had the best record of Hà Nội's urban districts in terms of social order) recorded 143 cases per month.[108] By May 1995, illegal construction in the four Hà Nội urban districts were occurring at the rate of about 1,000 cases a month, or 12,000 per year, or an average of 250 cases per district per month.[109]

The Dykes

The earlier pages have painted a partial picture of a rather weak enforcement of construction rules. A more balanced picture is closer to reality. There have been instances whereby the state is capable of enforcing rules and does not tolerate extended challenges to its authority. A famous example concerns the illegal construction along the Nghi Tàm dyke in the northeast of Hà Nội city. The dyke, however, stretches out from two ends of Nghi Tàm to Yên Phụ and Phú Thượng areas, and the whole stretch was beginning to be populated by illegal housing.[110]

Dykes surrounding or running through Hà Nội prevent or minimize flooding by the Red River during high rises of the water level. Hà Nội's dykes are in fact a key part of this defence system that protects many northern provinces south and west of the Red River. Building on the dykes can adversely affect their effectiveness, because the soil of the dykes would loosen from drilling and pilling work. From the late 1970s, despite being illegal, considerable construction occurred. Three types of violations were common: (1) construction without a licence; (2) construction beyond the dyke and beside the river, on state land; and (3) structures that broke the dyke or undermine its foundations. Type (3) was the most threatening to dykes.

An informant told me that the problem at Nghi Tàm began when the Hà Nội City authority decided in the early 1990s that the top surface of the dyke should be used as a major road and proceeded to pave and widen its top. This decision encouraged people to build residences and especially shops along the new road.[111] Branching out from the dyke road, people began to build streets, shops, and neighbourhoods on either side of the dykes, especially on the side between the dykes and the river. Neighbourhoods took shape without planning or authorization from the state, and all the houses were built without licences. When the squatting and illegal construction first occurred, no government agencies took action. Two agencies likely to be responsible, the wards and the Ministry of Irrigation, pushed the responsibility for taking action to the other, and neither did much to prevent the situation from getting worse.[112]

From July 1991 to March 1995, the Ba Đình District recorded ninety-four cases of illegal construction near and beyond the Nghi Tàm section of the dyke. In actual fact, however, more than 300 houses were illegally built along the dyke. They would have also been tolerated if not for the dangers they posed to the dyke, because they were Type (3) offences. A substantial number of houses were built with iron and cement, requiring drilling that weakened dyke foundations. Among the 300 houses, ten were hotels, thus indicating a substantial business interest — and perhaps grease money — on the issue.[113]

None of these more than 300 households possessed a "construction licence", but to take it literally would be to miss two points about clever officials and usurpation of authority. In the 1990s, the Hà Nội Chief Architect was the sole authority to vet construction plans and issue construction licences for projects around the dyke.[114] Contrary to this law, 70 of the more than 300 households were given "approval" by other government agencies, such as the Hà Nội Office of Construction, the Ba Đình District, and leading officials of the district and wards. The usurpers gave builders stamped official letters that allowed construction to proceed, although in fact only the Hà Nội Chief Architect had the authority to do so after having checked the safety aspects of the proposed construction project. The other 270 houses had no approval from anywhere. Furthermore, those with construction licences built houses of sizes and scale far greater than what were stated in the licences.[115]

Second, when they dealt with squatters, ward and district officials interpreted provisions of Decisions 4637 (1987) and 1431 (1992) liberally. These two Decisions gave amnesties to illegal houses on vacant public land, but whether amnesty applied to land beyond the dykes was not clear.

Land-use beyond the dykes was, however, also subjected to the authority of the Ministry of Irrigation. Disregarding the authority of the Ministry, local authority officials of the district and wards imposed "fines for existence" (which they kept as organizational income) on illegal builders without demanding demolition, a course of action provided by the amnesties. For instance, a vice-chairman of the Ba Đình District imposed a fine of 7.26 million đồng (equivalent to about US$700 then) in one such case. People then cited the receipts for the fines as legitimate state approval for their houses, and even sold the receipts in a black market to other people who used the receipts as "licences" for construction. The transfers were not questioned but were accepted by local authorities.[116]

In late 1994 the Hà Nội City ordered all construction at the Nghi Tàm area to stop, but compliance was poor. Fourteen households went ahead with their building plans after the order. Even though the ward had inspected and filed reports as many as six times, indicating that eviction action was likely to be taken, squatters and builders refused to budge. When officials came to remind them to move out, they merely promised to obey government orders, but secretly intensified building activity.[117]

With strong backing from the Central government just when the case was gaining international fame and causing considerable pressures and loss of "face" to the country, the Hà Nội City administration stood its ground. It sent out demolition teams that lopped off enough of the offending houses facing the dykes so that a minimum distance from the dyke was observed.

Curiously, however, while all houses facing the dyke suffered this act, house number 71 on Yên Phụ Road stood unaffected. Apparently, a person high in the state's hierarchy personally wrote to the ward to suggest a suspension of demolition of house 71 until "more thorough investigations" could be completed. "More thorough investigations" was usually the euphemism upper levels used to subtly order lower levels to leave things as they are. The high-ranking official knew that district officials had already filed eleven situation reports against house 71 and visited it many times to confirm that it infringed dyke regulations.[118] But only after several months of strong protests in the printed media about the case did the ward lop off the offending part of house 71 as well.[119]

CONCLUSION

The weak ability of the party-state in enforcing its housing regime in Hà Nội has been remarkable. The trend, as late as the mid-1990s, has been increasing instances of illegal construction, although pockets of compliance and strict enforcement exist, especially in the early 1980s. It seems that if the central government takes a strong stand against a construction issue, such as illegal construction at the dykes, then it has a good chance of having its regime rules observed. But similar instances that affect national interests are few. Many more instances of illegal construction occur at the everyday urban level, and enforcement of rules at that level has been hotchpotch. This is despite the party-state dominating the structure of power, which theoretically ought to facilitate the state in enforcing its rules strictly, through the network of ward authorities in Hà Nội. The fact is also that this illegal construction phenomenon has not been restricted to Hà Nội. In Đà Nẵng in the late 1990s, as the economy took off, increased housing needs and inflated prices led to a steep rise in illegal construction. The licensing process could not deal with these changes and the wards and other local authorities acted as the mediators between constructors and the state, so that things could work. This has also been the case in Hồ Chí Minh City in the past few years, in a number of former areas that the city authority has opened up for urban housing development.

People in Hà Nội might observe housing construction and renovation rules if the rules were easy to follow and, very important, if by abiding with the rules residents could meet basic and urgent housing needs. But instead, on many occasions, fence-breaking (*phá rào*)[120] seemed to be the only alternative in order to break through the bind of impractical rules and urgent needs. In other words, housing rules have received little respect because they have prohibited people from achieving a basic — and later desired — standard of housing, which also varied across time.

In order to deal with this situation, a range of informal methods has evolved in Hà Nội. These methods include residents pleading, lobbying, using political connections, bribing ward officials, and bribing district- and city-level supervisors in an effort to deter officials from enforcing the law. They also use guerrilla tactics, outmanoeuvering local officials and turning to their advantage, when they can, the very laws themselves. Informant C noted again:

> Under the housing decree, everybody is entitled to accommodation, and thus the government actually has no right to destroy a person's house, once it is completed, without consultation or compensation. So people take advantage of this loophole to construct their extension overnight so that by the time the government machinery comes back to work the next day the house is a *fait accompli*.

Ward officials are party-state officials, but societal influences on their behaviour are important; at least, these influences explain why at the everyday urban level, people lack strong respect for housing regime and construction rules. Ward officials were unable to enforce rules strictly because the socioeconomic situation in general and the housing situation in particular prescribe role conflicts for them. Many officials resolve their role conflicts in favour of their informal interests and obligations, such as corruption and the moral issue of allowing people a decent standard of housing, despite the rules. In that way, the boundaries of the party-state are renegotiated to create mediation space.

Thus, ward officials often help to conceal, legitimizing, or at least pretending to ignore fence breaking. They may also use informal ways to appeal for compliance or minimize the fence-breaking lest they get into serious trouble with their supervisors. There are also times they insist on implementing the housing rules. Out of this dynamic between residents and local ward officials have emerged informal understandings.

Mediation space in housing regimes of Vietnam impacts on our view of the Vietnamese political system by challenging the notion that the party-state is in control of society, and by also challenging us to rethink whether in Vietnam, state and society are separate identities. To be sure, in Vietnam the party-state is a separate organization from society; it is above society. At levels of state–society interaction above the ward, the party-state is the sole determinant of what kind of rules enter the housing regime and if it chooses to it can erect rules or make decisions without consulting society. At the everyday urban level, however, when the housing regime is enforced, the state may not necessarily get its way all the time, and agents of the party-state may side with society rather than their employers. In this way, the boundary between state and society becomes hazy and subjected to negotiation and influence by the situation.

Notes

1. This definition is adapted slightly from Benedict Kerkvliet's definition of a "land regime". See Benedict J. Tria Kerkvliet, *Land Struggles and Land Regimes in the Philippines and Vietnam during the Twentieth Century* (Amsterdam: Centre for Asian Studies, The Wertheim Lecture, 1997), p. 2.
2. Ngoc Mai, "Squatters swamp history's landmarks", *Vietnam Investment Review,* 12 June 2000, via vnnews-l.

3. See, for example, Alfred John DiMaio Jr., *Soviet Urban Housing: Problems and Policies* (New York: Praeger Publishers, 1974); Ivan Szelenyi, *Urban Inequalities under State Socialism* (New York: Oxford University Press, 1983); Sun Jin-lou and Liu Lin, *Zhu zhai she hui xue* [The Sociology of Housing] (Chi-nan: Shan-tung ren min chu pan she, 1985); Kazimierz Jose Zaniewski, "Housing Inequalities under Socialism: The Case of Poland", (Ph.D. dissertation, University of Wisconsin, 1987); John Sillince, ed., *Housing Policies in Eastern Europe and the Soviet Union* (London & New York: Routledge, 1990); Bengt Turner, József Hegedüs and Iván Tosics, *The Reform of Housing in Eastern Europe and the Soviet Union* (London & New York: Routledge, 1992); Peter Nan-shong Lee, "Housing privatization with Chinese characteristics", in *Social Change and Social Policy in Contemporary China,* edited by Linda Wong and Stewart MacPherson (Aldershot: Avebury, 1995), pp. 113–39.

4. John Sillince, "Housing Policy in Eastern Europe and the Soviet Union," in *Housing Policies in Eastern Europe and the Soviet Union*, p. 6.

5. Frank Carter, "Housing Policy in Bulgaria", in *Housing Policies in Eastern Europe and the Soviet Union,* p. 125.

6. Conversation with a Vietnamese researcher in the National Centre for Arts and Social Sciences, Fieldnotes 20 December 1996.

7. Minh Tuấn, Hương Thủy, "Hà Nội thí điểm cấp giấy chủ quyền nhà và đất" [Hà Nội pilots the issuing of ownership certificates for houses and land], *Đại Đoàn Kết,* 20 January 1997, pp. 1, 7.

8. *Vietnam News Brief,* "Illegal house constructions booms in HCM City", 29 July 2002.

9. Đoàn Lan, "Hà Nội: Công trình xây dựng được cấp phép chỉ đạt 40%" [Hà Nội: Only 40% of Construction projects are licensed], VN Express, 27 March 2004. http://vnexpress.net/Vietnam/Xa-hoi/2004/03/3B9D10A4/.

10. *"Tôi xin giấy phép làm gì, phải chạy lo đủ thứ giấy tờ, lên phường, quận, địa chính, cũng phải tốn kém thuốc nước, nhưng ngại nhất là phải chạy lên chạy xuống, chờ đợi, chầu chực, rồi còn thưa gửi nữa chứ. Thôi, làm luật là nhẹ người, chẳng phải thưa gửi ai."* Minh Tuấn, "Xây nhà không phép, lỗi của dân hay của chính quyền?", *Đại Đoàn Kết,* 6 May 2000, pp. 1, 7.

11. Trịnh Duy Luân and Nguyễn Quang Vinh, *Tác động kinh tế xã hội của Đổi mới trong lĩnh vực nhà ở đô thị* [Socioeconomic impact of đổi mới on urban housing) (Hà Nội: NXB Khoa học Xã hội, 1998), pp. 123–29.

12. Fieldnotes 21 November 1996.

13. DCD, "Nội dung phân cấp cho UBND Quận, UBND phường" [The contents of work delegated to people's committees of Districts and Wards], *Hà Nội Mới* (hereafter HNM), 12 May 1982, p. 2.

14. This incident took place in late 1995 on Đỗ Ngọc Du Street in Hà Nội, close to the junction with Đồng Nhân Street. It was not reported in the mass

media. The co-operative refused to comply with ward orders to desist, so ward officials sent out a team to demolish the illegal structures while a big crowd watched.

15. Nguyễn Đức Thà, "Xử lý những trường hợp xây dựng trái phép" [Dealing with cases of illegal construction], *HNM*, 13 April 1982, p. 2, and 14 April 1982, p. 2.

16. Conversations with a resident group head in Quỳnh Mai Ward, 31 January 1998, and with chairman of Ô Chợ Dừa Ward on 16 March 1998.

17. Conversations with a resident group head in Quỳnh Mai Ward, 31 January 1998.

18. Vương Thức, "Điều tra quyền sở hữu tư nhân về nhà của ở quận Đống Đa" [Survey on right of private ownership of housing in Đống Đa District], *HNM*, 31 January 1986, p. 3; Minh Tuấn, Hương Thủy, "Hà Nội thí điểm cấp giấy chủ quyền nhà và đất" [Hà Nội pilots the issuing of ownership certificates for houses and land], *Đại Đoàn Kết*, 20 January 1997, pp. 1, 7.

19. See DiMaio Jr., *Soviet Urban Housing*, pp. 27, 180–81.

20. Peter Nan-shong Lee, "Housing privatization with Chinese characteristics", in *Social Change and Social Policy in Contemporary China*, pp. 115–17.

21. Regarding confiscation of private houses in the Soviet Union between 1961 and 1962, see DiMaio Jr., *Soviet Urban Housing*, pp. 27, 180–81. For discussions of other features of the housing sector in the USSR, see Sillince, "Housing Policy in Eastern Europe and the Soviet Union", p. 37–44.

22. Ngô Huy Giao, "Từ một tiểu khu nhà ở …" [From a small housing area…], *Cứu Quốc*, 20 June 1975, pp. 6, 7; P.V., "Những việc cần làm ở khu tập thể Cầu Đất" [Necessary tasks at the Cầu Đất Housing Area], *Lao Động*, 27 July 1978, p. 12.

23. Trần Bình, "Những bước đi lên trong việc xây dựng nhà ở" [Improvements in housing construction], *HNM*, 1 April 1977, pp. 3, 4; Trần Hùng and Nguyễn Quốc Thông, *Thăng Long - Hà Nội: Mười thế kỷ đô thị hoá* [Rising Dragon-Hà Nội: Ten centuries of urbanization] (Hà Nội: NXB Xây dựng, 1995), pp. 138–39.

24. Before the late 1980s, housing statistics for Vietnam were scarce and were often of low quality. Statistics in this chapter are culled from newspapers, journal articles, and a few books; most of these sources are in Vietnamese. The figures in one source often conflict with those in another source. Official publications of social statistics usually give a hazy picture. For example, state expenditure on housing is usually grouped together with social welfare items. Statistics on particular years are often missing. When I tried to obtain coherently presented housing statistics from officials working in the city's housing sector, I encountered many obstacles, including a payment request,

which I could not ethically grant. Consequently, when preparing this chapter,
I have tried hard to make sensible use of those data that are available from
assorted and open sources.

25. The bombing of Hà Nội by the United States that occurred between 1965 to
1973 destroyed 17,000 housing units in Hà Nội. See Nigel Thrift and Dean
Forbes, *The Price of War: Urbanization in Vietnam 1954–1985* (London:
Allen and Unwin, 1986), pp. 147–51.

26. Nguyễn Văn Canh and Earle Cooper, *Vietnam under Communism, 1975–1982*
(Stanford, CA: Hoover Institution Press, 1983) p. 23, and Faith Keenan,
"Let History Judge: Struggle over houses recalls more divided days", *Far
Eastern Economic Review*, 31 December 1998, pp. 18, 20.

27. Trịnh Duy Luân and Nguyễn Quang Vinh, *Tác động kinh tế xã hội của Đổi
mới trong lĩnh vực nhà ở đô thị* [Socioeconomic impact of đổi mới on urban
housing], p. 59.

28. Phạm Trí Minh and Phạm Văn Nhiếp, "Mấy ý kiến về giải quyết nhà ở đô
thị" [A few opinions on resolving housing problems in urban areas], *TCCS*
6 (1987): 68–69.

29. *HNM*, "UBND Thành phố ra quyết định xử lý những người có nguồn tài
sản bất minh mua nhà và xây nhà có gia trị lớn" [City People's Committee
deals with people who have unclear sources of wealth and purchase or build
houses of huge value], 25 May 1983, p. 1; P.V., "Nhân dân nhiệt liệt hoan
nghênh biện pháp nghiêm minh, hợp tình hợp lý của chính quyền" [The
people warmly welcome measures of the political authority which are just
and reasonable], *HNM*, 26 May 1983, pp. 1, 4; Hiền Lương, "Nhắm trúng
đối tượng đấu tranh", *HNM*, 12 August 1983, p. 2; Hiền Lương, "Cuộc đấu
tranh tiếp tục", *HNM*, 14 August 1983, p. 2; and Nguyễn Đức Thà, "Quận
Hai Bà Trưng quản lý nhà ở theo kỷ cương và pháp luật" [Hai Bà Trưng
District manages houses according to the law and social discipline], *HNM*,
26 October 1983, p. 2.

30. Generally, to avoid attention from the state, before the 1990s it was important
for people not to appear rich or even slightly better-off than people around
them. Household savings were stashed at home, and there was a high level of
standardization in consumption patterns. Many informants in Vietnam told me
that good food (such as chicken) the family managed to obtain during those
times of economic difficulty had to be hidden from the neighbours' eyes,
because people were afraid of being investigated by the authorities. Thus,
the chopping of chickens had to be done on cloth laid on the floor, instead
of on the chopping board, which would have made a loud thud. Chicken
bones, unable to be swallowed, had to be disposed of in camouflage.

31. Phạm Trí Minh and Phạm Văn Nhiếp, "Mấy ý kiến về giải quyết nhà ở đô
thị" [A few opinions on resolving housing problems in urban areas], *TCCS*
6 (1987): pp. 66–67.

32. See Trần Bình, "Những bước đi lên trong việc xây dựng nhà ở" [Improvements in housing construction], *HNM,* 1 April 1977, pp. 3, 4.

33. At such times of severe shortage, the solution of subdividing houses into smaller parts was a very common practice resorted to. The house I stayed in (on about 30 sq. m. of land) in Hà Nội was the house of the second son of my house-mother. It was just beside the parents' house (60 sq. m. of land) but joined to it at the back. In front of my place was the house of the eldest son of the house-mother (15 sq. m). One generation ago, all three houses were one house and it occupied an area double their present sizes. In the mid-1980s half the land area was sold to finance rebuilding of the existing house, and further subdivided as the children grew up and set up families. The family could sell the land and renovate the houses even though the land and house were under dispute from rival claims within the clan. As the youngest son was to marry in 1997, the parents' house was renovated in 1996 to add two more storeys. In the house of a tailor who lived two doors away, the family moved there in 1995. Then, the second and eldest sons married in the same year, and the family bought over the adjacent areas, demolished the major part of the house and rebuilt it so that every member could live close to one another and still have solid walls that retained each nuclear family's privacy.

34. Ánh Ngọc, "Những yêu cầu chính đáng cần được giải quyết gấp ở một khu nhà tập thể" [Legitimate demands that need urgent solutions at a collective housing area], *HNM* ,7 April 1981, p. 2.

35. See Bùi Mạnh Trung, "Chung quanh vấn đề sửa chữa nhà cửa" [Around the problem of housing repair], *HNM,* 28 November 1979, p. 2.

36. Trần Quang, "Chất lượng nhà xây chưa tốt" [Quality of constructed houses still not good], *Đại Đoàn Kết,* 22 December 1982, p. 11.

37. Ánh Ngọc, "Những yêu cầu chính đáng cần được giải quyết gấp ở một khu nhà tập thể" [Legitimate demands which need urgent solutions at a collective housing area], *HNM,* 7 April 1981, p. 2; and Vương Thức, "Ở các khu nhà tập thể" [At the collective flat areas], *HNM,* 14 October 1988, p. 3.

38. See Vương Thức, "Điều tra quyền sở hữu tư nhân về nhà cửa ở quận Đống Đa" [Survey on right of private ownership of housing in Đống Đa District], *HNM,* 31 January 1986, p. 3, and Vương Thức, "Cần chấn chỉnh việc đăng ký và chuyển dịch nhà cửa" [Need to reorganize registration of housing and housing sale], *HNM,* 6 May 1988, p. 3.

39. The same handwritten notes and mutual trust system are commonly used in the transfer of ownership in many other types of valuable commodities, such as bicycle and motorcycle. For instance, in December 1995 I sold my bicycle to a second-hand bicycle trader I met by chance on Hà Nội's Đại Cổ Việt Street, and I was only required to write a note that said that the bicycle with a certain serial number was transferred to the buyer at a certain sum

of money. Similarly, when I bought a motorcycle in January 1997, I was only given the original licence papers belonging to a person residing in Đà Nẵng City in Central Vietnam, and three notes of previous transactions on the motorcycle since the original registration with the state. When I sold my motorcycle in 1998 I was not asked for ownership papers but the buyer trusted me because a friend he trusted had introduced me. No state taxes or levies were involved. Officially, the motorcycle still belongs to the person in Đà Nẵng.

40. Sun Jin-lou and Liu Lin, *Zhu zhai she hui xue* [The Sociology of Housing], (Chi-nan: Shan-tung ren min chu ban she, 1985), p. 73, and Peter Nan-shong Lee "Housing privatization with Chinese characteristics", p. 116.

41. Sillince, "Housing policy in Eastern Europe and the Soviet Union", pp. 44–47.

42. Thrift and Forbes, *The Price of War,* Ch. 7.

43. Lars Reutersward, "Vietnam", pp. 161–71, in *Housing Policy and Practice in Asia,* edited by Seong-Kyu Ha (New York: Croom Helm, 1987).

44. This practice was similar to the Soviet Union policy of "labour for housing" used to boost housing output in the 1960s. See DiMaio Jr., *Soviet Urban Housing,* pp. 109–10.

45. These variants were:
    1. the state used its capital to build completed houses and sold, rather than allotted, them to cadres and the people;
    2. the state collected some capital contribution by the people to build the basic parts of the houses, and the people completed the building on their own; and
    3. the state built the infrastructure in an area and allotted parcels of land for the people to build houses according to state-prepared architectural plans. This variant was somewhat similar to what people wanted in the Bãi Bằng paper company incident.

    See K.O., "Xây dựng nhà ở theo phương châm 'Nhà nước và nhân dân cùng làm'" [Construct houses under the policy of "state and people working together"], *HNM,* 8 March 1985, p. 3; Phạm Trí Minh and Phạm Văn Nhiếp, "Mấy ý kiến về giải quyết nhà ở đô thị" [A few opinions on resolving housing problems in urban areas], *TCCS* 6 (1987): 66–69, 80; Lao Động, "Mấy ý kiến của bộ trưởng Phan Ngọc Tường về vấn đề xây dựng nhà ở" [A few opinions of Minister Phan Ngọc Tường regarding the housing construction problem], 23 February 1984, p. 4.

46. The model was later extended to many other types of infrastructure construction all over the country. See ĐCSVN, "Nhà nước và nhân dân cùng làm" [State and people working together], *TCCS* 11 (1984): 6–9, 63; and Trịnh Duy Luân and Nguyễn Quang Vinh, *Tác động kinh tế xã hội của Đổi mới trong lĩnh vực nhà ở đô thị* [Socioeconomic impact of Đổi mới on urban housing], (Hà Nội: NXB Khoa học Xã hội, 1998), pp. 60–63.

47. *Nhân Dân*, "Hà Nội thêm nhiều lực lượng sửa chữa nhà cửa" [Hà Nội adds many new forces for repair of houses], 15 June 1977, p. 3.

48. K.O., "Xây dựng nhà ở theo phương châm 'Nhà nước và nhân dân cùng làm'" [Construct houses under the policy of "state and people working together"], *HNM*, 8 March 1985, p. 3.

49. Phùng Minh, "Từ đầu tháng 9-1987 thực hiện việc bán nhà ở" [Sale of houses starts from beginning of September 1987], *HNM*, 4 September 1987, pp. 1, 4. At the same time, there was also a suggestion from the grassroots that old flats that required urgent repairs should also be sold to the people so that they could repair their own flats. See Lưu Thị Thái Hà, "Cấp phường với công tác quản lý nhà" [Wards and their management of housing matters], *HNM*, 7 October 1988, p. 2. The state implemented this suggestion in 1994, but went further in deciding to sell most flats rather than only old flats that required repairs.

50. The enterprises lacked money to build high-rise flats to maximize land use, and therefore had to resort to this method. They therefore only collected fees for the land and for the infrastructure they provided. Once employees finished construction, the enterprises asked the city to issue the builders with land-use right certificates. See Trịnh Duy Luân and Nguyễn Quang Vinh, *Tác động kinh tế xã hội của Đổi Mới trong lĩnh vực nhà ở đô thị* [Socioeconomic impact of Đổi mới on urban housing] (Hà Nội: NXB Khoa học Xã hội, 1998), pp. 79–81, 115.

51. *HNM*, "Về việc mua bán nhà tư nhân" [On private transactions on houses], 24 March 1989, p. 1. Government organizations were asked not to engage in housing speculation activity when they built flats for their employees.

52. People's Committee of Hà Nội, "Quyết định về xây dựng, cải tạo nhà ở" [Decision on construction and re-construction of housing], *HNM*, 13 June 1990, p. 1.

53. Issued on 26 March 1991. SRV, "Pháp lệnh nhà ở" [Ordinance on Housing] in *Hệ thống hoá văn bản pháp luật về nhà ở, đất đai và thuế nhà đất* [Legal documents on housing, land, and land taxes systematized], by NXB Pháp Lý, (HCM City, 1991) pp. 7–23.

54. "Nhà nước khuyến khích và tạo điều kiện để mọi tổ chức, cá nhân tham gia vào việc duy trì và phát triển nhà ở. Tổ chức, cá nhân được kinh doanh nhà ở bằng việc xây dựng, cải tạo nhà ở để bán hoặc cho thuê và các hoạt động kinh doanh nhà ở khác theo quy định của pháp luật." Article 4 of SRV, "Pháp lệnh nhà ở" [Ordinance on Housing], in *Hệ thống hoá văn bản pháp luật về nhà ở, đất đai và thuế nhà đất* [Legal documents on housing, land, and land taxes systematized], pp. 7–23.

55. Trịnh Duy Luân and Nguyễn Quang Vinh, *Tác động kinh tế xã hội của Đổi Mới trong lĩnh vực nhà ở đô thị* [Socioeconomic impact of đổi mới on urban housing], pp. 26–30, 78–83.

56. Bùi Đình Nguyễn, "Xung quanh việc hoá giá nhà ở" [About the matter of monetizing value of houses], *Đại Đoàn Kết,* 3 December 1991, p. 7.

57. SRV, Thông tư số 27/LB-TT ngày 31-12-1992 của liên bộ Lao Động — Thương Binh và Xã Hội — Tài Chính — Xây dựng hướng dẫn thực hiện việc đưa tiền nhà ở vào tiền lương [Inter-Ministry Notice 27/LB-TT dated 31/12/1992 of Ministries of Labour-Veterans-Social Affairs, Finance, and Construction on guidance for implementation of policy to add rental monies to salaries].

58. "Regarding the sale of houses belonging to the state, the general principle is not to proceed impetuously, but to proceed one solid step at a time. We should first sell class three and four houses, and collective flats in suburban areas of cities, outer areas of the inner cities in order to gain experience." ("Đối với việc bán nhà thuộc sở hữu Nhà nước, nguyên tắc chung là không tiến hành ồ ạt, mà tiến hành từng bước vững chắc. Tổ chức bán trước các loại nhà cấp III, cấp IV, nhà ở các khu tập thể ngoại thành, ven nội để rút kinh nghiệm, ..."). SRV, Chỉ thị số 346/TTg ngày 5-7-1994 của Thủ tướng Chính phủ Về việc tổ chức thực hiện các Nghị Định của Chính phủ về "quyền sở hữu nhà ở và quyền sử dụng đất ở tại đô thị" và "mua bán và kinh doanh nhà ở" [Directive of the Prime Minister 346/TTg dated 5 July 1994 on implementation of Decisions of the Government regarding right to own houses, right to use land, and the purchase and trade in housing], (1994), Article 5.
From 1994 until the end of 1997, the Hà Nội City government managed to sell state-owned houses to about 350 families, about one-tenth the population size of an average Hà Nội ward. See Xây Dựng "Giám đốc Sở nhà đất Hà Nội trả lời phỏng vấn về công tác bán nhà theo Nghị Định 61/CP" [Director of the Hà Nội Housing Authority interviewed regarding work on selling houses under Decision 61/CP], September 1997, pp. 4, 13; Minh Tuấn, Hương Thủy, "Hà Nội thí điểm cấp giấy chủ quyền nhà và đất" [Hà Nội pilots the issuing of ownership certificates for houses and land], *Đại Đoàn Kết,* 20 January 1997, pp. 1, 7.

59. SRV, "Nghị Định của Thủ tướng Chính phủ về quyền sở hữu nhà ở và quyền sử dụng đất ở tại đô thị" [Decision of the Prime Minister on right to own houses and right to use land in urban areas], *HNM,* 21 July 1994, p. 2, and Thanh Mai, "Thực hiện Nghị Định 60, 61/CP của Chính phủ về nhà ở, đất ở trên địa bàn Hà Nội" [Hà Nội implements Decision 60, 61/CP of the Government on housing and land for housing], *HNM,* 25 February 1995, p. 1, 4; Tuổi Trẻ Thủ Đô, "Hà Nội: Bước ngoặt giải quyết nhà ở" [Hà Nội: turning point in solving housing problems], 20 November 1996, pp. 1–2.

60. E-mail from informant living in that area, 2 February 1999.

61. Thanh Niên, "Cấp giấy chủ quyền nhà đất chậm do quy định ngang nhau" [Issue of house and land ownership papers slow due to conflicting

regulations], 26 June 2002; Đỗ Lê Tạo, "Đưa thị trường nhà đất vào khuôn phép", *Lao Động Điện Tử,* 29 November 2002. http://www.laodong.com.vn/pls/bld/folder$.view_item_detail(51883).

62. I am ignoring here the years between 1954 and 1975 because the wars during much of that period created special conditions.

63. During the subsidy and rationing period (which ended in the late 1980s) animal husbandry was an important "hobby" of urban families to complement the household income as well as to provide meat dishes for important occasions. Lưu Phương, "Việc làm được ở khu tập thể Nguyễn Công Trứ" [Accomplishments at the Nguyễn Công Trứ collective flat area], *HNM,* 1 October 1975, p. 2; P.V., "Những việc cần làm ở khu tập thể Cầu Đất", *Lao Động,* 27 July 1978, p. 12.

64. *HNM,* "Thành phố đẩy mạnh cuộc vận động nếp sống văn minh, gia đình văn hoá mới" [The City pushes strongly the Cultured Way of Life and New Culture Family movement], 13 August 1977, p. 1; Thanh Long, "Chuyện số Nhà 55" [The story of House 55], *HNM,* 7 September 1977, p. 2; Văn Giáp, "Tiểu khu Long Biên vận động những người làm ăn không chính đáng chuyển sang sản xuất" [The Long Biên Small Area mobilizes people in illegitimate professions to switch to production], *HNM,* 7 January 1978, p. 3; Ánh Sáng, "Nhà máy chế tạo công cụ số 1 xây dựng khu tập thể văn minh" [The Number 1 Tools Manufacturing Factory implements a Cultured collective flat area], *HNM,* 18 January 1978, p. 2; Huy Lân, "Nếp sống mới ở khu tập thể nhà A10" [New way of life at Block A10 of a collective flat area], *HNM,* 11 January 1978, p. 2; P.T.L., "Cưới xin theo nếp sống mới" [Weddings that follow the new way of life], *HNM,* 29 January 1978, p. 3; Phương Sinh, "Nếp sống tốt ở một khu tập thể" [Good way of life in one collective flat area], *HNM,* 10 February 1978, p. 2; Phan Tất, "Tiểu khu Bông Nhuộm xây dựng số nhà văn hoá mới" [Bông Nhuộm Small Area implements new culture homes programme], *HNM,* 26 April 1978, p. 2; Nguyễn Đức Quang, "Khu phố Ba Đình: 7 tiểu khu và 10 khu tập thể được công nhận là tiểu khu và khu tập thể văn minh" [Ba Đình District: 7 Small Areas and 10 collective flat areas recognized as cultured areas], *HNM,* 5 June 1979, p. 1; *HNM,* "Hội nghị tổng kết phong trào nếp sống văn minh, gia đình văn hoá mới năm 1978 của Hà Nội" [Conference summed up movement on Cultured Way of Life, New Culture Family of Hà Nội in 1978], 19 January 1979, pp. 1, 4; *HNM,* "Thủ Đô Hà Nội tổng kết công tác nếp sống mới, gia đình văn hoá mới năm 1980 và nhiệm vụ năm 1981" [Hà Nội the Capital summed up work on New Way of Life, New Culture Family in 1980 and tasks for 1981], 14 April 1981, pp. 1, 4.

65. Quế Lan, "Không nên để tệ làm nhà trái phép phát triển" [Do not let the evil of illegal construction develop], *Đại Đoàn Kết,* 20 August 1980, p. 2.

66. *HNM*, "Tiểu khu Cống Vị xử lý một số nhà xây dựng trái phép" [Cống Vị Small Area dealt with a number of houses built illegally], 22 October 1980, p. 2.

67. Nguyễn Đức Thà, "Xử lý những trường hợp xây dựng trái phép" [Dealing with cases of illegal construction], *HNM*, 13 April 1982, p. 2 and 14 April 1982, p. 2.

68. "Cao Sà Lá" is a local nickname shortened from "*Cao* su, *Sà* phòng, thuốc *Lá*" meaning "Rubber, Soap, Cigarettes" that factories along the road manufactured.

69. Nguyễn Đức Thà, "Xử lý những trường hợp xây dựng trái phép" [Dealing with cases of illegal construction].

70. Ibid.

71. Ibid.

72. These were: thirty days for certificate of use of land, twenty days to approve building plans and for construction licence, and ten days for repair and renovation licence. *HNM*, "Về quản lý xây dựng nhà cửa ở thành phố" [On management of housing construction in the City], 16 April 1982, p. 2; *HNM*, "Rút kinh nghiệm về xử lý những trường hợp xây dựng trái phép" [Drawing lessons from dealing with cases of illegal construction], 25 May 1982, p. 3.

73. *HNM*, "Về quản lý xây dựng nhà cửa ở thành phố" [On management of housing construction in the City], 16 April 1982, p. 2.

74. *HNM*, "Rút kinh nghiệm về xử lý những trường hợp xây dựng trái phép" [Drawing lessons from dealing with cases of illegal construction].

75. Completed around 1976, the Trung Tự and Kim Liên collective flat areas have forty-one blocks of flats, each four to five storeys, with a total of 2,252 households and 12,186 people. The average living area was 6 sq. m. per person, thus the housing situation was better than Hà Nội's average in the 1980s.

76. In the Giảng Võ collective flat area, which also saw many cases of similar types of illegal construction, eighteen blocks of flats were reported to be sinking in 1997 because of the added but unsupported weight. Hà Thị Hồng, "Ai là người quản lí nhà lắp ghép cao tầng?" [Who is responsible for managing the prefabricated high-rise buildings?] *Xây Dựng*, September 1997, p. 38. See also Trần Hùng, "Một số suy nghĩ về 'Hà Nội cải tạo và xây dựng'" [A few thoughts about "Hà Nội being reconstructed and constructed"], *HNM*, 23 January 1983, pp. 1, 3.

77. Vương Thức, "Cần xử lý tệ làm nhà trái phép ở khu tập thể Kim Liên", [On the situation of illegal housing construction in the Trung Tự collective flat area], *HNM*, 23 May 1986, p. 3.

78. Decree 11/XDCB of Hà Nội UBND dated 9 April 1983, article 3 said that in the flat areas of four to five storeys, renovations must follow plans for the area, and the people should not construct and extend in front or behind

their flats at their own will. Vương Thức, "Về tình hình làm nhà trái phép ở khu tập thể Trung Tự" [On the situation of illegal housing construction in the Trung Tự collective flat area], *HNM*, 30 July 1985, pp. 3, 4.

79. Eighty-six of the flats involved before 1985 had average extensions of 4 to 6 sq. m, eighteen flats from 7 to 12 sq. m. Vương Thức, "Về tình hình làm nhà trái phép ở khu tập thể Trung Tự" [On the situation of illegal housing construction in the Trung Tự collective flat area].

80. Vương Thức, "Cần xử lý tệ làm nhà trái phép ở khu tập thể Kim Liên" [Need to deal with evil of illegal construction in the Kim Liên collective flat area], *HNM*, 23 May 1986, p. 3.

81. Until the late 1980s, state cadres used these coupons to obtain rations or buy controlled-price goods at state shops. Class "A" was the highest class with the most entitlements, and class "E" was the lowest.

82. Tung Phương, "Trách nhiệm của đảng bộ phường Kim Liên trước tệ xây dựng nhà trái phép đến đâu?" [What are the responsibilities of the Kim Liên Ward Party Branch regarding the evil of illegal construction?], *HNM*, 29 March 1989, p. 2.

83. "Các cơ quan có trách nhiệm như phường, ban quản lý nhà, đội quy tắc... chỉ lập biên bản để đấy. Cùng lắm là phạt chứ không tổ chức dỡ bỏ. Do đó ai thích làm cứ làm (!)" Vương Thức, "Cần xử lý tệ làm nhà trái phép ở khu tập thể Kim Liên" [Need to deal with evil of illegal construction in the Kim Liên collective flat area].

84. This method was widely used among the collective flat areas of Hà Nội. Trịnh Duy Luân and Nguyễn Quang Vinh, *Tác động kinh tế xã hội của Đổi mới trong lĩnh vực nhà ở đô thị* [Socioeconomic impact of đổi mới on urban housing] (Hà Nội: NXB Khoa học Xã hội, 1998), p. 132

85. "UBND quận, phường ra lệnh dỡ bỏ, nhưng lệnh không được thi hành hay phường tổ chức lực lượng đến cưỡng chế dỡ bỏ, thì gặp sự phản ứng gay gắt, quyết liệt. Có trường hợp đã dỡ bỏ nhưng vài ngày sau lại làm tiếp 'đàng hoàng' hơn." Vương Thức, "Về tình hình làm nhà trái phép ở khu tập thể Trung Tự" [On the situation of illegal housing construction in the Trung Tự collective flat area].

86. Hoàng Quí Thân, "Suy nghĩ nhân một vấn đề thời sự ở Kim Liên" [Some thoughts provoked by a current affair in Kim Liên], *HNM*, 12 March 1989, p. 1.

87. Vương Thức, "Về tình hình làm nhà trái phép ở khu tập thể Trung Tự" [On the situation of illegal housing construction in the Trung Tự collective flat area].

88. People's Committee of Hà Nội, "Quyết định của UBND Thành phố về việc xây dựng nhà ở và xử lý xây dựng trái phép" [Decision of the City People's Committee on housing construction and dealing with illegal construction] *HNM*, 4 November 1987, p. 3.

89. B.V., "Cuộc thảo luận về cấp phường chưa thể kết thúc được" [Debate on the ward still inconclusive], *HNM*, 23 September 1988, p. 2.

90. Vương Thức, "Việc xây nhà trái phép vẫn tăng" [Illegal construction still on the rise], *HNM*, 18 June 1988, p. 3; Vương Thức, "Ở các khu nhà tập thể" [At the collective flat areas], *HNM*, 14 October 1988, p. 3.

91. Trịnh Duy Luân and Nguyễn Quang Vinh, *Tác động kinh tế xã hội của Đổi mới trong lĩnh vực nhà ở đô thị* [Socioeconomic impact of đổi mới on urban housing], p. 131. A case study of one locality by the authors showed that many families did the extensions because others had done it and had simply been fined by the state without being asked to demolish the extensions ("fine for existence").

92. Lưu Thị Thái Hà, "Cấp phường với công tác quản lý nhà" [Wards and their management of housing matters], *HNM*, 7 October 1988, p. 2.

93. *HNM*, "Nhất bên trọng, nhất bên khinh" [Lop-sided], 25 December 1989, p. 2.

94. T.C., "Tuy muộn nhưng vẫn tốt" [Though late but still good], *HNM*, 11 March 1991, p. 2.

95. Fieldnotes 17 March 1997.

96. Fieldnotes 30 June 1997, and visits in springs of 1998, 1999, and 2004.

97. T.C., "Tuy muộn nhưng vẫn tốt" [Though late but still good].

98. Fieldnotes 30 June 1997, and visit spring 1999.

99. Visit to the neighbour, May 2002.

100. Vương Thức, "Đổi mới việc cấp phép xây dựng" [Reform the process of issuing construction licences], *HNM*, 26 August 1988, p. 3.

101. People's Committee of Hà Nội, "Quyết định về xây dựng, cải tạo nhà ở" [Decision on construction and re-construction of housing], *HNM*, 13 June 1990, p. 1.

102. Cases that occurred before 11 January 1972 were forgiven unconditionally. For cases that took place between 1972 and September 1985 (when the city had issued a regulation regarding the use of land) the city issued a warning and imposed a fine. For cases that occurred between September 1985 and October 1987 when Decision 4637 was issued, the city imposed a heftier fine calculated as a percentage of the total value of the construction project but not more than 10 per cent. For cases that took place after Decision 4637 came into effect, however, there was no "amnesty" if they had infringed on building regulations and were asked to stop construction. People's Committee of Hà Nội, "Quy định về việc cho phép sử dụng tạm thời đất và nhà trong đô thị và thị trấn" [Regulations for allowing temporary use of land and houses in urban centres and townlets], *HNM*, 18 June 1990, p. 2.

103. Thanh Thủy, "Thử xem tham nhũng cấp phường đến đâu!" [Let's see how deep corruption is at the ward level!], *HNM*, 1 July 1994, p. 2.

104. Ibid.

105. Thanh Chi, "Xung quanh việc xây dựng không phép" [Regarding construction without licences], *HNM*, 11 April 1994, p. 2.

106. Decision 677 of May 1994. Kim Dung, "Từ bảo vệ hành lang thoát lũ nghĩ đến giữ gìn trật tự đô thị" [Thinking about maintenance of urban social order from observing the protection of storm water drainage system], *HNM*, 8 July 1994, p. 2.

107. Thanh Mai, "Xung quanh việc thực hiện quyết định 1431 và phạt vi cảnh xây dựng không phép" [Regarding implementation of Decision 1431 on compounded punishments for construction without licences], *HNM*, 1 March 1993, p. 2.

108. Thanh Chi, "Xung quanh việc xây dựng không phép" [Regarding construction without licences].

109. Uyên Chi, "Xây dựng trái phép: Tiếng chuông báo động" [Illegal construction: the alarm bells], *HNM*, 11 November 1994, p. 3; Trịnh Duy Luân and Nguyễn Quang Vinh, *Tác động kinh tế - xã hội của Đổi mới trong lĩnh vực nhà ở đô thị* [The socioeconomic impact of đổi mới on urban housing], pp. 79–81.

110. Trần Quang Vũ, "Điều gì cản trở Hà Nội giải toả nhà xây trên đê" [Obstacles preventing Hà Nội from ridding the dyke of houses], *Đại Đoàn Kết*, 19 November 1994, p. 7.

111. Conversation with a journalist, 17 February 1998.

112. Kim Dung, "Từ bảo vệ hành lang thoát lũ nghĩ đến giữ gìn trật tự đô thị" [Thinking about maintenance of urban social order from observing the protection of storm water drainage system], *HNM*, 8 July 1994, p. 2.

113. Nguyễn Viết Cảnh, "Đằng sau sự bình yên của đê Nghi Tàm" [Behind the serenity of the Nghi Tàm dyke], *HNM*, 22 November 1994, p. 3. According to another source, the number of illegally built houses numbered more than 1,000. See N.S.P., "Thư Hà Nội" [Letter from Hà Nội], *Đất Nước* 36–37 (June–September 1995), pp. 19, 23.

114. Nguyễn Viết Cảnh, "Đằng sau sự bình yên của đê Nghi Tàm" [Behind the serenity of the Nghi Tàm dyke], *HNM*, 22 November 1994, p. 3.

115. Ngô Huy Giao, "Giữ vững kỷ cương phép nước và an ninh quốc gia" [Maintain social discipline and national security], *Đại Đoàn Kết*, 4 March 1995, p. 7.

116. A report for example cited the cases of Mr Đặng Văn Dân and Bùi Đình Xuyến. Other families used their licences. In that area, at least twenty-three licences were known to have been transferred. Then there was also the transfer of "ownership" of land freely among people there. A total of sixteen households had transferred 5,784 sq. m of land to others at a value of 1.233 billion đồng plus 83.8 cây of gold (1 cây was around US$500, 1995 prices). See Nguyễn Viết Cảnh, "Đằng sau sự bình yên của đê Nghi Tàm" [Behind the serenity of the Nghi Tàm dyke], *HNM*, 22 November 1994, p. 3.

117. Tổ phóng viên Ban bạn đọc, "Xung quanh vụ xây nhà vi phạm lệnh bảo vệ đê điều thuộc quận Ba Đình" [Regarding the cases of housing construction in Ba Đình District which offend the dyke protection ordinance], *HNM,* 3 March 1995, pp. 1, 3.

118. Ibid. According to the journal *Đất Nước*, the *Lao Động* (Labour) newspaper had suggested that the house belonged to the relative of a former head of state who handwrote the letter. See N.S.P., "Thư Hà Nội" [Letter from Hà Nội].

119. Conversation with a journalist, 17 February 1998.

120. This term was frequently used by Vietnamese to refer to action that went beyond or even against state laws, regulations, and socioeconomic regimes.

6

Conclusion

This book has looked at mediation space in several arenas of everyday life in Hà Nội. In reality, this mediation space exists — in parallel with compliance — in most arenas of non-political life in Vietnam. In many arenas not covered here, the agent of mediation may not be the ward but the issue would generally be similar: it is, how compliance is aborted, covertly or overtly, by co-operation between local officials and the people. Among the other arenas, the more well-known ones include taxation, smuggling, residential registration, driving licences, business registration, sale of prescribed drugs, illegal logging, the use of public space in parks, pornography, prostitution, and many others. Therefore, the scale of mediation is very wide across the country.

Several reasons account for mediation. One is inefficiencies of the administrative system. Chapter 1 pointed out complaints, from both the party-state and the people generally, on how the wards' inefficiencies diminished the party-state ability in managing society. Paradoxically, these were caused by features of the party-state itself, especially the lack of open competition in elections as well as the lack of regular checks on implementing officials, including those at the ward level. Chapter 2 examined the ward party-state machinery, which is a part of the countrywide administration system organized to manage society. Power in the ward party-state machinery is concentrated in a cluster of top party-state officials. Senior and leading officials of the ward party-state machinery are usually party members. Through paid volunteers at the sub-level of resident clusters and resident cells, the Vietnamese party-state can reach into every household to mobilize people to comply with party-state policies. More importantly, such a reach can be used to grasp the details of the private lives of troublesome individuals who might dare to challenge the party-state's political domination.

In Chapter 3, we saw that the election machinery and election process are firmly under the control of the party-state. Party officials occupy leading positions of the Vietnam Fatherland Front, the organization that screens candidates for elections at every level. Meanwhile, the same group of party-state officials run the election machinery and become the arbitrator in elections. Some of them even stand as candidates in the same elections. Consequently, only party-state approved candidates are elected to executive positions of the ward. It is rare for leading officials of the party-state to lose local elections, although that is more possible today than a decade ago. We saw that while the party-state machinery controlled many aspects of elections, it could not prevent certain anomalies. A significant number of people disagree with how elections are conducted. The result has been an "electoral tension", manifested from the late 1980s by calls from people for more choices and easing of the party-state's grip on nominations of election candidates. Despite voter discontent, however, voter turnout has been high and became even higher in recent elections. Local authorities have been excellent in ensuring this result for the central government. Their tactics include allowing proxy voting, which is contrary to the law. Still, party-state officials cite the high turnouts as proof of popular support for the political system. Allowing proxy voting, meanwhile, has contributed to ameliorating "electoral tension", which otherwise might become a significant political liability for the state.

More mediation — and thus more limits to party-state dominance — are present in the socioeconomic arenas analysed in Chapters 4 and 5. Chapter 4 analysed why the pavement situation on many streets has been anarchic and how the party-state has tried to restore order. In economically difficult times, many urban residents of Hà Nội relied on peddling and other small business activities in order to make a living. Often these activities obstructed pavement and roads, thus infringing on traffic laws. If ward officials had enforced these traffic regulations in a strict manner, many more people would have been unemployed and perhaps even greatly discontented — even angry — with the party-state. Instead, ward and police officials in Hà Nội have often neglected, overlooked, or sometimes even facilitated the operation of roadside and roaming vendors. By dusk, vendors on many streets of Hà Nội hang out to stake their economic space, contributing to the chaotic pavement and road situation and undoing the order that ward officials maintain during the day. Some mediation occurred because ward officials were sympathetic with vendors who were in financial difficulties. Hà Nội's ward authorities also give feedback to the city authority and ask the city to allow trading on many smaller streets during marketing hours rather than ban all such trade. At certain times, however, authorities insist on strict compliance with, and enforcement of, the rules. In the case of pavement management, such occasions arose during elections, important national meetings when the city was flooded with dignitaries, and periodic campaigns to bring public order to all traffic.

Chapters 4 and 5 also pointed to significant party-state domination. For management of pavement activities and catching illegal housing construction, the Vietnamese party-state at the central level and next level down — the central city/province — have the exclusive policy-making power. No form of widespread public consultations exists at the policy formulation stage; it is top-down. Participation by society in policy-making consisted of resistance to and evasion of unpopular policies that force the party-state to make changes.

Chapter 5 examined contested goals of the party-state and society regarding housing, another sensitive issue from the 1970s to the early 1990s. The socialist housing regime could not provide for the needs of an increasing and more demanding population, especially in Hà Nội. The restrictive and inadequate socialist housing regime faced resistance from people, who used connections to or their positions of power within the party-state to ask ward officials to mediate. Other means people used to evade the housing rules include nepotism, corruption, sympathy, and community acquiescence. Consequently, despite party-state bans, a significant amount of private, illegal housing construction occurred all over Hà Nội, reaching larger proportions within the last two decades. Again, this result has not necessarily been bad for the party-state and its relations with society. If wards and other specialist officials had faithfully enforced state regulations on constructions and renovation, much of the urgent demand for housing would not have been satisfied. That could have made the shortage of housing a huge source of popular discontent. Chapter 5 also showed that the cumulative effect of the large number of people evading housing regulations was to force state policy-making agencies to alter the regulations.

THE RESEARCH PROCESS

Fieldwork is part and parcel of area studies, and so is the learning of the vernacular language of the country being studied. In 1995, I went to Hà Nội to further strengthen my Vietnamese language capabilities. Participation in the daily life of the host country is, I still reckon, a quick way to master the language. But fieldwork, I believe, required more than participation. Living like an ordinary local was required and difficult, but the extra effort had its benefits.

Getting out of the library and seeking integration with the local community in Hà Nội was how I came to this topic I am writing on. One of my landladies or house-mothers was a resident group head. One evening, I got interested in what she was doing, as an old woman bending over a bunch of papers, name lists, and making entries in tables on paper carefully drawn by hands. This neighbourhood leader demonstrated pride in her work and I became curious. When asked, she said she was collecting charity donations from her neighbours, on behalf of the ward. "The ward? What's that?" With this germ of an idea, I talked to Vietnamese scholars and my supervisors about the feasibility of adopting "wards in Hà Nội" as my topic. With further observations of how, in Hà Nội, social discipline and respect for the law in many aspects of daily life were lacking, I made the connection between the problems of the wards and the important issue of basic-level implementation of state policies. Frequent, hours-long walks all over Hà Nội, preliminary research into newspapers, and repeated queries among friends helped me to identify a number of government policies worthy of investigation, from which I have chosen three to analyse in this book. Exchanges with foreign and Vietnamese academics demonstrated an almost complete void in the academic literature, both internationally and in Vietnam. This void is the lack of addressing of issues like local corruption and effectiveness of state governance. That was in 1995; the outbreak of the Thái Bình unrests in 1997 heightened the topic's relevance.

In view of the freshness of the topic, my approach to Vietnamese friends to talk about it had been met with surprises and cheers. Vietnamese friends said that at last, the topic of utmost importance in governance was going to be addressed. For the surprised friends, it was a wonder why a Singaporean (also considered "foreigners" in Vietnamese parlance but less so compared with those whose hair and eyes were not black) would be interested in the topic. The reason for the surprise is I think due to Vietnamese tending to divide research turf into "Vietnamese" and "non-Vietnamese". Topics on Vietnamese turf are, for either political or language capability reasons, done by Vietnamese only. Foreigners would have their list of pet topics, which however did not include local administration and mundane governance problems. Many of them expressed disbelief that I would be capable of pulling it off. With more than hard work and time, the language obstacle was soon overcome. Soon, speaking with fluency and some slang brought me closer to Vietnamese and into their confidence.

It was time-consuming because it involved spending much time to get to know people on a personal level, to the neglect of a broader sort of approach to relationships as well as concerns about the larger political, economic, and social issues. I however reckoned that getting qualitative data through interviews and in-depth knowledge of personal situations within the context of state–society relations would be more useful (and more practical) than attempts at gathering quantitative data of whole localities. The latter could not be achieved without strong, high-level political support and huge financial outlays; a graduate student like me had neither. Not that such quantitative data exist, or that they would be more effective as the qualitative data in throwing light on the issues of this book.

In this regard, foreign researchers usually have a hard time doing research in Vietnam. But in fact there is little reason for them to complain, because I soon discovered that Vietnamese researchers also faced obstacles of bureaucratic procedures and opaqueness similar to those put in the way of foreigners. A formal social research or survey request lodged with the city or provincial authority, or perhaps the district authority above any ward, is usually required before ward officials can allow researchers to work in or survey the locality. This procedure conforms to regulations regarding the conduct of social research by Vietnamese as well as by foreigners. In 1996, my sponsoring agency applied to the city or provincial level to grant me permission to work in a ward. The request was passed on to the district authority above that ward, and then to the ward authority. Even if both the city and district had agreed to my request, the ward had the right to reject it. In Vietnam most of the time upper level government authorities could only request, rather than order, lower levels to perform tasks that the law did not compel, and receiving researchers was a voluntary thing. Reasons that any ward might reject research requests include the fear of saying the wrong things to foreigners, as well as the intention to hide internal problems within the ward from the eyes of upper level officials and foreigners. In 1997, my request took five months to process because it had to meander down and up this bureaucratic ladder a few times. When the permit was granted, I was already more than half-way through my fieldwork period of stay in Hà Nội, and therefore I had to make a number of subsequent trips to Hà Nội to continue working with the ward. In 1999, I directly requested the ward for permission to interview more heads of resident group in the ward, but the people's committee chairman told me that the permit I had was obtained "long ago" (two years) and therefore it should be considered as expired, even though I protested and demonstrated that no expiry date was written on the permit. Being straight, I could not fathom that perhaps the ward chairman was asking for a bribe. In any case, I wanted to have a high ethical standard for this piece of work.

There are, however, informal ways that researchers can resort to. These ways are an additional demonstration of the methods of mediating the difficulties imposed by the bureaucratic state. Circumventing these bureaucratic obstacles requires a long period of close association and acquaintance with — and even assistance to — the locality and its officials. Most Vietnamese researchers would recommend to their foreign counterparts the informal access route, because formal meetings and a formal environment usually produce information that is not very useful. I discovered this quickly after I had the first formal work meeting with ward officials and was given speech after speech on the achievements of the locality. I switched to spending a considerable amount of time cultivating personal relationships with officials in two wards. This process spanned about three years. Ward officials and I usually avoided mention or talk of any sensitive topics while in the ward office. They were more likely to answer sensitive questions if asked in a confidential setting, such as during one of the dinners and lunches I hosted for them, individually as well as collectively. I also visited several officials at their homes, and even sponsored transport costs for a summer day vacation trip to a beach in Hải Phòng province for a ward's staff and their family members.

In view of the restrictions above, another research method I used was what Vietnamese like to call "street learning" or "learning in the dust" (*học bụi*). I did these formal interviews in the two wards, where I got to know ward officials personally, as well as in other wards. On the other hand, I asked questions of numerous friends who by random lived in various wards and across all urban districts of Hà Nội, and learned from these interactions about the problems there. Thus, getting out onto the streets to live, to observe, and to record life and the meanings it had for locals was rewarding. Since graduating, I have also visited Hà Nội once every few months to keep track of developments in the city with regard to local authorities. That the political system has not changed much, and that local authorities have more or less retained their ways, ensures that the approaches I have adopted to mediate state controls and the fieldwork experiences gathered in the past nine years continue to be relevant.

SELECTION OF WARDS AND CASE STUDIES

Some explanation regarding the biases in the sampling process is necessary. Admittedly, the selection of wards for analyses in this book was not systematic; neither was it the intention to satisfy as far as all possible criteria for survey that statistical studies prescribed. The initial approach I adopted was ethnographical — to penetrate a ward in a working-class district so deep that a unique view from the grassroots could be obtained. Given sordid research limitations described above, it was not possible to have wide-ranging and expensive surveys. While waiting for the research permit, I went to stay with friends in all districts and I could observe the same urban governance problems taking place in the same arenas of state–society contestation in all districts (except for a number of streets in Ba Đình District where state and government buildings and the houses of the top VCP members were located and thus needed maximum security and clearways).

Arena selection was influenced by the wish to reflect adequately the Janus-faced characteristic of Vietnamese state–society relations. Given the need to outline and analyse the structure and workings of the ward system, the arena of elections, which determined official selection, was selected as a natural pairing case. Together they would show the "tough" side of state–society relations. The arenas of housing construction and traffic order were the first choices to demonstrate the "soft" side, not just because they were easily witnessed on the everyday level, but also because they represented key demands of urban living; they were arenas where state–society contestations were sharp, and the state weak. Other arenas were also considered, such as control over social vices, smuggling, land use, zoning and requisition, satellite dishes, legal procedures, and so on (and there was a long list) but I reckoned that work, transport, and dwellings had to be the most pressing issues. In the end, it was thought that two case studies of the "soft" side would be sufficient so that the total view of Vietnamese state–society relations would be nicely balanced. I should emphasize it has not been the intention here to generalize that the state is strong or weak; the point is state strength and weakness (and conversely society) depends on the arena in focus.

The approach described above has its biases. One bias could be the urban nature of the arenas in a country that has more than 70 per cent of its population living in the rural area. Consider, however, that construction of new houses (with governance implications analysed in Chapter 5) tended to take place in the peri-urban areas as the cities expanded. Moreover, the same building regulations applied to the rural areas as well; these included construction, zoning, and land use restrictions (for example, the ban on conversion from agriculture use to residential use). Every commune had a people's committee to oversee these things, a mirror of the urban situation. The demand for daily commute from rural and peri-urban areas into the city was getting greater by the day as city demands for agricultural goods and excess rural labour increased. A second bias could be unrepresentativeness of the urban situation in view of the small sample. On this score, it is still difficult to overcome the research obstacles. On the other hand, a survey of newspapers from the major cities of Hồ Chí Minh City, Hà Nội, Đà Nẵng, and Cần Thơ would reveal similar problems of urban governance that impact in similar ways on state–society relations and elicit the same tactics and responses from both people and local officials. The four arenas chosen for study present themes and realities that exist in all those cities. They may occur in different time-frames in different cities, or may be concentrated in different parts of a city at different times because urbanization arrived at different timings. The issues in state–society relations nevertheless would be common to all so long as there are no fundamental changes in the parameters that shape state–society relations at the everyday level. As of 2005, the ward system still existed and operated in the same way as I first found them in 1995. The arenas are still being featured regularly as major urban governance problems by local newspapers. Thus, the biases in selection of wards and arenas exist, but the choices were carefully weighed and were the best under contemporary research circumstances.

Bibliography

BOOKS AND JOURNALS

Ali, Ashraf *Government and Politics of Big Cities: An Indian Case Study*. Delhi: Concept Publishing Company, 1977.

Andrusz, Gregory D. *Housing and urban development in the USSR*. London: Macmillan, 1984.

Ban chỉ đạo tổng điều tra dân số Việt Nam. *Kết quả điều tra mẫu nhà* [Results of survey of housing types]. Hà Nội: NXB Thống Kê, 1989.

Beresford, Melanie. *Vietnam: Politics, Economics and Society*. London and New York: Pinter Publishers, 1988.

————. "The political economy of dismantling the 'bureaucratic centralism and subsidy system' in Vietnam". In *Southeast Asia in the 1990s: Authoritarianism, Democracy and Capitalism,* edited by Kevin Hewison et al., pp. 215–36. St Leonards, NSW: Allen and Unwin, 1993.

Blowers, Andrew. *The Limits of Power: The Politics of Local Planning Policy*. Oxford: Pergamon Press, 1980.

Bùi Danh Lưu. "Kết quả bước đầu thực hiện Nghị Định 36/CP và Chỉ Thị 317/ TTg trong cả nước" [Initial achievements of the nationwide implementation of the 36/CP ordinance and the 317-TTg Instruction]. *Quản lý Nhà nước* 13 (1995): 9–12, 20.

Bùi Quang Khánh. *Hành-chánh địa-phương* [Local Administration]. Sàigòn: Học viện Quốc gia Hành-chánh, 1963.

Burchett, Wilfred and Norodom Sihanouk. *My War with the CIA: The Memoirs of Prince Norodom Sihanouk*. Harmondsworth, Middlesex: Penguin Books, 1973.

Burns, John P. *Political Participation in Rural China*. Berkeley: University of California Press, 1988.

Cẩm Ninh. "Cuộc nổi dậy Quỳnh Lưu" [The Quỳnh Lưu Uprising]. In *Gươm Thiêng* [The Sacred Sword], pp. 28–37. Số phát hành Ngày Quốc Hận 30-4, 1998.

Campbell, Adrian. "Regional Power in the Russian Federation". In *Local Government in Eastern Europe,* edited by Andrew Coulson, pp. 145–67. Hants and Brookfield: Edward Elgar. 1995.

Carter, Frank. "Housing Policy in Bulgaria". In *Housing Policies in Eastern Europe and the Soviet Union,* edited by John Sillince, pp. 170–227. London and New York: Routledge, 1990.

Cat@coombs.anu.edu.au. "Implications of Electoral Change?". *Seasia-list,* 3 December 1994.

Cattell, David T. *Leningrad: A Case Study of Soviet Urban Government.* New York: Frederick A. Praeger, Praeger Special Studies in International Politics and Public Affairs, 1968.

Chan, Anita, Richard Madsen, and John Unger. *Chen Village under Mao and Deng*, Expanded and Updated edition. Berkeley, CA: University of California Press, 1992.

Cheung, Peter Tsan-yin. "The Case of Guangdong in Central-Provincial Relations". In *Changing Central-Local Relations in China*, edited by Jia Hao and Lin Zhimin, pp. 207–37. Boulder, CO: Westview Press, 1994.

Coulson, Andrew. "From Democratic Centralism to Local Democracy". In *Local Government in Eastern Europe*, edited by Andrew Coulson, pp. 1–19. Hants and Brookfield: Edward Elgar, 1995.

Cục Thống Kê và Sở Văn hoá Thông tin Thành phố Hà Nội. *Thủ Đô Hà Nội: 30 năm xây dựng và bảo vệ chế độ Xã hội Chủ nghĩa* [Hà Nội the Capital: 30 years of building and protecting the Socialist system]. Hà Nội, 1984.

Đàm Trung Phương. *Đô Thị Việt Nam tập 1* [Urban areas of Vietnam, vol. 1]. Bộ Xây dựng Chương trình KC. 11. Hà Nội: NXB Xây dựng, 1995.

Đào Trí Úc. "Nghiên cứu về ý thức và lối sống theo pháp luật" [Research on consciousness and way of life that respect the law]. In *Xây dựng ý thức và lối sống theo pháp luật* [Build consciousness and way of life that respect the law], edited by Đào Trí Úc, pp. 3–33. Hà Nội: Đề tài Khoa học xã hội Cấp Nhà nước KX-07-17, 1995.

ĐCSVN. "Làm tốt cuộc Bầu cử Hội đồng Nhân dân và Ủy ban Nhan dân các cấp" [Organize well elections of people's councils and people's committees of all levels]. *TCCS* 4 (1977): 34–38.

———. "Thấu suốt nguyên tắc tập trung dân chủ trong quản lý kinh tế – xã hội" [Let the principle of democratic centralism penetrate management of the economy and society]. *TCCS* 7 (1983): 1–7.

———. "Nhà nước và nhân dân cùng làm" [The state and people working together]. *TCCS* 11 (1984): 6–9, 63.

———. *Chiến lược ổn định và phát triển kinh tế xã hội đến năm 2000* [Strategy to stabilize and develop the economy and society until year 2000]. Hà Nội: NXB Sự Thật, 1991.

DiMaio Jr., Alfred John. *Soviet Urban Housing:Problems and Policies.* New York: Praeger Publishers, 1974.

Đinh Gia Khánh. "Tổng Luận". In *Địa chí Văn hoá Dân gian Thăng Long - Đông Đô - Hà Nội*, edited by Đinh Gia Khánh and Trần Tiến, pp. 19–20. Hà Nội: Hà Nội Culture and Information Office, 1991.

Đinh Ngọc Vượng. "Đánh giá thực trạng hiểu biết pháp luật và thái độ đối với pháp luật của các tầng lớp dân cư" [Evaluation of the real standard of understanding of the law and attitudes towards the law among classes of people]. In *Xây dựng ý thức và lối sống theo pháp luật* [Build consciousness and way of life that respect the law], edited by Đào Trí Úc, pp. 202–12. Hà Nội: Đề tài Khoa học xã hội Cấp Nhà nước KX-07-17, 1995.

Đinh Văn Mậu et al. *Chính trị học đại cương* [An Outline of Political Studies]. HCM City: NXB Thành phố Hồ Chí Minh, 1997.

ĐLDVN. "Báo cáo Chính trị của Ban Chấp hành Trung ương Đảng do đồng chí Lê Duẩn trình bày tại Đại hội đại biểu toàn quốc lần thứ IV" [Political Report of the VCP Central Committee presented by Comrade Lê Duẩn at the Fourth VCP National Congress]. *Học Tập*, 22 December 1976, 37–12.

———. "Political Report of the Central Committee to the 4th Party Congress". In *4th National Congress: Documents*, pp. 45–46. Hà Nội: Foreign Language Publishing House, 1977.

Đỗ Bằng et al. *Tổ chức bộ máy nhà nước triều Nguyễn: Giai đoạn 1802–1884* [Organization of the state machinery during the Nguyễn Dynasty, 1802–1884]. Huế: NXB Thuận Hoá, 1997.

Đỗ Mười. "Quyết tâm giành thắng lợi trên mặt trận phân phối lưu thông" [Resolutely secures success on the front of distribution and circulation]. *TCCS* 7 (1981): 26–33.

Đoàn Trọng Truyến. "Vận dụng đúng đắn nguyên tắc kết hợp quản lý theo ngành với quản lý theo lãnh thổ, tăng cường một bước công tác quản lý kinh tế trong tình hình mới" [Use correctly the principle of combining management by specialization and management by geographical location, strengthen by one level the management of the economy in the new situation]. *Học Tập* 21, no. 8 (1975): 8–24.

———. "Cải cách hành chính địa phương trong cải cách nền hành chính nhà nước" [Reform of local administration in reforms of the state administration system]. In *Cải cách hành chính địa phương: Lý luận và thực tiễn* [Local administration reform: Theory and practice], edited by Tô Tử Hạ, Nguyễn Hữu Trị, and Nguyễn Hữu Đức, pp. 21–32. Hà Nội: NXB Chính trị Quốc gia, 1997.

DRV. "Pháp lệnh quy định thể lệ Bầu cử Hội đồng Nhân dân các cấp ngày 23 tháng 1 năm 1961" [Ordinance on Regulations of People's Councils elections at all levels, 23/1/1961]. In *Các văn bản về việc Bầu cử Hội đồng Nhân dân và Ủy ban Hành chính các cấp* [Documents on people's councils and Adminstrative Committees elections at all levels], by Ủy ban Nhân dân tỉnh Nam Định, pp. 4–26. Nam Định, 1961.

Đ.T. Phương. "Lecture on Development of Hà Nội". Institute of Sociology, Hà Nội, 5 May 1997.

Duara, Prasenjit. *Culture, Power, and the State: Rural North China, 1900–1942*. Stanford, CA: Stanford University Press, 1988.

Duiker, William J. *Vietnam: Nation in Revolution*. Boulder, CO: Westview Press, 1983.

Dương Xuân Ngọc and Nguyễn Chí Dũng. "Ảnh hưởng của kinh tế thị trường đối với hệ thống chính trị ở cấp phường" [The impact of market economy on the political system at the level of the ward]. *TCCS* 455 (1993): 51–53.

Economist. "Troublesome Christians", 15 November 1997.

Elliot, David W. P. "Political Integration in North Vietnam: The Cooperativization Period". In *Communism in Indochina: New Perspectives*, edited by Joseph J. Zasloff and MacAlister Brown, pp. 165–93. Massachusetts: Lexington Books, 1975.

———. "Institutionalizing the Revolution: Vietnam's Search for a Model of Development". In *Vietnamese Communism in Comparative Perspective*, edited by William S. Turley, pp. 199–223. Boulder, CO: Westview Press, 1980.

Elliot, David, "Socialist Republic of Vietnam". In *Marxist Governments: A World Survey*, edited by Bogdan Szajkowski, pp. 713–54. London: Macmillan, 1981.

Elliott, James. "The Future of Socialism: Vietnam, the Way Ahead?". *Third World Quarterly* 13, no. 1 (1992): 131–43.

Fall, Bernard B. *The Viet-Minh Regime: Government and Administration in the Democratic Republic of Vietnam*. New York: Institute of Pacific Relations and Southeast Asia Program, Cornell University, 1956.

Fforde, Adam. "The Political Economy of 'Reform' in Vietnam: Some Reflections". In *The Challenge of Reform in Indochina*, edited by Borje Ljunggren, pp. 293–325. Massachusetts: Harvard Institute for International Development, Harvard University, 1993.

Friedgut, Theodore H. *Political Participation in the USSR*. Princeton, NJ: Princeton University Press, 1979.

———. "The Soviet Citizen's Perception of Local Government". In *Soviet Local Politics and Government*, edited by Everett M. Jacobs, pp. 113–30. London: George Allen & Unwin, 1983.

Gibson, John and Philip Hanson, eds. *Transformation from Below: Local Power and the Political Economy of Post-Communist Transitions*. Cheltenham, UK, and Brookfield, US: Edward Elgar, 1996.

Gilison, Jerome. "Soviet Elections as a Measure of Dissent: The Missing One Percent". *American Political Science Review* 52, no. 3 (1968): 814–26.

Gillespie, John. "The Role of the Bureaucracy in Managing Urban Land in Vietnam". *Pacific Rim Law and Policy Journal* 5, no. 1 (1995): 59–124.

Ginsburgs, George. "Local Government and Administration under the Viet-Minh, 1945–54". In *North Vietnam Today: Profile of a Communist Satellite*, edited by P. J. Honey, pp. 135–65. New York: Frederick A. Praeger, 1962.

Ha, Seong-Kyu. "Introduction". In *Housing Policy and Practice in Asia,* edited by Seong-Kyu Ha, pp. 1–11. New York: Helm Croom, 1987.

Hà Thị Hồng. "Ai là người quản lý nhà lắp ghép cao tầng?" [Who is responsible for managing the prefabricated high-rise buildings?]. *Xây dựng*, September 1997, p. 38.

Hahn, Jeffrey W. *Soviet Grassroots: Citizen Participation in Local Soviet Government.* Princeton, NJ: Princeton University Press, 1988.

Harrop, Martin and William L. Miller. *Elections and Voters: A Comparative Introduction.* London: Macmillan, 1987.

Heng, Russell. "Vietnam 1992: Economic Growth and Political Caution". *Southeast Asian Affairs 1993,* pp. 354–63. Singapore: Institute of Southeast Asian Studies, 1993.

Hermet, Guy, Richard Rose, and Alain Rouquie, eds. *Elections Without Choice.* London: Macmillan, 1978.

Hiebert, Murray. *Chasing the Tigers: A Portrait of the New Vietnam.* New York: Kodansha International, 1996.

Higgs, Peter. "The Footpath Economy and Beyond: Factors Affecting Social and Economic Change in a District of Hanoi". Paper delivered at the Asian Studies Association of Australia Annual Conference held in Melbourne, 1996.

Hirszowicz, Maria. *Coercion and Control in Communist Society: The Visible Hand of Bureaucracy.* Brighton, Sussex: Harvester Press, 1986.

Hoàng Hữu Phê and Yukio Nishimura. *The Historical Environment and Housing Conditions in the "36 Old Streets" Quarter of Hanoi.* Bangkok: Division of Human Settlements Development, Asian Institute of Technology, Bangkok, 1992.

Hoàng Hữu Phê and Hans Orn, eds. *The Phường of Hanoi.* Vietnam Urban Transport Assistance Project. Hà Nội: Swedish International Development Agency, 1995.

Hoàng Quốc Việt. "Lời giới thiệu" [Introduction]. In *Về pháp luật và pháp chế Xã hội Chủ nghĩa* [On Law and socialist rule by law in Vietnam], pp. 3–4. Hà Nội: Sự Thật, 1964.

Hoàng Văn Hảo, ed. *Nhà nước và Pháp luật Xã hội Chủ nghĩa* [The State and Socialist Law]. Hà Nội: NXB Chính Trị Quốc gia, 1993.

Học Viện Chính trị Quốc gia Hồ Chí Minh. *Nhà nước và Pháp luật Xã hội Chủ nghĩa Tập I, II, III* [State and Socialist Law Volumes I, II, III]. Hà Nội: NXB Chính trị Quốc gia, 1993.

Học Viện Hành chính Quốc gia. *Về nền hành chính nhà nước Việt Nam: Những kinh nghiệm xây dựng và phát triển* [On System of Administration of Vietnam: Experiences in Building Up and Development. Hà Nội: NXB Khoa học và Kỹ thuật, 1996.

Honey, P. J. "Introduction". In *North Vietnam Today: Profile of a Communist Satellite*, edited by P. J. Honey. New York: Frederick A. Praeger, 1962.

Hồng Vy. "Hà Nội 'hậu 36/CP'" [Hà Nội post-36/CP]. *Giao thông vận tải*, 18 January 1996, p. 8.

Hữu Đức. "Về nâng cao hiệu lực của chính quyền địa phương" [On raising the effectiveness of the political authority of the ward]. *TCCS* 12 (1985): 70–75.

Hy Van Luong. "The Political Economy of Vietnamese Reforms: A Microscopic Perspective from Two Ceramics Manufacturing Centers". In *Reinventing Vietnamese Socialism: Đổi Mới in Comparative Perspectives,* edited by William S. Turley and Mark Selden, pp. 119–48. Boulder, CO: Westview Press, 1993.

International Committee for a Free Vietnam. "Prospects for democracy in Vietnam after twenty years of totalitarian misrule". Proceedings of a conference of the same name held by the International Committee for a Free Vietnam, May 1995.

Janos, Andrew C. "Preface". In *Authoritarian Politics in Communist Europe: Uniformity & Diveristy in One-Party States*. Berkeley: Institute of International Studies, University of California, 1976.

Jeong, Yeosnik. "The Rise of State Corporatism in Vietnam". *Contemporary Southeast Asia* 19, no. 2 (September 1997): 152–71.

Kelliher, Daniel Roy. *Peasant Power in China: The Era of Rural Reform, 1979– 1989.* New Haven and London: Yale University Press, 1992.

Kerkvliet, Benedict J. Tria. "Politics of Society in the Mid-1990s". In *Dilemmas of Development: Vietnam Update 1994,* edited by Benedict J. Tria Kerkvliet. Political and Social Change Monograph no. 22, pp. 5–43. Canberra: RSPAS, Australian National University, 1995.

———. "Village-State Relations in Vietnam: The Effect of Everyday Politics on Decollectivization". *Journal of Asian Studies* 54, no. 2 (1995): 396–418.

———. "Partial Impressions of Society in Vietnam". In *Đổi Mới: Ten Years after the 1986 Party Congress,* edited by Adam Fforde, Political and Social Change Monograph no. 24, pp. 47–49. Canberra: RSPAS, Australian National University, 1997.

———. *Land Struggles and Land Regimes in the Philippines and Vietnam during the Twentieth Century*. Amsterdam: Centre for Asian Studies, The Wertheim Lecture 1997.

———. "Land Regimes and State Strengths and Weaknesses in the Philippines and Vietnam". In *Weak and Strong States in Asia-Pacific Societies*, edited by Peter Dauvergue, pp. 158–74. Sydney: Allen and Unwin, 1998.

———. "Wobbly Foundations: Building Cooperatives in Rural Vietnam, 1955–1961". Conference paper presented at the International Conference on Vietnamese Studies, Hanoi, July 1998.

Khải Vinh. "Quản lý tốt đô thị để góp phần xây dựng lối sống đô thị lành mạnh" [Manage well the cities to contribute to building a virtuous urban way of life]. In *Lối sống trong đời sống đô thị hiện nay* [Present urban way of life], edited by Lê Như Hoa, pp. 147–51. Hà Nội: NXB Văn hoá Thông tin, Viện Văn Hoá, 1993.

Khoa Luật, Trường Đại học Tổng hợp Hà Nội. *Luật Nhà nước Việt Nam* [Laws on the state in Vietnam], pp. 110–13. 1994.

Kimura, Tetsusaburo. *The Vietnamese Economy 1975–1986: Reform and International Relations*. Tokyo: Institute of Developing Economies, 1989.

Kirkby, R. J. R. *Urbanisation in China: Town and Country in a Developing Economy 1949-2000 AD*. London and Sydney: Croom Helm, 1985.

Kohli, Atul and Vivienne Shue. "State power and social forces: on political contention and accommodation in the Third World". In *State Power and Social Forces: Domination and Transformation in the Third World*, edited by Joel S. Migdal, Atul Kohli, and Vivienne Shue, p. 294. Cambridge: Cambridge University Press, 1994.

Kolko, Gabriel. *Vietnam: Anatomy of a Peace*. London and New York: Routledge, 1997.

Lê Điều. "Chế độ dân chủ Xã hội Chủ nghĩa" [Socialist democracy]. *Học Tập* 6 (1976): 30–38.

Lê Đình Khiên. "Xác định thế nào là cán bộ quản lý hành chính nhà nước" [How to define a "state administrative cadre"]. *Dân chủ và Pháp luật* 6 (1996): 8–9.

Lê Đức Thọ. *Phấn đấu xây dựng Hà Nội trở thành thủ đô tin yêu của cả nước* [Let us struggle to build Hanoi into the beloved and trusted capital of the country]. Hà Nội: Sự Thật, 1985.

Lê Hồng Sơn. "Một số ý kiến về sửa đổi, bổ sung luật Bầu cử đại biểu HĐND và luật tổ chức HĐND và UBND" [A few opinions about amendments and expansion of the laws on election of people's councils and organisation of people's councils and people's committees]. *Dân chủ và Pháp luật* 8 (1998): 4–5.

Lê Kiến Quốc. "Ba mươi năm cải tạo và xây dựng kinh tế, phát triển văn hoá của nước Việt-Nam Dân chủ cộng hoà (1945–1975)" [Thirty years of reform and building of the economy, developing the culture of the Democratic Republic of Viet-Nam (1945–1975)]. *Học Tập* 8 (1975): 25–33.

Lê Quang Thưởng. "Thực trạng của hoạt động tuyên truyền giáo dục pháp luật ở nước ta hiện nay" [The present situation in our country on activities on mobilization and education regarding the law]. In *Xây dựng ý thức và lối sống theo pháp luật* [Build consciousness and way of life that respects the law], edited by Đào Trí Úc, pp. 183–201. Hà Nội: Đề tài Khoa học xã hội cấp Nhà nước KX-07-17, 1995.

Lê Thi. "Xây dựng mọi quan hệ đúng đắn giữa tập thể và cá nhân trong chế độ Xã hội Chủ nghĩa" [Build a correct relationship between the collective and the individual in the socialist regime]. *TCCS* 8 (1977): 54–61.

Lê Thị Túy. "Vấn đề được đặt ra từ lối sống Hà Nội" [The problem starts from the way of life in Hanoi]. In *Lối sống trong đời sống đô thị hiện nay* [Present urban way of life], edited by Lê Như Hoa, pp. 152–64. Hà Nội: NXB Văn hoá Thông tin, Viện Văn hoá, 1993.

Lee, Peter Nan-shong. "Housing Privatization with Chinese Characteristics". In *Social Change and Social Policy in Contemporary China,* edited by Linda Wong and Stewart MacPherson, pp. 113–39. Aldershot: Avebury, 1995.

Legge, J. D. *Central Authority and Regional Autonomy in Indonesia: A Study in Local Administration 1950-1960.* Ithaca: Cornell University Press, 1961.

Lev, Daniel S. "Judicial Institutions and Legal Culture". In *Culture and Politics in Indonesia,* edited by Claire Holt, pp. 246–318. Ithaca: Cornell University Press, 1972.

Li Tana. *Peasants on the Move: Rural-Urban Migration in the Hanoi Region.* Occasional Paper No. 91. Singapore: Institute of Southeast Asian Studies, 1996.

Lieberthal, Kenneth and Michel Oksenberg. *Policy Making in China: Leaders, Structures, and Processes.* Princeton, NJ: Princeton University Press, 1988.

Luo Xiaopeng. "Rural Reform and the Rise of Localism". In *Changing Central–Local Relations in China,* edited by Jia Hao and Lin Zhimin, pp. 113–34. Boulder, CO: Westview Press, 1994.

Lương Minh Cừ. "Về quyền sở hữu và quyền sử dụng ruộng đất ở Việt Nam trong thời kỳ quá độ lên chủ nghĩa xã hội" [On right to own and use farm land in Vietnam during the period of transition towards socialism]. *Khoa học xã hội* 26 (IV-1995). Trung tâm Khoa học xã hội và Nhân văn Quốc gia, Viện Khoa học xã hội tại thành phố Hồ Chí Minh, 1995.

Lý Công Uẩn (1010). "Royal Edict on the transfer of the capital" [Thiên đô chiếu]. In *Vietnamese Literature,* edited by Nguyễn Khắc Viện and Hữu Ngọc, pp. 199–200. Hà Nội: Red River, year unclear.

Malarney, Shaun Kingsley. "Culture, Virtue, and Political Transformation in Contemporary Northern Vietnam". *Journal of Asian Studies* 6 (1997): 899–920.

Mares, Peter. "Reporting Vietnam: True confessions of a foreign correspondent". In *The Mass Media in Vietnam,* edited by David G. Marr. Political and Social Change Monograph no. 25, pp. 146–63. Canberra: The Australian National University, 1998.

Marr, David G. "Where is Vietnam coming from?". In *Đổi Mới: Vietnam's Renovation Policy and Performance,* edited by Dean Forbes et al. Political and Social Change Monograph no. 14, pp. 12–20. Canberra: RSPAS, Australian National University, 1991.

———. *Vietnam Strives to Catch Up.* New York: The Asia Society, 1995.

——— and Christine Pelzer White. "Introduction". In *Postwar Vietnam: Dilemmas in Socialist Development,* edited by David G. Marr and Christine Pelzer White, pp. 1–11. Ithaca, NY: Southeast Asia Program, Cornell University, 1988.

McAlister, John T. Jr. and Paul Mus. *The Vietnamese and Their Revolution*. NY: Harper & Row, 1970.

Migdal, Joel S. *Strong Societies and Weak States: State-Society Relations and State Capabilities in the Third World*. Princeton, NJ: Princeton University Press, 1988.

———. "The state in society: an approach to struggles for domination". In *State Power and Social Forces: Domination and Transformation in the Third World*, edited by Joel S. Migdal, Atul Kohli, and Vivienne Shue, p. 15. Cambridge: Cambridge University Press, 1994.

Moise, Edwin E. "'Class-ism' in Northern Vietnam, 1953-1956". In *Vietnamese Communism in Comparative Perspective*, edited by William S. Turley, pp. 91–105. Boulder, Colorado: Westview Press, 1980.

Mote, Max E. *Soviet local and republic elections: A description of the 1963 elections in Leningrad based on official documents, press accounts, and private interviews*. Stanford University, Hoover Institution Studies 10, The Hoover Institution on War, Revolution, and Peace, 1965.

Ng Shui Meng. "Vietnam in 1981". In *Southeast Asian Affairs 1982*, pp. 377–94. Singapore: Institute of Southeast Asian Studies, 1982.

Người Xây dựng. "Quan Liêu" [Bureaucratism]. *Học Tập* 22, no. 10 (1976): 70–73.

Nguyễn Bim. "Một số ý kiến về xây dựng chính quyền cấp phường ở Hà Nội" [Some opinions on developing the ward level authorities in Hà Nội]. In *Tạp chí Quản lý Nhà nước*, no. 7, (1994): 25–26.

Nguyễn Đăng Dung. *Tổ chức chính quyền nhà nước ở địa phương* [Political authorities of the state at the local level]. Dong Nai: NXB Dong Nai, 1997.

Nguyễn Duy Gia. "Nhà nước và nền hành chính nhà nước Việt Nam - xây dựng và phát triển (1945–1995)" [The state of Vietnam and its system of administration: Building up and development, 1945–1995]. In *Về nền hành chính nhà nước Việt Nam: Những kinh nghiệm xây dựng và phát triển* [On the System of Administration of Vietnam: Experiences in Building Up and Development], edited by Học Viện Hành chính Quốc gia, pp. 5–14. Hà Nội: NXB Khoa học và Kỹ thuật, 1996.

Nguyễn Hữu Đức. "Về cơ cấu bộ máy chính quyền địa phương hiện nay" [On the present structure of local authorities]. In *Cải Cách hành chính địa phương - Lý luận và thực tiễn* [Local administration reform: Theory and practice], edited by Tô Tử Hạ, Nguyễn Hữu Trị, and Nguyễn Hữu Đức, pp. 96–106. Hà Nội: NXB Chính trị Quốc gia, 1998.

Nguyễn Hữu Trị. "Vấn đề chính quyền địa phương – những xu hướng cải cách" [The problem of local political authorities: Directors in reform]. In *Cải cách hành chính địa phương: Lý luận và thực tiễn* [Local adminsitration reform:

Theory and practice], edited by Tô Tử Hạ, Nguyễn Hữu Trị, and Nguyễn Hữu Đức, pp. 33–50. Hà Nội: NXB Chính trị Quốc gia, 1997.

Nguyễn Hữu Trị. "Vấn đề quản lý nhà nước ở đô thị và phương hướng đổi mới mô hình tổ chức chính quyền đô thị" [The problem of state management in urban areas and direction of change in the model for organizing urban political authorities]. In *Cải cách hành chính địa phương: Lý luận và thực tiễn* [Local adminsitration reform: Theory and practice], edited by Tô Tử Hạ, Nguyễn Hữu Trị, and Nguyễn Hữu Đức, pp. 245–63. Hà Nội: NXB Chính trị Quốc gia, 1997.

Nguyễn Khải. "Một người Hà Nội" [A Hanoian]. In *Một người Hà Nội: tập truyện* [A Hanoian: stories]. Hà Nội: NXB Hà Nội, 1990.

Nguyễn Lam. "Mấy vấn đề về tư tưởng chính sách kinh tế hiện nay" [A few problems on present ideology in economic policies]. *TCCS* 3 (1980): 1–10.

Nguyễn Mại. "Một số ý kiến về mối quan hệ giữa cải tạo thị trường và phân phối lưu thông" [A few opinions about the relationship between market reform, distribution, and circulation]. *TCCS* 6 (1985): 58–65.

Nguyễn Ngọc Minh. "Nâng cao ý thức tôn trọng và nghiêm chỉnh chấp hành pháp luật" [Raise the awareness in the respect for and proper carrying out of the law]. *TCCS* 6 (1977): 64–68.

―――. "Thời kỳ quá độ ở Việt Nam và vấn đề tăng cường hiệu lực của nhà nước Xã hội Chủ nghĩa" [The period of transition in Vietnam and the problem of strengthening the effectiveness of the socialist state]. In *Tăng cường hiệu lực nhà nước Xã hội Chủ nghĩa của ta* [Strengthen the effectiveness of our socialist state], by Viện Luật Học, Ủy ban Khoa học xã hội Việt Nam, pp. 11–43. Hà Nội: NXB Khoa học xã hội, 1983.

Nguyễn Niên. "Tăng cường pháp chế Xã hội Chủ nghĩa - biện pháp để nâng cao hiệu lực quản lý của nhà nước" [Strengthen socialist rule of law: measures to raise effectiveness of state management]. In *Tăng cường hiệu lực nhà nước Xã hội Chủ nghĩa của ta* [Strengthen the effectiveness of our socialist state], edited by Viện Luật Học, Ủy ban Khoa học xã hội Việt Nam, pp. 157–72. Hà Nội: NXB Khoa học xã hội, 1983.

Nguyễn Tiến Đoàn. "Về Đổi mới Chính quyền Địa phương từ ba cấp thành hai cấp" [On the reshuffle of the local authorities from three-tier to two-tier system]. *Quản lý Nhà nước* 12, no. 4 (1993): 17–19.

Nguyễn Tử Chi, "The Traditional Viet Village in Bắc Bộ: Its Organizational Structure and Problems". In *The Traditional Village in Vietnam,* edited by Phan Huy Lê et al., pp. 44–142. Hà Nội: Thế Giới Publishers, 1993.

Nguyễn Trung Thực. "Chiếc Ô" [The umbrella]. *TCCS* 4 (1980): 58–60.

Nguyen Van Canh and Earle Cooper. *Vietnam under Communism, 1975-1982.* Stanford, CA: Hoover Institution Press, 1983.

Nguyễn Văn Uẩn. *Hà Nội nửa đầu thế kỷ XX Tập 1-3* [Hà Nội in the first half of the twentieth century: vol. 1–3]. Hà Nội: NXB Hà Nội, 1995.

Nguyễn Vinh. "Xây dựng chế độ làm chủ tập thể Xã hội Chủ nghĩa" [To build the regime of socialist collective mastery]. *TCCS* 4 (1977): 25–33, 70.

Nguyễn Văn Thư. "Về đào tạo, bồi dưỡng cán bộ chính quyền địa phương trong giai đoạn hiện nay" [On training and cultivation of cadres of local authorities in the current situation]. In *Cải Cách hành chính địa phương: Lý luận và thực tiễn* [Local adminsitration reform: Theory and practice], edited by Tô Tử Hạ, Nguyễn Hữu Trị, and Nguyễn Hữu Đức, pp. 134–46. Hà Nội: NXB Chính trị Quốc gia, 1998.

Nguyễn Vĩnh Phúc. "Khu phố cổ Hà Nội" [The ancient quarters of Hanoi]. *Xưa và Nay* 3 (04), 1994.

Nguyễn Xuân Yêm. "Vi phạm hành chính và công tác giáo dục ý thức, lối sống theo pháp luật cho công dân" [Administrative offences and work on education for citizens to cultivate consciousness and way of life that respect the law]. In *Xây dựng ý thức và lối sống theo pháp luật* [Build consciousness and way of life that respect the law], edited by Đào Trí Úc, pp. 213–24. Hà Nội: Đề tài Khoa học xã hội Cấp Nhà nước KX-07-17, 1995.

Nhật Tâm. "Tệ ức hiếp quần chúng" [The evil of bullying the masses]. *TCCS* 6, (1980): 82–83.

N.S.P. "Thư Hà Nội" [Letter from Hanoi]. *Đất Nước* 36–37 (1995): 19, 23.

Oi, Jean C. *State and Peasant in Contemporary China: The Political Economy of Village Government*. Berkeley, CA: University of California Press, 1989.

Orttung, Robert. *From Leningrad to St. Petersburg: Democratization in a Russian City*. New York: St Martin's Press, 1995.

Page, Edward C. and Michael J. Goldsmith. "Centre and locality: functions, access and discretion". In *Central and Local Government Relations: A Comparative Analysis of West European Unitary States*, edited by Edward C. Page and Michael J. Goldsmith. London: SAGE, 1987.

Paine, Suzy. "The Limits of Planning and the Case for Economic Reform". In *Postwar Vietnam: Dilemmas in Socialist Development,* edited by David G. Marr and Christine P. White, pp. 91–94. Ithaca, NY: Southeast Asia Program, Cornell University, 1988.

Phạm Điềm. "Đấu tranh xoá bỏ tàn dư của tư tưởng pháp lý cũ, xây dựng ý thức pháp luật Xã hội Chủ nghĩa" [Struggle to abolish remnants of old legal thinking, build the socialist legal awareness]. In *Tăng cường hiệu lực nhà nước xã hội chủ nghĩa của ta* [Strengthen the effectiveness of our socialist state], edited by Viện Luật Học, Ủy ban Khoa học xã hội Việt Nam, pp. 247–76. Hà Nội: NXB Khoa học Xã hội, 1983.

Phạm Hưng. "Khắc phục những mặt yếu về pháp chế Xã hội Chủ nghĩa ở nước ta" [Overcome weaknesses of socialist rule of law in our country]. *TCCS* 10 (1986): 8–11, 20.

Phạm Minh Hạc et al. *Vấn đề con người trong sự nghiệp công nghiệp hoá, hiện đại hoá* [The human element in industrialization and modernization]. Hà Nội: NXB Chính trị Quốc gia, 1996.

Phạm Trí Minh and Phạm Văn Nhiếp. "Mấy ý kiến về giải quyết nhà ở đô thị" [A few opinions on resolving housing problems in urban areas]. *TCCS* 6 (1987): 66–69, 80.

Phan Hiền. "Mấy vấn đề về tăng cường pháp chế xã hội chủ nghĩa" [A few problems about strengthening socialist rule by law]. *TCCS* 10 (1985): 34–40.

Phan Huy Lê et al. *The Traditional Village in Vietnam*. Hà Nội: Thế Giới Publishers, 1993.

Phan Trung Lý. "Suy nghĩ về kết quả Bầu cử đại biểu Hội đồng Nhân dân ba cấp". *Người Đại Biểu Nhân Dân*, no. 9, May–June 1990, p. 45.

Phùng Văn Tửu and Ngô Văn Thâu. *Tìm hiểu Bầu cử đại biểu Quốc hội* [In search of understanding of National Assembly elections]. Hà Nội: NXB Pháp lý, 1992.

———. *Bầu cử đại biểu Hội đồng Nhân dân theo Luật Bầu cử đại biểu Hội đồng Nhân dân năm 1994* [Election of People's councils under the 1994 people's council elections law] (Tài liệu phục vụ cuộc Bầu cử đại biểu Hội đồng Nhân dân ngày 20-11-1994). Hà Nội: NXB Chính trị Quốc gia, 1994.

Pike, Douglas. "Informal Politics in Vietnam". In *Informal Politics in East Asia*, edited by Lowell Dittmer, Haruhiro Fukui, and Peter N. S. Lee, pp. 269–89. Cambridge: Cambridge University Press, 2000.

Pinkele, Carl Frederic. *Local Government and Politics in the People's Republic of China: 1949–1952*. Ann Arbor, Michigan: University Microfilms, 1974.

Porter, Gareth. *Vietnam: The Politics of Bureaucratic Socialism*. Ithaca: Cornell University Press, 1993.

Pravda, Alex. "Elections in Communist Party States". In *Elections Without Choice*, edited by Guy Hermet, Richard Rose, and Alain Rouquie, pp. 169–95. London: Macmillan, 1978.

Puddington, Arch. *Failed Utopias: Methods of Coercion in Communist Regimes*. San Francisco: ICS Press, 1988.

Pye, Lucian. "The Powers That Be". *Far Eastern Economic Review*, 9 September 1999.

Race, Jeffrey. *War Comes to Long An: Revolutionary Conflict in a Vietnamese Province*. Berkeley, CA: University of California Press, 1972.

Reutersward, Lars. "Vietnam". In *Housing Policy and Practice in Asia*, edited by Seong-Kyu Ha, pp. 159–74. New York: Helm Croom, 1987.

Rigby, T. H. "Politics in the Mono-organizational society". In *Authoritarian Politics in Communist Europe: Uniformity and Diveristy in One-Party States*, edited by Andrew C. Janos, pp. 31–80. Berkeley: Institute of International Studies, University of California, 1976.

Rosenthal, Donald B. *The Limited Elite: Politics and Government in Two Indian Cities*. Chicago: University of Chicago Press, 1970.

Ross, Cameron. *Local Government in the Soviet Union*. London and Sydney: Croom Helm, 1987.

Scientific conference on ancient Hanoi [Hội thảo khoa học về Hà Nội cổ] held on 7 June 1997 at the Pharmaceutical Faculty of the National University of Hanoi, organized by the Centre for Research on Vietnam and Inter-Cultural Exchanges.

Shoup, Paul. "The Limits of Party Control: The Yugoslav Case". In *Authoritarian Politics in Communist Europe: Uniformity and Diveristy in One-Party States,* edited by Andrew C. Janos, pp. 176–96. Berkeley: Institute of International Studies, University of California, 1976.

Shue, Vivienne. *The Reach of the State.* Stanford, CA: Stanford University Press, 1988.

Sikor, Thomas. "Village-state relations in Vietnam: the role of the local state". Conference paper presented at the Annual Meeting of the Association for Asian Studies, Boston, 1999.

Sillince, John. "Housing policy in Eastern Europe and the Soviet Union". In *Housing Policies in Eastern Europe and the Soviet Union,* edited by John Sillince. London and New York: Routledge, 1990.

———, ed. *Housing Policies in Eastern Europe and the Soviet Union.* London and New York: Routledge, 1990.

SRV. "Luật tổ chức Hội đồng Nhân dân và Ủy ban Nhân dân các cấp (1962)" [Law on Organization of people's councils and people's committees at all levels, 1962]. In *Tổ chức Nhà nước Việt-Nam Dân chủ Cộng hoà.* Hà Nội: NXB Sự Thật, 1971.

———. "Pháp lệnh nhà ở" [Ordinance on Housing]. In *Hệ thống hoá văn bản pháp luật về nhà ở, đất đai và thuế nhà đất* [Legal documents on housing, land, and land taxes systematized], by NXB Pháp Lý, pp. 7–23. HCM City, 1991.

———. "Quyết định số 94/HĐBT, ngày 26/9/1981 của Hội đồng Bộ trưởng Về Chức năng, nhiệm vụ và tổ chức bộ máy chính quyền cấp phường" [Decision 94/HDBT of the Council of Ministers on the role, tasks, and organization of ward political authority machinery]. In *Cẩm nang công tác chính quyền xã, phường,* by Nguyễn Trí Hoà and Nguyễn Thương Huyền. TP HCM: NXB Thành phố Hồ Chí Minh, 1994.

———. "Hướng dẫn số 469-TCCP, ngày 2-12-1981 của Ban tổ chức của Chính phủ Về việc thi hành Quyết định số 94-HĐBT ban hành ngày 26-9-1981 của Hội đồng Bộ trưởng quy định chức năng, nhiệm vụ và tổ chức bộ máy chính quyền phường" [Guideline number 469-TCCP dated 2 December 1981 of the Government Commission on Personnel regarding implementation of Decision 94-HĐBT promulgated on 26 September 1981 by the Council of Ministers on roles, duties, and organization of local political authority at the ward level]. In *Cẩm nang công tác chính quyền xã, phường,* by Nguyễn Trí Hoa and Nguyễn Thương Huyền. TP HCM: NXB Thành phố Hồ Chí Minh, 1994.

———. "Nghị Định số 46-CP ngày 23-6-1993 của Chính phủ Về chế độ sinh hoạt phí đối với cán bộ Đảng, chính quyền và kinh phí hoạt động của Các

đoàn thể nhân dân ở xã, phường, thị trấn" [Decision number 46-CP dated 23
June 1993 of the Government on activity allowances for party and political
authority cadres, and activity funding for people's organizations at the
commune, ward, and townlet level]. In *Cẩm nang công tác chính quyền xã,
phường*, by Nguyễn Trí Hoà and Nguyễn Thương Huyền. TP HCM: NXB
Thành phố Hồ Chí Minh, 1994.

SRV. *Luật Bầu cử đại biểu Hội đồng Nhân dân (Sửa đổi)* [Law on Election of
People's Councils (Amended)]. Hà Nội: NXB Chính trị Quốc gia, 1994.

———. "Luật tổ chức Hội đồng Nhân dân và Ủy ban Nhân dân" [Law on
Organization of the People's Councils and People's Committees (21 June
1994)]. In *Cẩm nang công tác chính quyền xã, phường*, by Nguyễn Trí Hoà and
Nguyễn Thương Huyền. TP HCM: NXB Thành phố Hồ Chí Minh, 1994.

———. "Quy trình hiệp thương lựa chọn, giới thiệu những người ứng cử đại
biểu Hội đồng Nhân dân. (Ban hành kèm theo Công văn số 193CV/MTTW
ngày 2/8/1994)" [Process of selecting and introducing candidates for election
to people's council — Appendix to Circular 193CV/MTTW dated 2 August
1994].

———. Chỉ thị số 346/TTg ngày 5-7-1994 của Thủ tướng Chính phủ Về việc
tổ chức thực hiện Các Nghị định của Chính phủ về "quyền sở hữu nhà ở và
quyền sử dụng đất ở tại đô thị" và "mua bán và kinh doanh nhà ở" [Directive
of the Prime Minister 346/TTg dated 5 July 1994 on implementation of
Decisions of the Government regarding right to own houses, right to use
land, and the purchase and trade in housing]. In *Tìm hiểu Các văn bản pháp
luật về bất động sản* [Understanding current legal documents regarding fixed
property], by Trần Huy Hùng and Trần Xuân Sơn, pp. 197–200. Hà Nội:
NXB Thống Kê, 1995.

———. "Thông tư số 27/LB-TT ngày 31-12-1992 của liên bộ Lao Động - Thương
Binh và xã hội – Tài Chính - Xây dựng hướng dẫn thực hiện việc đưa tiền nhà
ở vào tiền lương" [Inter-Ministry Notice 27/LB-TT dated 31 December 1992
of Ministries of Labour-Veterans-Social Affairs, Finance, and Construction
on guidance for implementation of policy to add rental monies to salaries].
Tìm hiểu Các văn bản pháp luật hiện hành về bất động sản [Understanding
current legal documents regarding fixed property], by Trần Huy Hùng and
Trần Xuân Sơn, pp. 91–95. Hà Nội: NXB Thống Kê, 1995.

———. "Nghị Định số 60/CP ngày 5-7-1994 của Thủ tướng Chính phủ về quyền
sở hữu nhà ở và quyền sử dụng đất ở tại đô thị" [Decision 60/CP dated 5 July
1994 of the Prime Minister on right to own houses and right to use land in
urban areas]. In *Tìm hiểu Các văn bản pháp luật hiện hành về bất động sản*
[Understanding current legal documents regarding fixed property], by Trần Huy
Hùng and Trần Xuân Sơn, pp. 172–86. Hà Nội: NXB Thống Kê, 1995.

———. "Nghị Định số 61/CP ngày 5-7-1994 của Chính phủ Về mua bán và kinh
doanh nhà ở" [Decision 61/CP dated 5 July 1994 of the Prime Minister on

sale, purchase, and trade in housing]. In *Tìm hiểu Các văn bản pháp luật hiện hành về bất động sản* [Understanding current legal documents regarding fixed property], by Trần Huy Hùng and Trần Xuân Sơn, pp. 187–96. Hà Nội: NXB Thống Kê, 1995.

———. *Hiến Pháp Việt Nam (Năm 1946, 1959, 1980 và 1992)* [Constitution of Vietnam, 1946, 1959, 1980 and 1992]. Hà Nội: NXB Chính trị Quốc gia, 1995.

———. Thông tư số 107/TCCP-ĐP ngày 3 tháng 8 năm 1994 của Ban Tổ chức – Cán bộ Chính phủ: Hướng dẫn kế hoạch thực hiện nhiệm vụ Bầu cử đại biểu Hội đồng Nhân dân các cấp nhiệm kỳ 1994–1999. (Notice 107/TCCP-ĐP 3/8/1994 of the Government Commission on Cadres and Organization to guide implementation of plans to carry out the people's council elections of all levels for the 1994–1999 term].

———. "Chỉ thị của Thủ tướng Chính phủ Về tăng cường công tác quản lý trật tự an toàn giao thông đường bộ và trật tự an toàn giao thông đô thị" [Directive of the Prime Minister on strenghening management of traffic order and safety on roads and urban traffic order numbered 317/TTg, promulgated 26 May 1995].

———. "Nghị Định của Chính phủ Về bảo đảm trật tự an toàn giao thông đường bộ và trật tự an toàn giao thông đô thị" [Decision of the Government on ensuring road order and safety and urban traffic order numbered 36/CP, promulgated 29 May 1995].

———. "Nghị Định của Chính phủ quy định xử phạt hành chính về hành vi vi phạm trật tự an toàn giao thông đường bộ và trật tự an toàn giao thông đô thị" [Decision of the Government on regulations for administrative punishments of behaviour against road safety and order and urban traffic order numbered 49/CP, promulgated 29 July 1995].

———. *Pháp lệnh về nhiệm vụ, quyền hạn cụ thể của HĐND và UBND ở mọi cấp* [Ordinance on tasks, specific powers of people's councils and people's committees at every level]. Hà Nội: NXB Chính trị Quốc gia, 1996.

———. *Quy chế hoạt động của Hội đồng Nhân dân các cấp* [Regulations on activities of all levels of people's councils]. Hà Nội: NXB Chính trị Quốc gia, 1996.

SRV State Planning Committee and General Statistical Office. *Vietnam Living Standards Survey 1992–1993*. Hà Nội, September 1994.

State Science Commission of Vietnam. *Hanoi, the capital of North Vietnam since 1954*. Research and Microfilm Publications, 1960.

Stone, Richard L. *Philippine Urbanization: The Politics of Public and Private Property in Greater Manila*. Dekaln, Illinois: Cenre for Southeast Asian Studies, Northern Illinois University, 1973.

Sullivan, John. *Local Government and Community in Java: An Urban Case-study*. New York: Oxford University Press, 1992.

Sun, Jin-lou and Liu Lin. *Zhu zhai she hui xue*. [The Sociology of Housing]. Chi-nan: Shan-tung jen min chu pan she, 1985.

Swearer, Howard R. "The Functions of Soviet Local Elections". *Midwest Journal of Political Science* 5, no. 2 (1961): 129–49.

Szelenyi, Ivan. *Urban Inequalities under State Socialism*. New York: Oxford University Press, 1983.

Tan Teng Lang. *Economic Debates in Vietnam: Issues and Problems in Reconstruction and Development (1975-1984)*. Research Notes and Discussions Paper No. 55 Singapore: Institute of Southeast Asian Studies, 1985.

Taubman, William. *Governing Soviet Cities: Bureaucratic Politics and Urban Development in the USSR*. New York: Praeger Publishers, 1973.

Taylor, Keith W. "Vietnamese Studies in North America". Paper presented at the International Conference on Vietnamese Studies, Hanoi, July 1998.

Taylor, R. H., ed. *The Politics of Elections in Southeast Asia*. Cambridge: Woodfrow Wilson Centre Press, Cambridge University Press, 1996.

Thạch Lam. *Hà Nội băm sáu phố phường* [Thirty-Six Streets of Hanoi]. Sàigòn?: Đời Nay, 1943.

Thành Nam. "Vui buồn trên đường Hà Nội" [Happiness and sadness on roads of Hanoi]. *Giao thông vận tải*, 19 December 1996, p. 8.

Thayer, Carlyle A. "Vietnam's Two Strategic Tasks: Building Socialism and Defending the Fatherland". *Southeast Asian Affairs 1983*, pp. 299–324. Singapore: Institute of Southeast Asian Studies, 1983.

———. "The Regularization of Politics: Continuity and Change in the Party's Central Committee, 1951–1986". In *Postwar Vietnam: Dilemmas in Socialist Development*, edited by David G. Marr and Christine White. Ithaca: Cornell Southeast Asia Program, 1988.

———. "Renovation and Vietnamese society: The changing roles of government and administration". In *Đổi Mới: Vietnam's Renovation Policy and Performance*, edited by Dean Forbes et al. Political and Social Change Monograph no. 14, pp. 21-33. Canberra: RSPAS, Australian National University, 1991.

———. *Political Developments in Vietnam: From the Sixth to Seventh National Party Congress*. Canberra: Department of Political and Social Change, Research School of Pacific Studies, Australian National University, 1992.

———. "Recent Political Developments: Constitutional Change and the 1992 Elections". In *Vietnam and the Rule of Law,* edited by Carlyle Thayer and David G. Marr, pp. 50–80. 1993.

———. "The Challenges Facing Vietnamese Communism". *Southeast Asian Affairs 1993*, pp. 349–64. Singapore: Institute of Southeast Asian Studies, 1993.

———. "Political Development in Vietnam, 1975–1985". Paper presented to a National Conference on "Vietnam: Ten Years On" organized by the Australia-Vietnam Society held at the Graphic Arts Centre, Sydney, New South Wales,

6–7 July 1985. Obtained from ftp://coombs.anu.edu.au/coombspapers/otherarchives/asian-studies-archives/vietnam-archives/politics/vietnam-polit-devel-75-85.txt on 20 July 1999.

Thayer, Carlyle A. "Mono-Organizational Socialism and the State". In *Vietnam's Rural Transformation,* edited by B. T. Kerkvliet and D. J. Porter. Boulder, CO and Singapore: Westview Press and Institute of Southeast Asian Studies, 1995.

Thrift, Nigel and Dean Forbes. *The Price of War: Urbanization in Vietnam 1954–1985.* London: Allen and Unwin, 1986.

Tố Hữu. "Mấy quan điểm cơ bản và mấy vấn đề lớn trong công tác phân phối, lưu thông" [A few basic points and a few big problems in the distribution and circulation of goods]. *TCCS* 8 (1980): 10–20.

Tô Tử Hạ. "Những vấn đề chung: Cải Cách hành chính nhà nước trong nền kinh tế chuyển đổi hiện nay" [General issues: Reform of state administration in the context of the present economic transition]. In *Cải Cách hành chính địa phương: Lý luận và thực tiễn* [Local Administration Reform: Theory and Practice], edited by Tô Tử Hạ, Nguyễn Hữu Trị, and Nguyễn Hữu Đức, pp. 7–20. Hà Nội: NXB Chính trị Quốc gia, 1998.

―――, Nguyễn Hữu Trị, and Nguyễn Hữu Đức, eds. *Cải Cách hành chính địa phương: Lý luận và thực tiễn* [Local administration reform: Theory and Practice]. Hà Nội: NXB Chính trị Quốc gia, 1998.

Toan Ánh. *Nếp Cũ: Tín ngưỡng Việt Nam* [Beliefs of Vietnam]. 2 vols. HCMC: NXB TP Ho Chi Minh, 1997.

Tổng Cục Thống Kê. *Động thái và thực trạng kinh tế - xã hội Việt Nam qua 10 năm Đổi Mới (1986–1995)* [Socio-economic dynamics and realities in Vietnam after 10 years of Đổi Mới, 1986–1995]. Hà Nội: NXB Thống Kê, 1996.

Tonnesson, Stein. *Democracy in Vietnam?* Report Commissioned by the Swedish International Development Authority (SIDA). Copenhagen: NIAS, 1993.

―――. "What the Vietnamese State Can Do". Paper presented to the State and Society network conference in Copenhagen, 27 September 1996.

Townsend, James R. *Political Participation in Communist China.* Berkeley, CA: University of California Press, 1967.

Trần Công Tuynh. "Đổi mới tổ chức chính quyền địa phương đảm bảo thắng lợi công cuộc cải cách nền hành chính". [Renewing the local authority organisation to ensure the success of the public administrative reform]. *Tạp chí Quản lý Nhà nước* 9 (1995): 11–14.

Trần Hộ. "Một số vấn đề về phân phối lưu thông" [A few problems on distribution and circulation]. *TCCS* 3 (1984): 27–33.

Trần Hùng and Nguyễn Quốc Thông. *Thăng Long - Hà Nội: Mười thế kỷ đô thị hoá* [Thăng Long – Hà Nội: Ten Centuries of Urbanization]. Hà Nội: NXB Xây dựng, 1995.

Trần Huy Liệu et al., eds. *Lịch sử thủ đô Hà Nội* [History of Hà Nội the Capital]. Hà Nội: NXB Sử Học, 1960.

Trần Lê. "Góp phần thực hiện tốt công tác quản lý kinh tế - xã hội của nhà nước ta" [Contribute towards management of economy and society of our state]. *TCCS* 9 (1986): 14–18.

Trần Nho Thìn, "Đổi mới tổ chức và hoạt động của Ủy ban Nhân dân Xã" [Reform the organisation and operation of the Commune People's Committee]. PTS dissertation submitted to the Viện Nghiên cứu Nhà nước và Pháp luật, Trung tâm Khoa học xã hội và Nhân văn Quốc gia and Bộ Giáo dục và Đào tạo, Hà Nội, 1996.

Trần Quốc Vượng and Nguyễn Vĩnh Long. "Hà Nội From Prehistory to the 19th Century". *Vietnamese Studies* 48 (1977): 9–57.

Trần Thế Nhuận. "Bàn về tập trung, phân quyền, tản quyền trong nền hành chính địa phương" [On centralizing, decentralization, and separation of power in the local administration system]. In *Cải Cách hành chính địa phương: Lý luận và thực tiễn* [Local Administration Reform: Theory and Practice], edited by Tô Tư Hạ, Nguyễn Hữu Trị, Nguyễn Hữu Đức, pp. 51–59. Hà Nội: NXB Chính trị Quốc gia, 1988.

Trần thị Tuyết. "Tác động của chiến tranh đến sự hình thành ý thức và lối sống theo pháp luật" [Impact of war on the shaping of consciousness and way of life that respect the law]. In *Xây dựng ý thức và lối sống theo pháp luật* [Build consciousness and way of life that respects the law], edited by Đào Trí Úc, pp. 132–41. Hà Nội: Đề tài Khoa học xã hội Cấp Nhà nước KX-07-17, 1995.

Trịnh Duy Luân. "Một số đặc điểm kinh tế - xã hội và nhà ở của người nghèo đô thị" [A few socio-economic and housing characteristics of the urban poor]. *Xã hội Học* 4 (48) (1994): 44–67.

Trịnh Duy Luân. "Vietnam". In *The Changing Nature of Local Government*, edited by Patricia L. McCarney, pp. 171–93. Toronto: Centre for Urban and Community Studies, University of Toronto, and International Office, Federation of Canadian Municipalities, 1996.

——— and Nguyễn Quang Vinh. *Tác động kinh tế - xã hội của Đổi mới trong lĩnh vực nhà ở đô thị* [The socioeconomic impact of đổi mới on urban housing]. Hà Nội: NXB Khoa học xã hội, 1998.

Trịnh Khánh Phong. "Nâng cao hiệu lực của chính quyền cấp phường" [Raise the effectiveness of local authorities]. In *Tăng cường hiệu lực nhà nước Xã hội Chủ nghĩa của ta* [Strengthen the Effectiveness of Our Socialist State], edited by Viện Luật Học, Ủy ban Khoa học xã hội Việt Nam, pp. 93–101. Hà Nội: NXB Khoa học xã hội, 1983.

Trịnh Thi. "Building blocks: Where is the Vietnamese identity in the new architecture?". *Heritage*, January/February 1996, p. 27.

Trường Hành chính Trung ương. *Những kiến thức cơ bản về quản lý nhà nước*. Tập đề cương bài giảng bồi dưỡng cho cán bộ chính quyền cơ sở [Basics of State management: Lecture outlines to train basic level political authority cadres]. Hà Nội: Sự Thật, 1989.

Truong Nhu Tang. *A Viet Cong memoir: An inside account of the Vietnam War and its aftermath*. New York: Vintage, 1985.

Turley, William S. "Hanoi's Domestic Dilemmas". *Problems of Communism* 29, no. 4 (1980): 42–61.

———. "Introduction". In *Vietnam Communism in Comparative Perspective*, edited by William S. Turley, pp. 1–10. Boulder, CO: Westview Press, 1980.

———. "Political Participation and the Vietnamese Communist Party". In *Vietnam Communism in Comparative Perspective*, edited by William S. Turley, pp. 171–97. Boulder, CO: Westview Press, 1980.

———. "Party, State, and People: Political Structure and Economic Prospects". In *Reinventing Vietnamese Socialism: Đổi Mới in Comparative Perspective*, edited by William S. Turley and Mark Selden, pp. 257–75. Boulder, CO: Westview Press, 1993.

———. "Political Renovation in Vietnam: Renewal and Adaptation". In *The Challenge of Reform in Indochina*, edited by Borje Ljunggren, pp. 327–47. Massachusetts: Havard Institute for International Development, Harvard University, 1993.

Turner, Bengt, József Hegedüs and Iván Tosics. *The Reform of Housing in Eastern Europe and the Soviet Union*. London and New York: Routledge, 1992.

Tyson, James and Ann Tyson. *Chinese Awakenings: Life Stories from the Unofficial China*. Boulder, CO: Westview Press, 1995.

United Nations Secretariat (Statistics Division) and United Nations Centre for Human Settlements (Habitat). *Compendium of Human Settlements Statistics 1983*, *Compendium of Human Settlements Statistics 1985*, and *Compendium of Human Settlement Statistics 1995*.

Ủy ban Nhân dân tỉnh Nam Định. *Các văn bản về việc Bầu cử Hội đồng Nhân dân và Ủy ban Hành chính các cấp* [Documents on Elections of People's Councils and Administrative Committees of All Levels]. Nam Định: 1961.

Văn Hiền. "Hoàn thiện pháp luật và tăng cường pháp chế Xã hội Chủ nghĩa" [Perfection of laws and strengthening socialist rule of law]. *TCCS* 7 (1982): 30–35.

Văn Tất Thu. "Phương hướng và giải pháp tổ chức, quản lý chính quyền địa phương" (Direction of solutions to problems of organisation and management of local authorities). In *Cải Cách hành chính địa phương: Lý luận và thực tiễn* [Local adminsitration reform: Theory and practice], edited by Tô Tử Hạ, Nguyễn Hữu Tri, and Nguyễn Hữu Đức, pp. 197–202. Hà Nội: NXB Chính trị Quốc gia, 1998.

Vasavakul, Thaveeporn. "Vietnam: The Changing Models of Legitimation". In *Political Legitimacy in Southeast Asia,* edited by Muthiah Alagappa, pp. 257–89. Stanford, CA: Stanford University Press, 1995.

Vasoo, S. *Neighbourhood Leaders' Participation in Community Development.* Singapore: Times Academic Press, 1994.

Viện Kiểm sát Nhân dân tối cao. *Bàn về pháp luật và pháp chế Việt-Nam* [On law and rule of law in Vietnam]. Hà Nội: NXB Sự Thật, 1964.

Viện Qui Hoạch Đô thị Nông thôn. *Cẩm nang dân số đô thị hoá Hà Nội* [Handbook on Urbanization and Population in Hanoi]. Hà Nội, 1992.

Viện Sử Học. *Lịch sử Việt Nam 1954-1965* [History of Vietnam 1954–1965]. Hà Nội: NXB Khoa học xã hội, 1995.

Vo Nhan Tri. *Vietnam's Economic Policy since 1975.* Singapore: Institute of Southeast Asian Studies, 1990.

Võ Văn Kiệt. "Transformation of private industry and trade in the south Vietnam: some practical problems". *Vietnam Social Sciences* 2 (1985): 47–63.

Vũ Đức Khiển. "Nâng cao hiểu biết và ý thức tôn trọng pháp luật của cán bộ, đảng viên" [Raise the understanding and consciousness among cadres and party members in respecting the law]. *TCCS* 1 (1988): 44–47.

Vũ Huy Từ. "Mấy ý kiến về cải cách thể chế của nền hành chính" [A few opinions on reforming administrative institutions]. In *Về nền hành chính nhà nước Việt Nam; Những kinh nghiệm xây dựng và phát triển* [On Vietnam's state administration system: Experiences in building and development], by Học Viện Hành chính Quốc gia, pp. 89–100. Hà Nội: NXB Khoa học và Kỹ thuật, 1996.

Vũ Minh Giang. "Xây dựng lối sống theo pháp luật nhìn từ góc độ lịch sử truyền thống" [Building the rule of law as a way of life from the perspective of history and tradition]. In *Xây dựng ý thức về lối sống theo pháp luật*, edited by Đào Trí Úc, pp. 116–31. Hà Nội: Đề tài Khoa học xã hội Cấp Nhà nước KX-07-17, 1995.

Vũ Quốc Thông. *Pháp chế sử Việt-Nam* [History of the Legal System in Vietnam]. Sài gòn: Tủ sách Đại học, 196?.

Vũ Trọng Phụng. "Household Servants" [Cơm Thầy cơm Cô]. *The Light of the Capital: Three Modern Vietnamese Classics,* translated by Greg and Monique Lockhart. Kuala Lumpur: Oxford University Press, 1996.

de Vylder, Stefan and Adam Fforde. *Vietnam: An Economy in Transition.* Stockholm: Swedish International Development Authority, 1988.

Wen, Simon Chu-Hsung. "A cross-national study on housing development in Asian transitional countries — Hong Kong, Korea (South), Singapore, and Taiwan (The Republic of)". Ph.D. dissertation, University of Michigan, 1988.

White, Stephen. "Economic Performance and Communist Legitimacy". *World Politics* 38, no. 3 (1986): 462–82.

Williams, Arthus Ross. "Center, Bureaucracy, and Locality: Central-Local relations in the Philippines". Ph.D. dissertation, Cornell University, 1981.

Womack, Brantly. "The 1980 county-level elections in China: Experiment in democratic modernization". *Asian Survey* 22, no. 3 (March 1982): 261–77.

————. "The Party and the People: Revolutionary and Postrevolutionary Politics in China and Vietnam". *World Politics* 39, no. 4 (1987): 479–507.

————. "Reform in Vietnam: Backwards Towards the Future". *Government and Opposition* 27, no. 2 (1992): 177–89.

Xây dựng. "Giám đốc Sở nhà đất Hà Nội trả lời phỏng vấn về công tác bán nhà theo Nghị Định 61/CP" [Director of the Hanoi Housing Authority interviewed regarding work on selling houses under Decision 61/CP], pp. 4, 13. September 1997.

————. "Chương trình phát triển nhà ở của Hà Nội đến năm 2000 và 2010" [Programme to develop housing in Hà Nội from now until 2000 and 2010], p. 9. November 1997.

Xie, Weizhi. "The Semihierarchical Totalitarian Nature of Chinese Politics". In *Comparative Politics* 25 (1993): 313–30.

Zaniewski, Kazimierz Jose. "Housing inequalities under socialism: the case of Poland". Ph.D. dissertation, University of Wisconsin, 1987.

Zaslavsky, Victor and Robert Brym. "The Functions of Elections in the USSR". *Soviet Studies* 30, no. 3 (1978): 362–71.

Zaslavsky, Victor and Robert J. Brym. "The Structure of Power and the Functions of Soviet Local Elections". In *Soviet Local Politics and Government*, edited by Everett M. Jacobs, pp. 69–77. London: George Allen and Unwin, 1983.

Zhao, Suisheng. "China's Central-Local Relationship: A Historical Perspective". In *Changing Central-Local Relations in China*, edited by Jia Hao and Lin Zhimin, pp. 19–34. Boulder, CO: Westview Press, 1994.

NEWSPAPER ARTICLES

Agence France Presse. "Communists retain firm grip on power". *South China Morning Post*, 28 July 1997.

———. "Vietnam warns against abuse of democracy in one-party polls", 1 February 2002.

———, "Communist Vietnam launches voters' website for one-party poll", 2 April 2002.

An Ninh Thủ Đô "Nhà ở vẫn là vấn đề gay cấn" [Accommodation still a thorny problem], 23 December 1996, p. 1.

Ánh Ngọc. "An Dương xây dựng nếp sống văn minh, gia đình văn hóa mới" [An Duong Ward builds the civilized way of life and new culture families]. *HNM*, 23 February 1979, p. 2.

———. "Những yêu cầu chính đáng cần được giải quyết gấp ở một khu nhà tập thể" [Legitimate demands which need urgent solutions at a collective housing area]. *HNM*, 7 April 1981, p. 2.

———. "Phường Cát Linh chăm lo đời sống" [Cat Linh Ward worries for livelihood of people]. *HNM*, 6 January 1982, p. 2.

Ánh Sáng. "Nhà máy chế tạo công cụ số 1 xây dựng khu tập thể văn minh" [The Number 1 Tools Manufacturing Factory Implements a Cultured Collective Flat Area]. *HNM*, 18 January 1978, p. 2.

AP. "Vietnam State Bank Seen Issuing De-Dollarization Laws Soon", 21 December 1998.

B. H. "Chùa Tràng Tín còn bị lấn chiếm đến bao giờ?" [When will encroachment of Tràng Tín Temple stop?]. *Đại Đoàn Kết*, 5 May 1997, p. 4.

B. V. "Cuộc thảo luận về cấp phường chưa thể kết thúc được" [Discussions on the ward level are still inconclusive]. *HNM*, 23 September 1988, p. 2.

Bích Hậu and Bích Hương. "Long đong ... hàng rong" [Hard times fall on *hàng rong*]. *Lao Động Hà Nội*, 17 January 1997, pp. 1, 10.

Bình Lưu. "Chuyện trật tự giao thông ghi ở cuộc họp" [A traffic affair at a meeting]. *HNM*, 6 November 1988, pp. 2, 4.

Bùi Bá Mạnh. "Đội tự quản giao thông nhân dân" [The traffic self-management teams of the people]. *HNM*, 17 April 1991, p. 2.

Bùi Công Lý. "Trật tự trong một số nhà" [Social order in a few houses]. *HNM*, 8 July 1987, p. 2.

———. "Thấy gì qua việc thi hành một vụ án" [Lessons from the execution of a court decision]. *HNM*, 30 September 1987, p. 4.

———. "Lý và tình từ bức tường ngăn" [Reason and compassion surrounding a wall]. *HNM*, 26 February 1988, p. 2.

Bùi Đình Nguyên. "Xung quanh việc hoá giá nhà ở". *Đại Đoàn Kết*, 3 December 1991, p. 7.

―――. "Có gì khác trong Luật bầu cử vừa được Quốc hội thông qua" [What's new in the election law just passed by the National Assembly]. *Lao Động Hà Nội,* 9 May 1997, pp. 1, 10.

Bùi Hiền. "Xử phạt hành chính như vậy đã đúng chưa?" [Is the issuing of administrative fine correct in this case?]. *Nhân Dân,* 4 December 1996, p. 3.

Bùi Mạnh Trung. "Chung quanh vấn đề sửa chữa nhà cửa" [Around the problem of housing repair]. *HNM,* 28 November 1979, p. 2.

Bùi Văn Sương. "Hà Nội có những chuyển biến tốt" [Hà Nội sees positive changes]. *HNM,* 5 June 1996, p. 3.

Cát Bình. "Vì sao việc giải phóng mặt bằng đường 18A chậm?" [Why is land requisition for road 18A slow?]. *Đại Đoàn Kết,* 1 June 1998, p. 6

Châu An Ninh. "Xóm liều - họ từ đâu đến?" [Risky neighbourhoods: where do the people come from?]. *Tuổi trẻ Thủ đô,* 14 May 1997, pp. 3, 7.

Chí Thành. "Tự do, dân chủ và pháp luật, kỷ cương" [Freedom, democracy, and law, discipline]. *HNM,* 25 October 1988.

―――. "Thấy gì qua ba vụ cưỡng chế phá bỏ các công trình xây dựng trái phép mới đây tại quận Hoàn Kiếm" [What can we learn from 3 recent cases of forced demolition of illegal construction in Hoàn Kiếm District?]. *HNM,* 3 June 1991, p. 2.

Chu Quang Hiếu. "Sai phạm đã rõ, sao để kéo dài?" [It is clearly wrong but why is it being perpetuated?]. *Lao Động,* 17 December 1996, p. 6.

D. L. T. "Người ứng cử đại biểu HĐND các cấp phải kê khai 5 loại tài sản". *Lao Động,* 19 March 2004, No. 79, http://www.laodong.com.vn/pls/bld/folder$.view_item_detail[95819].

Đại Đoàn Kết. "Vài nét về Khu phố Cửa Nam – Hà Nội" [A few characteristics of the Cửa Nam area], 10 December 1977, pp. 6, 7.

―――. "Một mất một còn?" [Win some, lose some?], 14 June 1998, p. 3.

Đại Đoàn Kết Cuối Tuần. "Chuẩn mực nếp sống Việt Nam: Đang & sẽ ..." [The good life benchmarks: Present and future]. *Xuân Đinh Sửu '97* issue, p. 12.

Đàm Minh Thụy. "Dân chủ là thực hiện việc trao toàn bộ quyền lực tối cao vào tay những đại biểu xứng đáng của nhân dân". *Lao Động,* 23 July 1992, pp. 1, 2.

Đào Quang Cát. "Về danh sách ứng cử viên" [About the list of candidates]. *HNM,* 3 November 1989, p. 2.

DCĐ. "Nội dung phân cấp cho UBND Quận, UBND Phường" [The contents of work delegated to people's committees of districts and wards]. *HNM,* 12 May 1982, p. 2.

Deutsche Presse Agentur. "Superstitious books seized and burned in Vietnam", 22 February 1999. Via Southeast Asia Discussion List, 24 February 1999.

Đinh Hương Sơn. "Lý và tình trong việc chấp hành pháp luật, bảo vệ trật tự và kỷ cương xã hội" [Reason and sentiments in carrying out the law, in protecting social order and discipline]. *HNM,* 12 February 1990, p. 2

Đinh Phố Giang. "Phường phải là đơn vị hành chính" [The ward has to be an administrative unit]. *HNM,* 22 January 1992, pp. 1, 4.

Đỗ Lê Tảo. "Đưa thị trường nhà đất vào khuôn phép". *Lao Động Điện Tử,* 29 November 2002, http://www.laodong.com.vn/pls/bld/folder$.view_item_ detail[51883].

———. "Ba tiêu chí trong hiệp thương". *Lao Động Điện Tử,* 16 February 2004, No. 47, http://www.laodong.com.vn/pls/bld/folder$.view_item_detail[92794].

Đỗ Ngọc Dương. "Cần có những biện pháp cụ thể và phù hợp thực tế để bảo đảm thực hiện nghị định 36/CP" [Need for specific measures closer to reality to ensure that 36/CP is implemented]. *HNM,* 30 October 1995, p. 2.

Đỗ Sơn. "Phường điểm về trật tự vệ sinh công cộng" [Model ward in public order and hygiene]. *An Ninh Thủ Đô,* 28 December 1986, p. 6.

Đoàn Lan. "Hà Nội: Công trình xây dựng được cấp phép chỉ đạt 40%" [Only 40% of building projects are licensed]. *VN Express,* 27 March 2004, http:// vnexpress.net/Vietnam/Xa-hoi/2004/03/3B9D10A4/.

Đông Phương. "Tổ trưởng dân phố - một trách nhiệm không nhỏ" [The head of the housing group — not an unimportant position]. *HNM,* 26 February 1997, p. 2.

Dương Bích Thủy. "Văn hoá thiếu ... văn hoá" [Cultural agencies lack ... culture]. *Tuổi trẻ Thủ Đô,* 26 March 1997, p. 4.

Dương Đức Quang. "Tản mạn về báo chí chống tiêu cực" [Rambling thoughts about newspapers against negativism]. *HNM, Tết Đinh Sửu,* 7 February 1997, p. 18.

Edwards, Adrian. "Vietnam reports high turnout in assembly elections". Reuters, 20 July 1997.

———. "Hanoi ablazed with red on eve of elections". Reuters, 21 July 1997.

———. "Former S. Vietnam Soldier elected to Assembly". Reuters, 28 July 1997.

———. "New Unrest In Vietnam, Southern Catholics Involved". Reuters, 10 November 1997.

H. K. "Quy định mới về cấp phép xây dựng ở Hà Nội" [New regulations on issuing of construction licences in Hà Nội]. *An Ninh Thủ Đô,* 3 January 1997, pp. 1, 10.

———. "Có hay không việc làm vi phạm pháp luật của ông chủ tịch UBND phường Thanh Xuân Bắc?" [Look at the illegal deeds of the Thanh Xuân Bắc Ward People's Committee Chairman!]. *Tuổi trẻ Thủ đô,* 11 June 1997, p. 3.

Hà Văn Vần. "Vất vả mà vẫn không được việc" [Tiring and yet nothing achieved]. *Nhân Dân,* 16 January 1976, p. 2.

Hải Yến. "Ngõ hay chợ?" [A lane of a market?]. *An Ninh Thủ Đô*, 8 April 1997, p. 5.

Hàm Châu. "Hà Nội mùa thu xây dựng". *Đại Đoàn Kết*, 2 September 1978, pp. 16, 17, 33.

Hiebert, Murray. "Letting off steam". *Far Eastern Economic Review*, 30 July 1992, p. 10.

Hiền Lương. "Nhằm trúng đối tượng đấu tranh" [In order to fight the right targets]. *HNM*, 12 August 1983, p. 2.

———. "Cuộc đấu tranh tiếp tục" [The struggle continues]. *HNM*, 14 August 1983, p. 2.

HNM. "Poem on the election", 7 April 1975, p. 2.

———. "Nominees for election to the People's Council of the City of Hà Nội", 24 April 1977, pp. 1, 3.

———. "Hội đồng Bầu cử Hội đồng Nhân dân thành phố công bố kết quả cuộc bầu cử ngày 15-5" [Election Council of the Hà Nội People's Council announced 15-5 election results], 19 May 1977, p. 1.

———. "Thành phố đẩy mạnh cuộc vận động nếp sống văn minh, gia đình văn hóa mới" [The City pushes strongly the Cultured Way of Life and New Culture Family movement], 13 August 1977, p. 1

———. "Về vấn đề phân phối nhà ở hiện nay" [On distribution of accommodation at present]. (Interview with Vũ Quốc Huy, Director of Public Works, Hà Nội), 27 November 1977, pp. 3, 4.

———. "Cửa Nam, Bạch Mai, Thụy Khuê, Kim Liên sẽ là những tiểu khu đầu tiên thành lập Ủy ban nhân dân tiểu khu, làm chức năng một cấp chính quyền cơ sở" [Cửa Nam, Bạch Mai, Thụy Khuê, Kim Liên will be the first Small Districts to have UBND as their local authority], 19 May 1978, p. 1.

———. "Hội nghị tổng kết phong trào nếp sống văn minh, gia đình văn hóa mới năm 1978 của Hà Nội" [Conference summed up movement on Culture Way of Life, New Culture Family of Hà Nội in 1978], 19 January 1979, pp. 1, 4.

———. "Tổ chức chính quyền mấy cấp trong nội thành?" [How many levels of local authority should we have in the inner city?], 3 October 1979, p. 2.

———. "Qua kiểm tra cung cấp lương thực ở khu phố Hai Bà Trưng" [Inspection of food supply in the Hai Bà Trưng District], 3 November 1979, p. 3.

———. "'Bung' sản xuất chứ không 'bung' buôn bán" ["Bursting" of production, not of trade], 16 January 1980, pp. 1, 4.

———. "Tiểu khu Cống Vị xử lý một số nhà xây dựng trái phép" [Cống Vị Small Area dealt with a number of houses built illegally], 22 October 1980, p. 2.

———. "Tổng kết hai năm hoạt động của chính quyền tiểu khu" [Review the activities of the Small District authority in the past 2 years], 17 December 1980, p. 1.

———. "Quyết định của Hội đồng Chính phủ về việc thống nhất tên gọi các đơn vị hành chính ở nội thành, nội thị" [Decision of the State Council on standardization of names of administrative units in cities], 6 January 1981, p. 1.

HNM. "Hội đồng bầu cử HĐND Thành phố công bố danh sách 190 người ứng cử HĐND Thành phố khóa VIII" [Election Council of Hà Nội People's Council announced list of 190 candidates for 8th City People's Council elections], 7 April 1981, p. 1.

———. "Danh sách những người ứng cử đại biểu HĐND thành phố khóa VIII" [Name list of candidates for election of the Eighth City People's Council], 8 April 1981, pp. 1, 4; 9 April 1981, pp. 1, 4; and 30 April 1981, pp. 1, 4.

———. "Thủ đô Hà Nội tổng kết công tác nếp sống mới, gia đình văn hóa mới năm 1980 và nhiệm vụ năm 1981" [Hà Nội the Capital summed up work on New Way of Life, New Culture Family in 1980 and tasks for 1981], 14 April 1981, pp. 1, 4.

———. "Về giao thông đường bộ" [On road traffic], 22 April 1981, p. 2,

———. "Các cấp chính quyền tập trung chỉ đạo để tổ chức tốt ngày bầu cử" [All levels of political authority focus on directing to organize well polling day], 23 April 1981, pp. 1, 4.

———. "Danh sách các vị trúng cử đại biểu HĐND thành phố khóa VIII" [Names of candidates elected into the 8th City People's Council], 30 April 1981, pp. 1, 4.

———. "Báo cáo của UBND trình HĐND thành phố khóa VIII về việc phân cấp quản lý cho chính quyền quận, phường" [Report of the People's Committee to the 8th City People's Council on decentralization of management to political authorities of the District and Ward levels], 17 June 1981, pp. 1, 2.

———. "Quận Hai Bà Trưng thu hồi 81.874 kg lương thực cấp sai tiêu chuẩn" [Hai Bà Trưng District takes back 61,674 kg of food given out to undeserving recipients], 8 July 1981, pp. 1, 4.

———. "Toàn thành phố có 154 đơn vị bầu cử cấp quận, huyện và được bầu 1.028 đại biểu HĐND quận, huyện, thị xã" [Hà Nội has 154 electoral units and will elect 1,026 for people's councils of district, prefecture and town level], 22 August 1981, p. 1.

———. "Phường Quán Thánh chuẩn bị bầu cử Hội đồng nhân dân" [Quán Thánh Ward prepares for people's council election], 3 September 1981, p. 2.

———. "Quận Hai Bà Trưng tổng kết kinh nghiệm hoạt động của UBND phường" [Hai Bà Trưng District reviews experiences of activities of its wards' people's councils], 25 September 1981, pp. 1, 4.

———. "Hàng vạn cán bộ làm công tác bầu cử được bồi dưỡng nghiệp vụ" [Tens of thousands of election cadres receive training for their tasks], 30 September 1981, pp. 1, 4.

———. "Quận Ba Đình đưa đoàn viên, thanh niên về 14 phường tham gia phục vụ bầu cử" [Ba Đình District sends youths and members of the HCM Youth League to 14 wards to help in electoral work], 2 October 1981, pp. 1, 4.

———. "Phường Hàng Trống chuẩn bị bầu cử" [Hàng Trống Ward prepares for election], 4 October 1981, p. 1.

———. "Trên 1 triệu rưỡi cử tri của thủ đô đi bỏ phiếu bầu đại biểu HĐND các cấp" [More than 1.5 million voters of the capital vote for people's council representatives of all levels], 4 October 1981, p. 1.

———. "Cử tri thủ đô hăng hái đi bỏ phiếu bầu đại biểu HĐND quận, huyện, thị xã, thị trấn và phường, xã" [Voters of the capital enthusiastically votes in representatives for people's councils of urban and rural districts, commune towns and towns, and wards and communes], 5 October 1981, pp. 1, 4.

———. "Chủ tịch Hội đồng Bộ trưởng Phạm Văn Đồng và các đại biểu Quốc hội Hà Nội gặp mặt cử tri" [Council of Ministers Chairman Phạm Văn Đồng and National Assembly deputies of Hà Nội meet voters], 5 January 1982, pp. 1, 4.

———. "Về quản lý xây dựng nhà cửa ở thành phố" [On management of housing construction in the City], 16 April 1982, p. 2.

———. "Rút kinh nghiệm về xử lý những trường hợp xây dựng trái phép" [Drawing lessons from dealing with cases of illegal construction], 25 May 1982, p. 3.

———. "Những điều cần biết để giữ gìn trật tự, vệ sinh công cộng" [What you should know in order to maintain public order and cleanliness], 28 January 1983, p. 2

———. "Hôm qua, 24-5: tiếp tục kiểm tra xử lý những người có nguồn tài sản bất minh mua nhà và xây nhà có giá trị lớn" [Yesterday 24–5: continued to deal with people who have unclear sources of wealth and who purchase or built houses of huge value], 25 May 1983, p. 1.

———. "UBND Thành phố ra quyết định xử lý những người có nguồn tài sản bất minh mua nhà và xây nhà có giá trị lớn" [City People's Committee deals with people who have unclear sources of wealth and purchase or build houses of huge value], 25 May 1983, p. 1.

———. "Mặt trận Tổ quốc các quận Hai Bà Trưng và Hoàn Kiếm hiệp thương về số đại biểu của các ngành, các đoàn thể tham gia HĐND quận khóa mới" [VFF of Hai Bà Trưng and Hoàn Kiếm Districts consult on the number of representatives allocated to all sectors and collectives participating in the next District People's Council], 14 March 1984, pp. 1, 4.

———. "Cử tri toàn thành phố hăng hái đi bỏ phiếu bầu cử HĐND hai cấp" [Voters of the whole city enthusiastically votes in elections for two levels of people's councils], 7 May 1984, pp. 1, 4.

———. "Quy tắc trật tự an toàn giao thông trong thành phố" [Regulations on traffic order and safety in the city], 15 May 1984, pp. 1, 3.

———. "Nhìn lại cuộc bầu cử đại biểu HĐND hai cấp" [Review of people's council elections of two levels], 25 July 1984, p. 2.

————. "Từng bước hoàn thiện cơ chế tổ chức ở cấp phường như thế nào?" [How to perfect the organization and system at the ward level step-by-step?], 29 August 1984, p. 2.

————. "Kết quả cuộc bầu cử đại biểu Hội đồng nhân dân thành phố khóa IX" [Results of Ninth City People's Council elections], 27 April 1985, pp. 1, 4.

————. "Quận ủy Hoàn Kiếm kiểm điểm 4 năm xây dựng cấp phường" [Hoàn Kiếm District Party Branch reviews 4 years of building up of the ward level], 4 June 1985, pp. 1, 4.

————. "Xử phạt những trường hợp vi phạm quy tắc vệ sinh, trật tự công cộng, trật tự an toàn giao thông của thành phố" [Penalties for offences against Regulations on public cleanliness and order, traffic order and safety of the City], 18 June 1985, pp. 1, 4.

————. "Quận ủy Hai Bà Trưng kiểm điểm bốn năm xây dựng cấp phường" [Hai Bà Trưng District Party Branch reviews 4 years of building up of the ward level], 23 June 1985, pp. 1, 4.

————. "Tạo điều kiện cho phường chuyển mạnh vào quản lý kinh tế, có kế hoạch, có ngân sách" [Make conditions possible for the wards to push strongly for planned and budgeted economic management], 26 June 1985, p. 2.

————. "Quận Đống Đa xử lý ngay những nhà làm trái phép của cán bộ thuộc quận trực tiếp quản lý" [Đống Đa District dealt with immediately cases of illegal housing construction by its own cadres], 30 May 1986, p. 1.

————. "Sơ kết đợt 1 tự phê bình và phê bình" [Preliminary conclusion of Stage One of Self-Criticisms and Criticisms], 25 July 1986, pp. 1, 4.

————. "Quy định của Hội đồng Nhà nước về cuộc bầu cử đại biểu Quốc hội khóa VIII," [State Council regulations on election of Eighth National Assembly Deputies], 17 February 1987, pp. 1, 4.

————. "Tâm sự cử tri" [Voters confide], 20 March 1987, p. 2.

————. "Họp cử tri ở một phường" [A ward voters' meeting], 14 April 1987, p. 1.

————. "Tranh chấp nhà cửa và hướng giải quyết" [Housing disputes and directions for resolution], 26 August 1987, pp. 3, 4.

————. "Chủ tịch UBND thành phố ra những quy định cụ thể nhằm bảo đảm thực hiện nhiệm vụ, quyền hạn của HĐND các cấp" [Chairman of City People's Committee promulgates specific regulations to ensure people's councils of all levels fulfil their obligations according to their powers], 19 May 1988, pp. 1, 4.

————. "Tai nạn giao thông chưa giảm" [Traffic accidents have not decreased], 9 August 1988, p. 1.

————. "Hội nghị bàn về công tác cấp phường" [Conference discussed work of the ward level], 1 September 1988, pp. 1, 4.

————. "Chủ tịch phường và những điều lo âu" [The ward Chairman and his worries], 16 November 1988, p. 2.

HNM. "Về việc mua bán nhà tư nhân" [On private transactions on houses], 24 March 1989, p. 1.

———. "Cuộc bầu cử có bảo đảm dân chủ hay không, quyết định ở bước hiệp thương, do MTTQ đóng vai trò chính" [Whether the elections are democratic is decided at the consultations stage led by the VFF] (Interview with Bùi Mạnh Trung, Vice-chairman, MTTQ Committee of the City of Hà Nội), 8 September 1989, p. 2.

———. "Về việc kiểm tra, xử lý xây dựng trái phép" [On inspection and dealing with illegal construction], 9 November 1989, pp. 1, 4.

———. "Công bố kết quả bầu cử và danh sách trúng cử đại biểu HĐND thành phố khóa X" [Official results of elections and list of elected representatives of the Tenth City People's Council], 24 November 1989, pp. 1, 4.

———. "Nhất bên trọng, nhất bên khinh" [Lop-sided], 25 December 1989, p. 2.

———. "Hội nghị toàn quốc về HĐND kết thúc tốt đẹp" [National Conference on People's Councils successful], 13 April 1990, p. 1.

———. "Về quản lý đường, hè phố" [On management of roads, pavements], 2 July 1990, p. 3

———. "Hội nghị về công tác xây dựng cấp phường" [Conference on building up the ward], 9 July 1990, p. 1.

———. "Hội nghị Toàn quốc về HĐND lần thứ III" [Third National Conference on the HĐND], 19 March 1991, p. 1.

———. "Tăng cường quản lý hè, đường phố ở thủ đô" [Strengthen management of pavements and streets of the capital], 23 December 1991, pp. 1, 3.

———. "Kết quả bầu cử đại biểu Quốc hội khóa IX tại thủ đô Hà Nội" [Election results for Ninth National Assembly in Hà Nội], 22 July 1992, p. 1.

———. "'Gia đình tôi không sai" [My family is not in the wrong], 9 September 1994, p. 3.

———. "Toàn thành phố có 99.55% cử tri đi bỏ phiếu" [99.55% of all voters in the whole city went to polls], 24 November 1994, p. 1.

———. "Thủ tướng Chính phủ họp với các ngành, đoàn thể bàn biện pháp triển khai Nghị Định 36/CP và Chỉ Thị 317/TTg về bảo đảm trật tự an toàn giao thông đường bộ và trật tự an toàn giao thông đô thị" [PM discussed with branches and organizations on measures to implement 36/CP and Directive 317/TTg on traffic order and safety on the roads and in the cities], 16 June 1995, pp. 1, 4.

———. "Thành phố cho dùng hè ở 57 tuyến phố để sắp xếp các hộ kinh doanh" [City allows traders to use pavements on 57 roads], 26 October 1995, pp. 1, 4.

———. "Trong cuộc bầu cử ngày 20 tháng 7 năm 1997 tại 175 đơn vị bầu cử" [The election of 20 July 1997 at 175 electoral units], 21 July 1997.

Hồ Hữu Xuân. "Hết hạn chưa?" [Is it expired?]. *Nhân Dân*, 16 January 1975, p. 2.

Hoàng Quí Thân. "Suy nghĩ nhân một vấn đề thời sự ở Kim Liên" [Some thoughts provoked by a current affair in Kim Liên]. *HNM*, 12 March 1989, p. 1.

Hồng Vy. "Tai nạn giao thông đường bộ chưa giảm" [Road traffic accidents have not decreased]. *HNM*, 19 February 1997, p. 2.

Hương Thủy. "Các đại lý xổ số sẽ bán vé ở đâu?" [Where would the agents of lottery sell their tickets?]. *HNM*, 10 July 1995, p. 3.

Hữu Mão. "Chọn người ra ứng cử ở một tổ dân phố" [Selection of election candidates in a resident group]. *HNM*, 22 March 1987, pp. 1, 4.

Huy Giang. "Chỉ có 6 đại biểu trẻ dưới 35 tuổi, 20 đại biểu nữ". *Tuoi Tre,* 28 April 2004 pp. 1, 3.

Huy Lân. "Nếp sống mới ở khu tập thể nhà A10" [New way of life at Block A10 of a collective flat area]. *HNM*, 11 January 1978, p. 2.

Huyền Trang. "Những điều bất thường ở Học viện Hành chính Quốc gia" [Unusual matters at the National Institute of Administration]. *Đại Đoàn Kết*, 1 May 1997, pp. 1, 6.

K. D. "Tích cực chuẩn bị cho ngày đầu thực hiện Nghị Định 36/CP của Chính phủ" [Enthusiastic preparations for the first day of implementation of 36/CP]. *HNM*, 29 July 1995, pp. 1, 4.

K. O. "Xây dựng nhà ở theo phương châm 'Nhà nước và nhân dân cùng làm'" [Construct houses under the policy of "state and people working together"]. *HNM*, 8 March 1985, p. 3.

———. "Giải quyết khiếu kiện về nhà đất ở quận Hoàn Kiếm" [Resolve complaints and disputes regarding land and houses in the Hoàn Kiếm District]. *HNM,* 29 May 1992, p. 3.

———. "Kết quả và những tồn tại cần giải quyết" [Results so far and remaining problems that need to be solved]. *HNM*, 24 February 1995, p. 3.

Kim Dung. "Qua một số chốt trật tự giao thông thuộc quận Hai Bà Trưng" [At a few traffic order hotspots in Hai Bà Trưng District]. *HNM*, 30 October 1988, p. 1.

———. "'57' làm được, phải giữ được" [Achievements of 57 must be maintained!]. *HNM*, 9 March 1992, p. 2

———. "Từ bảo vệ hành lang thoát lũ nghĩ đến giữ gìn trật tự đô thị" [Thinking about maintenance of urban social order from observing the protection of storm water drainage system]. *HNM*, 8 July 1994, p. 2.

———. "'Nhóm liên gia tự quản ở cụm dân cư số 2 phường Ngô Thì Nhậm" ["Self-managed family groups" in Cum no. 2 of Ngô Thì Nhậm Ward]. *HNM,* 22 September 1995, p. 2.

———. "Để nâng cao hiệu quả hoạt động của chính quyền phường, xã" [In order to raise the impact of the activities of the ward and commune authorities]. *HNM,* 20 June 1996, p. 2.

Kim Liên. "Tuyên truyền nhiều nhưng trật tự an toàn giao thông vẫn kém" [Much mass education but traffic order and safety still far from ideal]. *HNM*, 11 May 1994, p. 2.

L. H. "ĐBSCL: Dự kiến 50% chủ tịch HĐND, UBND các cấp tái cử" [Mekong Delta: 50% of People's Council and Committee Chairmen of all levels re-elected]. *Lao Động*, 24 February 2004, No. 55, http://www.laodong.com. vn/pls/bld/folder$.view_item_detail[93584].

Lan Thanh. "Nghèo vì giỗ, khổ vì đám" [Poverty by death anniversaries, misery by feasts]. *Phụ nữ Chủ nhật* 21, 7 June 1998, pp. 5, 9.

Lao Động. "Mấy ý kiến của bộ trưởng Phan Ngọc Tương về vấn đề xây dựng nhà ở" [A few opinion of Minister Phan Ngọc Tương regarding housing construction], 23 February 1984, p. 4.

———. "Hà Nội, TP Hồ Chí Minh, Khánh Hoà và nhiều tỉnh, thành phố đạt tỷ lệ bầu cử cao" [Hà Nội, TP Hồ Chí Minh, Khánh Hoà and many provinces achieved high voter turnout], 23 July 1992, p. 1.

———. "Cử tri Hà Nội,", 23 July 1992, pp. 1, 2.

———. "Vì sao không đền bù thoả đáng cho dân?" [Why are people not compensated appropriately?], 9 January 1997, p. 6

———. "Tổ chức lai bộ máy chính quyền đô thị", 7 April 2001, p. 3.

Lao Động Điện Tử. "Dự thảo cấm xe máy, ôtô – liệu có khả thi?" [Plan to ban motorcycles and motorcars – is it feasible?]. 1 November 2002. http://www. laodong.com.vn/pls/bld/folder$.view_item_detail[49325].

———. "17.3, hạn cuối loại đối tượng tham những hối lộ … khỏi danh sách ứng cử". 2 March 2004, No. 62, http://www.laodong.com.vn/pls/bld/folder$. view_item_detail[94244].

Lê Thanh Nghị. "Phát huy mạnh hơn nữa hiệu lực của HĐND các cấp ở thủ đô Hà Nội" [Bring into stronger play the effectiveness of people's councils at all levels of Hà Nội the capital]. *HNM*, 24 December 1985, pp. 1, 4.

Linh Anh and Huy Thục. "Nhà ở đô thị - thực trạng và kiến nghị" [Urban accommodation: Reality and suggestions]. *Nhân Dân,* 19 January 1997, p. 2.

Linh Lanh. "Chuyện 'vỉa hè Hà Nội" [The Pavement in Hà Nội]. *Đại Đoàn Kết,* 4 December 1985.

Lưu Băng. "Năm 1977, vấn đề xây dựng nhà ở có gì mới?" [In 1977, what's new in housing construction?]. *HNM,* 28 January 1977, p. 3.

Lưu Phương. "Việc làm được ở khu tập thể Nguyễn Công Trứ" [Accomplishments at the Nguyễn Công Trứ collective flat area]. *HNM,* 1 October 1975, p. 2.

Lưu Thị Thái Hà. "Cấp phường với công tác quản lý nhà" [Wards and their management of housing matters]. *HNM,* 7 October 1988, p. 2.

Lương Xuân Nội. "Xây dựng và quản lý nhà ở trong các đô thị" [Build and manage houses in the urban areas]. *Đại Đoàn Kết,*16 January 1997, pp. 1, 7.

Lý Hải. "Sửa chữa khuyết điểm" [Correct the shortcomings]. *HNM,* 23 July 1986, p. 2.

Lý Ngân. "Một bản án còn nhiều câu hỏi?" [A case that still has many unanswered questions]. *Đại Đoàn Kết,* 13 March 1997, p. 6.

Lý Phương Hiên. "Đội tự quản giao thông - trật tự phường Cát Linh" [The Traffic and Order self-management team of the Cát Linh Ward]. *HNM,* 8 January 1992, p. 2.

Lý Quốc Khánh. "Chính quyền xã Tấn Phú cường quyền với dân, vì sao?" [Why did the local authority of Tấn Phú Commune compel people?]. *Đại Đoàn Kết,* 13 January 1997, p. 6

Lý Sinh Sự. "Đâu lại đóng đấy" [Back to square one]. *Lao Động,* 23 February 1997, p. 1.

Lý Thanh Hằng. "Đừng để người dân quá thiệt thòi" [Do not let the people suffer too much]. *Lao Động,* 17 April 1997, p. 6.

Lý Tiến Dũng. "Hãy nhìn vào tận gốc vụ án Tamexco" [Looking at the root of the Tamexco affair]. *Đại Đoàn Kết Cuối Tuần,* 15 February 1997, pp. 1, 3.

———. "Cần chấm dứt những 'ơn nghĩa' trong hoạt động kinh doanh" [Need to stop "favours" in business activities]. *Đại Đoàn Kết Cuối Tuần,* 1 March 1997, p. 3.

———. "Trước giờ xét xử phúc thẩm vụ án Tamexco: Một mảng 'phần chìm' của tảng băng" [Before the hearing of the appeal of Tamexco: What is underneath the tip of the iceberg?]. *Đại Đoàn Kết Cuối Tuần,* 22 March 1997, pp. 1, 3.

———. "Pháp lệnh chống tham nhũng trình Quốc hội: Gia đình quan chức sẽ bị cấm kinh doanh?" [The Decree against Corruption before National Parliament: Families of officials will be barred from businesses?]. *Đại Đoàn Kết Cuối Tuần,* 19 April 1997, p. 3.

Lý Trần Hưng. "Một số điểm mới trong dự án sửa đổi, bổ sung Luật bầu cử đại biểu HĐND" [A few new points in the revision and amendments done to the Law on Elections of People's Councils]. *HNM,* 17 May 1989, p. 2.

M. H. "Phường Đồng Nhân đẩy mạnh giữ gìn trật tự hè đường" [Đồng Nhân Ward pushes strongly for order on sidewalks and roads]. *HNM,* 2 June 1995, p. 1.

Mai Hoa. "Hàng rong: chuyện nhỏ mà không nhỏ" [Hawkers: apparently small but actually big matter]. *An Ninh Thủ Đô,* 13 December 1996, p. 3.

Mạnh Hồng. "Có hay không việc làm vi phạm pháp luật của ông chủ tịch UBND phường Thanh Xuân Bắc" [Look at the illegal deeds of the Thanh Xuân Bắc Ward People's Committee Chairman!]. *Tuổi trẻ Thủ đô,* 14 May 1997, p. 3.

Mạnh Hùng. "Liên kết thực hiện Nghị Định 36/CP" [Joint implementation of 36/CP]. *HNM,* 28 July 1995, p. 1.

Minh Đức. "Trật tự an toàn giao thông" [Traffic order and safety]. *Nhân Dân*, 13 January 1997, p. 2.

Minh Hoàng, "Phường Cầu Dền bước đầu làm kinh tế" [Cầu Dền Ward takes first step into business]. *HNM*, 21 December 1982, p. 3; 22 December 1982, p. 3.

―――. "Ở phường Cầu Dền" [At the Cầu Dền Ward]. *HNM*, 28 December 1982, p. 3; 29 December 1982, p. 3.

Minh Ngọc. "Điều mong muốn chính đáng" [A legitimate wish]. *HNM*, 3 November 1989, p. 2.

Minh Quang. "Từ hòa giải ... đến việc xử lý nghiêm minh" [From reconciliation to dealing with matters justly and strictly]. *HNM*, 16 March 1991, p. 2.

――― and Phạm Hiếu. "Chuyện trang: xíchlô Hà Nội" [Special Report: the xichlo in Hà Nội]. *Lao Động*, 15 April 1997, p. 6.

Minh Tuấn. "Mong muốn năm 1997: Cuộc cải cách hành chính sẽ mạnh mẽ và hiệu quả hơn" [Wish for 1997: stronger and more effective administrative reforms]. *Đại Đoàn Kết*, 2 January 1997, pp. 1, 7.

―――. "Cải tiến thủ tục cấp giấy phép xây dựng - nhu cầu cấp bách" [Reform procedures to issue construction licences: an urgent need]. *Đại Đoàn Kết*, 17 February 1997, pp. 1, 7.

―――. "Mục tiêu chủ yếu của Nghị Định 36/CP vẫn chưa thực hiện được" [The main objective of 36/CP has not been achieved]. *Lao Động*, 4 March 1997, p. 3.

―――. "Tai nạn giao thông tăng không ngừng - vì sao?" [Why do traffic accidents keep increasing?]. *Đại Đoàn Kết*, 13 April 1998, pp. 1, 7.

―――. "Xây nhà không phép, lỗi của dân hay của chính quyền?". *Đại Đoàn Kết*, 6 May 2000, pp. 1, 7.

――― and Hương Thủy. "Hà Nội thí điểm cấp giấy chủ quyền nhà và đất" [Hà Nội pilots the issuing of ownership certificates for houses and land]. *Đại Đoàn Kết*, 20 January 1997, pp. 1, 7.

N. T. "Cần xem lại tội danh và điều luật áp dụng đối với Phó Chánh án Tòa dân TANDTC Bùi Văn Thấm" [Should review the charge and the law to be cited against Bùi Văn Thấm, Deputy chief justice of the Civil Court of the Supreme People's Court]. *Phụ Nữ Thủ Đô*, 25 December 1996, pp. 1, 4.

NĐT. "Hoạt động của HĐND từ khi có cơ quan thường trực" [Activities of the HĐND with a new Standing Committee]. *HNM*, 29 March 1991, p. 2.

Nghĩa Nhân. "Thu hút đông đảo nhân dân tham gia, giám sát bầu cử". *Vietnam Express*, 8 January 2004, http://vnexpress.net/Vietnam/Phap-luat/2004/01/3B9CEC98/.

Ngô Đồng Chiêm. "Cỗ Cưới" [Wedding party]. *Lao Động*, 7 January 1997, p. 5.

Ngô Huy Giao. "Từ một tiểu khu nhà ở ..." [From a Small Area housing area]. *Cứu Quốc*, 20 June 1975, pp. 6, 7.

Ngô Huy Giao. "Giao thông đô thị" [Traffic in urban areas]. *HNM*, 19 April
1981, p. 3;
———. "Giữ vững kỷ cương phép nước và an ninh quốc gia". *Đại Đoàn Kết*,
4 March 1995, p. 7.
Ngô Thanh Nhàn. "Nhà của người nghèo" [Houses of the poor]. *Lao Động Hà
Nội*, 6 December 1996, p. 3.
———. "Chuyện buôn nhà đất" [Sad tales about houses and land]. *Lao Động
Xã Hội*, 23 May 1997, p. 7.
Ngoc Mai. "Squatters swamp history's landmarks". *Vietnam Investment Review*,
12 June 2000, via vnnews-l.
Người Xây Dựng. "Từ một vụ cưỡng chế ..." [From a case of compulsory
demolition ...]. *HNM*, 10 June 1997, p. 4.
Nguyễn Bắc. "Mấy vấn đề ở một phường" [A few problems in a ward]. *HNM*,
4 June 1987, pp. 2, 4.
Nguyễn Chí Tình. "Vị trí cấp phường đang được thực tiễn khẳng định" [The position
of the ward is being confirmed by reality]. *HNM*, 28 June 1985, p. 2.
———. "Tạm cho sử dụng vỉa hè một số đường phố để quản lý người buôn bán".
[Allowing temporary use of pavement along a few roads in order to manage
traders]. *HNM*, 30 January 1991, pp. 1, 4.
Nguyễn Đình Tuế. "Thái độ bán hàng không đúng" [Attitude of the shop assistant
is not correct]. *Nhân Dân*, 12 January 1976, p. 2.
Nguyễn Đức Quang. "Khu phố Ba Đình: 7 tiểu khu và 10 khu tập thể được
công nhận là tiểu khu và khu tập thể văn minh" [Ba Đình District: 7 Small
Areas and 10 collective flat areas recognized as Cultured areas]. *HNM*, 5
June 1979, p. 1.
Nguyễn Đức Tha. "Qua hai năm xây dựng chính quyền phường Cửa Nam" [After
two years of operation of political authority in the Cửa Nam Ward]. *HNM*,
3 April 1981, p. 2.
———. "Xử Lý những trường hợp xây dựng trái phép" [Dealing with cases of
illegal construction]. *HNM*, 13 April 1982, p. 2; and 14 April 1982, p. 2.
———. "Phường Cửa Nam từ khi có chính quyền hoàn chỉnh" [After Cửa Nam
had a proper political authority]. *HNM*, 26 May 1982, p. 2.
———. "Quận Ba Đình tiến hành công việc phân cấp cho phường" [Ba Đình
District implements decentralization to ward level]. *HNM*, 16 June 1982,
pp. 2, 4.
———. "Phường Trúc Bạch với công tác thi hành án" [Trúc Bạch Ward implements
court verdicts]. *HNM*, 22 October 1982, p. 2.
———. "Chính quyền phường Đồng Xuân với chức năng quản lý xã hội" [The
Đồng Xuân Ward authority in management of society]. *HNM*, 3 November
1982, p. 2.
———. "Hiệu lực của chính quyền phường Ô Chợ Dừa" [Effectiveness of the Ô
Chợ Dừa ward political authority]. *HNM*, 26 November 1982, p. 2.

————. "Một năm thắng lợi của phường Cửa Nam" [One year of success for Cửa Nam Ward]. *HNM,* 2 February 1983, p. 2.

————. "Ở một phường mới thành lập" [At a new ward]. *HNM,* 4 May 1983, p. 2.

————. "Phường Nguyễn Trung Trực quản lý xã hội theo kỷ cương" [Nguyễn Trung Trực Ward manages society with social discipline]. *HNM,* 5 October 1983, p. 2.

————. "Quận Hai Bà Trưng quản lý nhà ở theo kỷ cương và pháp luật" [Hai Bà Trưng District manages houses according to the law and social discipline]. *HNM,* 26 October 1983, p. 2.

————. "Quận Hoàn Kiếm xử lý những trường hợp sử dụng nhà ở trái phép" [Hoàn Kiếm District deals with illegal uses of houses]. *HNM,* 8 February 1984, p. 2.

————. "Vài nét về hoạt động của chính quyền cấp phường ở quận Hoàn Kiếm" [A few characteristics of the activities of the wards of Hoàn Kiếm District]. *HNM,* 4 April 1984, p. 2.

————. "Phường Lê Đại Hành: quần chúng tham gia quản lý xã hội" [Lê Đại Hành ward: the masses participate in management of society]. *HNM,* 20 February 1985, p. 2.

————. "Phường Ô Chợ Dừa" [Ô Chợ Dừa Ward]. *HNM,* 18 June 1986, p. 3.

————. "Từ công tác quản lý nhà cửa ở một phường" [Learning from housing management in one ward]. *HNM,* 8 July 1988, pp. 2, 4.

————. "Chuyện thường gặp ở tiểu khu" [A common affair in Small Areas]. *HNM,* 29 October 1997, p. 2.

Nguyễn Hoài. "Thế nào là con người mới?" [What kind of person is a new person?]. *Nhân Dân,* 10 December 1976, p. 5.

Nguyễn Huy Đức. "Tiện nghi nhà ở tại Hà Nội" [Housing amenities in Hà Nội]. *HNM,* 19 September 1982. p. 3.

Nguyễn Mẫn. "Tai nạn giao thông vẫn cần nhắc lại" [Need to remind people about traffic safety]. *Lao Động Hà Nội,* 18 April 1997, p. 8.

Nguyễn Mạnh Cường. "Mấy nét chủ yếu về sự hoạt động của các tổ công tác tại các phường" [A few main characteristics of the activities of the special teams at the wards]. *HNM,* 22 June 1984, p. 2.

————. "Xây dựng cấp phường ở thị xã Sơn Tây" [Building up the ward level in Sơn Tây Town]. *HNM,* 7 June 1985, p. 2.

Nguyễn Ngọc Minh. "Tính chất, nhiệm vụ, quyền hạn của UBND" [Nature, duties, and powers of the people's committee]. *HNM,* 16 March 1984, p. 2.

————. "Làm thế nào để nâng cao hiệu quả hoạt động của Hội đồng Nhân dân" [How to raise the effectiveness of activities of people's councils]. *HNM,* 20 March 1984, p. 2.

Nguyễn Quang Hoà. "Có thể giảm tai nạn giao thông?" [Can traffic accidents be reduced?]. *HNM,* 20 January 1989, p. 3.

Nguyễn Quang Hoả. "Vỉa hè, đường ..." [Pavements, Roads ...]. *HNM,* 16 August 1991. p. 3.

———. "Lục cục '36'" [Internal conflicts of "36"]. *HNM,* 18 October 1995, pp. 1, 3.

Nguyen Thang. "Foreign firms slam currency control decree". *Vietnam Investment Review,* 26 October 1998, p. 15.

Nguyễn Thành Lập. "Độ phức tạp tại các nút giao thông trong thành phố" [The complexity of the traffic junctions in the City]. *HNM,* 2 November 1988, p. 2.

Nguyễn Thị Nương. "Vì sao những lộn xộn trên vỉa hè Hà Nội kéo dài?" [Why does the disorder on Hà Nôi's pavements still exist?]. *Đại Đoàn Kết,* 12 November 1988, p. 7.

Nguyễn Tiến. "Lời tự thuật của người phạm tội 'đưa hối lộ" [The confession of the person who bribed an official]. *Đại Đoàn Kết,* 3 March 1997, pp. 1, 6.

Nguyễn Tiến Đạm. "Truy tố Bùi Văn Thấm về tội 'Lợi dụng ảnh hưởng đối với người có chức vụ quyền hạn để trục lợi' là không chính xác" [Incorrect to charge Bùi Văn Thấm with using an official position and authority to influence to seek profit]. *Đại Đoàn Kết,* 26 December 1996, pp. 1, 6.

Nguyễn Triều. "Trên một trục đường trọng điểm" [Along the axis of a few busy streets]. *HNM,* 9 November 1988, pp. 2, 4.

Nguyễn Trường Giang. "Quán Thánh, 2 tháng thực hiện NĐ36/CP" [Two months of 36/CP at Quán Thánh Ward]. *HNM,* 9 October 1995, p. 2.

Nguyễn Tuấn. "Phát huy hiệu lực chính quyền trong việc kiểm tra, xử lý các trường hợp xây dựng, sử dụng nhà trái phép" [Bring into play effectiveness of political authority in inspections and dealing with illegal construction and uses of houses]. *HNM,* 10 June 1983, p. 2.

Nguyễn Văn Cừ. "Biện pháp đẩy nhanh tốc độ xây dựng nhà ở ở thủ đô" [Measures to speed up construction of accommodation in the capital]. *HNM,* 12 February 1982, p. 3.

———. "Phát huy mọi tiềm năng xây dựng nhà ở" [Use every potential in building accommodation]. *HNM,* 29 October 1982, p. 3.

Nguyễn Văn Lợi and Trần Nhâm. "Kinh nghiệm của chúng tôi" [Our experience]. *HNM,* 23 February 1979, p. 2.

Nguyễn Văn Truyền. "Nghĩ về mô hình cưới hiện nay" [Thinking about the new model of wedding]. *Tuổi trẻ Thủ đô,* 24 April 1997, p. 6.

Nguyễn Văn Vương. "Kẻ côn đồ ngang nhiên hành hung người vô tội" [Gangsters openly assaulted people but deemed innocent]. *Lao Động,* 2 January 1997, p. 6.

Nguyễn Văn Xây. "Rất cần 'ba kiểm tra trong thực hiện chỉ thị 57" [Real need for "three checks" in implementing Directive 57]. *HNM,* 5 March 1992, p. 1.

Nguyễn Viết Cảnh. "Đằng sau sự bình yên của đê Nghi Tàm" [Behind the serenity of the Nghi Tàm dyke]. *HNM,* 22 November 1994, p. 3.

Nguyễn Xiển. "Nhiều Đại biểu tham luận về phương hướng và nhiệm vụ kế hoạch Nhà nước năm 1975: Tăng cường quản lý nhà nước" [Many representatives discuss the direction and tasks for the 1975 State Plan]. *Nhân Dân,* 3 January 1975, p. 2.

Nguyễn Xuân. "Phô ... chợ!" [Street ... Market!]. *HNM,* 11 June 1982, p. 1.

Nhân Dân. "Ý kiến bạn đọc" [Readers' Opinions], 15 January 1976, p. 2.

———. "Hà Nội nêu cao trách nghiệm của đảng viên trong công tác lưu thông, phân phối lương thực" [City of Hà Nội stresses party members' responsibility in the circulation and distribution of food stuffs], 25 May 1977, p. 5.

———. "Hà Nội thêm nhiều lực lượng sửa chữa nhà cửa" [Hà Nội adds many new forces for repair of houses]. 15 June 1977, p. 3.

Nhóm Phóng Viên Hà Nội Mới. "Ngày khởi đầu" [The first day]. *HNM,* 2 August 1995, pp. 1, 3.

Nhóm PV Nội Chính. "Lần đầu tiên một nguyên thẩm phán TAND Tối cao bị tuyên phạt 24 tháng tù giam" [The first time a former judge in the Supreme People's Court jailed for 24 months]. *Lao Động,* 25 February 1997, pp. 1, 7.

———. "Cần xem xét trách nhiệm của các phường sở tại" [Need to ascertain the responsibility of the ward authorities]. *Lao Động,* 20 March 1997, pp. 1, 7.

Như Trang. "Chủ tịch UBND không được giữ chức quá 2 nhiệm kỳ". *VN Express,* 17 March 2004, http://vnexpress.net/Vietnam/Xa-hoi/2004/03/3B9D0B85/.

———. "Giảm 34 ứng cử viên đại biểu HĐND cấp tỉnh". *VN Express,* 29 March 2004, http://vnexpress.net/Vietnam/Xa-hoi/2004/03/3B9011A2/.

———. "Một số cán bộ chủ chốt không trúng cử HĐND". *VN Express,* 28 June 2004, http://vnexpress.net/Vietnam/Xa-hoi/2004/06/3B9D3FF7/.

P. Linh. "Giải quyết vướng mắc trong bầu cử đại biểu HDND 3 cấp". *Lao Động,* 5 April 2004, No. 94, http://www.laodong.com.vn/pls/bld/folder$. view_item_detail[97397].

P. Q. "Hoàn Kiếm nhân điển hình cơ quan xí nghiệp tự quản thực hiện NĐ 36/ CP" [Hoàn Kiếm District uses self-management model for state agencies and enterprises in implementing 36/CP]. *HNM,* 10 August 1996, p. 1.

———. "Liên kết trường - phường một mô hình cần được nhân rộng" [School-Ward alliance: a model that needs to be spread widely]. *HNM,* 15 November 1996, p. 2.

———. "Có 417 trường hợp lấn chiếm Hồ Tây" [417 cases of encroachment of West Lake]. *HNM,* 9 December 1996, p. 1.

P. T. L. "Cưới xin theo nếp sống mới" [Wedding that follow the new way of life]. *HNM,* 29 January 1978, p. 3.

P. V. "Nhung việc cần làm ở khu tập thể Cầu Đất". *Lao Động,* 27 July 1978, p. 12.

———. "Nhân dân nhiệt liệt hoan nghênh biện pháp nghiêm minh, hợp tình hợp lý của chính quyền" [The people warmly welcome measures of the political authority which are just and reasonable]. *HNM,* 26 May 1983, pp. 1, 4.

P. V. "Phường Quang Trung với hai công tác trọng tâm" [The Quang Trung ward and its two major tasks]. *HNM*, 26 February 1985, p. 2.

———. "Phường Hàng Bồ xây dựng nếp tự quản đường phố, làm chủ số nhà" [Hàng Bồ ward builds self-managed streets and houses]. *HNM*, 12 March 1986, p. 2

———. "Quy hoạch xây dựng và quản lý xây dựng ở thủ đô" [Development plans and construction management in the capital]. *HNM*, 13 February 1988, p. 3.

———. "Tranh luận sôi nổi về sửa đổi Luật tổ chức HĐND và UBND" [Lively debates on amendments to Law on organization of People's Council and People's Committee]. *HNM*, 29 June 1989, pp. 1, 4.

———. "Tai nạn giao thông vẫn còn nghiêm trọng" [Traffic accidents still at serious level]. *HNM*, 14 July 1989, p. 3.

———. "Chồng chéo hay gian lận?" [Overlapped or cheating?]. *HNM*, 6 November 1991, p. 3.

———. "Không bỏ được cấp phường" [The ward cannot be abolished]. *HNM*, 30 October 1991, p. 2.

———. "Sơ kết một tháng thực hiện Nghị Định 36/CP của Chính phủ" [Preliminary review of the first month of implementation of the government's 36/CP]. *HNM*, 14 September 1995, p. 1.

———. "CA phường Ô Chợ Dừa làm tốt vai trò nòng cốt thực hiện NĐ 36/CP" [Ô Chợ Dừa Ward police performs its pillar role well when implementing 36/CP]. *HNM*, 2 October 1996, p. 2.

———. "Kiểm tra xử lý 431 trường hợp xây dựng sai phép và không phép" [Check on 431 cases of building projects which infringed or did not have permits]. *HNM*, 3 January 1997, p. 1.

———. "Đừng để cái sảy nảy cái ung" [Do not let the prickly heat become an abscess]. *Đại Đoàn Kết*, 20 January 1997, p. 6.

——— and Quang Nghĩa. "Hơn 5000 lượt thanh niên, thiếu niên và các lực lượng an ninh tham gia tuyên truyền giáo dục nếp sống mới, lao động xây dựng thủ đô và kiểm tra trật tự trị an ở nơi công cộng" [More than 5,000 youths, children and security forces participate in mass education on the new way of life, labour to build the capital, and checks on order and security in public places]. *HNM*, 20 April 1983, p. 1.

People's Committee of Hà Nội. "Quy định tạm thời về nhiệm vụ, quyền hạn của Ủy ban nhân dân tiểu khu" [Temporary regulations on duties and powers of Small Area People's Committees]. *HNM*, 21 December 1978.

———. "Báo cáo của UBND trình HĐND thành phố khóa VII về việc phân cấp quản lý cho chính quyền quận, phường" [City People's Committee submits report to 7th City People's Council on delegation of management duties to District and Ward political authorities]. *HNM*, 17 June 1981, pp. 1, 2.

————. "Quyết định của UBND thành phố về nhiệm vụ, quyền hạn của chính quyền địa phương" [Decision of City People's Council regarding duties and powers of local political authorities]. *HNM,* 15 August 1986, pp. 2, 4.

————. "Dự thảo bản quy định về việc xử lý các vi phạm, tranh chấp trong sử dụng nhà cửa ở các quận, phường, thị xã, thị trấn" [Draft of regulations on dealing with offences and disputes on use of houses in districts, wards, towns and townlets]. *HNM,* 4 September 1987, pp. 1, 3.

————. "Quyết định của UBND Thành phố về việc xây dựng nhà ở và xử lý xây dựng trái phép" [Decision of the City People's Committee on housing construction and dealing with illegal construction]. *HNM,* 4 November 1987, p. 3.

————. "Quyết định của UBND Thành phố Hà Nội về xử phạt vi cảnh đối với những trường hợp vi phạm quy tắc vệ sinh, trật tự công cộng, trật tự giao thông" [Decision of the Hà Nội People's Committee on penalties for commune nuisances in cases of offences against health, public order, traffic order regulations]. *HNM,* 3 January 1988, pp. 1, 2.

————. "Quy định về việc phạt vi cảnh đối với những vi phạm trật tự an toàn giao thông trong thành phố Hà Nội" [Regulations on penalties for common nuisance offences against traffic order and safety in Hà Nội]. *HNM,* 8 October 1988, p. 3

————. "Quyết định xử phạt các trường hợp vi phạm quy tắc vệ sinh, TT của thành phố" [Decision to punish offences against public health and social order in the City]. *HNM,* 19 January 1989, p. 2.

————. "Quyết định xử phạt các trường hợp vi phạm quy tắc vệ sinh, trật tự công cộng của thành phố" [Decision to punish offences against City regulations on health and public order]. *HNM,* 15 February 1989, pp. 1, 4.

————. "Quyết định về việc xây dựng, cải tạo nhà ở" [Decision on construction and re-construction of housing]. *HNM,* 13 June 1990, p. 1.

————. "Quy định về việc cho phép sử dụng tạm thời đất và nhà trong đô thị và thị trấn" [Regulations for allowing temporary use of land and houses in urban centres and townlets]. *HNM,* 18 June 1990, p. 2.

————. "Về một số biện pháp về quản lý và phát triển nhà ở" [A number of measures to manage and develop housing]. *HNM,* 29 April 1994, pp. 1, 3.

Phạm Như Cương. "Tham nhũng, một khuyết tật bẩm sinh của quyền lực?" [Corruption: a flaw that is innate in power?]. *Đại Đoàn Kết,* 9 January 1997, pp. 1, 2.

Phạm Thế Duyệt. "Về vấn đề 'Nhà 30 Quang Trung và 84 Hàng Bạc" [Regarding house 30, Quang Trung Street, and house 84, Hàng Bạc Street]. *HNM,* 14 December 1989, p. 1.

Phan Tất. "Tiểu khu Bông Nhuộm xây dựng số nhà văn hóa mới" [Bông Nhuộm Small Area implements new culture houses programme]. *HNM,* 26 April 1978, p. 2.

Phan Thị Bội Hoàn. "Phường Kim Liên với chỉ thị 57" [Kim Liên Ward and Directive 57]. *HNM,* 13 January 1992, p. 2

Phan Thị Hồng Sinh. "Khi xác định rõ nhiệm vụ của tổ chức đảng ở đường phố" [When the tasks of the Party on the street level is clear]. *Nhân Dân,* 22 February 1997, p. 3.

Phan Tưởng. "Phường Quang Trung làm gì và làm như thế nào để công tác bảo vệ an ninh trở thành phong trào quần chúng" [What and how did the Quang Trung turn work on security into a mass movement?]. *HNM,* 2 June 1982, p. 2.

————. "Trật tự và an toàn giao thông của thành phố hiện nay" [Traffic order and safety in the city at present]. *HNM,* 8 September 1982, p. 2.

————. "Phường Phúc Tân bảo vệ tài sản XHCN, giữ gìn kỷ cương xã hội" [Phúc Tân Ward protects socialist property, maintains social discipline]. *HNM,* 12 January 1983, p. 2

————. "Sau hai năm lập lại trật tự hè, đường phố ở quận Hai Bà Trưng" [After two years of restoring order on the pavement and roads in Hai Bà Trưng District]. *HNM,* 13 October 1993, p. 2.

Phùng Minh. "Từ đầu tháng 9-1987 thực hiện việc bán nhà ở" [Sale of houses starts from beginning of September 1987]. *HNM,* 4 September 1987, pp. 1, 4.

Phương Sinh. "Nếp sống tốt ở một khu tập thể" [Good way of life in one collective flat area]. *HNM,* 10 February 1978, p. 2.

Quang Hiệu. "Vi phạm tăng, tai nạn cũng tăng" [Offences and accidents increased]. *Lao Động,* No. 110, 19 April 2004, http://www.laodong.com.vn/pls/bld/folder$. view_item_detail[98743].

————. "6 tháng gần 300 người chết vì TNGT" [300 dead in traffic accidents in 6 months]. *Lao Động Điện Tử,* 12 July 2004, No. 194.

———— and Đức Trung. "3 năm nữa ra đường chỉ còn đi … bộ" [Three more years and there will only be space for … walking]. *Lao Động,* 7 December 2000. http://www.laodong.com.vn/pls/bld/folder$.view_item_detail[106559].

Quang Huy. "Phường Cống Vị: Giải quyết việc làm cho dân" [Cống Vị Ward finds employment for its people]. *HNM,* 28 June 1985, p. 3

————. "Phường Cửa Nam chăm lo đời sống nhân dân bằng con đường phát triển kinh tế" [Cửa Nam ward takes care of the people's livelihood via economic development]. *HNM,* 2 August 1985, p. 2.

Quang Nguyễn. "Mở rộng đường Hùng Vương – Cầu Giấy có dễ hay không?" [Widening Hùng Vương – Cầu Giấy Road: easy or not easy?]. *HNM,* 24 February 1993, p. 2.

Quế Lan. "Không nên để tệ làm nhà trái phép phát triển" [Should not let illegal construction develop]. *Đại Đoàn Kết,* 20 August 1980, p. 2.

Quốc Khánh. "Thanh tra cần có quyền năng pháp lý thực sự" [The Inspectorate needs to have real legal powers]. *Đại Đoàn Kết,* 23 February 1998, p. 6.

Quỳnh Chi. "Quy định mới về đăng ký hộ khẩu" [New regulations on residential registration]. *An Ninh Thủ Đô*, 5 June 1997, p. 4.

Quỳnh Trang and Anh Thơ, "Có phải ông chủ tịch phường Thanh Xuân Bắc coi thường pháp luật?" [Is not Thanh Xuân Bắc Ward chairman disrespecting the law?]. *Lao Động Hà Nội*, 2 May 1997, p. 10.

————. "Biết là sai - bao giờ sửa?" [When will the wrong be corrected?]. *Lao Động Hà Nội*, 13 June 1997, pp. 1, 6.

Reuters. "Assembly Vice-Chairman views People's Council elections", 21 September 1994.

————. "Adultery charge trips Vietnam Assembly candidate", 2 July 1997.

————. "Cheating reported ahead of Vietnam election", 16 July 1997.

————. "Leaders change in Long An Province", 7 May 1998.

————. "No more freebie mobile phones", 11 May 1998.

————. "Vietnam reports major increase in goods smuggling", 27 May 1998.

————. "Deal with complaints of people, Vietnam party says", 28 May 1998.

————. "Vietnam party chief hints at internal strife", 6 July 1998.

————. "Hà Nội to set out fines for illegal dollar use", 20 May 1999.

S. H. "Phường Hàng Bài càng làm, càng thấy sáng" [Hàng Bài does it better every time]. *HNM,* 10 September 1982, p. 2.

Saigon Times Daily. "City annuls 830 invalid legal documents". Via Reuters, 7 May 1998.

————. "Can Tho customs chief prosecuted". Via Reuters, 29 May 1998.

————. "Customs chief's son found guilty". Via Reuters, 29 May 1998.

————. "Police detain anti-smuggling official". Via Reuters, 12 June 1998.

————. "Traffic accidents kill 3,300 in first half". Via Reuters, 30 July 1998.

————. "Study says Vietnam poverty lower than thought". Via Reuters, 26 April 1999.

SRV. "Quy định tạm thời về nhiệm vụ, quyền hạn của Ủy ban nhân dân tiểu khu" [Temporary regulations on tasks and powers of the Small Area People's Committee]. *HNM,* 28 December 1978, pp. 1, 4.

————. "Quy định của Hội đồng Chính phủ về việc thống nhất tên gọi các đơn vị hành chính ở nội thành, nội thị" [Decision of State Council on uniform names for administrative units in the inner and outer city]. *HNM,* 6 January 1981, p. 1.

————. "Luật tổ chức Hội đồng nhân dân và Ủy ban nhân dân, 9/7/1983" [Law on Organization of People's Councils and People's Committees, 9 July 1983]. *HNM,* 12 July 1983, pp. 1–3.

————. "Luật bầu cử đại biểu Hội đồng nhân dân" [Law on Election of People's Councils]. *HNM,* 15 January 1984, pp. 1, 2.

————. "Quy chế hoạt động của Hội đồng nhân dân các cấp" [Regulations on activities of People's Councils of all levels]. *HNM,* 24 November 1987, pp. 2, 3.

SRV. "Luật sửa đổi bổ sung Luật bầu cử đại biểu Hội đồng nhân dân" [Law (Amended) on Elections of People's Councils]. *HNM,* 8 May 1989, pp. 2, 3.

————. "Dự án sửa đổi, bổ sung Luật tổ chức Hội đồng nhân dân và Ủy ban nhân dân" [Project to amend and expand on the Law on Organization of People's Councils and People's Committees]. *HNM,* 5 June 1989, pp. 2–3.

————. "Luật tổ chức Hội đồng nhân dân và Ủy ban nhân dân" [Law on Organization of People's Councils and People's Committees]. *Nhân Dân,* 17 July 1989, pp. 3, 4.

————. "Pháp lệnh nhà ở" [Ordinance on Housing]. *HNM,* 10 April 1991, pp. 1, 3.

————. "Nghị Định của Thủ tướng Chính phủ về quyền sở hữu nhà ở và quyền sử dụng đất ở tại đô thị" [Decision of the Prime Minister on right to own houses and right to use land in urban areas]. *HNM,* 21 July 1994, p. 2.

T. C. "Tuy muộn nhưng vẫn tốt" [Though late but still good]. *HNM,* 11 March 1991, p. 2.

T. H. "Kết thúc phiên tòa xét xử vụ án buôn lậu qua biên giới Long An" [Conclusion of trial of smuggling across the borders of Long An]. *Đại Đoàn Kết,* 14 May 1998, pp. 1, 6.

Thái Hoàng Vũ. "Lại bàn về giáo dục lối sống đô thị" [About education for urban way of living, again]. *Nhân Dân,* 8 May 1997, p. 6.

Thanh Chi. "Trật tự đô thị, một việc cấp bách" [Urban order: an urgent matter]. *HNM,* 18 March 1991, p. 2.

————. "Nhìn lại công tác xử lý XD trái phép ở quận Hoàn Kiếm năm 1993" [Reviewing how illegal construction in Hoàn Kiếm District in 1993 had been dealt with]. *HNM,* 3 January 1994, p. 2.

————. "Xung quanh việc xây dựng không phép" [Regarding construction without licences]. *HNM,* 11 April 1994, p. 2.

————. "Trật tự giao thông đô thị ở Hà Nội trước và sau NĐ 36/CP" [Urban traffic order in Hà Nội before and after 36/CP]. *HNM,* 16 October 1995, p. 2.

Thanh Hùng. "Trật tự, kỷ cương đô thị lại bị buông lỏng" [Urban order and discipline are loose again]. *HNM,* 4 September 1992, p. 2.

Thanh Lan. "Lực cản từ cơ chế" [The obstruction is from within the mechanism]. *Đại Đoàn Kết,* 19 February 1998, pp. 1, 7.

Thanh Long. "Chuyện số Nhà 55" [The story of House 55]. *HNM,* 7 September 1977, p. 2.

Thanh Mai. "Xung quanh việc thực hiện chỉ thị 57" [About implementation of Directive 57]. *HNM,* 6 January 1992, p. 2.

————. "Thực hiện chỉ thị 57 ở một con đường" [Implementing Directive 57 on one road]. *HNM,* 8 January 1992, p. 3.

————. "Vì sao có các vụ tranh chấp kéo dài?" [Why do disputes take too long to resolve?]. *HNM,* 13 January 1992, p. 2.

————. "Hồ Tây đang bị lấn chiếm!" [West Lake is being encroached upon!]. *HNM,* 13 July 1992, p. 2.

————. "Xung quanh việc thực hiện quyết định 1431 về phạt vi cảnh xây dựng không phép" [Regarding implementation of Decision 1431 on compounded punishments for construction without licences]. *HNM,* 1 March 1993, p. 2.

————. "Thực hiện Nghị Định 60, 61/CP của Chính phủ về nhà ở, đất ở trên địa bàn Hà Nội" [Hà Nội implements Decision 60, 61/CP of the Government on housing and land for housing]. *HNM,* 25 February 1995, p. 1, 4.

————. "Quản Lý xây dựng ở quận Ba Đình" [Management of construction in Ba Đình District]. *HNM,* 8 November 1995, p. 3.

————. "Phát triển cho Hà Nội 'Thiên Niên tuổi'" [Development of Hà Nội for the millennium]. *HNM,* 9 December 1996, p. 3.

Thanh Thủy. "Thử xem tham nhũng cấp phường đến đâu!" [Let's see how deep corruption is at the ward level!]. *HNM,* 1 July 1994, p. 2.

————. "Nhà chung cư" [Collective houses]. *An Ninh Thủ Đô,* 10 January 1997, p. 4.

Thế Gia. "Nói thêm về bài học qua vụ án Tamexco" [More about the lessons drawn from the Tamexco case]. *Nhân Dân,* 15 March 1997, p. 5.

Thịnh Giang. "Chẳng lẽ người Hà Nội cứ cam chịu mãi cảnh giao thông như thế này?" [Do Hanoians really want to continue to tolerate the present traffic situation?]. *Nhân Dân,* 15 January 1997, pp. 1, 7.

Thu Hương. "Các cấp, ngành, đoàn thể tích cực triển khai thực hiện Nghị Định 36/CP" [All levels, branches, and organizations enthusiastically prepares to implement 36/CP]. *HNM,* 31 July 1995, pp. 1, 4.

Thu Huyền. "Nhiều dự án, thiếu nhà ở" [Many projects, but insufficient homes]. *Lao Động Điện Tử,* 16 February 2004, No. 47, http://www.laodong.com. vn/pls/bld/folder$.view_item_detail[92798].

Thu Phương. "Lại chuyện vỉa hè Hà Nội" [It's the Hà Nội pavement story again]. *Đại Đoàn Kết,* 7 November 1989, p. 5.

Thu Thủy. "Xíchlô thành phố Hồ Chí Minh sau một năm cấm đường" [The Trishaw in Hồ Chí Minh City after one year of road ban]. *Lao Động,* 21 December 1996, p. 6.

Thurber, David. "Vietnam votes for National Assembly". *Associated Press,* 19 May 2002.

Thủy Hùng. "Trật tự đô thị ở phường Tràng Tiền" [Urban order at the Tràng Tiền Ward]. *HNM,* 26 February 1993, p. 2.

Thủy Linh. "Chị chủ tịch phường" [Sister Chairwoman of the Ward]. *HNM,* 19 August 1982, p. 3.

————. "Tham gia tự quản hè, đường phố, giữ gìn TTVV sạch đẹp" [Participate in self-management of pavements and streets, keep them orderly, hygienic and clean]. *An Ninh Thủ Đô,* 18 March 1997, p. 6.

Tiến Chính. "Không nên hỏi: 'Tồn tại hay không tồn tại?" [We should not ask "Should it or should it not exist?]. *An Ninh Thủ Đô*, 9 December 1996, pp. 1, 3.

Tiến Phú and Phan Tưởng. "Qua 2 năm lập lại trật tự hè, đường phố" [After 2 years of restoring order on pavements and roads]. *HNM*, 29 October 1993, p. 2.

Tô P. V. "Cần xử lý nghiêm những kẻ coi thường pháp luật" [Need to deal strictly deal with people who disrespect the law]. *Lao Động Hà Nội*, 1 January 1997, p. 6.

Tô phóng viên Ban bạn đọc. "Xung quanh vụ xây nhà vi phạm lệnh bảo vệ đê điều thuộc quận Ba Đình" [On the cases of illegal construction against the dyke decree in the Ba Đình District]. *HNM*, 3 March 1995, pp. 1, 3.

Tô PV Điều Tra. "Dân đòi hỏi quá đáng, hay thực hiện chưa công bằng" [Do the people demand too much, or is the implementation unfair?]. *Đại Đoàn Kết*, 21 April 1997, pp. 1, 7.

Tôn Xuân Thích. "Phường Tràng Tiền giữ gìn trật tự công cộng" [Trang Tien Ward keeps public order]. *HNM*, 28 October 1988, p. 2.

Trần Bình. "Những bước đi lên trong việc xây dựng nhà ở" [Improvements in housing construction], *HNM*, 1 April 1977, pp. 3, 4.

Trần Đạo. "Làm thế nào kiềm chế sự gia tăng tai nạn giao thông?" [How to stop the increase in traffic accidents?]. *Nhân Dân*, 24 June 1997, p. 3.

Trần Đình Chính. "Chuyện thường ngày ở phường Phương Liên" [Everyday occurrences in Phương Liên ward]. *Nhân Dân*, 6 March 1997, pp. 1, 7.

Trần Đoàn Vũ and Lý Quang Khang. "Chúng tôi sẽ dạy thế nào?" [How should we carry on teaching?]. *Lao Động*, 9 January 1997, p. 2.

Trần Dũng and Vũ Long. "Từ phường Hàng Bông ... đến phường Phan Chu Trinh" [From Hàng Bông Ward ... to Phan Chu Trinh Ward]. *HNM*, 19 April 1983, pp. 2, 4.

Trần Hoàng Trâm. "Một trong 5 phường khá nhất thành phố" [One of 5 best wards of the City]. *An Ninh Thủ Đô*, 15 June 1986, p. 3.

Trần Hùng. "Một số suy nghĩ về 'Hà Nội cải tạo và xây dựng" [A few thoughts about "Hà Nội being reconstructed and constructed]. *HNM*, 23 January 1983, pp. 1, 3.

Trần Quang. "Chất lượng nhà xây chưa tốt". *Đại Đoàn Kết*, 22 December 1982, p. 11.

————. "Tiếp tay chuyển dịch tài sản đang tranh chấp" [Given a hand in selling an assert under dispute]. *Lao Động*, 28 November 1996, p. 6.

Trần Quang Vũ. "Điều gì cản trở Hà Nội giải toả nhà xây trên đê". *Đại Đoàn Kết*, 19 November 1994, p. 7.

Trần Quế Thương. "Phường Hàng Đào thực hiện có hiệu quả chỉ thị 57 của UBND Thành phố" [Hàng Đào Ward implements effectively Directive 57 of the City People's Committee]. *HNM*, 17 January 1992, p. 2.

————. "Nhìn lại hai tháng thực hiện chỉ thị 57 ở Quận Hoàn Kiếm" [Review of two months of implementation of Directive 57 in Hoàn Kiếm District]. *HNM,* 28 February 1992, p. 2.

Trần Sơn. "Đỗ xe ở Hà Nội - bài toán nan giải" [Parking in Hà Nội: a complex problem]. *Pháp luật và đời sống,* 28 October 1996.

Trần Thông. "Sớm có biện pháp" [We should act early]. *Đại Đoàn Kết,* 27 May 1981, p. 2.

Trọng Nghĩa. "Có thể bảo đảm an toàn giao thông được không?" [Can traffic safety be assured?]. *HNM,* 24 July 1981, p. 3.

Trung Thành. "Tìm giải pháp đồng bộ cho nhà ở đô thị đến năm 2000" [Looking for coordinated solutions for urban housing between now and the year 2000]. *Đại Đoàn Kết,* 14 May 1998, pp. 1, 7.

Trương Duy Nhất, "Đâu là uy lực của tòa?" [Where is the authority of the Court?]. *Đại Đoàn Kết,* 22 May 1997, pp. 1, 7.

Tuấn Anh. "Nỗi niềm những người làm kinh tế vỉa hè" [The feelings of those working in the pavement economy]. *Lao Động Hà Nội,* 10 January 1997, pp. 1, 7.

Tung Phương. "Trách nhiệm của đảng bộ phường Kim Liên trước tệ xây dựng nhà trái phép đến đâu?" [How far is the responsibility of the Kim Liên Ward Party branch in the problems of illegal construction?]. *HNM,* 29 March 1989, p. 2.

Tuổi Trẻ. "Hội nghị về HĐND và UBND: Nâng cao quyền của HĐND và năng lực quản lý của UBND" [Conference on people's councils and people's committees: Raise the power of people's councils and management ability of people's committees], 29 September 1998, pp. 1, 14.

Tuổi Trẻ Thủ Đô. "Hà Nội: Bước ngoặt giải quyết nhà ở" [Hà Nội: Turning point in solving housing problems], 20 November 1996, pp. 1–2.

Tường Anh. "Tổng kiểm tra, duy trì kết quả thực hiện chỉ thị 57/UB về giữ gìn trật tự hè, đường" [General inspection to maintain results of Directive 57/UB on maintaining order on pavements, roads]. *HNM,* 16 September 1992, pp. 1, 4.

Tường Phan. "Những bài học phản diện" [The other lessons]. *HNM,* 26 May 1983, p. 4.

UBND Hà Nội. "Quy định về việc phạt vi cảnh đối với những vi phạm trật tự an toàn giao thông trong thành phố Hà Nội" [Rules on compounded fines for traffic offences in Hà Nội]. *HNM,* 8 October 1988, p. 3.

————. "Quyết định xử phạt các trường hợp vi phạm quy tắc vệ sinh, TT của thành phố" [Decision to punish offences against Regulations on public cleanliness and public order of the City]. *HNM,* 19 January 1989, p. 2.

————. "Quyết định xử phạt các trường hợp vi phạm quy tắc vệ sinh, trật tự công cộng của thành phố" [Decision to punish offences against regulations on public cleanliness and order of the City]. *HNM,* 15 February 1989, pp. 1, 4.

Uyên Chi. "Xây dựng trái phép: Tiếng chuông báo động" [Illegal construction: the alarm bells]. *HNM,* 11 November 1994, p. 3.

Văn Chiểu. "Nên tổ chức chi bộ theo tổ dân phố" [Should organize party cells parallel to resident groups]. *HNM,* 7 May 1997, p. 2.

Văn Giáp. "Tiểu khu Long Biên vận động những người làm ăn không chính đáng chuyển sang sản xuất" [Small District Long Biên mobilized people to go into production work]. *HNM,* 7 January 1978, p. 3.

Văn Thành. "Tai nạn giao thông vẫn là nỗi lo của mọi người" [Traffic accidents are still everybody's worry]. *HNM,* 30 August 1991, p. 3.

Việt Anh. "Gần 2,000 ứng cử viên bị loại khỏi danh sách bầu cử". *VN Express,* 21 April 2004, http://vnexpress.net/Vietnam/Xa-hoi/2004/04/3B9D1DF5/.

Vietnam Economic News. "Full Breakfast But Empty Lunch". Via Reuters, 22 June 1999.

―――. "Road Accidents Now Claim 6,000 Lives Per Year". Via Reuters, 7 July 1999.

Vietnam Express. "Nội dung chính và những điều còn tranh cãi trong Luật Bầu cử đại biểu HĐND", 5 July 2003, http://vnexpress.net/Phap-luat/2003/07/3B9C96B7/.

Vietnam News Agency. "Hội đồng Bộ trưởng hướng dẫn thi hành Luật tổ chức Hội đồng nhân dân và Ủy ban nhân dân" [State Council guides on implementation of Law on Organization of People's Councils and People's Committees]. *HNM,* 3 May 1984, pp. 1, 4.

―――. "National Assembly closes fifth session", 12 June 1999. Via Vnnews-l, 13 June 1999.

―――. "National Assembly Office explains elimination of three candidates", 17 May 2002.

Vietnam News Brief. "Over 100 parliamentary candidates accused of wrongdoings", 21 June 2002.

―――. "Illegal house constructions booms in HCM City", 29 July 2002.

Vĩnh Yên. "Đầu xuân gặp nữ chủ tịch phường" [Meeting the ward Chairwoman at the start of spring]. *HNM,* 8 March 1994, p. 2.

―――. "Cần giữ cho hè thông, đường thoáng ở mọi nơi, mọi lúc" [Every pavement and road needs to be clear at all times]. *HNM,* 31 July 1995, p. 2.

Voice of Vietnam. "Former party official Pham Van Dong discusses party problems". Via Reuters, 16 May 1999.

―――. "Vietnam officially announces election results". 27 May 2002.

Vũ Đình Hoành. "Sau gần 20 tháng thực hiện chỉ thị 57" [After close to 20 months of implementation of Directive 57]. *HNM,* 9 July 1993, p. 2.

―――. "Làm gì để thực hiện Nghị Định 36/CP của Chính phủ có hiệu quả cao?" [What is to be done to ensure implementation of 36/CP of the government is highly effective?]. *HNM,* 1 August 1995, pp. 1, 4.

Vũ Minh. "Hãy cố gắng khắc phục nguyên nhân chủ quan" [Let's try to overcome the subjective causes]. *HNM,* 19 April 1981, p. 3.

Vũ Minh Tâm. "Trò phù thủy của dự án 'Làng phong cảnh'" [The magic in the "Landscape Village' project]. *Đại Đoàn Kết,* 16 April 1998, pp. 1, 7.

Vũ Ngọc Anh. "Hiệu lực quản lý của chính quyền" [Management effectiveness of state authority]. *HNM,* 19 March 1989, p. 1.

Vũ Phùng. "Có những điểm gì mới trong Luật tổ chức Hội đồng nhân dân và Ủy ban nhân dân" [What's new in the Law on Organization of People's Councils and People's Committees]. *HNM,* 15 July 1983, p. 2; 16 July 1983, p. 2.

Vũ Quang Du. "Cưới ở Hà Nội qua số liệu thăm dò gần đây [Looking at weddings in Hà Nội through some recent statistics]. *Hà Nội Mới Chủ Nhật,* 2 March 1997, p. 3.

Vũ Tất Tiến. "Hiệu quả của một cuộc vận động" [Effectiveness of an instance of mobilization]. *HNM,* 22 November 1996, p. 2.

Vương Nguyễn. "Để dân an cư" [In order that the people live peacefully]. *HNM,* 21 December 1990, p. 3.

Vương Phan. "Phường Tràng Tiền: Những cố gắng và các mặt tồn tại" [Trang Tien Ward: efforts made and shortcomings remaining]. *HNM,* 24 September 1986, p. 2.

Vương Thức. "Chống làm nhà trái phép ở quận Ba Đình" [Fight against illegal construction of houses in Ba Đình District]. *HNM,* 4 October 1983, p. 3.

———. "Chuyện nhà cửa ở phường Hàng Bồ" [Housing matters in Hàng Bồ Ward]. *HNM,* 15 November 1983, p. 3.

———. "Những dãy nhà phía nam thành phố" [Rows of houses south of the City]. *HNM,* 20 January 1984, pp. 3, 4.

———. "Về tình hình làm nhà trái phép ở khu tập thể Trung Tự" [On the situation of illegal housing construction in the Trung Tự collective flat area]. *HNM,* 30 July 1985, pp. 3, 4.

———. "Chuyện nhà, chuyện cửa ở phường Hàng Bài" [Housing matters in Hàng Bài Ward]. *HNM,* 25 October 1985, p. 3.

———. "Tìm việc làm cho dân" [Looking for work for the people]. *HNM,* 10 January 1986, p. 2.

———. "Điều tra quyền sở hữu tư nhân về nhà cửa ở quận Đống Đa" [Survey on right of private ownership of housing in Đống Đa District]. *HNM,* 31 January 1986, p. 3.

———. "Cần xử lý tệ làm nhà trái phép ở khu tập thể Kim Liên" [Need to deal with evil of illegal construction in the Kim Liên collective flat area]. *HNM,* 23 May 1986, p. 3.

———. "Hè đường kêu cứu" [The pavement is calling for help!]. *HNM,* 14 March 1987, pp. 1, 4.

———. "Những cuộc tranh chấp trên sân thượng - mái bằng" [Disputes regarding roof yards and roofs]. *HNM,* 8 May 1987, p. 3.

Vương Thức. "Hộ khẩu với việc quản lý nhà" [Residential registration and housing management]. *HNM*, 9 October 1987, p. 3.

————. "Cần chấn chỉnh việc đăng ký và chuyển dịch nhà cửa" [Need to reorganize registration of housing and housing sale]. *HNM*, 6 May 1988, p. 3.

————. "Việc xây nhà trái phép vẫn tăng" [Illegal construction still on the rise]. *HNM*, 18 June 1988, p. 3.

————. "Đổi mới việc cấp phép xây dựng" [Reform the process of issuing construction licences]. *HNM*, 26 August 1988, p. 3.

————. "Ở các khu nhà tập thể" [At the collective flat areas]. *HNM*, 14 October 1988, p. 3.

————. "Trước những đòi hỏi của cuộc sống" [In the face of demands of living]. *HNM*, 3 November 1989, p. 3.

————. "Tranh chấp nhà cửa ở quận Hoàn Kiếm" [Housing disputes in Hoàn Kiếm District]. *HNM*, 13 April 1990, p. 3.

————. "Việc nhà, việc cửa ở quận Hoàn Kiếm" [Housing matters in the Hoàn Kiếm District]. *HNM*, 18 July 1990, p. 3.

Xinhua News Agency. "Vietnam Promotes Grassroots Democracy". Via Reuters, 14 May 1998.

————. "Traffic accidents claim 15 lives a day in Vietnam". Via Reuters, 6 July 1998.

Xuân Hà. "Giải quyết nạn hàng rong quả thật không dễ!" [Really not easy to solve the *hang rong* problem!]. *Lao Động Hà Nội*, 10 January 1997, p. 2.

Xuân Quyết. "Thêm một cách nhìn về tai nạn giao thông" [One more way to look at traffic accidents]. *Nhân Dân*, 8 February 2001, pp. 1, 5.

Xưởng Thương Binh Quận Hoàn Kiếm. "Hiệu lực chính quyền ở đâu?" [Where was the effectiveness of the political authority?]. *HNM*, 9 June 1987, p. 3.

Index

About the author

David Koh is Fellow at the Institute of Southeast Asian Studies in Singapore. He is the Coordinator of the Institute's Regional Strategic and Politics Programme. He started his working life as a social surveyor, then a salesman, and then a copywriter, while receiving early training, since childhood, in his family's little sundries shop. After graduating from the National University of Singapore, he worked with the Singapore Ministry of Foreign Affairs for two years, before finding his niche in Vietnam studies. He is trilingual in English, Mandarin, and Vietnamese.